DATE DUE

FEB 1 6 1998	

BRODART   Cat. No. 23-221

KARL MANNHEIM
AND THE
CRISIS OF LIBERALISM

DAVID
KETTLER
AND
VOLKER
MEJA

KARL MANNHEIM

AND THE

CRISIS OF LIBERALISM

THE
SECRET
OF
THESE
NEW
TIMES

Transaction Publishers
New Brunswick (U.S.A.) and London (U.K.)

Library of Congress Catalog Number: 94-47504
ISBN: 1-56000-188-7
Printed in the United States of America

Library of Congress Cataloging-in-Publication Data

Kettler, David.
    Karl Mannheim and the crisis of liberalism : the secret of these new times /David Kettler, Volker Meja.
        p. cm.
    Includes bibliographical references and index.
    ISBN 1-56000-188-7 (alk. paper)
    1. Mannheim, Karl, 1893–1947. 2. Sociologists—Germany—Biography. 3. Sociology—Germany—History. 4. Knowledge, Sociology of. 5. Political science. II. Meja, Volker. I. Title.
HM22.G3M3253 1995
301'.092—dc20   94-47504
                                                                        CIP

Contents

Acknowledgments

Because this book represents a rethinking of work started in 1964 and reported in many publications, it is difficult to acknowledge in full the many sources, critics, and funding agencies whose contributions are recombined here. The text draws on the following earlier publications: "Culture and Revolution: Lukács in the Hungarian Revolutions of 1918/ 1919", *Telos* 10(1971):35-92 (Kettler); "The Sociology of Knowledge and the Critique of Ideology", *Cultural Hermeneutics* 3 (1975):57-68 (Meja); "Karl Mannheim's Sociological Theory of Culture," *Canadian Journal of Sociology* 5,4 (1980):405-32 (with Nico Stehr); *Karl Mannheim*. London: Tavistock and New York: Methuen, 1984 (with Nico Stehr); "Karl Mannheim and Conservatism: The Ancestry of Historical Thinking," *American Sociological Review* 49,1 (1984): 71-85 (with Nico Stehr); "Settling with Mannheim," *State, Culture, and Society* 1,3 (1985):225-37; "The Reconstitution of Political Life: The Contemporary Relevance of Karl Mannheim's Political Project," *Polity* 20, 4 (1988):623-647; "Rationalizing the Irrational: Karl Mannheim and the Besetting Sin of German Intellectuals", *American Journal of Sociology* 19,6 (1990): 1441-73 (with Nico Stehr) ; "Their 'Own Peculiar Way': Karl Mannheim and the Rise of Women," *International Sociology* 8,1 (1993): 5-55; "Studying Mannheim: Projects, Negotiations, Settlements," paper presented at the 31st Congress of the International Institute of Sociology at the Sorbonne, 21-25 June 1993; "'That typically German kind of sociology which verges towards philosophy': The Dispute about *Ideology and Utopia* in the United States," *Sociological Theory* 12,3 (1994):279-303.

Financial support has come from the Social Science Research Council, The Rockefeller Foundation (Bellagio), the Social Sciences and Humanities Research Council of Canada, the Fulbright Senior Research Program, the Netherlands Institute for Advanced Studies, the Research Committees of the University of Alberta, the Memorial University of Newfoundland, and Trent University, as well as the Bard College Center. We gratefully acknowledge this support. In lieu of many critics and friends, we thank Kurt H. Wolff, whose questions started us on our inquiries, and Éva Karádi and Anna Wessely, who challenged us to think again when we thought we had said enough. Nico Stehr graduated from the team when other important work absorbed his time; but he remains a silent partner in the undertaking.

Glossary

AA   Authors' Archives

AJP   Alvin Johnson Papers, Yale University

BG   Badisches Generallandesarchiv, Karlsruhe

BK   July 25, 1938, letter Karl Mannheim's to Alfred Weber. Bundesarchiv, Koblenz, Germany.

CUL   Oscar Jászi Papers, Columbia Unversity Library, Rare Books and Manuscript Library, New York City.

DL   Deutsches Literaturarchiv, Marbach

EEEP   Earle Edward Eubank Papers, Regenstein Library, University of Chicago

ES   "Die Entstehung der intellektuellen Gruppen aus der sich wandelnden Gesellschaftsstruktur." Unpublished manuscript by K. Mannheim (1934–5), in possession of Edward Shils, Chicago.

JCBM   J.C.B. Mohr (Paul Siebeck) Verlag, Tübingen

KMP   Karl Mannheim Papers, University of Keele Library, Keele, Staffordshire.

LSRM   Laura Spelman Rockefeller Memorial Acrchives, Rockefeller Foundation Archive Center.

LP   A.D. Lindsay Papers, University of Keele Library, Keele, Staffordshire.

LWP   Louis Wirth Papers, Regenstein Library, University of Chicago

MP   Michael Polanyi Papers, Regenstein Library, University of Chicago.

MTAK   Magyar Tudományos Akadémia Könyutára, Kézirattár (Library of the Hungarian Academy of Sciences), Budapest.

NR   Archives of Nina Rubinstein, New York City.

NRI   Interviews with Nina Rubinstein in New York City on October 31, 1987, and December 17, 1987.

PT   Paul Tillich Papers, Andover Theological Library, Harvard University, Box 601 #999–1010.

RB   Read Bain, "Remarks on Mannheim's *Ideology and Utopia.* In LWP/ 67:2

RF   Rockefeller Foundation Archive Center.

RKP   Routledge & Kegan Paul Archives, London

RL   Interview with Richard Löwenthal (June 4, 1986), in possession of Reinhard Blomert, Berlin.

RM   Robert M. MacIver, "*Ideology and Utopia. A Critique of Mannheim.*"
      In LWP/67:2
SP   Karl Mannheim, "A Syllabus on Power." Prepared for the Moot, Janu-
      ary, 1942. AA.
TP   Talcott Parsons, "The Role of Ideas in Social Action". In LWP/9:9
UF   Karl Mannheim's Personalakten, Johann-Wolfgang-Goethe Uni-
      versität, Frankfurt/Main.
UH   Rupert-Karls-Universität, Heidelberg.
WB   November 22, 1979, letter from W. Baldamus, in possession of Nico
      Stehr, Edmonton.

Introduction: The Biography of a Project

To reflect on Karl Mannheim is to address fundamental issues of political enlightenment. Mannheim's driving determination, as he wrote to the political scientist Oscar Jászi, was "to learn as a sociologist by close observation the secret (even if it is infernal) of these new times." Mannheim's aim was "to carry liberal values forward" (CUL). His problem remains irresistible to reflective people at the end of the twentieth century. Mannheim's project was to link thinking to emancipation despite strong evidence against the connection. This book is a sympathetic biography of Mannheim's paradoxical—and paradigmatic—project.

In its theoretical reflections, sociological thought cannot long escape ambivalence about the processes of rational ordering to which it belongs. It has understood itself as integral to a new civil mastery whereby humanity's purposes are formulated and pursued by a methodical, self-critical (and thus self-transforming) collective knowledge, and whereby social relations are continually changed to function in congruence with that knowledge. Enlightenment and sociology are born twins. Yet sociological theory has also been haunted by the conviction that while the rational is decisive, it is not enough. Whether we locate its beginnings in Adam Ferguson's civic humanist misgivings about the commercial civil society he analyzed and affirmed, Comte's passion for an unconditional worship to ground the positive age, Durkheim's ingeniously nonrational foundations for the most sophisticated social differentiations and systematizations, or Weber's personalist and decisionist complements to rationalization, classical theory has never fully trusted the mental, institutional, and organizational patterns that it has both displayed and identified as the marks of modern society. Sociologists have conceded to the opponents of their discipline and its world a profound lack in enlightenment thinking. But claims for some all-embracing alternative mode of thinking or relating—whether in the name of ancient virtues, traditional pieties, or romanticisms of various kinds—have been assiduously resisted. The great theoretical models have embodied theoretical

1

and social strategies for managing or harnessing or constitutionalizing a limited openness to antithetical considerations, claiming that their integrative designs can provide the recognition of deep, ineluctable, prerational necessities without which no measure of rationality can be secured. Rationalizing rather than eradicating the irrational has been a central formative theme for sociological theory during the 200 years of its history.

Generations of sociological theorists are distinguishable by the diverse forms of anti-Enlightenment challenges and temptations they have confronted, and intergenerational learning is most promising when a newer generation turns to an older one confronted with comparable tasks. Judging from recent trends in the sociological literature, the present problem-constellation is defined by talk and events that antiquate the two long-dominant sociological strategies for comprehending rationalization and secularization. Marxist and non-Marxist theories of irreversible, cumulative—indeed, progressive—social development appear grounded on misconceptions of what can be known and what can be expected to make a difference in the world. Both established strategies for inclusive rational ordering are stymied by religious outbreaks they cannot master, disruptions of familiar forms of organization, neoromantic oppositions based on blood and belonging, and naturalistic justifications of power and its effects. These confrontations resemble the problem constellation at the beginning of the twentieth century.

The similarities between the two intellectual landscapes explains why many sociological theorists are retracing the moves of that earlier generation, trying again to see what happened: what the classical theorists attempted and in what ways they failed. Such retrieval differs from the academic initiatory rite institutionalized as "history of sociological theory." Nor is past thought treated as simply a quarry for present science. Because sociologists no longer confidently know that they know better, they explore new ways of looking at Durkheim and Weber and Simmel. They deconstruct received opinion about texts and strike new bargains with old authors. The aim is to read interactively in order to learn. In this book, a member of the second founding generation, Karl Mannheim, is subjected to such scrutiny.

Karl Mannheim was born in Budapest in 1893. He earned a degree in philosophy at the university there, with a thesis on the structure of epistemology. In 1919, after the successive collapses of the two postwar revolutionary regimes in Hungary, Mannheim settled in Germany. He had already spent one of his student years there, attending Simmel's lectures in cultural philosophy and sociology, and now established himself as a private scholar in Heidelberg. He attended Alfred Weber's seminars and worked closely with Emil Lederer, and these two sociologists sponsored his successful licensing as authorized tutor (*Privatdozent*), on the strength of his sociological study of German conservatism in the nineteenth century. He gave seminars for five years in Heidelberg, until he was called, after several noted publications and a brilliant debut at the German Sociological Congress in 1928, to succeed Franz Oppenheimer as professor of sociology at Frankfurt. As a recently naturalized citizen and Jew, he was ousted by one of the first National Socialist decrees, in April of 1933. Invited to London by Harold Laski, acting for an elite committee organized to rescue outstanding scholars victimized by the Nazis, Mannheim spent the next ten years as lecturer at the London School of Economics. In the middle of the war, then, he was appointed to the new professorship in the sociology of education at the University of London. He died in 1947 at the age of fifty-three.

During this stressful and brief intellectual career, Mannheim produced much work highly regarded by his contemporaries, and he twice published major books that set the agenda for extensive discussions within and among several disciplines. It is still impossible to think critically about the sociology of knowledge without reflecting on *Ideology and Utopia*. And the continuing debates about planning continually return to *Man and Society in an Age of Reconstruction*. These books have had careers in several countries, at different times. In its German original, *Ideology and Utopia* attracted fascinated reviews from Hannah Arendt, Max Horkheimer, Herbert Marcuse, Paul Tillich, and other outstanding representatives of the younger intellectual generation. In its English version, it has had a long, if flawed, career in the United States, after a disputed reception that helped initiate the careers of Edward S. Shils, Robert K. Merton, and C. Wright Mills. His work on crisis, reconstruction, and planning began as a German-language reflection on the German disaster, addressed primarily to emigrants, but then figured in the English wartime debate on planning, thanks to the interest of A.D. Lindsay, T.S. Eliot, and Bronislaw Malinowski. It intrigued John Dewey and Louis Mumford in the United States, and it stimulated Karl R. Popper,

Friedrich Hayek, Robert A. Dahl, and Charles E. Lindblom to make influential responses. Major collections of other works by Mannheim, including writings left unpublished at his death, have appeared during the past fifty years, generating periodic reconsideration. The case of Karl Mannheim is not closed.

Mannheim developed his sociology of knowledge in a series of writings culminating in *Ideology and Utopia*, a volume of connected essays first published in Germany in 1929 (Mannheim 1929, 1936a). Through his sociology of knowledge, Mannheim attempts a social-scientific way of encountering and partly transcending the irrational elements in all thought bearing on social constitution. The hidden integrative force of such elements in structures of thinking, he argues, is evident from the disorientation effected by political strategies that expose the worldviews of opponents as nothing but ideologies or utopias. While this subversive insight was first loosed on the political world by Marxism, it soon became common property among all parties in Weimar Germany, according to Mannheim, generating a crisis of mutual distrust and poisoning political processes dependent on self-confident reflection, inquiry, debate, and settlements that could be defended in public. The sociology of knowledge promises to break through the impasse by fostering among the parties a realistic assessment of the social situation common to all, paradoxically beginning with a sociological neutralization of the insight into ideology and utopia. If sociology can disinterestedly show how contrasting styles of practical social knowledge are without exception grounded in unacknowledged wishes derived from diverse social locations, the common consciousness among politically active strata about this piece of highly interesting theoretical social knowledge—itself based on a commitment to synthesis sociologically imputable to the intelligentsia as stratum—can gradually expand to grasp the wider social diagnosis that it implies. Universal awareness of ideology and utopia would undergo a decisive change in function, from a paralyzing political poison to organon for a knowledge-oriented but not conflict-free politics.

With the destruction of these hopes in 1933, Mannheim turned to "planning for freedom" as the motif of his writings in exile, beginning with a German-language essay collection published in 1935 and much enlarged in English in 1940 as *Man and Society in an Age of Reconstruction* (Mannheim 1935a; 1940). The National Socialist dictatorship, he now argues, exploits a socially unconscious mass response to a worldwide crisis in the institutions of liberal civilization, involving the obsolescence of its regulative social technologies—from markets to parliaments to elitist humanistic education. Mannheim pleads for a preemptive move to a planned social order that strategically utilizes, instead of vainly resisting, the new social technologies that undermine the spontaneous self-ordering of the previous epoch. A discriminating, consensual reconstruction could save many human qualities and diversities earlier privileged by liberalism, unlike the violent homogenization imposed by communist or National Socialist control through command. Without anachronistic confidence in obsolete forms of liberalism, planning for freedom would rely as far as possible on manipulated field controls (more recently known as steering by induced self-regulation) and other unbureaucratic techniques for coordinating activities that proceed best when experienced as spontaneous. Timely action guided by awareness of the impending crisis taken by leading strata whose positions are still sheltered from the full force of the devastating changes underway, notably the English elite of gentlemanly professionals, can tame the processes that would otherwise destroy the old liberal civilization and condition mass populations for dictatorial domination. Planning for freedom presupposes a reorientation among traditional elites, their acceptance of a sociological diagnosis of the times and their willingness to learn prophylactic and therapeutic techniques. But Mannheim's planning scheme also counts on deep continuities at prerational levels of commitment among his elite audience, commonly religious. Mannheim was never simply a rationalist.

Mannheim's forced exile, following the fatal outcome of the Weimar crisis he still addressed with muted optimism in his 1929 writings, led him to abandon his earlier claims about the catalytic political mission of a relatively unattached intelligentsia wielding a disinterested sociology of knowledge. Weimar intellectuals were politically articulate, inured to crisis-consciousness, and persuadable that party conflict merited their care. Although increasingly deaf to reason, the parties other than the National Socialist shared the ancient Western hope that, despite appearances, an unseen humane order hovers over the chaotic surface of historical events. However powerless in the ordinary sense, intellectuals might be made to matter in their own right, as illuminators and mediators. In England Mannheim thought he had found a world of self-absorbed scholar-hobbyists comfortably chatting with secure elites who saw little reason to reconsider conventional wisdoms and who smoothly coopted their occasional naysayers. In Weimar Germany, he wrote to counter a crisis where, in his view, all principal political actors were being demoralized by disclosure of partisan irrationalities behind their reasonings. In the England of 1936, by contrast, Mannheim reported himself smothered by the confidence in vested prejudices pervasive in the political class. Instead of counteracting universal distrust, the sociology of knowledge now had to unsettle self-assurance, to foster a sense of crisis that could lead this comparatively intact elite to look to the sociological teachings of an outsider like himself for diagnostic and therapeutic help. This shift in emphasis, amounting almost to a reversal, leaves confusing tracks in the English version of *Ideology and Utopia*.

The prime victims of this confusion were American sociologists, because they were the most responsive English-speaking audience for Mannheim's sociology of knowledge. Since they resonated to neither the German nor the English rhetorical sonorities discordantly compounded in *Ideology and Utopia*, they typically abstracted isolated elements from the work and molded them to fit their own intellectual strategies, dismissing the remainder as historically conditioned excess. Mannheim's *Man and Society in an Age of Reconstruction*, in turn, was received during the first decades after its publication by a subgroup among American social scientists who treated his sociology of knowledge as largely irrelevant, except for its most commonplace cautions against the dangers of deceptive ideologies, and sifted out accessible generalizations about social technologies for problem-oriented planners and educators. *Ideology and Utopia* and *Man and Society in an Age of Reconstruction* thus soon dwindled to the status of minor classics, superceded scientifically, but useful for pedagogical exercises in academic curricula.

Mannheim's position as a seminal theorist is by no means secure. Important passages in his best-known political work, abstracted from the diagnosis of global crisis and trust in an immovable British political culture that pervade them, bring him close to authoritarian panaceas now patently obsolete. His philosophical interests and speculative methods make him suspect to empirical sociologists; and his respect for Weberian social-scientific ideals antagonizes antipositivists. It is only as Mannheim's political perplexities become pertinent again and as the simplistic disciplinary oppositions lose plausibility that the undeniable presence of Mannheim at the starting points for compelling questions can be acknowledged, and the riddles of his achievements and failings can be recognized as bearing directly on those of the present.

While it remains worthwhile to assess Mannheim's contributions to specialized subdisciplines—the sociological study of political ideologies, culture, organization, planning, politics, education, women, intellectuals, generations—our book, instead, investigates the design that brought him to all these matters. The suggestion of a design is not meant to indicate that there is some grand unified theory to be found or an elegant dialectical progression through Mannheim's works. There is, rather, a search for alternatives, a complex sensibility and a distinctive openness to hard findings about the social world. The story of Mannheim is a story of working at social theorizing. He writes essays but aspires to synthesis and system; he wants to dig empirically and dig deep but he feels called to give concrete advice; he cannot stop reflecting on the place and role of intellectuals but he takes as a model the knowledge of the practical actor who commands a situation.

Political thinking and thinking about politics figure in Mannheim's thinking, even when he seems to be putting them aside. His preoccupation with ideologies derives from the conviction that political knowledge is decisive to the most fascinating and determinative processes in human life. He expects his findings to bear on the matters ideologies are about and not only on what ideologies do in society. In consequence, this book begins with an interpretation of Mannheim's political interest. Since that interest poses problems about the nature of knowledge, the opening is by no means intended to unveil and expose discrediting "ideological" compulsions. Attention shifts, instead, to Mannheim's humanistic efforts to circumscribe the knowledge required for human life and to his conclusion that sociological study has displaced the humanities as its method. Mannheim's thought flourishes in that belief. Then comes the crisis that undermines the plausibility of his intellectual strategy. Mannheim's efforts to restore his project require him to cope with disillusionment and exile, and to negotiate with alien modes of thinking. Issues of education increasingly overshadow his political inquiries, and the book ends with the question of how one can learn from Mannheim.

Mannheim belongs to a cultural generation and exhibits a style that values hints and allusions and multiple meanings, even while he acknowledges the authority of rigorous method and the power of firm evidence. To follow after his thinking requires patience and tolerance for essayistic experimentation.[1] A characteristic feature of Mannheim's thought is a willingness to reopen questions prematurely closed by others, to keep alternatives in reserve, to let difficulties find solution later. Although Mannheim's conception of sociology's disciplinary design professed allegiance to Max Weber's specialist model, he located this design, in his reflections as in the discussions he eagerly sought, in a wider context that comprehended not only multiple academic disciplines but also the essayistic literary world of political controversy and cultural commentary.

Mannheim consistently professed to value openness. This commitment is implicit in his rationales for publishing collections of essays instead of systematic works. In 1928, for example, Mannheim arranged the publication of his two essays on "Historicism" and "The Problem of a Sociology of Knowledge" together with a new essay on Max Weber in book form.[2] When the publisher, Paul Siebeck, asked Mannheim to rework the two previously published essays to make a more novel and integrated whole, Mannheim replied: "As for the reworking of the two other essays, this could not be radical in any case, if only because these works represent a searching, experimenting penetration of the contemporary intellectual condition; and the author's changes in position, his intellectual adventures, must not be disguised" (Mannheim to Siebeck, October 1, 1928. JCBM).

In both the German and the English versions of *Ideology and Utopia*, Mannheim insists that the constituent essays must be accepted as distinct and overlapping experiments. In a letter to Louis Wirth, indignantly disputing the critical review of *Ideology and Utopia* by Alexander von Schelting in the *American Sociological Review*, Mannheim protests that von Schelting "suppresses the fact that the author expressly says that he is on the search, that a number of systems are at work in a single human being, and that therefore he himself—relying on the new method of 'experimental thinking'—does not cover over the inconsistencies that arise" (Mannheim to Wirth, December 28, 1936. LWP/7:11).

This preference for the essay mode is not the product of diffidence. Mannheim's theoretical assertions were aggressive enough. But he considered systematic works premature. He writes in *Man and Society in an Age of Reconstruction*:

I feel that we should not aim at absolute consistency at too early a stage, when our main task is rather to break the old habits of thought and to find the new keys to the understanding of the changing world.... The politician, if he is to gain a following, is forced to draw up a clear and definite programme. But if there is to be a science of politics and of society, there must be no obligation to find a definite solution before the time is ripe. The sociologist must be able to say: "Thus far have I come and no further: the rest I leave to my successors." (Mannheim 1940: 33)

There are new reasons for probing the records of Mannheim's search, especially since the theoretical approaches that had so confidently declared his work anachronistic and hopelessly eclectic have themselves fallen on hard times. The self-aware and self-critical rhetorical constituents in his thinking, his sensitivity to cultural contexts, his informed skepticism about Marxist historical ontologies, his experiments with dialectics that eschew more than provisional syntheses, his recognition of multiple modes of knowing, and other features of his unfinished thinking repay critical attention. And that requires a reconstruction of his project as a whole. Karl Mannheim's most influential works turn on two distinct conceptions, the "sociology of knowledge" and "planning for freedom," and they are generally considered apart. Yet they form a common project for reconstituting political knowledge.

Notes

1. Mannheim never published anything but essays. His best-known works, *Ideology and Utopia* and *Man and Society in an Age of Reconstruction* are collections of essays, different in English and German, and are each expressly announced as assembling "thought experiments" exploring related but not necessarily consistent theoretical possibilities. Five of his more ambitious treatises were left unfinished and unpublished, except for portions worked into essays. The five works are: "The Distinctive Character of Cultural-Sociological Knowledge" and "A Sociological Theory of Culture and its Knowability (Conjunctive and Communicative Thinking)," both published in *Structures of Thinking* ([1922–24] 1984); *Conservatism* ([1925] 1986); the original "Sociology of Spirit," revised by his editors and published as "Toward the Sociology of the Mind" in *Essays in the Sociology of Culture* (1956); and *Freedom, Power and Democratic Planning* (1950).
2. Mannheim failed to deliver the manuscript of the book and it was therefore never published. The originally proposed title, *Wissenssoziologische Analysen zur gegenwärtigen Denkweise. Drei Essays über M. Weber, Troeltsch und Scheler*, was later changed by Mannheim to *Analysen zur gegenwärtigen Denklage. Drei Untersuchungen über M. Weber, Troeltsch, und Scheler*. Cp. Mannheim's letter to Paul Siebeck of October 12, 1928 and Siebeck's letter to Mannheim of May 28, 1929 (JCBM), and the first edition of *Ideologie und Utopie* (Mannheim 1929: 215).

1

Politics as a Science

Karl Mannheim often commented on the social condition of the out-sider who stands on the margin of an integrated social field or on the boundary between two or more. No condition was more familiar to him. While the position of a Jewish student and young intellectual in the Budapest of 1910 may have been "marginal" only when viewed from the nationalist perspective his self-enclosed circle of assimilated Jews disdained, twice in his life he underwent the experience of exile and twice had to find a voice and a language appropriate to a newcomer. He left Hungary in 1919, after the failures of the social liberal and Soviet regimes, when the White reaction often conflated Jewish origins and complicity with Béla Kun; and he fled Germany for England in 1933, after the National Socialist decree excluding almost all Jews from the civil service deprived him of the Frankfurt professorship that he had only recently gained.

But it was not only force of circumstance that brought him to the boundary. Already as a young man in Budapest he had chosen an intel-lectual place for himself between proponents of reform based on social science, led by Oscar Jászi, and advocates of cultural renovation grounded on an aesthetic philosophy, under Georg Lukács. And during his Ger-man academic career, he prided himself on standing between sociology and philosophy, as well as between the exciting world of intellectual criticism and the exacting world of academic rigor.[1] Mannheim's En-glish writings include reflections on the role of the refugee, and on his special mission as a mediator between European and Anglo-Saxon in-tellectual modes of thinking; and he aimed his work at creating conjunc-tions between sociology and education, between the preoccupations of practical reformers and those of the university (Mannheim 1940: 3-27).

Mannheim was not satisfied to enjoy the ironic distance and insights his sometime teacher Georg Simmel ascribed to the boundary condition (Simmel 1968: 509–12; Honegger 1993). He believed it also creates a unique opportunity to mediate antithetical forces and to work for syntheses—indeed, that it implies a mission to do so. In his accounts of the sociology of knowledge, the inquiry for which he is best known, he emphasizes that the very possibility of this approach to ideas and culture depends on the existence of a social stratum whose members have lived in diverse cultural and social settings and are now situated where they can experience that diversity (Mannheim [1922–24] 1982: 255–71; Mannheim [1925] 1986:117–21). But the aim of their intellectual labors should not be the impressionistic relish of diversity he found in Simmel (Mannheim [1918] 1985), but to foment a common spirit in society.

This preoccupation with bridging mutually alien worlds, overcoming conflicts, and cultivating comprehensive unities gives his thought a political cast and provides one source of his interest in political thinking. Mannheim's two best-known works treat materials of primary interest to political writers. In *Ideology and Utopia*, he subjects complexes of political ideas to sociological interpretation, and in *Man and Society in an Age of Reconstruction* he proposes a design for reorganizing the social order to overcome the crises that afflict public life. In both books, however, he disregards primary concepts of political discourse and slights many issues central to political theory. In Mannheim's writings, questions of rational public policy displace questions of legitimate authority, justice, citizenship, or the best constitution. We find ideology and sociology instead of political theory, and, especially in his later writings, elites instead of governors, techniques of social control instead of law, command or coercion, questions of integration and coordination instead of power and resistance. Precisely because of this systematic recontextualization and reconceptualization of political issues, the view from political theory offers exceptional insight into Mannheim's ambitions for sociology.

Some writers have objected that Mannheim epitomizes a twentieth-century betrayal of political theory, and that his work is vitiated by subordination of human action to social process.[2] Such sweeping arguments reify a distinctive cultural formation institutionalized in localized academic traditions. The defining features of theories about politics are not, as many academic political theorists contend, the moral problem of obligation or the question of the best constitution or any theme from the conventional curriculum. It is more appropriate for political theorists to pay close attention to any sustained attempt to depict a structured relationship between politics and knowledge; and it is best to recognize that such attempts will differ markedly in the concepts and problems made central, the approaches found appropriate, and the criteria for justifying theoretical claims. Mannheim's engagements with political thinking cannot be dismissed with a formula, although his commitments to sociology as institutionalized cultural formation undoubtedly limit his contributions to political thought.

Questions about what actors can know and how they can know it have special weight in political inquiry. They refer, for example, to that "recognition" without which authority is inconceivable; they refer to responsibility; and they refer to the distinctive capacity for judgment that all political theories locate somewhere in political life and that is supposed to vindicate the coercion and violence that are everywhere features of that sphere. When political theorists are secure in their answers to questions about the nature of knowledge, they construct new questions that presuppose those answers—as with older inquiries about natural law or recent Anglo-American moral philosophizing on political themes. But if the problems of knowledge themselves require new solutions, traditional topics are recast to reflect these fundamental investigations.

The theme of knowledge enters the understanding of political thought at two levels. First are the problems that arise when theories are construed as structures of knowledge, not bodies of opinion. And second are the questions arising from tasks assigned to knowledge in the political world. Mannheim thought that a sociological approach, grounded on the boundary position of the social type of the "intellectual," could break through the impasse he found blocking thinking in both dimensions. What appears to Mannheim as a Copernican new insight into the nature of political knowledge requires a substantial reformulation of traditional political concepts and relations. Mannheim proposes the sociology of knowledge not only as a critique of prevailing traditions of political thought—charging them with illusions about political knowledge and about their knowledge about that knowledge—but also as an opening to the authentic constitutive problems of liberal, conservative, and socialist political thought. Beyond sociology of knowledge as exposé of ideological distortion, then, Mannheim offers it as a way towards political knowledge.

Mannheim's political interest developed over a period of years. In his earliest writings he is dismissive of the political domain. Following German antimaterialist currents, and especially his Hungarian mentor, Georg Lukács, he sets out to oppose the incorporation of ethical and aesthetic issues in a uniform positivist system that restricts the range of the thinkable by its methodological dogma. Envisioning instead a pluralist universe of diverse spiritual projects, he seeks to restore the legitimacy of humanist concerns by uncovering their respective places in disparate domains, each yielding its own kind of knowledge in its own way. In the context of these discussions, the political sphere originally appears un-interesting—an arena for the adjustment of narrow interests devoid of spiritual meaning. The position dramatically changed when Lukács ex-trapolated a Communist program from the "revolutionary culturism" entailed by the antipositivism they shared. Mannheim shrank from this consequence but abandoned his disparagement of political relations.

Mannheim's "Letters from Exile" (1924) illustrate his movement to-wards a reassessment of politics. In sum, political responsibility is equiva-lent to bearing witness. As one of the Hungarians who left home after the establishment of the "White" regime in 1919, Mannheim distinguishes between the emigration and the exile. The emigration, he maintains, in-cludes many afraid to stay because of their unthinking participation in the brief Soviet regime. Others have better reasons to fear. But the "exile," he contends, comprises the self-exiled like himself, someone who could re-main in Hungary without harassment but "thinks that bridging the gap between his own viewpoint and that of the regime is impossible." This genuine exile "has an important 'national goal.' It saves and keeps alive the free spirit of the Hungarian mind and awakens the conscience of the Hungarian people.... The soul of the Hungarian people is for freedom, moral rebirth and is opposed to corruption.... We love our people more than these criminals." Admittedly, such inspirational writing is far from Mannheim's substantial work, but there is an intriguing parallel between this notion of "exile" and the recurrent motif of "homeless" intellectuals comprising distinct political-cultural formations of persons responsible for serving their people by faithfully serving the spirit.

Mannheim's reassessment of politics comes with a redrawing of the boundaries of the political. Eventually he finds an element of political thinking in all thought other than the strictly technical. In the transitional methodological reflections leading up to the sociology of knowledge, he already takes practical political knowledge (as in Machiavellian statesmanship) as paradigm for all qualitative, nonpositivist thinking:

> While natural-scientific knowledge abstracts completely from the specific situation of the knowing subject, practical-political knowledge gains its distinctive character precisely from the fact that it gains knowledge from within situations and acts with situations in view... [T]he special capacity of the concrete, prescientific practical actor consists in perspectivistically bringing the given facts into an order relevant to himself and to his own situation. (Mannheim [1922–24] 1982:158)

Mannheim's emphasis on practical judgment generates an interest in understanding ideas that address political matters in the narrow sense. By reinterpreting them in a sociological context he means to incorporate and to correct earlier political thought. The aim is a knowledge about political thinking and substantive political matters that is patterned methodologically on practitioners' thinking, but includes social and philosophical dimensions conventionally excluded.

When "political" is taken in a broad sense to refer to all "activity aiming at the transformation of the world" in conformity with a structured will (Mannheim [1929] 1952:214), as Mannheim urges, the sociological interpretation of works in philosophy and sociology reveals the political character of the intellectual activities they document. When he traces his own pedigree to the philosophy of Hegel (Mannheim [1925] 1986) and to the sociology of Max Weber (Mannheim [1929a] 1993), Mannheim is not denying the political design of his work. He treats his predecessors—now heedless of disciplinary classifications—by linking them to intellectual projects defined by liberal, conservative, and socialist political ideologies. To view Mannheim in the context of political thought, then, is to take him as he saw himself.

Mannheim and the Liberal Style of Thought

To classify Mannheim as a political partisan who fits neatly into one of his own categories of ideological ideal types—as conservative, liberal, or socialist—would be to close one's thinking to the principal challenge implicit in all of his essays, the challenge to work patiently amidst discontinuity, complexity, and novelty. Yet Mannheim's political thought has an identifiable point of departure and reference: the internal debates about liberalism attending the rise of "social liberalism" since the end of the nineteenth century. In his native Hungary, such debates split the "Second Reform Generation" influential in his youth, and brought into prominence Oscar Jászi, second only to Georg Lukács in his influence on Mannheim's early intellectual development. The author Mannheim later claims as his own philosopher, John Dewey, was the foremost American voice of "social" or "new liberalism." As Alfonso Damico says in his study of Dewey, "The belief that mutual aid, not merely mutual forbearance, marks the good society is crucial to the new liberalism. To make liberalism a more reform-oriented political theory, its proponents attack the individualism of classical liberalism" (Damico 1978; Dewey [1930] 1962, [1935] 1960; Collini 1979: 13–50; Sklar 1988:33–40). Mannheim's refusal to align himself with any competitor of liberalism places implicit limits on his political experimentation; his place in the history of twentieth-century liberalism clarifies central motifs in his thinking.

In a typically ambiguous memorandum, undated but originating in the mid-1930s, Mannheim takes note of an "uneven development of [my] attitudes and thought: while my intellect recognizes that liberalism is obsolete, my attitudes remain on a liberal plane" (KMP). A decade earlier, in his work on conservative thought, Mannheim had assigned special importance to a distinction analogous to that between attitudes and thinking. He there distinguishes between the determinate patterns of consciousness through which humans mediate their experiences of the world, on the one hand, and, on the other, their conceptualized thinking. He takes the underlying patterns as embodying formative will; they constitute the animating principles of a "style." "Structural analysis" of a doctrine, he argues, involves the discovery of the stylistic principle giving it structure and therewith direction. The "style" is a plan. In *Conservatism*, he also takes up the possibility of "thought" that does not rest upon such a structured mode of experiencing, but he treats it as a surface phenomenon, incapable of securing authentic knowledge. Anything like Mannheim's reported "disproportion between thought and attitudes," on this analysis, would call for skepticism about his conviction of the obsolescence of liberalism.

During his Weimar years, Mannheim was influenced by Marxian socialist theory, and he recognized other contestants in the ideological field as well, but his deeper analyses constantly come back to a fundamental opposition between liberal (or progressive) and conservative political thinking and to the need for synthesis between them. In his study of conservative thought, Mannheim offers a revealing contrast between the formative principles of liberal and conservative thinking. Although *Conservatism*, written for his university habilitation under conditions of political pressure from the nationalist Right, is artfully designed to communicate with conservative readers, the further development of Mannheim's theorizing builds on the liberal side of the comparison.

Mannheim claims that liberalism is conditioned by a consciousness of the possible, not the actual; that it experiences time as the beginning of the future, not as the end of the past or as eternal now. Matters to be understood are placed in the context of a projected future or in essential relationship to some universal ideal norm, not in the context of their past or of some immanent tendency. Liberals, according to Mannheim, think of their fellows as contemporaries, as associates in a temporal continuum, not as compatriots sharing some communal space with past and future. Structuralism is a liberal way of organizing knowledge: the liberal seeks to understand things as rationalized and subject to purposive control. The conservative, in contrast, pursues interpretive intuition and appreciation. Liberals, moreover, experience the world as abstraction, explicable by universal theories, while conservatives respond to concrete, unanalyzed complexities. Tied to this, in Mannheim's view, is liberalism's vision of complex entities as accumulations of individual units and its perception of time as a cumulation of discrete moments. Mannheim emphasizes the one-sidedness of theories based on liberal experiences and insists on the corrective value of conservatism, but the synthesis he proposes is asymmetrical. Defining situations in terms of a "next step," structural analysis, theoretical comprehension, the perception of generations and contemporaneity are the major presuppositions of his subsequent work. His critiques of rationalism, ahistorism, and individualism address substantive points of liberal doctrine requiring adjustment, but the liberal elements constitute the structure and plan of his inquiry. Judged by his own indicators, his style of thought is predominantly liberal.

Like John Dewey, Mannheim distinguishes between an old liberalism and a new, and dismisses only the former as anachronistic and philosophically inadequate. Even in his practical political creed he builds on the tradition of the reformist movement led in the Budapest of his youth by Oscar Jászi. Writing to Jászi in 1936, in response to his criticism of

Mensch und Gesellschaft, the original German version of *Man and Society*, Mannheim says:

> I am an old follower of yours and the impressions of my youth of the purity of your character are so profound that all reproofs I find paternal and they touch me deeply.... I find the basic difference between the two of us in one thing. In my opinion, both of us are "liberal" in our roots. You, however, wish to stand up against the age with a noble defiance, while I, as a sociologist, would like to learn by close observation the secret (even if it is infernal) of these new times, because I believe that this is the only way that we can remain masters over the social structure, instead of it mastering us. To carry liberal values forward with the help of the techniques of modern mass society is probably a paradoxical undertaking; but it is the only feasible way, if one does not want to react with defiance alone. But I am also familiar with such a way of reacting, and it is probably only a matter of time until I join you in it. (Mannheim to Jászi, November 8, 1936. CUL)

Mannheim's many departures from his liberal "roots," even when presented as tough-minded concessions to historical imperatives, can best be understood through his search for an inclusive and philosophically grounded way of comprehending liberal calls for reason, reconciliation, responsibility, and personal development. But the letter to Jászi shows the important respect in which the parallel to Dewey fails. Far from serving as point of departure, as with Dewey, democracy is not highly valued in Mannheim's versions of "new liberalism." Democratic institutions are instruments or social facts; the liberal task is to foster reasonableness in their operations. Mannheim's conception builds on continental liberalism, always uneasy in its alliances with democratic forces.

Social Liberalism in Budapest

When Mannheim arrived at the University of Budapest in 1912, he followed a well-established path that took him from a club for reform-minded students, the Galileo Circle, to its sponsoring lodge of liberal Freemasons and on to the meeting rooms and lectures of Jászi's Society for Social Science. The reformers avowed themselves "socialists" rather than "individualists" on questions of economic organization, but they stressed that their advocacy of planning and regulation had nothing to do with class struggle or class revolution, not to speak of the dictatorship of the proletariat or the abolition of the state. The state, they thought, must be strong, liberal, parliamentary, and democratic. Oscar Jászi wrote in 1908:

To raise humanity to the highest conceivable level of morality, science, aesthetics, and hygiene—that is the objective. The way to it is through ever greater mastery of objects by the human spirit. The principal idea of socialism, thoroughgoing planful cooperation, is undoubtedly a more scientific idea than the main idea of individualism.... But at the same time there must not be missing that quantum of freedom which determines goals, makes discoveries possible, changes antiquated conditions, precludes arbitrary rule, and allows the advancement of the best.[3]

In support of these objectives, the reform group lent its support to the Socialist Party in campaigns for democratic suffrage and political liberalization. Democratization was reconciled with the requirements for "scientific" policy by confidence in the influence of a dedicated and enlightened intelligentsia. Their authority was to be exercised, above all, through their contributions to creating an educated mass public. At the opening of a "Free School for Social Studies," soon to be expanded into a program of Workers' Schools supported by the socialist trade unions, Jászi emphasized the nonpartisan but also political character of this activity:

We must...make every effort to work out a new morality, a new ethics in place of the decaying old religious or metaphysical one. A new morality, founded on science and human solidarity.... One more word about the road to this end.... [It] can only be the road of free inquiry. The road knows neither dogmas nor party-truths. No socialist party-truths either, needless to add. (Horváth 1966: 135)

And indeed, radical intellectuals repeatedly praised these schools for moderating the unthinking socialist enthusiasm of the masses. While the Socialist leadership saw in the Workers' Schools an instrument for organizing and mobilizing the hitherto unpolitical industrial workers, the lecturers themselves hoped for a different kind of popular education and stressed the complex and technical character of problems encountered in managing social change, implying that solutions of these problems require leadership by the well-educated. Shortly before the First World War, Jászi founded the Radical Party. Speaking to a membership meeting, he said:

Guidance for the ideal politician can only come from the Platonic ideal: an age must come when public life is controlled by philosophers, when persons of complete theoretical knowledge and complete moral purity take the lead. (*Pester Lloyd*, December 31, 1918)

Mannheim rejected the philosophical arguments and cultural premises supporting these social liberal pronouncements when he became absorbed in Lukács' Sunday Circle after 1916. But variations on the substantive political themes recur throughout his work; and in the 1930s he reasserted virtually the whole creed as his own. This provides an additional reason for placing his work in the liberal tradition.

Structural Problems of Liberalism after Mill

The characterization of the liberal tradition offered in this sketch of the style of thought and the practical political creed that were Mannheim's points of departure will not satisfy those who define liberalism exclusively in terms of "negative freedom" or "distrust of political power" or "individual consent." But an adequate conception of liberalism as a tradition precludes abstracting isolated points from Locke's *Second Treatise*, Smith's *Wealth of Nations*, or Mill's *Liberty* and treating these as touchstones. The story of liberalism is a story of adjustments in classical conceptions, as they are placed in new contexts designed to meet changing conceptions of theoretical knowledge, as well as developments in other, not hitherto political, studies variously taken as relevant to political theorizing by successive liberal theorists .

In his study of John Stuart Mill and the constitution of liberalism as a tradition, Robert Denoon Cumming identifies deep structural problems confronting modern attempts to think philosophically about liberalism. Cumming suggests that liberalism since Mill has been preoccupied with method, that it has been taken up with a process of adjusting creedal principles to a novel set of considerations about ways of holding, discussing, and legitimating political opinions. Taking Mill as the representative liberal, Cumming highlights two features characteristic of liberal ventures in political philosophy: first, the liberal political thinker defines his own intellectual situation as a period of "transition" or "crisis" requiring a major reinterpretation of the "tradition" comprising historically liberal ethical ideals and political ideas; second, the modern liberal believes that in political thought as in politics conflicts are surmountable, that they represent "differences of opinion...resolvable by some kind of transition and adjustment" (Cumming 1969: 16).

In the work of John Stuart Mill, these two assumptions run through the essays, treatises, and journalistic writings that variously confront the interrelated methodological issues that Mill identifies as central to his concerns:

In politics, though I had no longer accepted the doctrine of [James Mills'] *Essay on Government*...as a scientific theory, though I ceased to consider representative democracy as an absolute principle, and regarded it as a question of time, place, and circumstances; though I now looked upon the choice of political institutions as a moral and educational question more than one of material interests...; nevertheless, this change in the premises of my political philosophy did not alter my practical political creed as to the requirements of my own time and country. I was as much as ever a radical and democrat for Europe, and especially for England. (Mill 1924: 110)

The three central problems, interpreted as structural by Cumming, are:

1. the relationship between political ideas and the requirements of scientific theory: can political ideas be recast so as to reveal them as the outcome of scientific inquiry, or, if not, how can they be thought of as subject to rational assessment and choice?
2. appropriateness to time, place, and circumstances: is a theory of history the proper context for moral and political decision and, if so, does this not imply a relativism destructive of the constitutive dedication to the values proper to human nature?
3. the question of the extent to which political teachings, as pedagogical components of a political order valued for its character-building, are themselves matters of "moral cultivation" and education: is political discussion to be governed by its ethical effects on both discussants and auditors, as in rhetorical conceptions of political knowledge, and, if so, what is to prevent political ideas from becoming either wholly unrealistic or starkly manipulative?

Mill failed to solve these problems, and, indeed, Cumming concludes that liberalism appears condemned to "a certain eagerness for elaborating...methodological precepts and remedial programs for the construction of the science of politics—without actually constructing it" (Cumming 1969: 12).

Yet the liberal thinkers represented by Jászi believed they could solve Mill's three structural problems.

1. They thought that science, in the broad sense they gave the term, generates and vindicates their doctrine. As suggested by Jászi's distinction between scientific principles and ethical purity, the knowledge needed may be distributed between distinct sciences of means and ends. Methods of knowing may differ for differing classes of objects, but in principle the whole forms a unified structure comprising universally valid relationships between the subjects and objects of knowledge, and it provides the means for answering without prejudice the questions human-

kind must address. Formulations of both kinds of knowledge, moreover, are equally theoretical, logical, and demonstrable to unbiased intelligence. For these continental liberals, in short, idealist philosophy provides a conception of knowledge that overcomes the difficulties created for Mill by his empiricism, while retaining the empirically founded social sciences.

When scientific intellect addresses the social and political realm, according to this theory, it finds *itself* as underlying principle. Things make sense because they are ordered by knowledge. There are two qualifications. The knowledge constituting the empirical social world may be radically imperfect and incomplete. And events in the social world may be dominated for a time by irrationality. Force and ignorance have consequences. Civilization is an achievement of progress, not a metaphysical given. This conception arises as philosophically informed supposition in Kant's *Idea for a Universal History*, but now appears to these thinkers a matter of scientific knowledge yielded by the sociological inquiries following Comte and Spencer. As knowledge becomes more complex and complete, the supervision of affairs by those initiated in sociological knowledge becomes ever more feasible, but also more necessary.

Knowledge can have effect in the world, they believe, because scientific method and philosophy rally those who share in knowledge self-confidently around rational public policies. Those most victimized by irrational oppression can accept the authority of the knowledgeable segment of society because mass education popularizes scientific legitimacy and because they directly benefit from alliances between organizations of protest and educated progressives. Democratization, accordingly, destroys the power of obscurantist privilege and opens the way to rational solutions. Like their counterparts in Germany, England, France, and the United States, the Hungarian reformers believed in the imminence of a popular scientific culture.

The dark fears of the tyranny of the majority that had distracted J.S. Mill are now ascribed to insufficient confidence in the cumulative character of social rationalization, failure to recognize that steady refinements in the division of labor elevate popular needs and beliefs. Industrial workers disciplined by their roles in engineered industrial workplaces and organized in strategy-minded unions, for example, need not be feared as a mob threatening to civilization. Jászi thought that experience with Marxist social movements before the Boshevik upheaval confirmed the feasibility of "rule in the state by laboring peasants and worker masses, under the leadership of the genuine, truly creative intellectuals" (Jászi 1923:12). Knowledge can be power because power depends on opinion and opinion can be cultivated.

2. The liberals of Mannheim's youth thought themselves exempted from the difficulties that distressed their predecessors by advances that had been made in both theory and practice. This does not mean that they saw the validity of theoretical knowledge as being relative to time and place. While development and progress are vital elements in the social sciences and while the attainment of knowledge itself progresses over time, normative criteria are timeless and universal. In the end, Jászi maintained, the formal norms of validity derive from principles implicit in the conception of a rational and free humanity. Political knowledge consequently addresses different problems and possibilities at different times and places, but the standards that define them as problems or possibilities are themselves universal. Epistemology is not historical in principle.

3. Similarly, the alleged strains between rhetorical uplift and scientific communication—the pedagogical and cognitive functions of theory, the contributions of knowledge to spiritual progress and utilitarian improvement—are referred to a confused or defeatist frame of mind. Participation in knowledge, Jászi thought, provides self-command and command over events. Knowledge can be inculcated in degrees and by stages, and the simplifications required by popularization need not compromise the standards constituting genuine theoretical knowledge.

A high level of material civilization, if wrought by free social actors, according to this doctrine, affords resources for cultural creativity and leisure for cultural appreciation. There is no conflict between social organization for moral improvement and innovative productivity. Choices experienced as dilemmas during the harsh early years of the new civilization now appear compatible, matters of preferences and timing. Persistent agonizing over the choices is a technique of obscurantist propagandists, whose hostility to progress in fact stems from the interests of the privileged or, at best, from a sensibility appropriate enough to poetic or religious genius but not entitled to deflect progressive reason. While important strategic questions of relations between moral education and intellectual interests remain, they can be answered by political knowledge if posed in rational and specific ways. The questions are not viewed as threats to the structure of knowledge itself. The combination of idealist philosophy and positivist sociology appeared to Jászi and his followers to overcome the philosophical quandaries of liberalism since Mill.

Those familiar with Thomas Mann's *The Magic Mountain* may hear the sermonizing of the progressive Freemason, Settembrini, in all this and turn away in impatience. Such reaction, however, is not helpful for understanding Mannheim. He is undoubtedly moved by the considerations the dark Jesuitical Bolshevik, Naphta, puts before the ingenuous Hans Castorp.[4] Georg Lukács was more important to Mannheim's intellectual formation than Oscar Jászi. But Mannheim does not imagine that negations of enthusiastic bourgeois progressivism are solutions, nor is he prepared to repose in the ironic, Olympian distance. For the liberal reformers, the most important new studies requiring recontextualization of liberal elements are sociological. Mannheim distanced himself from this intellectual structure, under the influence of Simmel and Lukács, by emphasizing the importance of other historical and cultural studies. But his shift evidenced his conviction that Jászi's liberalism sacrifices vital interests of personal fulfillment because of its deference to a social science he considered positivist and hostile to spirituality. That is, after all, a liberal objection to the prevalent form of liberalism.

During all the phases of Mannheim's work, his writings display in classical form the characteristic themes Cumming leads us to expect in liberal thinking. He rejects the methodology utilized by the liberals and consequently reopens the questions they thought to have resolved with its help: (1) Beginning with his doctoral dissertation on epistemology, Mannheim recurrently sought to relate his cultural and critical inquiries to the philosophical delineation of knowledge and especially to the requirements of scientific theory; (2) the themes of history and historicism are even more pervasive in Mannheim's work, as are (3) his efforts to specify how the culture-forming and pedagogical qualities of theoretical beliefs and utterances affects their status as theory. Throughout his life, Mannheim described his work as a work of transition necessitated by a crisis in the liberal tradition and order, and he made it his avowed objective to develop a synthesis that would acknowledge and comprehend the partial legitimacy of each of the bitterly contending and mutually incomprehending parties making up the theoretical and political fields. His central questions ultimately turn on the character of scientific political knowledge. The topics of Mannheim's studies indicate his lifelong preoccupation with the constitutive structural problems of liberal political thinking, and this provides a third, deeper, reason for emphasizing his relations to liberalism.

Science and Politics as Vocation

In the core chapter of *Ideologie und Utopie*, "Is Politics as a Science Possible?,"[5] Mannheim exposes the longing for a science of politics as a typical feature of bourgeois liberal-democratic thought. Yet the essay associates Mannheim with the search. He observes that liberalism created the "systemic location" for a science of politics, just as it formed institutions like parliaments, electoral systems, and the League of Nations, to rationalize political conflict. As expounded in liberal doctrine, these conceptions are vitiated by a misleading "intellectualism" that overvalues the cognitive power and practical efficacy of abstract thinking oriented to universal laws. What is needed, Mannheim argues, is a more adequate conception of what it means to grasp and to govern the political world by reason. He clearly does not advocate an abandonment of the underlying design.

The continuity between Mannheim's thesis and the liberal objective is made graphic by his extended metaphorical use of the term "platform." In criticizing the liberal theory of knowledge, Mannheim remarks, "it was thus the foremost aim of this style of thought to create a purified platform of universally valid knowledge which is knowable and communicable by all" (Mannheim [1929] 1952: 147). Such knowledge cannot be. But there can be a science of politics after all and a "platform" where it will operate. Moreover, Mannheim claims, this locus of political knowledge involves persons whose wills are free from constraints, who have political choice or decision before them (Mannheim [1929] 1952: 141).

The spatial metaphor is important here, linking bodies of knowledge with forums for action. Mannheim is talking about a place to stand where knowledge and choice matter, and that commands the field of political life. Established liberal conceptions of political science and parliaments are poor designs for such a platform. Mannheim's proposals for political education offers a better one:

> But should there not and could there not be a form of political awakening that speaks to the comparatively free will which is and should to an ever greater degree become the foundation of the modern intellectual stratum. Would we not simply be

giving up a significant achievement of European history precisely in the critical moment when the part machine threatens to overwhelm us, if we did not make the attempt to strengthen the tendencies which enable us to make decisions on the basis of prior comprehensive orientation? Is political awkening only possible by way of strict discipline? Is not a will that has incorporated criticism also a will, and even a higher form of will, which should not be readily renounced...Or must it be assumed that only preparation for an insurrection is to be deemed political action? Is not the continual transformation of conditions and people also action?...And is it to be assumed that precisely the will which seeks to establish a dynamic equilibrium, which has comprehensive vision, lacks a tradition and form of cultivation appropriate to it? Would it not be in the general interest to create new centers of political will quickened by critical conscience? There exists the need for a platform where that which is necessary for such a critical orientation...can be taught in way which presupposes people still searching for solutions, people who have not yet committed themselves. (Mannheim [1929] 1952: 160. Cp. Mannheim 1936a: 163)

But if the difficulties that Mill had identified have not been solved by the proposals of Jászi and his generation, how can the comprehensive vision for such a science come about and gain validity as well as achieve a political effect? Mannheim originally intended "Is Politics as a Science Possible?" to serve as a point of departure for *Ideology and Utopia*, and thus as a programmatic introduction to a sociology of knowledge offered as "organon" for such a science. Mannheim's diverse writings in sociology of knowledge are linked by the conviction that the new inquiry is central to any strategy for creating a rapprochement between politics and reason. He always maintained that it has important transformative effect on its practitioners: the sociology of knowledge calls intellectuals to their vocation of striving for synthesis. It changes their relationship to the parties contending in society, giving them distance and synoptic vision (Kettler 1967). But Mannheim's conception of the specific ways the sociology of knowledge affects the state of political knowledge fluctuated and changed. There are three principal models: (1) Sociology of knowledge as a pedagogical but also political mode of encountering and acting upon the other forces that make up the political world, serving as a mediating force that reorients all vital participants in the political process and generates the synthesis that makes possible the "next step" in a sequence of human activities having intrinsic value; (2) sociology of knowledge as an agency of enlightenment, comparable to psychoanalysis, freeing men and women for rational and responsible choices by uncovering unrecognized compulsions and enabling them to gauge realistically the consequences of their actions; and (3) sociology of knowledge as a weapon against prevalent myths and as a method for freeing social science from bias, so that it can master the fundamental public problems of the time and guide appropriate political conduct.

Before 1932, Mannheim's work fluctuates between the first two versions: afterwards, and especially after 1933, the third increases in importance. All three versions can best be understood in the context of the quest for an adequate philosophical mode for liberalism. The shifts in emphasis among them during his English career depend on his accommodation to patterns of thinking in his new English-speaking audiences, on changes of Mannheim's diagnosis of the main obstacles to effective political knowledge, as well as on his changed assessment of the prospects for knowledge, planning and rational rule. With his later conception of "thought at the level of planning," he comes close to claiming success in the search for a science able to "contribute," as he writes to Louis Wirth on the outbreak of the war in 1939, "both to the interpretation of the appalling events and to the right action" (Mannheim to Wirth, September 17, 1939. LWP/7:11). Like John Stuart Mill, whose *Logic* provides Mannheim with a key concept in his work on planning, Mannheim comes close to Comte in his ultimate celebration of rule by scientific social knowledge. Unlike Mill, he never drew a persuasive line of separation between his late thought and positivist authoritarianism. This failure was due in part to his biographical destiny, and in part to the state of sociology, the discipline he selected to legitimate his work.

Notes

1. A programmatic statement can be found in Mannheim's "Announcement" (1929) on the occasion of taking over the editorship of the *Schriften zur Philosophie und Soziologie*, originally founded by Max Scheler and published by Friedrich Cohen, Bonn. There Mannheim writes, "Collaboration between the two disciplines [philosophy and sociology] should not obliterate boundaries, yet mutual stimulation should be one aspiration. Neither displacing the initially philosophical context of inquiry with sociology nor burying empirical methods under empty speculation in the social sciences can be desirable. Cooperation can have but one purpose, namely that philosophical questions become a part of this newest level of world orientation in science and life, and that sociology in the attempt to permeate reality empirically keeps its investigative impulses always uniformly centered. Philosophy gives up if it does not deal with contemporary problems, sociology if it loses the center of its inquiry" (AA).
2. Sheldon Wolin, Hannah Arendt, and Robert Nisbet have emphasized the contrasts between the presuppositions underlying sociological concepts and the humanist political tradition. For an influential statement, see Wolin (1960: ch.10).

3. Jászi (1908). Quoted in Horváth 1966: 290.
4. On the resemblance between Naphta and Mannheim's most admired mentor, Georg Lukács, see Marcus-Tár (1982).
5. Because the English translation revises several concepts and formulations pertinent to the present context, including the title of the essay, we are retranslating from the German original: "Ist Politik als Wissenschaft möglich?" (Mannheim ([1929] 1952).

2

Idealism, Romanticism, and Sociology

Thinkers properly begin the pursuit of knowledge, according to Mannheim, by attempting to grasp the intellectual situation of their own time. The starting point is defined by the prevailing "problem constellation," the questions and issues widely discussed by recognized thinkers. Moreover, Mannheim concedes a presumption in favor of approaches gaining strength in a thinker's own generation, ways of thinking among literary intellectuals and political thinkers as well as academic scholars. If there is conflict or incoherence, thinkers must attempt to clarify the scene, but they may not deny their complicity in the intellectual uncertainties of their peers.

There was no shortage in Mannheim's generation of young thinkers yearning for truths more humane and inspiring than those provided by academic scholarship; and the calls for renewal of culture or community and for a politics of wisdom and greatness were clichés of cultural journalism. What distinguishes Mannheim is his intellectual conscience. Moved by Romantic protests against rationalism and positivism, he nevertheless refuses to dismiss the achievements or methods of the burgeoning sciences. The goal of a comprehensive vision to overcome the crisis of disorientation he diagnoses inspires him, but he seeks a mediating way, aspiring to conciliate and coordinate discordant spiritual powers.

Despite his eagerness to encompass the diversity of knowledge, Mannheim cannot, of course, accept all the knowledge claims of all thinkers whose works he examines. But he characteristically challenges claims only in part, querying the depth, scope, or duration of their validity. Much of Mannheim's work is devoted to classifying types of knowledge, mapping the routes appropriate to diverse ways of knowing (Mannheim [1922] 1964). The dispute about Max Weber's method that framed Mannheim's first sociological efforts was not about "methodology" in the narrow sense; the issues also concerned types, range, and scope of knowledge (Frisby 1976; Wagner and Zipprian 1994). Because of the narrow connotations of the term "method," it is better to accentuate the etymologically related but normally dead metaphor of "ways" to capture Mannheim's image of knowledge as a multilevelled, boundless terrain traversed by many approaches. His earliest philosophical position, influenced by neo-Kantian and phenomenological teachings, is pluralistic, insisting on irreducible differences in ways of knowing things irreducibly different. But even when he believes himself to have found a way of articulating theoretically what he had initially described as only a longing for metaphysical unification, he insists that the philosophy of history that provides dialectical synthesis cannot be deduced or imposed by some all-comprehending superlogic. It emerges from the variegated flow of ordinary disciplined intellectual life. In practice, then, Mannheim remained catholic in his determination to find some truth in all current systems of belief and, above all, in his respect for the findings of all disciplined inquiry. If there is eventually to be a comprehensive knowledge, it will have to embrace all inquiries, show the foundations of their distinctive achievements, and vindicate its own claims by standards as demanding as established ways of knowledge.

During his years of expounding and justifying a sociology that would provide comprehensive orienting knowledge to enable actors to take the "next step," Mannheim nevertheless insisted on the value of other kinds of sociological investigations, including those patterned on the physical sciences. And during the most productive years of his life, he thought that his preferred sociology would come about through interaction with those complexes of political ideas he designated by the commonly dismissive term "ideology," but treated in a way that transformed the function of the concept. Mannheim saw himself interacting with a field of intellectual forces and objectifications, for which no English word serves as well as the German *Geist*, intervening strategically to redirect creative energies active there, to recontextualize and thus reinterpret existing achievements, as well as to inspire innovation. Despite his talk of synthesis and later of planning, Mannheim envisioned an inherently unfinished formative process no one could control.

His willingness to negotiate with competing thinkers equipped him to address the larger Budapest intellectual community with philosophical explanations of Lukács' cultural project during the middle war years, presenting the public face of the Sunday Circle. After his emigration from Hungary, he strove first to find a place in a philosophical scene more differentiated and technically demanding than the intense belletristic ambience of Lukács' Sunday Circle, his first audience. Surprisingly, this brought him to the new academic discipline of sociology, on the one hand, and to political reflections in a politicized culture whose partisan institutions and ideological complexity does not permit the luxury of tacit participation he had enjoyed in the prewar unity of Hungarian oppositionists.

Dilemmas of Culture

Karl Mannheim's first German publication was a 1920 review of Georg Lukács' *Theory of the Novel*, a work he had already read in manuscript, as a devoted young follower of the author. Lukács maintains that Goethe's *Bildungsroman, Wilhelm Meister*, is an attempt to mediate between idealist and romantic views of the world. Both have valid insights into the human condition, but each confutes the other. Idealists see the abyss between the ideal that reason can know and the reality encountered by experience; and they call for a life of heroic and self-denying service to the unattainable ideal. Romantics reject idealism as a devitalizing indifference to the sensations and energies of life, and they contend that acting in the world as if it could or should meet the demands of abstract reason leads to violence against the human soul and to chaotic failures. Romantics focus instead on the refinement of sensibility, seeking an opening to spirituality and experience, to move the soul toward fulfillment. Idealists counter that the romantic course leads to subjectivism, disillusionment, or submission to brute facts glossed over by bogus spirituality. Goethe sought a way out of the impasse, Lukács contends, by leading Wilhelm Meister through a self-transformational social development, alternating between the contrasting emphases; but Goethe's effort collapses because he cannot consistently present Wilhelm Meister as fulfilling the commitments entailed by each successive social identity while simultaneously recognizing that their meanings are only provisional. Writing in 1914, Lukács views Goethe's failure as a symptom of persistent cultural crisis, and he looks ahead to the new, authentically grounded culture signalled by the revolutionary writings of Dostoyevsky.

Mannheim shared with more than one philosophical generation in Germany the idea of reconciling, in a philosophically apt way, the romantic insight into the flux of all things and the idealist vision of a rational order. The philosophical journal that published his Lukács review brought into collaboration a group of thinkers ranging from Heinrich Rickert and Max Weber to Edmund Husserl and Friedrich Meinecke and graphically signalled a similar ambition on every volume: an embossed head of Heraclitus and the bold title *Logos*. Lukács published in it, as did Mannheim himself; and the journal *Szellem*, which Lukács had originated and where Mannheim got his start, was to have been an Hungarian pendant to *Logos*, similar to one that saw several editions in Russian. Like the other serious scholars assembled by *Logos*, Mannheim recognized that agreement on common themes is not the same as an agreed way.

Lukács' dramatic statement of the issues profoundly touched Mannheim in his early years. He began writing to Lukács before he was twenty, and one of his letters of that time expresses his heartfelt determination to immerse himself in the life of Dostoyevsky, "since I feel that a knowledge of his life promises solutions" (Mannheim 1971:98). The problems for which he seeks solutions are much like those Lukács formulated with such polish, except that for Mannheim questions about guiding one's life are increasingly subordinated to questions about the possibility of the necessary knowledge. By the time he reviewed Lukács' work, he had long given up the hope for some unmediated, Dostoyevskian access to the soul, earlier proclaimed a precondition for criticism, and he had greatly refined the philosophical definition of his central concerns. But he did not yet call himself a sociologist.

Mannheim's way to sociology began with a youthful rejection of the sociology promoted by Oscar Jászi. Mannheim was principal author of the only publication issued by the "Free School for Studies of the Human Spirit," a lecture and seminar series that grew in 1917 out of the Sunday Circle inititiated by Lukács that proudly asserted the standpoint of the German *Geisteswissenschaften* against the *Sozialwissenschaften* disseminated by the Free School of the Society for Social Science. According to the anonymous introduction to Mannheim's pamphlet, the new "Free School" was distinguished, first, by the fact that its lectures "seek to express the point of view that recognizes the problem of transcendence (in opposition to the materialism that is already receding into

the past), the unconditional validity of principles (in opposition to relativistic impressionism), the pathos of normative ethics" (in opposition
to an anarchic worldview) (Mannheim 1918). Second, the sponsoring
group rejected the aim of popularizing knowledge, speaking only to
"those who no longer require the primer knowledge provided by lectures that are never more than introductory." The operations of the Free
School for Humanistic Studies exemplify its program. The lecture and
seminar series presupposes that "the culture of Europe is turning, after
the Positivism of the Nineteenth Century, once again towards metaphysical idealism." "It is not a matter of new knowledge alone, but of a *new
culture.*" And this reborn culture is carried by "the type of European
now in the making." In this context, the Free School at work is a cultural
creation: "The lectures are to help [these new Europeans] find themselves and to gather strength from the consciousness of [constituting] an
new generational community." Since the task is to clarify the objectives
and to mobilize the resolve of individuals already implicitly committed
to the work of renovating culture, appeals to a mass audience would
make no sense. The "generation" is destined for its mission; only "consciousness" is needed.

This "culturist" conception polemicizes against the lecture series associated with Jászi's Society for Social Science, since the latter was an
institute for popular enlightenment. Politically, the social scientists sought
to fulfill an ideal of rational leadership: by exposing social evils and
their causes and by proposing effective remedies, intellectuals create a
progressive public opinion that acts for change. For Lukács, Mannheim,
and their associates, in contrast, intellectuals do not require the collaboration of nonintellectuals. What intellectuals do on their own—in their
Free School, for example—has consequences for all because it revolutionizes the culture, a domain with more profound effects than the surface arenas of clashing social interests. Yet it is inaccurate to characterize
the conflict between the followers of Jászi and Lukács as a clash of
political objectives. While the Russian and German exemplars of the
culturist group were politically conservative, revulsion against resur-
gent Hungarian anti-Semitism combined with hopes of imminent transformation in a stagnant Hungary brought the two groups of intellectuals
into the practical alliances exemplified by their collaboration on the new
journals *Nyugat* (The West) and *Huszadik Század* (Twentieth Century).
No substantial segment of the Hungarian "Generation of 1900," over-

whelmingly Jewish in origin, betrayed the common foundation myth of emancipation (Lukács 1988: 138). They clashed over its actualization.

Mannheim's inaugural lecture for the Free School, "Soul and Culture," (Mannheim [1918] 1964) documents the inclusiveness of his aspirations, as well as offering an authentic interpretation of the group's program. He opens with two surveys to circumscribe the position: a catalogue of persons and movements to which the lecturers' collective claims affinity and a preliminary calendar of tenets. The first list begins with Dostoyevsky, "one with us in worldview and sense of life," and Kierkegaard, "with the same ethical convictions as we"; then follow the philosophers, Lask and Zalai, and two journals, the German *Logos* and Lukács own short-lived *Szellem*.[1] Paul Ernst and Alois Riegl appear as sources for "our aesthetic views," and the survey concludes "that in our artistic culture we could well use as our slogan Cézanne, the new French lyric poetry—especially the movement of the Nouvelle Revue Française—and Béla Bartók or Endre Ady...and the Thalia theater movement." "Naturalism and impressionism in art" as well as "Marxism in sociology" Mannheim lists as movements that have been "factors in our development" that the members of the group have outgrown, "although we do not want to forget what they taught us." The impression formed by the name-slogans is reinforced by Mannheim's doctrinal summary: "Our ethical and aesthetic convictions are marked by a firm normativism, unbound by academic rules. Our worldview is characterized by an idealism aspiring toward metaphysics, but far removed from the strained idealism of dogmatic religion" (Mannheim [1918] 1964:68).

Turning from general slogans, Mannheim contends that the unity of the group can best be understood as a shared perspective on culture. Making a crucial distinction, they see *subjective* culture as the activity of the soul, "striving to realize itself through a medium alien to it," and *objective* culture as comprising "all the concrete manifestations of the spirit, as transmitted...in the course of historical development as a legacy of humankind." The problem is to relate these aspects to one another. Mannheim follows Simmel in seeing a tragic discordance. Hegel's comforting synthesis lacks philosophical warrant and offers no help for the human soul. Although highest worth attaches only to the self-realization of the soul, the soul can attain fulfillment—save in a few chosen individuals who have special mystical gifts—only through some "work" (in the sense used by Meister Eckhart). An ever widening gap between the subjective and objective dimensions of culture results from this external dependency of the creative soul. The tragedy of culture is that the accumulation of works past and present becomes ever more independent of the experiences and activities of the soul.

This autonomy of objective culture derives from several paradoxical attributes of cultural work. To order the inchoate energies and experiences of the soul, the act of creation requires submission to the laws governing the medium used; and such submission introduces into the work something alien to its source in the soul. The fulfillment the soul seeks, even demands not only an exteriorizing and ordering of its experiences, but also communion through the work with other souls. Yet the qualities in the work that make communication possible, its attributes as social event, bring additional external factors into culture, as it comes under the sway of the heterogeneous and soulless forces that shape history. A deep yearning of the soul is also satisfied by the fact that the work can live and be deepened beyond the lifetime of its creator. But this capacity for transcending time is no less paradoxical than the other inherent attributes of the work, because it also makes possible the perpetuation of techniques and the imitation of works after all meaning and life have left them. Culture, in short, tends towards "misdevelopment," towards inauthenticity.

Mannheim then moves to a scheme of three stages for this misdevelopment, correlating patterned changes in subjective and objective culture. Each historical period manifests progressively greater distance between the soul and the work, while corresponding to one of the implicit "intentions" (*Wollen*)—a concept borrowed from Riegl—animating the diverse modes of human activity. At the first stage, cultures are religious and whole. The soul addresses itself to "primeval facts" and the "creator is occupied directly with the soul itself. While it cannot be comprehended, it is actually present to him." Second come artistic cultures, "when human efforts are applied to the best and most thorough working of the material." The third stage brings a culture that is aesthetic and critical. A strong "feeling of estrangement" comes to the fore; "the discrepancy between forms and substances becomes increasingly clear"; and the critic flourishes while the creative artist is impotent.

Not surprisingly, Mannheim argues that the culture of his time has reached the crisis of the third stage. The need is to bring it through. The soul is at its furthest remove from fulfillment, although cultural actors are exercising a genuine and thus valuable "intention." "An aesthetic culture...directs its contributors exclusively to their special capacity for appreciating form as such, to the detriment of their other capabilities and immersion in life." Culture then becomes a *golem*, taking on a life that dominates its human creators: it has "no more relation to the soul than has a parasite to its host," and individuals are condemned "always to feel that the contents they encounter are alien and no parts of themselves, and impelled to remain aloof from these contents because incapable of judgment." But the moment of crisis also promises a vital turning-point:

> The alienation becomes visible to the individual when here and there a soul is already shaken by new experiences, the primeval facts of the soul. Only then is it evident that the old contents no longer speak to us and that the old forms have become strange. We now live in such an epoch...[W]hile the new contents appearing on the horizon are as yet unformed, their lightning-like immediacy makes obsolete much that is old (Mannheim 1918 [1964]:75).

Mannheim underlines the assertion in the pamphlet's introduction that it is precisely his generation, "knitted together by a common development and shared sense of life," that can fulfill the promise implicit in the cultural crisis. The generation must heed "the signal of the renewal of culture," become fully conscious of itself and thus of its mission, and—in that very process—transform its relation to culture and thus the culture itself. Wild experiments in search of new forms and new creativity will not help; they will not transform the situation. The injunction of the historical moment must be heeded; the generation must prepare the way by performing the task of criticism assigned to it. "Even if it is never granted to us to see the new contents shaped by a new form," he perorates, "we know we will have accomplished something if we prepare the way for the new culture, for which we so yearn, by as complete an understanding as possible of the old" (Mannheim 1918 [1964]:84).

Despite resemblances between the pattern of Mannheim's argument in "Soul and Culture" and Lukács' well-known Marxist interpretation in *History and Class Consciousness*—self-conscious action by those appropriately situated in a world-historical crisis revolutionizes the world—Mannheim kept his distance from Marxism until after the publication of *History and Class Consciousness* in 1923. When he writes on Lukács in 1921, he harks back to writings antedating his mentor's abrupt conversion to communism. Mannheim's culturist enthusiasm has dampened, and his vision of apocalyptic meanings in the historical moment has gone, but the centrality of the cultural problem remains and social analysis remains suspect. His review of *The Theory of the Novel* (Mannheim [1920] 1993) sums up what Mannheim thought at the outset of his independent intellectual career about contradictions between idealism and romanticism, especially in the domain of knowledge, and about ways of mastering the apparent impasse.

He praises Lukács, first, for recognizing that each of the many ways of knowing a given object is autonomous and has its own logical structure. An aesthetic view of an object's form, for example, requires that the elements of form are recognized as spiritual entities, interconnected by relations appropriate to such entities, and not by the causal linkages required if the object were to be explained as a physical field of force. Such pluralism respects the idealist concern for logical order and structural analysis, but it avoids the reductionism inherent in the modern search for universal abstract laws that has led idealism in its neo-Kantian form to assimilate all knowledge to the model of science. Second, Mannheim celebrates Lukács' attempt to find a level of interpretation able to account for the emergence of the plurality of inquiries and reveal the reasons for the variety of logics. Mannheim speaks of this level as a metaphysical one, but agrees with Lukács that it will take the form of a philosophy of history. This form accords with modern romanticism, with its acute sensibilities for historical experience, but avoids the subjectivism and relativism with which historicism has come to be linked.

Mannheim thus lays out the two central issues of reductionism and relativism that occupy his philosophical speculations and that he carries forward into his subsequent sociological work. The autonomy of the various domains of knowledge counters the reductionist tendency to bring everything down to a fundamental unified science of the analytically simplest parts, like psychology or materialist sociology. The "metaphysics" projected differentiates itself into these autonomous activities, and its theory interprets them "from the top down." The possibility of such an integrative philosophy, in turn, counters relativism, while acknowledging diversity and change. In keeping with the *Logos* program—and in reminiscence of "Soul and Culture"—Mannheim signals the hope that a way can be found to perform what Hegelian dialectics promised, despite the collapse of the Hegelian system.

His publication of the review may also have been intended as a gesture of support for Lukács, who was in perilous exile as former commissar of education in the communist Kun regime. But the tribute to Lukács disregarded what Mannheim knew to be Lukács' departures from the position established in *The Theory of the Novel* (Mannheim [1920] 1993). Lukács proclaimed himself a Marxist in 1918 and published several of his remarkable Hegelian renderings of Marxist theory in Hungarian periodicals before the end of the six-month Soviet interlude. Although Mannheim accepted appointment as university lecturer from Lukács in 1919, notes of his philosophy course he then prepared indicate no breach with the pre-revolutionary Sunday Circle approach (Karádi and Vezér 1985; Kettler 1971; Gábor 1983; Gluck 1985; Löwy 1979; Congdon 1983; Kadarkay 1991). Mannheim was fascinated by Lukács' *History and Class Consciousness* when it appeared in 1923, after he had already immersed himself in sociological problems, but he never accepted the book's revolutionary teachings. Nor was he satisfied, as his thinking matured, that Lukács' earlier Hegelianism, oriented primarily to Hegel's aesthetic writings, comprehended enough of modern knowledge to serve him as more than an inspiration. Lukács inspired his philosophical searches for alternatives to the neo-Kantian rationalism taught at the University and presupposed by Jászi's formulation of progressive liberalism, but it was Jászi who remained Mannheim's model in political thinking.

Sociology and Culture in Heidelberg

While Mannheim never followed Lukács in his conviction that the communist revolution signified the redemptory crisis promised in "Soul and Culture," he did move towards Lukács' belief that the destiny of culture and thus the recovery of the deep knowledge needed for fulfillment was linked to the social and political awareness of those destined to carry it forward. In Heidelberg he developed a renewed interest in issues central to progressive social scientists, but he addressed them by methods designed to meet the romantic objections that had originally drawn him away from progressive social science. With the dispersion and disillusioning of the culturist "generation" embodied in the Sunday Circle, Mannheim turned to a more cosmopolitan search for a context to give meaning to his identity as an intellectual.

Mannheim (1921–22) offered an initial interpretation of his place in the postwar intellectual scene in his two "Letters from Heidelberg" written in Hungarian for an emigré literary audience. Still writing as a Budapest intellectual, he is struck by the historical decentralization of German cultural life. But the distinctive local tendencies are now mingling, he reports, and Heidelberg offers a microcosm. There is value in the immediacy of contact among intellectuals within such manageable boundaries, although there is also some "provincialism" in the bad sense, first because individuals are not stimulated to experiment beyond the limits of comfortable bourgeois ways of living, however audacious their thinking, and second, because rare individuals possessing political or prophetic gifts, like Max Weber, cannot manifest their powers on a sufficiently large stage.[2]

Mannheim's epistolary essay portrays the spiritual condition of the "thin layer" of "progressive German intellectuals," as seen from the distance provided by an intellectual in exile. He writes with irony about the pervasiveness of idiosyncratic programs among a disoriented but prolific and enthusiastic intelligentsia. In language that strikes familiar chords in the 1990s, Mannheim observes:

> One discovers rhythm, the other dance, the third education, and still others faith, God, Blacks, style, unity, or the theater. And whatever someone accidentally seizes upon becomes the center of the universe, the foundation stone of rebirth, the promised land of all life to come, for which he alone is the apostle.... This is why the German intellectual lacks distance. He does not recognize the difference between great and small because he imagines that he is always in the midst of grandiose actions.

Nevertheless, Mannheim avows that these are the people he loves and among whom he belongs. Moreover, he believes they are preparing something that will become of paramount importance. In these letters, the "intellectual" is not a sociological construct but a member of a culturally scattered cosmopolitan community, whose members know, address, read, recognize, and judge one another, even when they cannot meet to talk, and whose centering on matters of the spirit makes them barely comprehensible to the rest of the world. He speaks of such humanistically educated intellectuals as a "caste," and hyperbolically traces a prominent contemporaneous confusion in thought to the fact that the caste lines are not marked by external signs, as in China and India: "I respect the exertions (which may in time acquire some meaning) but simultaneously despise the lies of those who try to fulfill the Romantic dream—under nationalist or racist slogans or under the banner of the class struggle—that they are at one with the race or class for which they articulate representative programs." Intellectuals have their own distinctive goal, he maintains. Their struggles and yearnings are properly directed to finding a "home," a world in which the spirit can be secure.

Mannheim portrays Heidelberg as polarized between an intellectual grouping centered on the sociological legacy of Weber and another constituted by the charismatic force of the poet Stefan George—one, Protestant, progressive, scientific, and the other, Catholic in sensibility, reactionary, aesthetic. Mannheim's history of misgivings about the philosophy and culture underlying the Hungarian sociologists' version of liberalism and his devotion to the cultural preoccupations of the Sunday Circle might make it seem likely that he would gravitate to the pole opposed to sociology. But Mannheim's comment on the Stefan George circle suggests an important difference between the literary antipositivist movement in which Mannheim had come of age and what he encountered in Heidelberg, and it indicates some of his reasons for turning instead to Max Weber's brother, the cultural sociologist Alfred Weber. He claims that the George circle, despite its many merits and accomplishments, ultimately fails to contribute to the transformation of life and the radical renewal of spirit that he considered necessary. Their humanism proves too literary and conventional. They pose the problem of spiritual homelessness but "their solution is a closing of the eyes. To comfort themselves with the feeling of rootedness, they isolate themselves, wrap themselves in cultural stuff, and—neglecting to include the world among their own objects—alienate themselves." An ordinary thunderstorm, he concludes, would suffice to dispel the illusion of strength created by the sheltering hills, and to expose this antiprogressive circle as flagging symbols of a bygone era.

For Mannheim, as for Lukács, the involvement in culture was bound up with the conviction that the old cultural contents had become obsolete and lifeless, and thus with a passionate attention to history as the locus for radical renewal. The problem was to find the historically apt way of attending to history. The "Heidelberg Letters" show Mannheim reluctantly taking leave from the aesthetic and metaphysical investigations of his Hungarian years, but they also evidence his continued feeling for the thoughts and cultural experiences that first shaped him. He never abandons his first questions, but he finds that "the world" must be more clearly recognized in the search for answers. Moreover, his choice entails a move from the company of intellectuals, taken as an undifferentiated literary company. "On one side," he writes, "is the university, on the other the boundless literary world" (Mannheim 1921–22). The academic discipline he considers most competent to comprehend the situation is sociology. Compared to the illusory cultural haven inhabited by the Stefan George circle, sociology appeared as a place for historical understanding and practical development.

Sociology was a strong and growing intellectual and spiritual force, and for that reason alone required attention. Yet there was also much about it that was threatening. Sociology belonged to the social progress that was inimical to the cultural renewal Mannheim craved, and it propagated methods and standards of knowledge that scorned the spiritual intentions constitutive of authentic cultural works. For the antipositivism and metaphysical yearnings that Mannheim brought to Heidelberg from Budapest, the idea of a *cultural* sociology involves a puzzle, if not a paradox. How can a sociology comprehend culture and contribute to its renovation, when it appears as the organon of intellectual methods hostile to culture? The question then was whether there could be a sociology in the service of culture, a study of humans as historically socialized beings that would act against social ossification of creative individuals. Only such a sociology might make intellectuals "feel that they exist and that they are important and effective" without the deceptive shelters from the world that secluded the followers of Stefan George and rendered them romantic in the bad sense. A cultural sociology, to fit Mannheim's requirements, must be a way of relating to culture consonant with the forces renewing culture. The old idealism can offer no help, since it is as dead as the materialism that was its counterpart. But the cultural crisis is nevertheless an opportunity for beginning anew. Mannheim and his Budapest fellows disavowed "impressionist" delight in the sheer manifold of possibilities. Yet they saw no alternative to working on the problems raised in one's time and used the cultural resources most prominently available.

Mannheim's assimilation of sociology began with two philosophically oriented inquiries into the character and methods of cultural sociology. Never published during his lifetime, although lightly corrected shortly before his death, the two treatises, one dated 1922 and the other approximately 1924, do not so much mark successive stages in Mannheim's thinking, as they explore two alternatives Mannheim never stopped trying to balance. The first derives from existentialist phenomenology and the second from post-Hegelian philosophy of history. While Mannheim rejects monopolistic claims of epistemology or methodology generalized from modern physical science, he insists that intuition indifferent to structure or methodical verification cannot secure controllable or effective knowledge. Phenomena, he maintains, are ultimately knowable because they can be referred to a "logic" or "systematization" appropriate to one of a plurality of autonomous domains each built on an underlying reality. Mannheim leaves unresolved, a matter for intellectual experimentation, whether such substructures must be approached by a direct perception of essences or by an understanding of their respective places within a historical development with a knowable meaning. Both possibilities appear in Mannheim's earlier work, and each predominates in one of the treatises in *Structures of Thinking* (Mannheim [1922–24] 1982).

The two treatises illustrate what Mannheim called his "essayistic-experimental attitude" and they exemplify his "conviction that a given theoretical sketch may often have latent in it varied possibilities which must be permitted to come to expression in order that the scope of the expression may be truly appreciated." Like the diverse essays comprising *Ideology and Utopia*, the two parts of *Structures of Thinking* hold in suspension the choice among "relativistic possibilities," "activistic-utopianism," and a "harmonious-synthetic solution" to the basic problems about culture and society posed by Mannheim. Mannheim pleaded against those who held *Ideology and Utopia* to the standard of a unified system, "As long...as a connection between ideas is still in the process of growth and becoming, one should not hide the possibilities which are still latent in it but should submit it in all its variations to the judgment of the reader" (Mannheim 1936a:47–48n). Many later readers of the English version of *Ideology and Utopia* have dismissed Mannheim's essayistic professions as admissions of philosophical failure or vain efforts to disarm criticism. But the contrasting strategies so clearly laid out in the constituent parts of *Structures of Thinking* make it clear that the "essayistic-experimental attitude" is integral to Mannheim's general project. His works must be read in full awareness of these inner tensions.

The problems at the heart of the crisis—the *relativism* fostered by the recognition that "truths" change in time, and the *reductionism* implied by attempts to comprehend such changes by uncovering underlying biological, social, or economic causes—are exacerbated, to all apearances, by the sociological treatment everywhere in the air. Mannheim states and accepts that challenge in *Structures of Thinking*, and the systematic character of these writings brings out the experimentation with ontological and historicist alternatives artfully disguised in his earlier essays. The questions he brings to cultural sociology are not only whether culture can be discussed without obscuring its dependence on the world (as the George circle does) or undermining its character as culture (as positivist sociology does), but also whether such inquiry can uncover a logic of cultural objects and establish the inner relationship between that logic and ultimate spiritual reality.

Cultural sociology must be faced, Mannheim contends, because it cannot be bypassed in any defense of the integrity of the individual's cultural experience against the relativizing effects of historicism and analyses of *Weltanschauungen*. Sociological interpretation of culture is grounded in a theoretically fecund human capacity to grasp the functional aspect of human doings, to fix their place in the world of social actions and relations. The cry, Mannheim avers, will also be heard as a call. Cultural sociology assumes a central place in structures of knowing after philosophy, having dissolved the supremacy claims of established value schemes, discovers "culture" as the process of creating value, after sociological concepts encompass the lived world, and after the interplay of society and culture appears as disturbance to participants centered in either domain.

An underlying question is whether authentic individual experience is possible or whether all such experiences are nothing more than passive accommodation to a collective force, for which the individual does not count. "Is there a way of solitude?" Mannheim asks, "Are there spheres within us which must, because of their essential nature, always remain alone? Does the historical-social course of things change anything in the fate of being human?" Historicism has loosened the sense of established order; everyone believes everything could have been and has been different. Although at first only external structures are viewed historically, in time the feeling of historical determination comes to apply to everything; "our very self is abandoned; it is as if we are suspended above ourselves" (Mannheim [1922-24] 1982:121-22). But the sailor, the historian, and the pure sociologist of culture (exemplified by Georg Simmel) act out of the same impulse. They have all three found a way

> of abandoning oneself, of separating the social and historical self from the substantial one, and of experiencing our humanity as such, purely in itself. And just as the homelessness which was empirical-historical at first (and which at first had us roaming through cultural and historical places and times) metamorphosed into the ultimate homelessness of being human, so does the most rigorous structural analysis of social consciousness transcend itself in the direction of new substantive insights, until finally we reach the ultimate point where it is still possible to stand, a sociological *cogito ergo sum*, something that can no longer be doubted. (Mannheim [1922-24] 1982:122)

In the present age, the human spirit cannot find its home in any cultural production, except, paradoxically, in the heroic acceptance of homelessness, and so in the cultural-sociological work which is the characteristic form of this acceptance. Mannheim gives special attention to Georg Simmel's "pure" cultural sociology in this connection because it persistently follows after and interrogates the cultural work of the socialized person, yearning to uncover a residue purely human and spiritual, something transcending social determination. This metaphysical longing cannot attain its ostensible objective, yet Mannheim preferred Simmel's exploration of the "relativist possibilities" to arbitrary and unearned leaps of faith. Such sociology of culture is an expression of decadence, a function of the lack of immediate and vital relationship to culture. It is a crippled way of relating to culture in a crippled age; the major consolation is that it manifestly does not penetrate deeply or destructively into its object.

The earlier of the two treatises, "The distinctive character of cultural-sociological knowledge" opens with the contrast between philosophical and sociological considerations of culture and so directly with relativism. "Immanent" interpretations address the claim of the object to be "valid"—as a binding law, a just action, a beautiful object, a true proposition—while nonimmanent interpretations locate the object in some different context. Sociological interpretation, a nonimmanent approach to culture, can neither confirm nor deny the validity of cultural productions whose social meanings it expounds. Validity is accessible by phenomenological methods to uncover the ontologically grounded principles it requires. Understood as a nonimmanent interpretation, cultural soci-

ology neither implies nor fosters relativism. To say that a social mentality corresponds to another is not a causal explanation. Nor can it affect
the claim of a cultural manifestation to be true, good, or beautiful. Cultural sociology offers a valid interpretation of cultural creations insofar
as they are a function of social interactions, but cannot thereby judge
their worth. It is dependent, in fact, on philosophical and other disciplines to specify its objects of study: cultural sociology cannot itself
determine whether a noise is music or a sight is art. And it cannot ascer-
tain whether something thought is knowledge.

In "Soul and Culture," Mannheim casually thanks Marx for having
broached the problem of base and superstructure, relating historically
given cultural manifestations to an underlying stratum, before confidently identifying the deeper stratum with the process of cultural evolution itself, not social or economic development. Both treatises in
Structures of Thinking return to the problem of Marxism. In the earlier
of the two, Mannheim seems unequivocal. Anticipating critics of his
own later writings, who will speak of "Mannheim's paradox," Mannheim
insists that "it will never be possible to construct a sociological critique
of human reason" (Mannheim [1922-24] 1982:82), and he charges Marx
with undermining his own theory by failing to distinguish his claims
about the social nature of ideas from the immanent level of interpretation which alone can validate any claims.

Yet Mannheim is less certain than he first appears. "Dynamic" sociology of culture, going beyond Simmel's pure sociology, promises to
bridge the distance between culture and society, although still without
reducing one to the other. Dynamic cultural sociologists find a congruence between the "style" articulated in a given cultural production and
the "worldview" appropriate to some social condition or location. Spirit
is related to spirit, and the interpretation of worldviews mediates between the two poles of cultural sociological interpretation. While the
cultural sociologist offers neither a systematic metaphysical explanation for the "logic" or "structure" he finds in the intermeshed growth of
culture and society nor a concept of progress towards some end of history, he nevertheless proposes elucidations like those essayed by the
older philosophers of history, whose inheritance he claims. Worldviews
are interlinked and changing, and in their historical development they
constitute a "higher" reality to which the cultural sociologist refers what
he interprets. On this view of the matter, there appears to be ever less

occasion for an immanent encounter with cultural objects as such. The knowing participant in a culturally charged and socially articulated history transcends both cultural insider and sociologist.

Written several years later, "A sociological theory of culture and its knowability (Conjunctive and communicative thinking)" reflects Mannheim's deep study of Lukács' *History and Class Consciousness.* Mannheim departs from the earlier acceptance of incommensurable realities and the diverse modes of knowing appropriate to them. He opens instead by denying that there can be a purely philosophical or immanent doctrine of method. Methodological doctrine properly arises from reflection on methodical inquiry. Such reflection turns up a sociological rather than philosophical self-orientation for inquirers, situating them within a structure ultimately comprehensible to philosophy of history. The approach offends against the modes of critical reflection decreed by established philosophy, but conventional objections derive from an incomplete, unhistorical idealization of physical science, best understood as expressions of bourgeois designs on the world. When philosophers condemn doctrines that recognize historically conditioned, nonuniversalistic knowledge, they are unwarrantedly imposing their rationalistic prejudices on all knowledge of cultural reality.

Disavowing the line of reasoning he adduced against Marx in "The distinctive character of cultural sociological knowledge," Mannheim offers two reasons for denying that admission of historical relativity necessarily undermines a knowledge claim. First, he maintains, some matters can be grasped only by knowledge bound to a time and a place, and the designation "relativistic" is consequently irrelevant, since its meaning is constituted by an inapplicable contrast model of universality. Second he inconsistently looks forward to a philosophy of history that will situate particularistic complexes of knowledge within an ontologically grounded developmental sequence, transcending their relativism. But such a reversal cannot be forced; it can only be sensed as an integrative undercurrent in the work actually under way. Mannheim's experiment in his 1924 treatise essays this tendency.

The historical understanding of culture is the achievement of the "whole human being," not of the narrow capacities sufficient for bourgeois calculation and its theoretical counterpart. Its possibility is given, according to Mannheim, by a convergence between the old anticapitalist spirit, carried by conservative social strata, and the new anticapitalism of the proletariat, attuned to bourgeois rationalism while anticipating a utopian disruption of that order. The cognitive capacities of these strata are not reducible to class interests. Cultural sociology does not deal in causal analyses. While bias in inauthenthic thinking is traceable to interest, its uncovering is a commonplace. Essential perspectivism, the special problem of cultural sociology, must be imputed instead to a socially differentiated collective mode of experiencing the world, engaging oneself with it, willing a world fit for one's socialized existence. This dimension is constitutive for the structures of thinking.

Mannheim describes all knowing as an appropriation of something encountered, letting us orient ourselves to it and enabling us to respond. Everything we encounter we come upon while pursuing some intention, and the will we apply to the world imparts a perspective to the resultant knowledge. Mannheim goes beyond the visual metaphor. Touching and being touched are central to the experience that grounds knowledge, and he uses the term "conjunctive knowledge" to designate acts of knowing close to this source, shaping and interpreting the world within which we are at home. Such knowledge is qualitative, judgmental, situational— and it belongs neither to the isolated individual nor to universal human faculties. Conjunctive knowledge concerns communities, constitutes communities, is borne by communities. The structure of knowing has three levels. The deepest is the primordial contagious encounter with some reality met as we act on the will we share with a community; the second is the structuring of an orienting response to that encounter, commonly through language and always with communal resources; and the third, conceptual and even theoretical in character, reflects on the implicit practical knowledge of the second level—the knowledge-in-action that constitutes cultural formations and the stylistic systems they comprise. According to Mannheim, theoretical knowledge prepares the "next step" in the inner development of a stylistic system, arising out of what has been done.

Mannheim uses this approach to account for the prevalence of philosophical theories of history in his time, none adequate in itself, but all portending a new development. Although all cultural systems change, as their accomplishments generate new requirements, many do not require a theoretical understanding of historical development. Crucial symbols and structures change meanings without recognition of the process, and stories of olden times are told as if the past were an adjoining room.

But at the present, the dynamism of things is everywhere evident. Culture must now understand itself as historical because culture has spawned a mode of knowing, a relation to vital realities, that threatens the possibilities of community and the creation of values, and thus all culture. Without a historical interpretation linking past, present, and future, the practical concept of a "next step" may itself be lost.

It is "communicative knowledge" that poses this threat to "conjunctive knowledge" and its culture. Participants in various conjunctive communities devise a language restricted to material or utilitarian aspects to achieve the narrow shared understandings they require, especially for practical objectives. Through its immanent logic, communicative language constitutes the knowledge found in the physical sciences, technology, commerce, and utilitarian calculations—in short, the elements of society not community (Tönnies), civilization not culture (A. Weber). Mannheim does not think that historical theorizing can or should expunge communicative knowledge. Philosophy of history will encompass it in a wider context of developing meanings and thereby contribute the next step that the present generation, according to Mannheim, appears destined to prepare, the reconstitution of cultural community based on a new, differentiated, and inclusive spirit.

Mannheim cannot doubt that such theoretical innovation is possible, notwithstanding the sway of communicative knowledge, because he believes he himself has been simply going along with what is going on among cultural sociologists, critics of ideology, interpretive psychologists, historians of artistic styles, and others. Underlying this converging theoretical work he finds participation in a common cultural formation he calls *Bildungskultur*. Joined in activities conditioned by the older humanistic education they share, here are individuals from diverse social groupings, prominently including such "outsiders" as Jews and members of strata little affected yet by the spirit of communicative culture. They ground theoretical reflections on the experiences constituting the life-situations of the groups they variously represent. Broadening the bases of their cultivation is a typically receptive sensibility fostered by their admixture. Because they are dependent on such foundational social experiences, they are not free-floating above society, yet the mutual distance resulting from their cultivation and lack of homogeneity allows for comparisons, combinations, and choices that justify speaking of this group as comparatively socially unattached. The *Bildungskultur* extrapolates from the possibilities generated by conjunctively grounded cultural experiences and reflects on the interplay of such possibilities. What it cannot do, according to Mannheim, is to generate new cultural possibilities of its own.

To matter, the historical and interpretive studies produced by this intermediate stratum must link with the ways other groups experience their lives, and thus their studies must include the socioeconomic shape of things, since this increasingly dominates experience. The conjunctively apt mode of proceeding within the novel and imperfect conjunctive community formed by *Bildungskultur* is paradoxically an adaptation of sociology, a discipline generated by communicative knowledge. But cultural sociologists do not use sociological thinking like ordinary sociologists, who have fashioned it on the model of the natural sciences. In seeking qualitative interpretation and aspiring to philosophy of history, inquirers consciously grounded in the *Bildungskultur* aim at a cultural not a civilizational sociology. Their knowledge can only be properly appraised by connoisseurs inside the conjunctive community. But this qualification applies to all conjunctive knowledge and implies no denigration of the validation achieved. For those who have conjunctive access to it, the validity of interpretations depends on three tests, Mannheim asserts. First, a profound evidentiary feeling arises when an account of something has gotten to the essence of the matter. Second, the authenticity of an interpretation can be scrutinized for signs of bias. Third, a valid interpretation will establish itself among connoisseurs, and it will last. But Mannheim knows that these tests are not decisive. Whether an interpretation provides knowledge depends on its ability to orient those who accept it and to guide their responses to their reality. And this can be judged only by a future interpretation, itself subject to no other sorts of checks.

In sum, Mannheim projects a process whereby the activity of cultural sociology will prove in time to delineate a comprehensive philosophy of history. The validity of this philosophy would be secured by the fact that it will have grown unforced out of disciplined inquiries into the historical rise and character of human cultural achievements, and especially the various forms of knowledge. Such a philosophy, he expects, will provide the metaphysical ground upon which all validity is ultimately founded. The possibility already projected in Mannheim's Lukács review reappears, now expressly linked to sociological work. But the philosophical construction resembles a Kantian regulative ideal. Not reliably known, the philosophy of history appears as a reasonable projection from what is known; it makes sense of things from an aesthetic as well as ethical standpoint. The meanings ascribed to history are provisional, but the regulative ideal clarifies interrelations among varieties of knowledge—without superceding them or displacing the disciplines that have brought them into being.

A Cultural Sociology

Unlike the methodological essays on sociology of culture, *Conservatism: A Contribution to the Sociology of Knowledge* (Mannheim [1925] 1986)—the work that earned Mannheim his habilitation as licensed tutor at Heidelberg in 1925—appears as a disinterested, empirical study of an ideological pattern within a specific historical context, monographically exemplifying the methods of sociology of knowledge, taken as a new academic specialty.[3] Modest in its theoretical claims, it avoids speculations about philosophy of history or reflexive scrutiny of epistemological premises or implications of its own proceedings. None of his other investigations concentrates so exclusively on materials from the past or attends so discriminatingly to the ideas of particular thinkers. In the introductory remarks on method, moreover, Mannheim treats the great methodological controversies with diplomatic tact. To all appearances, Mannheim has put his more adventurous ideas aside, while presenting his supervisors, Alfred Weber, Emil Lederer, and Carl Brinkmann, with a scholarly study far removed from his mental experiments with existentialist and post-Hegelian ideas. If anything, he leans here towards an empirical and explanatory approach, stressing the need for the new discipline to uncover causal linkages between social and cognitive phenomena and warning against the propensity, elsewhere prevalent in the cultural sciences, to be satisfied with interpretive elucidations of congruences among meanings in diverse domains. The ingenuity with which Mannheim works out this analysis, without reductionism of the ideas or arbitrary sociological imputations, has led many sociologists to consider the work on conservative thought as his outstanding achievement, as a paradigm for empirical research into the social genealogy of political beliefs.

But *Conservatism* also manifests Mannheim's preoccupation with political *knowledge*, not belief alone, and his continuing hope that a method can be devised to transcend ideology and establish such knowledge without sacrificing scientific devotion to evidence or disinterestedness. The full text, never published in his lifetime, shows that Mannheim designed his work on conservatism to serve simultaneously as empirical study and as self-justifying *exemplification* of several ways of political thinking he presents as characteristically conservative in structure. The idea behind Mannheim's study is that the enduring distinction between the natural and historical sciences, as well as the most influential approaches contesting the second of these domains have their historical progenitors in the conservative movement of nineteenth-century Germany. Screened through a conservative "style of thought," his findings about the genealogy of historicist thinking appear as a legitimation of that thinking, including its appearance, in a dramatic change of function, as the method of modern revolutionary thought.

Experimenting with "sociology of knowledge" as the most strategic subdivision of the genuinely "cultural" sociology, *Conservatism* shows how subtly Mannheim tried to balance his inclination towards broad speculation about ultimate meanings, in the manner of Hegel, with his admiration for specific social scientific analyses, like those of Max Weber. The wider ramifications emerge only when the study, in its entirety, is subjected to an interpretation informed by awareness of Mannheim's literary apprenticeship in the school of Georg Lukács. Yet whatever may emerge on closer scrutiny, the surface level represents a substantial part of Mannheim's objective in the effort. For Mannheim, sociological explications of cognitive phenomena have intrinsic interest, apart from the larger issues such inquiry raise, and he repeatedly returns to the problems of analytical technique first explored in this work. Moreover, Mannheim sought institutional legitimation as practitioner of the newly established academic discipline of sociology, acknowledging that opportunities for initiating new departures presupposed such recognition.

Conservatism is provocative in any case because of its political subject matter, controversial for a cultural sociologist. Expounding a thesis that appears as an unargued assumption in his subsequent reliance on political ideologies as points of reference in interpreting the whole domain of thinking connected to existence, Mannheim maintains that political thinking has become fundamental only since the French Revolution because the state has only assumed a central place in society since then. Moreover, he establishes a conceptual link between political ideologies, as novel cultural formations, and the activities and designs of actual political parties. It is the struggle among the parties, broadly considered, that constitutes the political reality of the state and the context within which ideologies take form and change. Before conservatism emerged as a political force, he argues, there could be no conservative ideology. In making the clash of political convictions central to the organization of worldviews, Mannheim changes his earlier approach to the study of *Weltanschauungen* by recognizing conflict and structural changes. Conservative ideology crystallizes out of the psychological attitude of traditionalism among social actors (and some observers) who experience the liberal ascendancy as harmful, but can neither ignore the advances of rationalization nor simply respond to them only in private. Like all examples of the novel cultural formation, "ideology," the conservative one accords with the orienting mode specifically appropriate to the newly rationalized state-centred societies, displacing traditional and religious ways of assigning meanings to the experienced world. Viewed from the social history of ideas, then, conservatism offers an efficacious practical orientation to the politicized and rationalized world, even while it reasserts spiritual as well as material interests damaged by rationalization. Like its principal adversary, conservatism belongs to the new time. The political conflict epitomizes the cultural situation.

After situating conservatism in political history, Mannheim explicates an inner structure common to the diverse and changing manifestations of this ideology. Such a morphological "structural analysis," Mannheim stresses, must not confuse what he calls a "style of thought" with either a theoretical system or a political program. Structural analysis uncovers a characteristic formative attitude towards human experience, as it exists before reflective elaboration, a rootedness in concrete experience and locales, as well as a special sense of continuities in time. Above all, the conservative style rejects constructions of human relations as subject to rationalistic universal norms and it disdains Enlightenment doctrines of natural law.

Mannheim's most ambitious level of analysis traces a part of the formative history of conservatism, with the aim of distinguishing decisive stages and variations in its development and showing empirically how the sociological and morphological attributes uncovered in the first two treatments interact to shape a historical style and movement. In a preliminary prospectus, Mannheim projects eight stages for this development, but he writes only about two in any detail. In the more finished of the completed sections, he draws on the writings of Justus Möser (1720–1794) and Adam Müller (1779–1829) to present a form of conservatism in which the political perspective of "estates" hostile to the modern bureaucratic or liberal state interacts with the romantic thinking originating among the preachers' sons who form the new post-Enlightenment intelligentsia. The second historical analysis treats Friedrich Karl von Savigny (1779–1861), foremost exponent of historical jurisprudence, whose work is explained as embodying the fastidiousness with which an officialdom having aristocratic connections reacted against schemes of universal codes or universal rights. Although Mannheim's subjects are jurists, legal issues do not interest him. Instead, he examines the conceptions and methods of knowledge they develop to replace the abstract, universalistic thinking they identify with natural science, capitalism, state-formation, and other manifestations of liberal rationalization.

In the first of three conservative ways of thinking Mannheim distinguishes, he identifies the community-bound (*seinsverbundene*, *gemeinschaftsgebundene*) thinking exalted by Savigny with the cognitive activity of elucidation (*Klären*). If the thought is integral to a community to which the thinker is deeply committed "with his total personality," then his elaborated thinking only clarifies and explicates what is already in the deepest sense inarticulately known by those to whom he addresses his thoughts. This conception, which Mannheim traces back from Savigny to Justus Möser, is similar to the "conjunctive" thinking that Mannheim had made paradigmatic for cultural sociology. In *Conservatism*, too, Mannheim extrapolates from Savigny to the undertakings more typical of cultural sociology in his own day. This fixes one characteristic of the academic context addressed by his own work.

The conservative paradigm for a second conception of the function of thinking, Mannheim finds in Adam Müller. Mannheim calls this conception "mediation." Its principal attributes are that it finds relations of mutual opposition everywhere, and that it equates thinking with the active judgment of practitioners expounding efficacious solutions to conflicts by respecting the parties in dispute. Mannheim considers this way of thinking an important alternative to the "rational-progressive" conception of understanding that he characterizes as depending exclusively on the systematic subsumption of particulars under general laws, and he stresses its practical character. Its effectiveness depends not only on its insight into the contesting forces and its partial accommodation to both, but also on an aesthetic sense of the fitness of a judgment to the state of the opposition to which it is applied. Such judgment meets the practical problem but it does not thereby eradicate the opposition or subject it to logical systematization, as in the Hegelian dialectic. Müller himself, Mannheim notes, was regrettably schematic, given to forced reductions of all oppositions to male-female polarities; and he first romanticized and later—once in Austrian service—reified the locus of mediation. Despite Müller's corruption of the design, Mannheim considers the conception fruitful. It contributes to the subsequent development of dynamic thinking and proves able to manage antinomies.

Mannheim uses the term "synthesis" to refer to the judgments distinguishing this way of thinking, but he stresses that the character of each synthesis depends on the standpoint from which it originates, or, more actively, on the design it implements. There is movement towards accommodation and incorporation of opposites, but no reintegration into a new totality superceding the old opposition, as is supposed to happen in fully dialectical thinking. In the intellectual field of his own time, Mannheim finds this impulse to mediation present in a curiously introverted form. *Lebensphilosophie*, he believes, absolutizes the twofold experience of moving through a world of opposites and making vital judgments, and thus has little to propose about the reality itself. It nevertheless displays its breeding, so to speak, by its opposition to liberal rationalism in all its forms.

Mannheim presents the history of conservatism as a succession of points of concentration, each of which represents a synthesis of the partial, partisan type he associates with Müller. The opposition between liberal rationalism and conservative impulses and traditions enter into each characteristic combination, in keeping with the achieved stage of development and other historical circumstances, with the conservative elements predominating. Mannheim indicates a plan for treating later stages, when conservatism increasingly fails to comprehend the movement of events, but his survey stops far short of these. In the interpretations of his own time scattered throughout the text, conservatism appears either as an integral protagonist in a political-intellectual field that also contains liberal and socialist partisans or as an ensemble of elements in "the contemporary state of thinking." In either case, Mannheim depicts a confrontation among seemingly irreconcilable opposites but not, as in *Ideology and Utopia* a few years later, a crisis. Diverse possible combinations strive for supremacy, but the contestants are held in bounds, and movement continues. There is no impasse. The insistence that liberal and conservative elements, although opposed, can never be wholly divorced from one another inheres in Mannheim's conception of conservatism as a way of rationalizing traditionalist impulses.

Every actual turn of events—in short, the practical movement through time—appears as a product of mediation in Müller's sense, as outcome of judgments that severally gain enough support to be provisionally effective without denying their partisan starting points or presuming to eliminate or absorb opposition. This view will be recast a few years later, in *Ideology and Utopia*, as a process of material political exchanges (*Realdialektik*), but there the process will have to cope with what appears to Mannheim as the emergence of crisis and immobilization, as well as a more urgent theoretical demand for higher unification of opposites through recontextualization of the whole. The contrast with this later work brings the comparative modesty and skeptical moderation of *Conservatism* into clearer focus. In some contexts, perhaps, one might be justified in speaking of a sober optimism.

On its face, *Conservatism* asks its readers to take it as a disinterested study integrating sociological and morphological approaches for the limited purpose of explaining conservatism as a structure of thinking. But here, as in several other writings, Mannheim uses the literary device of making his essays exemplify the subject matter they are ostensibly viewing at an analytical distance, a device also present in "The Problem of a Sociology of Knowledge" and "Is Politics as a Science Possible?" for example, as well as the second of the essays collected in *Structures of Thinking*. The essays deal analytically with "sociology of knowledge" or a "situational thinking dialectically mediating between theory and practice" or "dynamic sociology of culture," and they then proclaim, more or less explicitly, that they have displayed the features of the approach under consideration and in some way made it good. *Conservatism* is more complex, first because the argument is also designed to make sense to an empirical scientific perspective and, second, because Mannheim analyzes and appropriates more than one form of conservative thinking. From Savigny, he derives a model that validates social knowledge by the authenticity of its social roots; from Müller, he takes a conception of practical knowledge rendered adequate by its capacity for making concrete judgments in situations marked by contradictions that cannot be resolved; and from Hegel he abstracts an ideal of a dialectical method capable of generating genuine syntheses that overcome contradictions. The first two of these standards he hopes to satisfy in what he says about the genealogy and structure of historicist thinking. The last and most ambitious standard is left standing as an aspiration.

Mannheim's study repeatedly returns to the bearing of conservatism on the intellectual situation of his own time, and he couches his findings in terms designed to influence that situation, as well as explain it. Conservative thinking, he contends, is a progenitor of opposition to natural science models in intellectual life and liberal-capitalist rationalizations in social knowledge. But showing the historical rootedness of historicism counts as a conservative argument for its authenticity, in Savigny's sense, especially since those roots lie in the progenitors of conservative thought. Balancing morphological and sociological methods, as well as characterizing the present state of thinking as a tense, unstable balance between conservative and progressive (socialist as well as liberal) elements, exemplifies dynamic mediation in the quasi-Romantic sense of "synthesis" that Mannheim identified with Müller. Mannheim's academic exercise, in other words, has a level of meaning in which it speaks beyond the discipline, to offer a justification for Mannheim's larger theoretical interests in philosophy of history, even in its Hegelian-Marxist variant, but in a justificatory idiom inoffensive to the academics comprising his primary constituency.

The text remains dramatically unresolved because Mannheim abruptly closes the survey after Savigny, although much of the discussion looks ahead to the undone section on Hegel.[4] In anticipatory passages, Mannheim asserts that dialectical thinking successfully rationalizes what romantic and Enlightenment thought had achieved, integrating it into a single comprehensive theory of development under conservative auspices, and that this discovery was subsequently transmuted by Marx into an organon for the thought of a class better placed to counter capitalist-liberal rationalization. This speculative denouement of conservatism is the most audacious current in Mannheim's study, because it proposes a relationship between conservatism and the new historicism that supercedes the other two aspects of conservative thinking and submerges the political contents of conservatism. From this point of view, Mannheim's analysis of conservatism pivots around the concept of change in function (*Funktionswandel*), adapted from Max Weber. The conservative contributions undergo a radical and paradoxical change in function, once separated from their originating historical context. The surprising point of the study, if we focus on this extrapolation, is the historical obsolescence of conservatism and the grounding of its socialist successor's claims on the dialectical reversal of conservatism's crowning intellectual achievement. Such a paradox is implicit in tantalizing passages, but it is not developed. Mannheim never wrote the section on Hegel.

Mannheim's fascination with Hegel's dialectic is checked by his uncertainty about Hegel's philosophy, his suspicion that Lukács may well be correct in treating Marxist revolutionary thought as Hegel's rightful heir, and by his deep respect for the achievements of Max Weber. Mannheim consistently accepted Lukács' argument that the socialist form of dialectical thinking depends on a commitment to the modern industrial proletariat as the concrete social force destined to take the next step in history, a commitment Mannheim never made. Mannheim's problem, if he was to follow through with the projections arising from his philosophical reflections, was to find an alternative way of earning the right to the dialectical integration that Hegel had grounded on conservative commitments and metaphysical reasonings, and Marx on socialist commitments and economic analysis. He could not accept either. Denied such a way, Hegelian dialectics remained an uncompleted sketch for him, an aspiration. Accordingly, the level of argument which a "literary" search for meanings below the academic surface uncovers does not take Hegelian form; Mannheim does not claim to offer a reconciliation between the methodological currents he combines or between the ideological themes he treats. The "syntheses" remain at the stage of "mediated" thinking. In *Conservatism*, as in the rest of his work, his business with Hegel remains unfinished.

But the same applies to Weber. Mannheim brings Weber into *Conservatism* by a curious route, and he differentiates himself from him in a way equally revealing. In analyzing Savigny's reliance on irrational forces as ultimate guarantors of social meaning, Mannheim goes back to the writings of an earlier German jurist, Gustav Hugo (1764-1844). Hugo's thought, in turn, he characterizes as representing a hard, hopeless acceptance of a world of facts in which all principles are relative and all developments ultimately fortuitous. Mannheim accounts for such bitter tough-mindedness by a situation in which two competing social strata are evenly balanced and the observer uses the insights of each to discredit the other: "Here value-freedom, the absence of utopia, become, as it were, the test of objectivity and proximity to reality" (Mannheim [1925] 1986:175). He calls this state of mind *Desillusionsrealismus*, and he finds its exact parallel pervading German thinking in Max Weber's time. In its modern form, this realism acknowledges socialist exposures of liberal illusions, but then turns the method of disillusioning against socialist utopianism as well. Max Weber, according to Mannheim, is the most important representative of this style of thinking, and his conceptions of reality and scientific method are deeply marked by this fundamental attitude.

Mannheim does not expressly extend the parallelism to himself, but it is deeply interesting to see how he accounts for Savigny's movement beyond the realism of Hugo: "Between Hugo's and Savigny's ways of reasoning we have the defeat at Jena, foreign rule, and the wars of liberation, which transformed theoretical discussion into real discussion and a national uprising...into reality" (Mannheim [1925] 1986: 179). The difference rests on "a generational distinction." This side of the case, Mannheim says, also has contemporary application, and on this matter he attaches his deepest concerns and convictions to generational destiny:

> In periods like ours, in which self-reflectiveness and a many-sided relativism are reducing themselves to absurdity, as it were, a fear grows up instinctively about where all this will lead. How can relativism be overcome in history? If we can learn from the example of Savigny, the answer would have to be: not by way of immanent theory but by way of collective fate—not by a refusal to think relativistically, but by throwing new light on new, emerging contents. Here the fact of the generational growth of culture is of immense significance. Although considerable individual latitude is possible, it can be phenomenologically ascertained that the newly arising faith has quite a different character in the most recent generation than it has in those who, coming from an earlier generation, do not take part in this upsurge. (Mannheim [1925] 1986:180)

Such a vitalist principle of distinction between his own generation and that of Weber, although it echoes a theme already present in "Soul and Culture," could not be a satisfactory clarification of his relationship to Weber. Hegel and Weber represent alternative proposals for resolving the tensions between rationalist idealism and irrationalist romanticism, transcending an ideological choice between liberalism and conservatism. Mannheim aspires to redirect Weber's way to lead it close to Hegel's objectives.

Notes

1. Lukács and his circle were nicknamed *Szellemkék* or "Sprites," from *Szellem*, the spirit.
2. In his brief account of Max Weber in the first Heidelberg letter of 1921, Mannheim admires Weber's "unlimited" social and economic knowledge and his evident calling for a career as a "political leader," and he regrets that confinement in the university and the town blocked Weber's energies and led to his being known "as nothing but a scientist."
3. Mannheim (1927) published a German excerpt, "Das konservative Denken," and he oversaw the preparation of a different English extract, "Conservative Thought" (in Mannheim [1927] 1952). The title of the *Habilitationsschrift* is *Altkonservatismus: Ein Beitrag zur Soziologie des Wissens*. The full text is in Mannheim [1925] 1986.
4. Mannheim's essayistic manner extends even to this scholarly submission. Between the text and the notes to the manuscript of *Conservatism* submitted to the faculty, Mannheim introduces a page that repeats a familiar theme: "The present work is only part of a still incomplete book; many an unevenness in exposition and treatment may be excused by this fact."

3

Mannheim's Weimar Project:
Ways of Knowledge

In his lecture on "Politics as a Vocation," Max Weber (Gerth and Mills 1958) distinguishes between words in politics and in science, likening the former to weapons for overpowering opponents and the latter to ploughshares for cultivating knowledge. Mannheim offers the sociology of knowledge as a way of bringing about the biblical transformation of swords into pruning hooks prophesied by Isaiah. He claims that the sociology of knowledge constitutes the "organon for politics as a science." It provides an instrument for operating on the ideological views active in politics so as to give them a new character, constituting a field of knowledge with a structure appropriate to this dimension of reality and to the work that knowing performs in it. Although Mannheim nominally defers to Weber's conception of politics as a sphere governed by choices no knowledge can dictate, his conception of the political involvement implicit in gaining insight into political situations shifts the meaning of the Weberian formulas he invokes. Political knowledge takes on elements of Hegelian consciousness. Mannheim credits Weber with uncovering that the Marxist method for exposing the social provenance and function of political ideas applies no less to the proletarian view of the world. But rendered nonpartisan, the method can now reveal its constructive powers. While the disillusioning discoveries of the earlier generation have to be preserved, they gain new positive functions. When Weber quotes Isaiah's admonition to watchmen in the night, he intends to reproach those who wait in vain for prophets of salvation instead of soberly meeting the demands of the day. Mannheim uses the same passage to call intellectuals to a mission of guardianship (Weber 1922:613; Mannheim [1929] 1952:143).

Mannheim's appropriation of the Weberian legacy belongs to his characteristic strategy for claiming a place in sociology by striking intellectual bargains with predominant figures defining the field. His inaugural lecture as *Privatdozent* at Heidelberg was called "The Contemporary State of Sociology in Germany," and he subsequently promised his German publisher a book on "Analyses on the State of Contemporary Thought," to contain essays on Max Weber, Ernst Troeltsch (Mannheim [1924] 1952) and Max Scheler (Mannheim [1925] 1952). The intended volume was never published, undoubtedly because Mannheim preferred to use the materials assembled for the Weber essay as centerpiece in *Ideologie und Utopie*. But the papers on Troeltsch and Scheler,[1] published independently, lay out his position on the prospects for philosophy of history and sociology of knowledge, and they take up the conclusions of his more systematic unpublished studies without exposing the full philosophical underpinnings expounded there.

Instead of providing such a systematic approach, Mannheim accepts the works of Weber, Troeltsch, and Scheler as achievements that demarcate the starting position in the field and he presents his distinctive counterproposals as extensions or corrections of these seminal works. While negotiating with his publisher, Paul Siebeck, Mannheim insists that he would not, as Siebeck had suggested, rewrite the essays to unify the book. They must retain their diversity, he contends, as conscientious responses to the diverse strategic initiatives comprising German sociology in its unresolved state. Mannheim's sociological career is marked by the attempt to gain recognition for intellectual mediation as a form of innovative leadership.

The essay arising out of his preparations for the Max Weber chapter in the proposed "Analyses of the State of Contemporary Thought," and published in *Ideologie und Utopie*, "Is Politics as a Science Possible?", argues that the comprehensive social knowledge capable of diagnosing the historical situation and grounding a scientific politics is generated by social interpretation of the clashing ideologies rending the political terrain. To understand why Mannheim thought that such study could provide an "organon for politics as a science," and not simply a chapter in the social history of ideas, it is necessary to review the argument of Mannheim's most technical philosophical work, "Structural Analysis of Epistemology," first published as his dissertation in Hungarian in 1918, and 1922 in German translation (Mannheim [1922] 1953). The rhetorical strategy in the subtext of *Conservatism* might have fascinated a literary readership, if Mannheim had published more than a version condensed for specialists; but Mannheim had earlier developed a philosophical argument for his expansive conception of knowledge.

Structures of Knowledge

Mannheim claims that the "structural analysis" of the "theory of knowledge" is less designed to offer a distinctive theory of knowledge than to lay down the forms, constituent elements, and objectives comprising every epistemology. The theory of knowledge is not a substitute for methods of knowing appropriate to the various inquiries, but a justificatory, legitimating inquiry that explains how something that is thought can be considered knowledge. It answers the Kantian question, *"How* is knowledge possible?," not *"what* knowledge is possible?" Epistemology cannot judge other inquiries, since its own claims rest on foundations no more secure than theirs. In a striking departure from the Cartesian conception, the theory of knowledge is taken as one of many constellations in the spiritual firmament, capable of shedding its own glow upon the others; it is not the lens through which the universe is scanned.

The primary consequence of Mannheim's conception, and its point, is to deny the claim that thought, if it is to count as knowledge, must conform to a system of propositions possessing universal logical properties and validating procedures. His argument disputes neo-Kantian criticism of substantively rational aesthetic, ethical or religious judgments on the grounds of their emotional contents or historical particularity, as well as positivist strictures against knowledge claims that lack empirical verifiability. But Mannheim also rejects neoromantic contentions that respect for structure or critical discipline precludes the discovery of vital, necessarily intuitive truths. The structural analysis of theories of knowledge uncovers the criteria used by theories of knowledge to qualify a thought as knowledge and—because theories of knowledge are a kind of knowledge too—it provides an example of the effects that can be achieved by subjecting thoughts to such a legitimating procedure.

In addition to the philosophical schools and political creeds corresponding to the competing idealist and romantic worldviews, Mannheim is thinking about the "impressionistic" literary intelligentsia, and how they treat ideas. He speaks of "a brilliant and often profound world of independent scholars and connoisseurs, who, however, often dissipate their energies in untestable vagaries because they lack inner or outer constraining bonds" and he contrasts it to "the scholarly world of academic teachers who are masters of their subject but are remote from the living center of present-day life" (Mannheim [1924] 1964:263. Cp. Mannheim [1924] 1952:98). Insights that touch vitally on life are neither arbitrary nor above criticism. They can be operated upon within appropriate normative frameworks constituting forms of knowledge, and thus kept from evanescing in vague impressions.

To consider something thought as something known entails consequences. First, we acknowledge that it has its place within a structured universe of thinking, interlinked with other thoughts about a specifiable dimension of existence. A judgment about the meter of a poem, for example, now appears as an aesthetic judgment, related to other judgments about forms. Second, we are led to inquire about the method of criticism and validation appropriate to it. The method itself depends on the structure in question and is not given by the conception of knowledge. But the propriety of subjecting thought to appropriate criticism is thereby established, even when the thought is in spheres not normally considered "theoretical." Third, we render thought normative when we legitimate it as knowledge, that is, as entitled to set the standard for thinking about what it is thinking about. It ceases to be a statement that is merely internal to the inquiry to which it belongs and subject to the methods of correction appropriate to that sphere; it becomes a valid claim. If we want to know something about the meter of a poem and not just what aestheticians or critics think about it, we must apprehend judgments as expressions of knowledge.

Mannheim offers a conception of knowledge designed to alter our attitudes and responses to many kinds of statements about many kinds of subjects, opening us to the possibilities for orderly and testable thinking about matters generally considered accessible only by inchoate intuition or inspired supposition. He does not provide novel methods for judging, but gives new reasons for paying attention to the methods already in use or under consideration among those knowledgeable in the diverse domains. Knowing, Mannheim writes in "On the Interpretation of *Weltanschauung*," "is gaining a kind of possession of 'something out there' that provides a point of orientation for us and allows us mastery over it" (Mannheim [1921] 1964:138. Cp. Mannheim [1921] 1993:174). In German as in English, Mannheim's language suggests a strong connection between knowing and purposing. Although the terms of appropriation and command need not refer to pragmatic uses in any narrow sense, knowing appears as an activity within a design. The theory of knowledge explains the elements involved and their precise relationships.

For every epistemology, according to Mannheim, the key elements are always a subject and an object of knowledge. To explain the relationship between them, theory of knowledge requires the assistance of a "foundational science," notwithstanding the claims of many theorists that they are proceeding without presuppositions. He finds only three disciplines capable of such service. Psychology characterizes subject, object, and their interconnections in the language of psychological events; logic construes them as patterns of necessary relations; and ontology uncovers the structural unity of the ultimate ground upon which all three elements rest. Although Mannheim declares himself neutral in regard to the conficting epistemological possibilities, he implicitly endorses ontology. His structural analysis of theories of knowledge exemplifies the ontological approach to knowledge claims.

Mannheim contends that every such claim can on reflection be referred to some "systematization" in which it is "at home." These domains of knowledge need not coincide with historical disciplines. But they can be delineated, because each possesses a unifying animating spirit, a "will to discipline," a purposive design, or a meaningful plan. Knowledge exists, on this theory of the relationship, when the knower connects with the aspect of things upon which a given structure of knowledge is grounded. Mannheim speaks of "premises" in this connection, but uses the logical term in an extended sense when he explains that these are "premises that a person, so to speak, has to accept, acknowledge, approve, and is party to whenever he states a theoretical concept in a meaningful way or somehow directs his attention to it" (Mannheim [1922a] 1964:172–173. Cp. Mannheim [1922] 1953:20).

We reflect on what we think—or on what someone claims to know— by becoming aware of the context where it belongs and by thinking ourselves into that context. Once oriented, we know how to characterize and to test the thought claimed as knowledge in the manner appropriate to the context-domain. As the example of Mannheim's structural analysis of theories of knowledge is meant to show, such insight also recognizes the limitations of the domain, its inability to impinge on the autonomy of others. A contestable judgment of propriety forms the core of epistemological assessment.

Mannheim distinguishes three classes of systematizations with distinctive structures. Art contains systematizations in which integrity of form counts but different conceptions do not exclude or even criticize one another; science, in contrast, comprises strictly logical systematizations for which, in principle, there are unequivocally correct questions and answers; and philosophy is intermediate between them. Philosophical inquiries, according to Mannheim, must presuppose the possibility of correct solutions if there is to be a point to their pursuit; but competing proposals can never be wholly rejected, even if their contribution to knowledge cannot yet be specified. Some philosophical questions are so urgent for humankind that judgments may not be postponed until solutions are found. Approximations and circumscriptions must serve, provided that they are properly grounded in their domain.

Mannheim's ontological theory of knowledge offers three tests for the legitimacy of a knowledge claim. First, it performs the mastering and orienting functions of knowledge. Second, it is authentically grounded in the existential domain about which knowledge is claimed. And third, it has properties congruent with the structure of the systematization to which it belongs; that is, the concepts formulating the claim and the relationships between them must fit the respective type of reality. Both treatises published in *Structures of Thinking* exemplify the approach, "The distinctive character of cultural sociological knowledge" by distinguishing immanent from functional aspects of culture, and "A sociological theory of culture and its knowability" by differentiating between conjunctive and communicative knowledge. In the philosophical dissertation where Mannheim develops the tests, they gain in discursive force—despite their formulation in his metaphorical language of "place" and "home"—from Mannheim's professional analyses and criticisms of respected philosophical doctrines, as well as his sophisticated invocations of Husserl, Heidegger, and other authorities.

But our present interest in Mannheim's epistemological tests derives from their reverberations in his later arguments about social and political knowledge. His strategy for transcending reductionism and relativism depends on the possibility of crystallizing structures of thinking out of the sea of opinion, mapping them, then linking them in a coherent design. The method of "structural analysis" exemplified in his comparative study of epistemologies is used to this end.

Two shifts mark Mannheim's turn from his more general attempt to establish ontological grounds for the constitution of cultural knowledge to the more specific design for uncovering the social bases of ideologies. He increasingly treats social reality as the last knowable reality and thus considers the social identity of cultural formations, including knowledge, as indicating their place in the order of things; and he views that knowledge-grounding social reality as undergoing constant historical change. In his dissertation on theories of knowledge he expressly denies the possibility of history in any form serving as a foundational science in the manner of psychology, logic, or ontology. But the abandonment of this unargued assertion returns to his parallel fascination with the possibility of a philosophy of history as a comprehensive frame of reference for all interpretation. And the elevation of theoretical history expresses Mannheim's responsiveness to the exciting competition between Marxist theories of ideology, given unprecedented subtlety by Lukács, and the more spiritual cultural sociology of Alfred Weber and Max Scheler. Although Mannheim never arrived at a satisfactory philosophical statement of his historicist option, the regulative ideal of a dynamic social ontology presided over the best-known phase of his work.

Correspondingly, conflicting social-political ideologies comprise the core cultural and spiritual formations of the modern age. Mannheim thus turns away from the conception of epochal worldviews of his earlier explication of cultural sociology as a specialized discipline. His own historical social ontology itself now appears as a function of the competition among the liberal, conservative and socialist ideologies from which it springs. Acknowledging that the construction of experience as political in structure cannot be shown to be more than an approach historically appropriate to the present, he denies that this limitation jeopardizes its status as genuine knowledge if there is a method appropriate to the domain for testing and improving specific knowledge claims. The possibility of a comprehensive social knowledge about the interrelationships among the ideological forms of social knowledge, grounded on an understanding of their interconnections at other levels of social reality, promises a new way of knowing and a new way for society.

The novelty in Mannheim's approach to the sociology of knowledge is neither the social interpretation of political ideas nor its extension to a wide range of cultural productions not usually considered political. These he accepts as the achievements of a line of thinkers, culminating in Marx and Weber. Mannheim makes two distinctive claims. First is the conception of ideologies as cognitive structures. They are variously flawed, limited, perspectivistically one-sided, subject to drastic correction from other perspectives, and nevertheless productive of knowledge. Mannheim does not understand the structure of ideologies as an organization of recommendations and claims built around some central "value," as is commonly done; he emphasizes their implicit "ontologies" and "epistemologies." Nor does he assume that ideologies have a standard form differentiated primarily by assumptions about human nature; instead, he stresses their diverse conceptions of historical development and of the relationship between knowledge and action.

The second original claim is that sociology of knowledge bears on the substantive issues addressed by ideologies and that it contributes directly to political orientation. It does so, in Mannheim's view, not because knowledge of social genesis can in itself determine judgments of validity, but because comprehensive inquiry into it will foster a synthesis of the valid elements in the ideologies, relocating them in a developmental context that will not so much falsify the ideologies as cognitive structures as render them obsolete—displacing them with a new comprehensive vision.

The word "method" derives from the Greek word for "way." Although in present usage method refers primarily to the procedures followed in inquiry, there is an older sense, preserved in some contexts, in which it indicates the topics or "places" an inquiry must traverse to reach its objective. Mannheim's sociology of knowledge is a method for attaining political knowledge in the second of these senses. By requiring investigators to explicate the diverse intellectual formations competing in the ideological field, correlating them with one another and with the social situation within which the ideological field is located, the study carries inquirers through the matters they must consider before they can diagnose their own time. And it is a method or way in a third sense: inquirers who pursue this course gain a new readiness for comprehensive knowledge. They are freed from illusions about ideologies and experience a new form of mastery.

Sociology of Knowledge

The essays published in 1929 in *Ideologie und Utopie* should be taken together with Mannheim's work on conservatism, his presentation on

"Competition as a Cultural Phenomenon" to the Sixth Congress of German Sociologists in Zurich 1928 that initiated the sociology of knowledge dispute (Mannheim [1929] 1993. See Meja and Stehr 1982, 1990), and his handbook article on the sociology of knowledge, published in 1931 (Mannheim [1931] 1952). In all these writings, there is the characteristic recognition of plurality in the intellectual field, along with a new emphasis on competition among intellectual designs, and there is the notion of an intellectual strategy for furthering a synoptic perspective that will give the competitors an awareness of a common direction and some shared conception of meaning. The overview may even render the contests anachronistic.

Mannheim's strategy involves two steps. First, the variety of ideas in the modern world is classified according to a scheme of historical ideological types, few in number, in keeping with Mannheim's thesis that the ideological field has moved from a period of atomistic diversity and competition to a period of concentration. Liberalism, conservatism, and socialism are the principal types. Second, each of these ideologies is interpreted as a function of some specific way of being in the social world, as defined by location within the historically changing patterns of class and generational stratification. Liberalism is thus referred to the capitalist bourgeoisie in general, and various stages in its development are referred to generational changes. Similar analyses connect conservatism to social classes harmed by the rise of the bourgeoisie to power, and socialism to the new industrial working class.

Each of the ideologies is said to manifest a characteristic "style" of thinking, a distinctive complex of responses to the basic issues systematic philosophy has identified as constitutive of human consciousness, such as conceptions of time and space, the structure of reality, human agency, and knowledge itself. The political judgments and recommendations on the surface of purely ideological texts must be taken in that larger structural context. Not every ideology elaborates such a philosophy, and the elaborated philosophies associated with an ideology may not provide an adequate account of the underlying ideological structures. Such philosophies are ideological texts like others, and require structural analysis and sociological interpretation to be fully comprehended. The style of thinking is most apparent in the way concepts are formed, according to Mannheim, and in the logic by which they are interlinked. These are the features that must be uncovered to identify the distinctive style.

Each of the styles, in turn, expresses some distinctive design upon the world vitally bound up with the situation of one of the social strata present in the historical setting. Mannheim is emphatic in his original German texts, but not in his later English revisions, that this design cannot be equated to a group "interest," because he disavows the theory of motivation associated with the stress on interest. He speaks of the "aspirations" of groups or of other social entities in this connection, but he does not hold that testimony by group representatives about demands or wishes is necessarily definitive. The sociologist of knowledge has no direct authoritative information about the formative will he postulates as the principle of integration and immanent development in ideological wholes. The self-explanations offered by groups in their ideologies and utopias are the starting points for knowledge about underlying styles and principles, along with such social theories as may be available to expound the logic of their social location, not excluding theories of interests.

The sociologist of knowledge works back and forth between these two sources to uncover the interpretation he seeks. The very definition of a generational unit that may serve as a point of reference in the social interpretation of an ideological phase, for example, depends on evidence that a given historical experience has in fact become a central point of reference for the cohort that has experienced it. Similarly, the definitive importance of certain social or political demands for a given social group—or indeed the saliency of social identity to social knowledge—cannot be established without using information about ideas associated with the group to elucidate other sociological or historical data, or without moving in the opposite direction. Mannheim, aware of the potential circularity, denies that it is damaging to his undertaking, since he is striving less for causal explanations of social belief or social knowledge than for explications of such knowledge in the context of a comprehensive or "total" view of the society undergoing change.

It is the view of the "totality" that is the objective. Sociology of knowledge seeks to give an account of the whole ideological field, in its historical interaction and change, together with an account of the historically changing class and generational situations that the ideologies interpret to the groups involved. To have a method for seeing all this, according to Mannheim, means to be able to see in a unified and integrated way what each of the ideologically oriented viewers can only see in part. It is to have the capacity for viewing the situation as a whole.

Mannheim's essay on politics as a science illustrates this procedure. In it he compares the contrasting ideological conceptions of the relationship between theory and practice, and explicates the differences by situating each ideology in a distinct social location. The exercise in sociology of knowledge tacitly introduces the concepts Mannheim then uses to characterize politics and the role of knowledge in it. Many readers object that Mannheim's analyses presuppose a sociological philosophy of history that is not sufficiently expounded or defended, but Mannheim defends his historical interpretation as elicited by his critical confrontations with ideologies and validated by the synthesizing consequences of the encounters. The concept of "situation" has special importance for him. To comprehend a piece of the historical world as a situation is to see it as a foresightful and perspicacious political actor might see it. The concept already appears in this form in Hegel's lectures on aesthetics, where the world as situation refers to the world as possessing moral significance, as a scene for action. A situation comprises a complex of factors and conditions; it is charged with meaning: opportunity and prospects, threat or promise.

In elucidating situations, then, sociologists of knowledge and ideologies seek the same kind of knowledge. Both pursue the intellectual means for effective political action. But sociologists have a larger view than ideologists, a synoptic vision. They can diagnose their time. And, Mannheim insists, they are no mere spectators. Spectators could not, in any case, read situations. That presupposes a will or design. But the precise character and source of the will directing the style of sociological thinking troubles Mannheim in these writings, and it is one of the important features about which the various essays venture different experiments.

Although Mannheim acknowledges that key concepts of the sociology of knowledge derive from the Marxist social theory he accepts as the explication of proletarian socialist ideology, he maintains that the terms and analytical procedures undergo a change in design when they become part of the sociology of knowledge. No longer utilized as a technique for discrediting and demoralizing opponents, the new understanding brings out the cognitive capabilities of ideologies even while uncovering the ideological character of social knowledge. These differences make it impossible to consider the proletariat and its revolutionary social purposes as the force behind sociology of knowledge.

Nor can sociology of knowledge be seen as animated by the universalist and rationalist designs Mannheim considers congruent with the social location of the capitalist bourgeoisie and identifies as the social principle of liberalism, because sociology of knowledge emphasizes the historically bound nature of social knowledge as well as the residue of volition and choice in all understanding. After excluding, for similar reasons, the other primary social styles and their social authors, Mannheim suggests—since he has no doubt that the sociology of knowledge is an irresistible force—that it must express the design specific to the urbane and educated intellectual stratum bringing it into being and actively responding to it.

Mannheim's emphasis on the cognitive worth of ideological knowledge in dynamic competition calls into question the necessity for sociology of knowledge as a force for integration. If the conflict of ideologies in an age of concentration and competition is grounded in the social realities of the time, the process itself should manifest the inner truth of this reality. The political process of competition would be the locus of all the knowledge required for politics, generating and monitoring the realism that is socially necessary. So understood, politics would correspond to the liberal parliament as a forum for rational disputation and as an institutionalization of the mechanisms by which knowledge is tested and validated. Such an outcome is too "rationalistic" for Mannheim. He draws on Marxism for a conception of politics as a process of dialectical interplay among factors more "real" than the competing opinions of liberal theory. But none of the political forces is bearer of a transcendent rationality, historically destined to reintegrate all the struggling irrationalities in a higher, pacified order. The contesting social forces and their projects in the world are complementary and in need of a synthesis that will incorporate elements of their diverse social wills and visions.

The ideological field is in a state of "crisis," incapable of immanent dialectical development. Several of the ideological contenders set forth their claims in terms so absolute that they imply the annihilation of all opponents and make for mindless acts of violence, without realistic hope of revolutionary reconstitution. All ideological contenders, moreover, use the concept of ideology in its purely destructive form to disorient and discredit their opponents, thereby mutually undermining their confidence in their own understandings and aspiration and opening another way to pointless violent direct action. Under these conditions, Mannheim denies that a *Realpolitik* can function without a contribution from thinking that transcends ideological perspectives. A sociology of knowledge is needed to generate such thinking. Constitional legalism will not serve. Only a sociology of knowledge can generate an experience of interdependence.

Sociology of knowledge renders diverse knowledge types legitimate, even while restricting the scope of the claims of each. The legitimating and constituting function of the sociology of knowledge is analogous to the functions of the democratic constitutional and legal systems in the juristic theory of Hans Kelsen. Sociology of knowledge and Kelsen's constitutionalism both offer a civilizing framework that denies the universality of claims put forward by competing political actors, while granting them legitimacy as partisan participants in an unresolvable competition. But the differences between them are great and bear on a major issue in dispute during the Weimar years, the reconstitutive powers of the law.

Mannheim's work stays on the margin of this dispute, from his use of Max Weber's sociology of law as paradigm for sociology of culture in his first treatment of the discipline (Mannheim [1922–24] 1982), to his exclusion of all but juristic writers from his study of conservatism, to denigrating all forms of legalism as aspects of liberal indifference to the irrationalities of power and conflict. What Kelsen entrusts to the legal manifestation of the democratically organized sovereign state, Mannheim would put on a basis of comprehensive, intercommunicated social knowledge about the common historical situation. For Mannheim, Kelsen exemplifies the "idealist" attempt to generate a normative order without reference to the actual situation and to impose it upon social existence from "above." The normativizing activity of the sociology of knowledge, in contrast, is as rooted in the same cultural and political developments as the conflicts it is designed to regulate and the crisis has the capacity to overcome. This gives it an authenticity and connectedness no legal structure can claim. It offers a genuine constitution (Burke 1945: 341ff.).

Two Conceptions of Ideology

Mannheim distinguishes three features as distinctive of knowledge in its various types. There is first a quality of authenticity, a rootedness in some lasting relationship to a dimension of reality. Aesthetic knowledge, for example, rests on a responsiveness to form, and form has real existence, in the special way that meanings exist in the world. In his studies in *Structures of Thinking* on the sociology of culture as a mode of knowledge, Mannheim seeks to uncover comparable structured attitudes and ontological objects to account for the possibility of the knowledge examined there. Second, then, knowledge is situated within an integrated structure, distinguished by its manner of forming concepts and by its logic. The whole class of the physical sciences, for example, operates with univocal universal concepts interlinked in deductive logical systems, while the cultural sciences use descriptive concepts connected in less determinate but clearly patterned ways. Third, knowledge provides what Mannheim calls "orientations" to a given domain, and knowledge can be applied, recalled, and transmitted. Transient impressions and idiosyncratic intuitions thus cannot count as knowledge, although systematizations will differ in the degree to which they can find uses for such mental acts. Mannheim's conception of sociology of knowledge as organon for a science of politics builds upon all three features of this theory of knowledge. The uncertainty of the tests that it generates, and Mannheim's difficulties in rendering them persuasive to professional colleagues, however, explain his unresolved doubts about his novel and preferred conception of sociology as "organon" for politics as a science and thus his continued, parallel interest in a more narrow, discipline-oriented characterization of sociology of knowledge.

For the second alternative, the sociology of knowledge appears as a specialized subdivision of applied sociology, and the validity of its findings and theories is subject to standards appropriate to this value-free discipline. While the emergence of the subdiscipline may be accounted for by social theory, the integrity of its practitioners and the value of their work depend on their submission to disciplinary norms. Sociology of knowledge as discipline is reminiscent of Mannheim's philosophical position before his projection of a philosophy of history as unifying ground for thought. It implies a pluralism of autonomous modes of knowledge, moreover, that casts doubt on the cognitive role of the movement towards synthesis in the ideology-process, as that movement is envisioned by the design of the sociology of knowledge as organon.

Ideology, in the more limited approach, appears as false consciousness, a view of the world distorted by the effects of unconscious social compulsions. Even in the introductory essay of *Ideologie und Utopie*,

Mannheim keeps open the possibility of associating his own concept with this skeptical connotation of the term. A criterion of false consciousness is presupposed by the "evaluative" concept of ideology, as distinguished from a "non-evaluative" one, since it is in the former that ideology appears as something categorically different from knowledge. The "non-evaluative" concept of ideology, in contrast, epitomizes a conception of sociology of knowledge as a superior but complicitous collaborator in the ideological process. Mannheim in one place suggests a dialectical movement between these conceptions at successive levels of analysis, but he does not work out a persuasive statement of this presumed development, and the designs emerge as incompatible alternatives.

The conception of sociology of knowledge as discipline is closer to Max Weber's categorical distinction between scientific words as ploughshares and political words as swords. The continued attractiveness to Mannheim of the former possibility owes much to his unfinished business with Weber: his attraction to Weber's teachings about empiricism, rigor, and intellectual asceticism always coexists with his fascination with historicist and phenomenological approaches. Mannheim hopes to achieve a dialectical change in function (*Funktionswechsel*) of Weber's social interpretation of culture, but he has no philosophical confidence in an Hegelian dialectical logic to serve that objective. In methodological reflections, he insists that the change could be achieved by the weight of evidence that Weber would have had to acknowledge. This consideration weighs against the attempt to ground comprehensive social knowledge on the historical and social identity of intellectuals. In Mannheim's alternative approach, the focus shifts to a disciplinary structure embodied in the professional community of social scientists.

The two currents in Mannheim's thinking about the sociology of knowledge have caused difficulties for his many commentators, who have been curiously unwilling to take seriously Mannheim's admission of inconsistencies in his work, or even to explore systematically what he might have meant when he insisted on his right to pursue alternate possibilities. His German contemporaries reacted to the more ambitious conception of the sociology of knowledge as organon, while later writers, especially English-speaking ones, have concentrated on his notion of the sociology of knowledge as (also) a positive discipline, a specialization in academic sociology.

The problems are compounded by the fact that Mannheim does not explore the alternatives in separate essays. While there are differences in emphasis from essay to essay and a shift in emphasis after the 1920s, the conceptions are frequently intertwined. Mannheim sometimes speaks of them as representing, in effect, his maximum and minimum programs. But this formula does not cover the case, since the sociology of knowledge as discipline differs from the sociology of knowledge as organon precisely on the two points that have been noted as Mannheim's distinctive contributions: the cognitive character of ideologies and the role of the sociology of knowledge in generating a substantive theory of history. The countercurrent in Mannheim's thinking functions rather as a fallback position, designed to preserve what he insists are uncontestable findings and practices of the sociology of knowledge, while avoiding theoretical and political difficulties associated with his more ambitious design.

To speak of "program," "position," and "political difficulties" in this connection is to recall Mannheim's programmatic concern with the liberal objective of showing how discursive reason can be in command of power. The liberal project links the two currents: if the sociology of knowledge cannot be the organon for a synthetic and reconciling understanding of the direction and meaning of historical development, providing a scientific grasp of the situation in which all parties will recognize themselves, then it can at least be a propaedeutic for scientific social theory, a prophylactic against ideologies that promote enlightenment. Mannheim's work in this domain must be understood as an ingenious, conscientious, and determined pursuit of the hunch that the way through the crisis of liberal civilization must go beyond the relativizing insights of fashionable cultural and political commentary that exposes the historical and social conditioning of all cultural productions, including knowledge. He is thinking this problem through, building on a philosophical model of knowledge derived from phenomenological speculation and elaborated in his essay on the structural analysis of epistemology. He emphasizes throughout a regulative ideal of philosophy of history, inspired above all by Hegelian readings of Marx, as well as the paradigmatic realism of Max Weber, whose intellectual strategies strengthen Mannheim's professionalism when his speculations draw him close to the belletristic and pseudophilosophical devices of the cultural essayists. And his thinking is conditioned by a strong sense of political responsibility amid changing readings of the political situation.

It is Mannheim's paradoxical thesis, in the main current of his Weimar thought, that ideologies count as knowledge by virtue of the fact commonly used to discredit them. Precisely because they are each rooted in the perspective specific to some social group, they are authentically connected to the real processes of social existence and to the way knowledge arises and works within it. Each group, of course, sees different threats and possibilities in the situation and needs to know different things about it. That is why ideologies are perspectival. But each does know something, and knows it well. In his explication of such knowledge in *Structures of Thinking*, he speaks of "conjunctive" knowledge, and means by this a knowledge "in touch" with things and shareable only among knowers similarly situated and somehow in contact with one another, or among connoisseurs situated so as to develop a special sensibility for the historical variety of such knowledge.

In his work on conservatism, specifically in the exposition of Savigny's conservative distinction between a law rooted in a communal sense of justice and a law derived from juristic systematization, Mannheim elaborates a similar conception of a way of thinking attached to collective forms of life. Mannheim's awareness of the positive sense attached to a showing of social roots in conservative thought and his own experimenting with that sense are expressed dramatically in one terminological choice, involving a concept central to his subsequent approach. He first introduces one of the key concepts of his sociology of knowledge, "*seinsverbundenes Denken*," when characterizing the more conservative of the two types of legal thinking distinguished by Savigny (Savigny 1892). One type of thinking is "abstract thinking, detached from the organic," and it operates with rigorous definitions, restricted to mere elaborations of form. "*Seinsverbundenes Denken*" in law, by contrast, is constituted by the recognition "that the knowing subject must be existentially rooted in the community in which the living, always changing law is to be found" (Mannheim [1925] 1986: 159). Mannheim thus establishes a terminological association between the thinking integral to the life of a community and the ultimate origination of modern historicism in the conservative movement against rationalization. Both are rooted in concrete existence, in contrast to strictly definable, logically systematized formal abstractions.

Mannheim subsequently uses the term he introduces in the Savigny discussion to describe the quality common to all thought subject to sociological interpretation, but the continuities with Savigny's conservative idea do not extend to the notion that only communities bound by soil and tradition can possess such knowledge.[2] In his first formulations of the distinction between "conjunctive" and "communicative" thinking in *Structures of Thinking*, he comes close when he suggests that the communicative type, produced by social modernization and rationalization, obliterates interpersonal human meanings. In the sociology of knowledge experiments in *Conservatism*, however, he already refers authentic social knowledge to the collective experiences of social classes in complex industrial societies, and this takes him far from conservative praise of communal ways of thought. The positive connotation of existential rootedness, nevertheless, remains an important characteristic in his thinking.

This criterion is vital to the distinction between "partial" and "total" concepts of ideology proposed by Mannheim in the first essay of *Ideologie und Utopie* . Partial ideology derives from intellectualist distrust of purposive discourse, but it suffices to comprehend self-interested manipulative designs in political expressions. But total ideology constitutes a way of knowing. Mannheim is concerned above all with the authentic cultural phenomenon corresponding to total ideology, a concept designating a style of thought inherent in a social and historical location. While an analyst applying the partial concept would uncover the interested motive underlying, for example, a newspaper editorial welcoming a measure of unemployment as an incentive to productivity, Mannheim would have investigated, as Gunnar Myrdal has done, the ideological context that gives meaning to such concepts as "unemployment" and "productivity" and the social and historical roots of this ideology. An analysis grounded on the concept of total ideology would lead not only to the powers and historical limitations of bourgeois political economy but also to the competing presence of what Marx had called the "political economy of the proletariat." Study of the "total ideology" opens the way to the ideological field and to the historical situation of which it is a part. Sociology of knowledge, on this reading, is concerned with establishing a vital connection to this underlying historical situation.

As is often the case at key points in Mannheim's argument, there is a paradox here. Like other forms of social knowledge, the synthetic achievement of the sociology of knowledge depends for its cognitive integrity on its rootedness in the social reality it explicates. Yet sociology of knowledge is grounded in a social stratum comparatively detached from the parties contesting the social terrain. The question is whether the style of thought peculiar to intellectuals can be authentic or whether it is bound to be a superficial, surface phenomenon. In many of his essays, Mannheim accepts this paradox without comment, letting the literary familiarity with dialectical ironies carry the burden of the argument. In other places, however, he concedes the need to present intellectuals as disciplined by constraints that his theory of their social location alone would not account for. Impatience with the superficial "impressionism" of the sophisticated and relativist intellectuals and distrust of the romantic indiscipline of antirationalist literary intellectuals had been, after all, starting points for his own work.

Mannheim's well-known formula of "socially unattached intellectuals" (sozial freischwebende Intelligenz), like "Seinsverbundenheit," first appears in Conservatism. Similarly too, familiarity with the earlier use complicates the interpretation of the later writings, rendering the texts richer in ambiguities. Mannheim introduces the expression to identify the proponents of romanticism, but quickly notes that the same social formation had also promulgated Enlightenment thought. Such intellectuals have been caretakers of the world of the spirit since the eighteenth century. While they remained true to the Enlightenment, Mannheim maintains, they kept up a connection with the bourgeois class from which most of them sprang, but when they reacted against rationalism, impelled by ideal reasons alone, they found themselves in "sociological as well as metaphysical alienation and isolation" (Mannheim [1925] 1986:117).[3] Only then did the intellectuals display the full mixture of qualities peculiar to this social formation, above all "an extraordinary sensitivity combined with moral unsteadiness, a constant readiness for adventure and obscurantism" (Mannheim [1925] 1986: 117-18). "These unattached intellectuals," Mannheim also observes, "are the archetypical apologists, 'ideologists' who are masters at providing a basis and backing for the political designs whose service they enter, whatever these may be" (Mannheim [1925] 1986:118).

But this stratum is also the locus of philosophical reflection on history and comprehensive reading of the times, initiating in its romantic phase the line of thinking that carries forward through Hegel, Treitschke, and Marx to the German sociology of Mannheim's own time. "This is certainly the positive side of their activities," he writes, "for there must and should always be people who are not so bound by their immediate ties that they care only for the 'next step'" (Mannheim [1925] 1986:118). But this productive achievement comes about, when "socially unattached intellectuals, with their inherent sense of system and totality, bind themselves to the designs of social forces which are concretely manifest" (Mannheim [1925] 1986: 214, n.150). There must be, in other words, a tie to a social reality more effective than their spiritual state, if the socially unattached intellectuals are to perform their larger spiritual tasks. A requirement for such social commitment stands in a problematic relationship to Mannheim's later view that the social stratum has a decisive role precisely by virtue of its unique capabilities for openness and choice, allowing it to generate a synthesis out of incompatible ideologies. The difference is shaped by nuances, but lets Mannheim preserve a more ironic view of intellectuals.

This distrust is echoed in Mannheim's subsequent reading of fascism as the ideology of a stratum of intellectuals who are "outsiders," as well as in his warning that an ideology and political enterprise designed by intellectuals on their own behalf could only be a fascist one (Mannheim [1929] 1952:123). This paradox about authenticity and his ambivalence about intellectuals are clearly among the considerations that keep alive for Mannheim an alternative theory about the sociology of knowledge and its relationship to ideology, and brings the alternative to the fore when fascism gains ascendancy, first in large circles of the academic and extramural intelligentsia and then, overwhelmingly, in the cultural domain as a whole. Nevertheless, he never abandons the argument, at least while writing in Germany, that intellectuals must become aware of their distinctive mission by gaining consciousness of themselves as a group. Mannheim's post-Marxist analysis draws on the idea of a historically privileged social location while rejecting the notion that one ideology possesses a monopoly of knowledge. The recourse to intellectuals remains decisive for him because they are uniquely haunted by ideology as a problem.

Karl Mannheim specified his debt to Marxist social theory and declared his independence from Marxist ideology in an address to Dutch students in October 1932. He credits "proletarian thought" with originating the method of sociological self-interpretation, "the method of deriving one's historical mission from the vantage point of one's sociological situation" (Mannheim [1932] 1993:72). But he rejects the con-

tention that social classes are the only entities capable of such consciousness, insisting that the sociological way to self-awareness has become
common property of many types of social groups. His professed aim is
to free the intelligentsia from the misconception that it must either count
as class or be nothing, to free intellectual life from the tyranny of partisan ideologies, among which the Marxist is the most seductive. "In times
like ours," he writes, "when the intellectual has long since cast off the
presumptuousness of a theocentric emissary of God, but is rather tempted
to regard himself as a sociologically irrelevant nullity, it is our supreme
duty, not to destroy the proletarian socio-logic, but to confidently sur-
mount it by taking account of the independent position of intellectuals
in present-day society" (Mannheim [1932] 1993: 74). Mannheim then
claims that sociology of knowledge achieves this purpose, expanding
on his principal theses in *Ideologie und Utopie*. To prepare the way for
his contention that the cognitive and transformative qualities Marxists
ascribe to proletarian class consciousness are shared by the reflexive
social awareness of other types of social formations, Mannheim adduces
the case of women. The emancipation of women provides a model for
undermining the intimidating monopoly of class theory.

"We see woman," Mannheim says, "becoming more conscious of her
own being. She has begun to reflect about herself." She had been thought
about before, of course. Everyone has always known about women: what
she is able and what she is obliged to do. But these were the thoughts of
men, expressing the preferences of "her partner, or rather: her opponent." "Man occupied the dominant position and could express his
thoughts, while woman lacked a consciousness of her own, and accepted
his thoughts about her as binding truth, both in her spiritual life and in
her conduct." Now this has changed. The central fact revealed by Marxism about thinking in the economic sphere applies to all social relations:
types of social actors interpret all others from their own points of view,
generating misleading ideologies. Once woman recognizes that she has
not been governed by her own thoughts, that action appropriate to her
position cannot be adequately guided by the designs of those who benefit from imposing an ideology on her, "she attempts to live her life as a
new, independent being" (Mannheim [1932] 1993:73).

The general insight into ideology is necessary but it is not sufficient.
Turning to psychoanalytic language, Mannheim says that there are "inhibitions" that obstruct full consciousness and corresponding action;

many women, in fact, "talk a great deal about emancipation, but only in order to abreact their inhibitions without bringing themselves to act." These inhibitions, he maintains, are a function of particular social situations, and they can be counteracted by a "socioanalysis" that clarifies their sources and operations. Sociology cannot tell whether a society wholly free of such inhibitions is possible, but Mannheim assures his listeners that progress is possible, "such conditions can be consciously promoted." He offers women a vital interest in the destiny of intellectuals. Because the sociology to which he aspires is, in his own view, best understood as the explication of intellectuals' consciousness, he devotes the remainder of his lecture to that theme.

Speaking to fledgling intellectuals at a time when political commitment seemed inescapable, he struggles to strike a balance between partisan politics and the intelligentsia's historical mission. Mannheim maintains that political parties are organs of social classes, and, consequently, that the intelligentsia "is not in a position to form its own party." He continues:

> Anyone who believes that a party of intellectuals is necessary has got the diagnosis of intellectuals wrong. It would be a complete accident if anything at all reasonable came of this. And that can hardly be the basis for gaining consciousness. Above all, it has to be recognized that there is no group that is as divided internally (bank manger, professor, "yellow press journalist," bohemian), and that this division is a division according to *classes*. More than that: the formation of a party of intellectuals would inevitably lead to fascism. This, of course, is hardly something to be desired. But the intellectual should recognize, on the other hand, that he belongs to a specific class. And to this class he must go, not to submerge himself as a pseudo-member in a class in which he does not feel at home, but honestly and with full conviction. And he must join its party. (Mannheim [1932] 1993:75-76)

But this advice cannot be Mannheim's last word because he also wants to emphasize the distinctive qualities common to intellectuals, as well as the reactions they provoke. Mannheim seems caught in a contradiction and seasons his conclusion with sarcasm:

> Julien Benda...laments that the uncommitted thinker is becoming extinct and that everything turns political. However, Benda appears to be mistaken. Politization also entails an important advantage. The traditional cult of the exclusively self-oriented, self-sufficient intelligentsia is in the process of disappearing; and let us be straightforward about the fact that we can no longer bear this aesthetic type: we must finish with this socially aimless, socially useless thinking. It is absolutely essential that the intellect become combative, if not after the fashion of contemporary Germany, where one first bashes each other's head in and only then begins to

think! Fundamentally, the intellectual should recognize that his intellectual identity prescribes certain duties: he must learn to cherish the fact of his intellectual education as an obligation. The danger of politicization, however, is the encapsulation of free thought under the constraint from church, state, or class organization. All of these merely desire a restrained or functionary form of thinking. Therefore I say: join the party which is the organic expression of the class, but do not think as a functionary but as a free man! I refrain from giving advice on which particular party to choose: you must decide for yourself, because that is precisely what makes you an intellectual. Join the ranks, but maintain the freedom of living thought—and you shall experience for yourself how soon you will be kicked out on the streets. (Mannheim [1932] 1993:79)

Mannheim hedges. Even the dictatorial parties need intellectuals to guide the reorientations required by the times and to devise arguments for the uncommitted. But this does not allay his pessimism. While the distinctive vocation of the intellectual in a class-centered society is clear, its fulfillment is uncertain. There is no reliable institution to mediate the contradiction between the political organizations that the responsible intellectual may not ignore and the mental activity that in fact constitutes the intellectual.

In sum, Mannheim's work constantly balances his central proposal against objections he cannot disregard. It may be objected that intellectuals cannot be the source of a distinctive creative political design of their own, since they are the elaborators of all ideologies, in the service of all social impulses and natural apologists for all groups. Mannheim counters that even such justifications raise social and political impulses to a level above brute conflict. They bring clashes of interest and struggles for power into the sphere of the spirit and thereby reproduce and develop the cultural inheritance. Their conversation with that field, moreover, and their exchanges with one another in the language of the educated, notwithstanding their differing ideological affiliations, take on added weight when there is dramatic concentration and polarization of competing ideological forces.

Because the intellectuals are situated where the ideologies make their competing claims in the most sophisticated ways, they are well placed to acknowledge the plurality of ideologies and to assess their intellectual force. Mannheim illustrates this point in his own practice by citing with respect Lukács, Lenin, and even Stalin, on the left, and Othmar Spann and Vilfredo Pareto, on the right. The prime social class competitors themselves, in contrast to the intellectuals, become ever more rigidly organized and steadily more distrustful of "their" intellectuals. They

are satisfied that the time has come for confrontation instead of competition over the public interpretation of reality, and they find that intellectuals, whatever their ideological profession, jeopardize the combativeness
of the parties to which they adhere. All this weakens the links between
many intellectuals and the vital principles animating the predominant
ideologies. They come to an increasing awareness of their distance from
the actively engaged organizations and their commonality with other
intellectuals.

But that raises the objection that such distancing will turn intellectuals into mere skeptics and relativists, into pessimists about all action, or
into fideists in defiance of their own knowledge, tendencies Mannheim
finds even in the works of Dilthey, Simmel, Weber, and Scheler. The
new generation, however, has witnessed the innovative political achievements of the postwar period and, as a member of that generation,
Mannheim professes belief in rational action. He avoids concrete political references, but seems hopeful about the Weimar political situation.
As late as 1932, he speaks about a politics of conflict and compromise
among contesting interests and ideologies in a tone markedly more positive than the political commentary of almost all of his academic colleagues (Mannheim 1932a: 38).[4] Such passages must be balanced, of
course, against other passages proclaiming a great crisis in political and
social life. But in their bearing on the question of the purposiveness of
the intellectuals, the two readings of the political situation converge in
their effects. Promise and threat together stimulate the intellectuals to
action on their own behalf, Mannheim thought. The special mission of
the intellectuals is to work for "synthesis": to cultivate a political life in
which the "next step" in the historically conditioned line of development can be taken with minimal loss to old achievements in culture and
maximal enlistment of all social energies. Intellectuals are to bring about
what liberal ideology had claimed for the market place of ideas and
parliament—except that they understand and show what needs to be
done in a world that is far more complex, irrational, and activist than the
world projected by liberalism.

And Mannheim contends that there are historical precedents for intellectuals assuming a mediating role. Even if there has never been a
prior instance of a mediation among all ideologies present in a competitive field, according to Mannheim, the multitude of ideological ventures
that crowded the field after the breakdown of the old monopolistic con-

trol over the public interpretation of social life exercised by the Church were successfully concentrated into a few by synoptic thinkers like Stahl and Hegel, for the conservatives, and Marx, for the socialists. He finds, moreover, that the work of thinkers like Ernst Troeltsch and Alfred Weber, who address the political public as well as the academy, indicates that a sense of integrative mission is in formation.

Mannheim speaks of these matters in a language adapted from Marxist conceptions of class consciousness. The point of the discourse is not only to show that the developments described are in fact under way, but also to make intellectuals recognize that his interpretation makes sense of their own experiences, lives, and aspirations, and thus to bring them to acknowledge that they share in this mission. Their own subsequent interventions, in turn, proceeding through the findings of the sociology of knowledge, would not merely uncover new information about things in the social world. By redefining the situation in ways that directly involve the vital energies of the competing ideological parties, they would be changing the contours of the entire political field and the character of the competition.

Notes

1. The published essays contain Mannheim's responses to Ernst Troeltsch's *Der Historismus und seine Probleme* (1922), Georg Lukács' *Geschichte und Klassenbewußtsein* ([1923] 1968), and Max Scheler's *Versuche zu einer Soziologie des Wissens* (1924).
2. The textual situation is complicated by the fact that Mannheim uses both *"Seinsverbundenheit"* and *"Seinsgebundenheit,"* almost everywhere interchangeably. In one passage in his 1931 encyclopedia article, "Wissenssoziologie," Mannheim differentiates between them, although without explanation: "The direction of research in the sociology of knowledge may be guided in such a way that it does not lead to an absolutising of the connectedness to existence (*Seinsverbundenheit*) but that precisely in the discovery of the existential connectedness of present insights, a first step towards the resolution of existential determination (*Seinsgebundenheit*) is seen" (Mannheim [1931] 1952:259). In this passage, Mannheim apparently takes advantage of a nuance of difference between the two German expressions. They have different ranges of connotations. *"Verbundenheit"* extends to freely chosen and morally binding ties, while *"Gebundenheit"* reaches out towards compulsion. *Seinsgebundenheit* thus refers to an objective and comparatively strict linkage between the conditions under which thought exists in the world and the makeup of the thought itself; *Seinsverbundenheit* also expresses such linkage, but takes it more nearly as a function of the subjective commitments and identifications of those who bear the thought in society, and accordingly as less firmly fixed. In articulating the con-

trast, then, Mannheim insists that awareness of the social commitments constitutive of social knowledge will counter the mechanical and alienated forms of those commitments, operating as uncontrollable constraints. The English translation incorporated in *Ideology and Utopia* omits the distinction between Seins-*verbundenheit* and Seins*gebundenheit*, rendering them both as "situational determination." Cp. Mannheim 1936a:271. See Meja 1975:7 and Simonds 1978:27.

3. This is one of the few interpretations that Mannheim changed when he published a portion of the text in German (Mannheim 1927). The purely "immanent" sources of the development from Enlightenment to romanticism are now presented as responses to social and political developments. The difference is important, not least because the question of spiritual and intellectual creativity is a touchstone for his mentor Alfred Weber.

4. See Mannheim's claim, in his *Encyclopaedia of the Social Sciences* (Mannheim 1935b) entry on Tönnies, that it was an achievement of the Weimar Republic to have recognized the value of sociology in the education of its citizens.

4

The Politics of Synthesis

According to Mannheim's introductory statement of purpose, his objective in *Ideologie und Utopie* is to break through the crisis of distrust crippling political life. The essay on politics as a science, on the relation between theory and practice, he places at the center of the book. *Ideologie und Utopie* is a political book in the context of Weimar. Yet direct evidence to place Mannheim in the Weimar political spectrum is meager. He counts as a refugee from Hungary for some years, but he was never a leftist political emigré. He arrived in Germany as a refugee from Hungarian authorities, ostracized as a minor beneficiary of Lukács' tenure in the education portfolio of the Soviet regime. But on the balance of the evidence, Mannheim stayed true to the nonpolitical "culturist" program of the original Sunday Circle during the months of communist rule in Hungary.[1] His personal loyalty to his communist friends led him to take risks to help them escape, but Béla Balázs spoke scornfully of an approach by Mannheim and Hauser to the reconstituted Sunday group in Vienna, charging that they had abandoned the group when most of its members committed themselves to the Revolution and wanted to return only when the Revolution seemed indefinitely postponed. Although Mannheim was allowed to join the discussions during his 1920 Vienna visit, undoubtedly because of closer personal ties and higher intellectual standing with the group, Balázs' dismissal of Hauser, "We can no longer have contacts which are not also alliances," applies equally to Mannheim (Karádi and Vezér 1985: 126–27; cp. Gábor 1983:8; Congdon 1983:175). Like Hauser, Mannheim never subordinated his thinking to partisan commitments, and the lack of such loyalty was Balázs' standard for exclusion. Mannheim's favorable review of Lukács' *Theory of the Novel* (Mannheim [1920] 1993) may have been a gesture of solidarity when Lukács was in mortal danger of extradition to Hungary on murder charges, but nothing in the review acknowledges that Lukács had been dedicated to the Bolshevik cause since December 1918. Since the issue of *Logos* in which the review appears is dated 1920, and is otherwise given over to articles on Spengler's *Decline of the West*, first published in 1918, time constraints alone do not explain Mannheim's failure to acknowledge the political coloration Lukács had given the philosophy of history Mannheim praises.[2] Lukács would not have countenanced the omission. Ignoring Lukács' partisan preoccupations, Mannheim says nothing to distinguish his position from that encapsulated in the motto of a campaign for Lukács among German literary figures: "Not the politician, but the human being and thinker Georg von Lukazs (*sic*) must be defended."[3] Mannheim is included on a list of "future leaders of democratic Hungary" compiled in 1922 by Mihály Károlyi, the leader of the short-lived first Hungarian Republic; and Hungarian scholars credit Mannheim with authorship of an uncharacteristically florid article aligning himself in 1924 with the purely political opposition to the Horthy regime. Despite these faint, uncertain hints of a liberal political profile, Mannheim overwhelmingly translated his Hungarian loyalties into personal, family matters.

If the dramatic events leading to Mannheim's departure from Hungary do not define his German political identity or clarify his central political concerns, his Hungarian experience nevertheless bears importantly on his most important political concept. The puzzle about Mannheim's reliance on the intelligentsia to conduct a politics of synthesis is not his general concept of the intellectual, but his sense of the sociologically diverse group as bearer of a collective mission. Mannheim's vision derives from non-Western models. In cohesiveness, mutual recognition, patterns of conduct, and self-conception, his Budapest generation has more in common with oppositional cultural formations in the Russian Empire (and its—largely Jewish—emigration) and among dissident nationalities in Austria-Hungary than with the West European literary or professional types Mannheim exclusively covers in his unfinished major study on "The Problem of the Intellectuals: Its Past and Present Role." As Mannheim (1940:82n.) notes in a later work, surprisingly crediting a Cambridge don for the reference to Masaryk's *Spirit of Russia* (1919), the term "Intelligentsia" originates in Russia. Peter Nettl writes:

> The word "intelligentsia"…captures the subtle increase in exacerbation over the word "intellectual": while the latter may develop from a social stratum into a col-

lectivity under certain favorable circumstances, an intelligentsia is more of a self-conscious collectivity *ab ovo*. In other words, in the Russian context the relationship between dissent in ideas and a sociopolitical role is historically much more strongly marked. (Nettl 1969:95; cp. Beloff 1985:402; Brym 1980:42–48; Williams 1976:141)

Like the English word, neither the transliteration from the Russian nor the German *"Intelligenz"* normally have these wider connotations in German usage, except when the reference is to Russians at home or in exile (Weber [1906] 1989). With its enthusiasm for Dostoyevsky and its Russian connections, Mannheim's Lukács fellowship has been characterized as "East" rather than left or right of the Jászi Sociological Society.[4] Mannheim had every reason to move "West," but nothing he found there quite corresponds to the notion of intellectuals with a "mission." And it is among the predominantly Jewish "ideologists of the Russian Left," that one more commonly finds Mannheim's characteristic architectonic conception that "political theory [has] to be developed as only one facet of a general weltanschauung embracing at least philosophy, sociology, anthropology, psychology and biology" (Frankel 1981). Mannheim's idea of using sociology to transcend such ideological activity and to attain "synthesis" also implies self-transcendence for a type of intellectual that was as alien and mystifying a phenomenon in Germany as in London (cp. Horowitz 1988).

Mannheim's political project, in short, requires him to sever himself from his roots in the Jewish Budapest "Generation of 1900," with its constitutive ambivalences about the East. The commitment to academic sociology marks the shift. His search for functional equivalents of the intelligentsia that his approach nevertheless requires later brings him, paradoxically enough, close to Christian circles in both Germany and England. But in Weimar Germany, the group that best illuminates his conception of synthesis is rarely recognized by Mannheim in his German writings.[5] The present chapter is in part devoted to a thought experiment, comparing Mannheim's design for reconstituting Weimar political thought with the constitutional politics of moderate Socialist advocates. Most of them shared his enthusiasm for sociology and his scepticism about Marxist ideology. And they resemble him too in paradoxically pursuing the holistic visions emblematic of the "intelligentsia" through professional work in professional identities. They sought to remake the role of lawyer as Mannheim sought to redefine the vocation of the sociologist. In both cases, an established discipline was expected to serve the reconstitution of the political world.

Politics at a Distance

Mannheim's experiences during his decade at the University of Heidelberg, from 1920 to 1930, reinforced his inclination to avoid political partisanship. When he was proposed for habilitation in 1925, the Inner Senate of the University objected to his being licensed as *Privatdozent* because he lacked German citizenship. His academic sponsors, Emil Lederer and Alfred Weber, defended Mannheim "as a man who has never exposed himself politically in the past and will not, to judge by his general attitude and inclinations, ever do so in the future";[6] and his German publications before his habilitation were technical and apolitical enough. The university and the authorities of the Baden state government eventually decided the issue in Mannheim's favor. His naturalization, however, was debated at intergovernmental levels for another three years.

The official exchanges concerning Mannheim's naturalization illustrate not only the difficulties confronting an alien Jew aspiring to an academic career, but also the obstructions barring such a person from influence on established political elites. Under the naturalization law of the time, any exception to a twenty-year probationary period required the agreement of all state governments. Baden had requested Mannheim's naturalization after only eight years residence on the grounds of his exceptional qualifications and accomplishments, as well as his culturally German background. Bavaria and Württemberg witheld consent. In the confidential exchanges of 1929, the official from the Württemberg Ministry of the Interior at one point writes:

> I see in the ever more common generous naturalization of ever larger numbers of Eastern foreigners of alien stock (*fremdstämmige Ostausländer*) a serious threat to German interests, especially at present, when it must be feared that professions which should be kept German, notably university teaching, will become foreign through and though (*Durchfremdung*).

Bavaria's Ministry adds:

> Dr. Mannheim is, moreover, an Eastern foreigner of alien stock. He has been in the country only eight years. The ever more common intrusion of Eastern elements (who are undesirable in any case) into German university careers must gradually lead to a flooding of German culture by foreign elements (*Überfremdung deutscher Kultur*). In view of the large number of well qualified domestic candidates, many forced to struggle bitterly for survival, I see no justification for bringing in foreigners to educate our German academic youth, especially ones originating in a culture essentially alien to the German one.

The official from Baden knows how he must speak to his colleagues, and presumably to the officials in the federal Chancellory as well, for whom this correspondence is eventually intended:

> Although I share the views of the others, that overpopulating university careers with Eastern elements is undesirable in general, I think that exceptions are justified where outstanding and professionally recognized achievements are present and the promise is great. Although Dr. Mannheim is a Jew, his case is not that of an Eastern foreigner in the usual sense, since his native city Budapest is to be considered as belonging to the German cultural domain in certain respects, in view of Hungary's former membership in the Austro-Hungarian Empire. (BG)

Diplomacy eventually triumphed, and Mannheim enjoyed four years of German civic rights.

In the Heidelberg Faculty of Social Sciences, the forbidden expression of the "political" was a breach of decorum as defined by mandarin custom. Mannheim's principal academic sponsors were in fact both secure in their professional standing despite their support of parties of the Weimar coalition. Alfred Weber, like his brother Max, was a founding member of the Democratic Party (DDP). But the rhetoric of the DDP, like that of the Conservatives, spoke the pathetic language of a national unity transcending parties, respectful of academic tradition and continuities of state (Pois 1976). Emil Lederer, on the other hand, was a socialist, the nominee of the Independent Socialist Party (USPD) to the "Socialization Commission" of December, 1918, and briefly Austrian Minister of Socialization a year later.[7] But Lederer had exceptionally strong support in the ministry for universities, and his public functions in professional roles were in any case different from participation in partisan conflict. The academic work had to be recognized as free from "political" overtones, and Marxist ideas not conforming to grudgingly accepted "scientific" varieties precluded certification. Mannheim was protected by Lederer, but his disputed civic status gave him ample reason for circumspection. To function as public intellectual, he first had to secure his place in the academy.

Within the German Sociological Society, too, acceptability was increasingly defined by the struggle against historical materialism, and especially against any "unmasking" of the "ideological" characters of respectable thinking. During the first decade of the century, the term "sociology" had been loosely associated with Marxism, and the small group that formed the new society, avowing their loyalty to Max Weber's program, vigorously sought to dispel these associations and to render the discipline academically legitimate. The central figures were Werner Sombart, Ferdinand Tönnies, and Leopold von Wiese, although Alfred Weber also had considerable influence (König 1984; Käsler 1981). The political upheavals of 1918–19 forced the question of Marxism on the sociological agenda with new urgency, and the emerging profession responded through a series of set-piece "disputes." The proceedings of the Fourth Congress of German Sociologists, which took place in Heidelberg in 1924 while Mannheim was at work on his sociological studies there, illustrate the character of the conflict during the first years of the Weimar Republic.

As at the Third Congress in 1920, the organizers staged a confrontation between the Austrian Marxist, Max Adler, and an opponent known to share the official, "unpolitical" conception of professional sociology. In 1920, the opponent had been Hans Kelsen; in 1924, it was Max Scheler. Angry heckling led by Alfred Weber punctuated Adler's talk, and the dynamics of the occasion are suggestive for understanding Mannheim's strategies in the same forum four years later. Adler argues that Scheler's philosophical speculations on relations between cultural contexts and modes of knowing lack reference to dynamic social forces, and that Scheler's teachings, typified by his plea for Western openness to Eastern capacities for suffering and contemplation, reveal the inability of "bourgeois science" to face realities damaging to its world. Adler recalls that his distinction between "bourgeois" and "proletarian" social policy (*Sozialpolitik*) had already caused an uproar the day before, and he continues: "For there is such ressentiment associated with the terms 'bourgeois and proletarian' among bourgeois scholars, that it is scarcely possible to have a calm discussion." Someone rises to the bait and calls out, "And what about proletarian scholars?" Adler calmly—even pedantically—insists that "proletarian science" is not interest-bound and that scientific method is universal: the difference lies in proletarian readiness to comprehend the social forces making for progressive change. His distinction explains, he contends, the sudden fascination in bourgeois-educated publics with the decline of culture, as well as the Orient—"even in those circles where Orientals are not in general so very popular." Moreover, bourgeois scholars now extenuate the old "Yellow Peril" and even flirt with it, "because it might help to avert the Red Peril, if also at the cost of white independence." Alfred Weber interrupts to charge rabble-rousing ("*Volksversammlung!*") and is answered by protest and applause. Adler proceeds with his contrast between "stationary" and "evolutionary" thinking, and he evokes another angry response when he mockingly recalls the contrasts between contemporary political imagery and that of the recent past. It is now good form, he notes, to speak about the cultural "muck" (*Schlamm*) of the times, while the same intellectual leaders had failed to notice the muck in which hundreds of thousands died, but spoke instead of the "genius of war." At this point, Scheler and Weber both burst out in rage, and the hall is in an uproar. From the chair, von Wiese cautions the speaker to abstain from value judgments. Adler agrees but observes that while it is not considered a value judgement to see nothing but muck in revolutionary outbreaks, it is an altogether different matter when war and oppression are at issue (Adler [1922] 1982).

Mannheim's presentation at the 1928 Congress of German Sociologists was a triumph, notwithstanding unmistakable echoes of Adler's Austro-Marxist approach to social knowledge. Audaciously competing with his co-presenter, Leopold von Wiese, he won a respectful hearing for a complex thesis, arguing that knowledge in the social and political domain is connected to existence (*seinsverbunden*) and thus varies according to social location. His distinction between static and dynamic thinking and his claim that only dynamic thinking can recognize the characteristics of social knowledge and adapt itself to them recalls Adler on proletarian science. But Mannheim meticulously avoids combative political slogans and distances himself from Marxism. The present is constituted by competition among three alternative interpretations of existence, and only a new "synthesis" will provide the core of common knowledge indispensable to all the competitors. Yet Mannheim's senior colleague, Alfred Weber, concludes his polite but dissatisfied comment with the question, "Is all this anything more than a brilliant rendition of the old historical materialism, presented with extraordinary subtlety?" But Werner Sombart, the president of the German Sociological Society, when his turn comes, offers Mannheim an opportunity to exculpate himself. He postulates that historical materialism denies the objectivity of existence and the reality of the spirit while Mannheim affirms them (Meja and Stehr 1990:90–92). "Is that right?" he asks, and the minutes record, "[Dr. Mannheim agrees]." So Mannheim is reassuring and the seniors are divided.

The more interesting response comes from a succession of younger, politically sophisticated academics delighted by Mannheim's presentation. Not only Emil Lederer but also his former colleague on the Socialization Commission, Robert Wilbrandt, are unqualified in their praise: while Adolf Löwe and Norbert Elias eagerly pick up Lederer's contention that Mannheim's argument trenchantly recognizes the dynamic character of modern society and the need to overcome the static war from antiquated positions in favor of a dynamic problem-solving openness to changing facts and uncertain terms of conflict (Meja and Stehr, 1990: 92–99; Elias 1990).

This response provides an important clue to the political bearing of Mannheim's social theorizing. Lederer used his influence with the reformist Prussian Ministry of Culture and Science during the next year to secure Mannheim the professorship at Frankfurt; and Löwe became Mannheim's lifelong friend and occasional collaborator, associated with him in Frankfurt in the Christian Socialist circle around Paul Tillich and in London in the Moot social Christian discussion group. Mannheim achieved recognition from moderately leftist sociologists as a new and powerful champion. His political reference group was not on the right. The ugly shared assumptions and common language in the intergovernmental correspondence about Mannheim's naturalization indicates the gulf separating the conservative political audience Mannheim hoped to reach through *Conservatism* from someone like himself and from his sophisticated subtext about inner connections between conservative and radical ideas. With the rise of novel types of rightist intellectuals at the end of the decade, Mannheim's reception on the right briefly changed, but his dismay at the favor shown *Ideologie und Utopie* in the circle around the periodical *Die Tat* confirms where Mannheim's project belongs.[8]

Dynamic Synthesis: Advocacy and Sociology

Mannheim was welcomed by sectors of the moderate left who shared his interest in neoromantic critiques of liberalism and rationalism (Söllner 1984). Like Mannheim, they were intrigued but troubled by Carl Schmitt's arguments about the irrational foundations of order. What they had in common, and what attracted them to Mannheim, was a search for a way to rationalize the irrationalities conservative writers celebrate, without losing their energy and dynamism. Unlike the ideologists of the Democratic Party, they denied that a feeling of national community could overcome conflict and channel social energies. And they could not accept the revolutionary socialist thesis of the presence *(Aktualität)* of a dialectical revolutionary overturn (Lukács [1924] 1971). In political terms, their problem was to explore the synthesis constituted by the legal order and political life of Weimar, given their shared reaction against individualist constitutional or social theory. Mannheim's conception of a process manifesting itself simultaneously in polarization and synthesis, as well as his conception of a dynamic mediation to manage the tensions without dissolving them, have parallels and resonance among these thinkers (Mannheim [1925] 1986).

The reception of Mannheim's *Ideologie und Utopie* reveals the affinities. The major reviews written by younger social theorists on the left were critical, sometimes aggressively so. Nevertheless, the group of writers attempting to revitalize stereotyped socialist thinking was remarkably interested in the book. Rudolf Hilferding had established the journal *Die Gesellschaft* to give Social Democracy a forum for theoretical reflection. After 1928, he left it largely under the control of the Frankfurt sociologist, Albert Salomon, who sought contributions from his peers among the younger generation of social thinkers (Fraenkel 1968: viii). In the two issues following the appearance of Mannheim's book, *Die Gesellschaft* published four essays devoted largely to *Ideologie und Utopie*. Paul Tillich, Herbert Marcuse, Hannah Arendt, and Hans Speier all had important objections to Mannheim's arguments; but all agreed that he had hit upon the essential agenda items, and none was satisfied to write him off as a bourgeois opponent of scientific Marxism. A one-sided way of summarizing what made Mannheim seem so relevant, if not completely right, to these members of the leftist intelligentsia can be taken from a furious characterization of his work by a hostile socialist writer of the older, scientistic kind: "The organizational goal of the social order is surrendered (by Mannheim) to Savigny."[9] The *Gesellschaft* critics were intrigued by precisely these conservative elements.

There is a striking coincidence between a passage in Mannheim's *Conservatism* and a theme in the doctoral dissertation of a leading younger contributor to both *Die Justiz* and *Die Gesellschaft*. In a "historical note on the concept of political conservatism" Mannheim ([1925]

1986:77–82) reviews the work of three predecessors, beginning with Friedrich Julius Stahl, in 1863, and closing with Gustav Radbruch's influential treatise on legal philosophy (Radbruch 1914).[10] Mannheim credits Radbruch with uncovering the systematic correspondences between the operating ideologies of political parties and comprehensive worldviews conditioning thought in domains not considered political. Mannheim and Radbruch shared not only a conception of actual party doctrines as a locus of social knowledge but also the goal of a structured but dynamic mediation among irreducibly partial perspectives ranging from the revolutionary left to the right. The same aspects of Radbruch's work are the point of departure for the doctoral dissertation by Franz L. Neumann (1923), who later studied with Mannheim in London, when both were refugees. Problems of ideology and synthesis, as well as the recovery of conservative elements, comprise the common problem nexus.

Neumann's topic is the relationship between the state and legal punishment. A truly sociological theory of the state, he maintains, is all but indistinguishable from a sociology of political parties, because the state is constituted by the activities of the parties. An inquiry into contrasting theories of punishment leads to conflicting partisan conceptions of the state. Now that the Social Democracy is a prime bearer of state power, according to Neumann, there is a contradiction between the constructive conception of the state appropriate to the Social Democratic Party and that party's continuing individualistic conception of punishment, a legacy from its time in opposition. One objective of the dissertation is to reconsider the reasons for the present gap between the socialist and conservative theories of punishment, reassessing the conservative idea of punishment as a necessary ethical establishment in a state embodying the ethical idea.[11] The second task is to generate a more adequate socialist theory. In both respects, Neumann draws on Radbruch:

> Until recently, socialism was substantially individualistic. Its ideology was the manifestly individualistic ideology of freedom.... A major task in the reconstruction of the party program was precisely the revision of demands like these, put forward by the Social Democracy in its capacity as opposition party without reference to the idea of socialism. Since the Social Democracy has been called to co-participation and co-responsibility in the aftermath of war and revolution, a change in its spirit is under way, removing it ever further from that individualistic starting point. (Radbruch 1922:16–17, quoted by Neumann 1923:9)

Similarly, in his brief conclusion, Neumann builds on Radbruch's findings that oppositions among party viewpoints are ineradicable because they reflect the ineluctability of conflicting values not only in the state but also in each individual, so that "no principle can be actualized in pure form." Neumann continues: "It is the task of legal policy—and especially of legal policy in a democratic state—to create a balance, a synthesis. This yearning for synthesis is intrinsic to our times" (Neumann 1923:108).

Neumann never gave this conception of "synthesis" theoretical form during the ten years following his dissertation. Its explication is implicit in his legal writings on labor law and the Weimar constitution; and these writings themselves, as moves in contests over legal doctrine, function in the "legal policy" of the Social Democratic Party (Luthardt 1986). In this work, Neumann followed a senior colleague, Hugo Sinzheimer, who had already laid down an influential theory of labor law before the First World War and figured importantly as Social Democratic member of the Constitutional Committee of the Constituent Assembly of 1919–20 (Kahn-Freund 1981; Sinzheimer 1976; Kettler 1984). While Mannheim's paradigm for achievable synthesis was a competition that concentrated ideological polarities while generating sufficient self-reflective capabilities to bring about a common public interpretation of the situation, Sinzheimer looked to the "collective agreement" between capital and labor.

For Sinzheimer, collective agreements forged by nonstate collective forces and incompatible with the rationalized, individualistic, property-oriented structures of bourgeois civil law epitomize social creativity in law. Out of this social innovation, he maintained, a labor law steadily displacing the civil code grounded on property and individual contract was growing. Interacting with the mass organization of labor into unions and its mobilization within an increasingly democratized political sphere, this development would cumulatively transform the entire constitution of economic and political life, rendering it more just and more oriented to the human personality. Like Mannheim's competitive reconstitution of the political situation, the theory grounded on the model of the collective agreement institutionalizes conflict. It purports to reconcile fundamental changes with limits defined by partisan commitments to refrain from violence. Both theories count on the possibility of rendering formally stable concepts and institutions more dynamic through "changes in [their] function."

For Sinzheimer, political development proceeds through a series of transitory but effective normative structures, each expressing the power relations between the principal contesting parties. As in collective agreements, the differences between parties are not denied. They are partially mediated by an agreement whose terms, binding for a limited time only, are enforceable by processes responsive to changes in the power realities that ground the agreements—for example, adjudication by courts with representative lay assessors, hearings before multiple-partite tribunals, arbitration. When agreements expire by their own terms or when they are rendered invalid by superior authority, the process of renegotiation is ultimately governed by tests of strength. Ordering principles are grounded upon constitutional settlements that have merely functional and political validation: they do the job and they are not forcibly resisted by any party.

In a deeper, more speculative sense, this practical foundation derives its meaning from a Marxist philosophy of history. But a decisive characteristic of this approach—as with legal theory in general—is that questions about such ultimate meanings are systematically relegated to the outermost margin of concern. The actual work of sustaining and improving agreements is comprehended within the terms of professional juristic discourse, however much this may be expanded to recognize social processes and power relationships normally obscured. Analogously, Mannheim hoped for ultimate philosophical validation of the composite synthesis he attempted to achieve, but his mode of inquiry and discourse was also designed to put ultimate questions aside. Theoretical approaches are characterized as much by the questions they choose not to address as by their active concerns.

An article in the same volume of *Die Gesellschaft* as the first extended reviews of Mannheim's *Ideologie und Utopie* illustrates Neumann's applications of Sinzheimer's approach beyond the specialized sphere of labor law.[12] It interprets the Weimar Constitution in the light of the political situation after the Social Democratic gains in the election of 1928 and before the onset of the economic crisis. Juxtaposing this legal-theoretical study to Mannheim's contemporaneous works helps to bring out the important structural parallels. A central quality of both the juristic and the sociological designs is that they are not critical but constructive theories. Radical criticisms of the rationalized structures of modernity—sciences, political theories, markets or liberal constitutional states—are conceded and even extended. But the aim is a reconstitution, incorporating the irrational factors cited by critics, reconceiving the structures as full of inner tensions, historically episodic and dynamic. In these respects, the new social legal doctrine of the political constitution sought by Neumann resembles the new sociologically reflective political discourse pursued by Mannheim.

Neumann's topic in 1929 is a liberal constitutionalist proposal to regularize the power of the highest court to review the validity of statute law under the Weimar Constitution (Neumann 1929). His critique depends on an exposé of the ideological constitution of legal doctrine and his juristic alternative depends on confidence in the lawmaking, ordering capacities of authentic social and political processes directly grounded in the contest of the two principal organized partisan social forces. Central to his argument is a contrast between the world of liberal rights and a democracy that is in principle social. Certain legal institutions belonging to the former world, he maintains, are guaranteed by the Weimar Constitution, but their functions, meanings, and effect are now to be controlled by the cumulative process of democratic transformation, in and out of the democratic legislature. These processes may not be overruled by courts applying what is now nothing but the defensive ideology of the bourgeoisie, appearing in its public-law guise as natural law competent to override decisions grounded in the actually existing democratic social and political constitution.

To show the dangerous tendency of the courts, Neumann cites judicial extension of constitutional guarantees of property to include all "objects and rights that form economic resources or wealth" (Neumann 1929:524). Such judgments deny the sociological recognition of the property right as a divisible "bundle of functions" and thus exclude developments consonant with the "modern socialist theory of private law" of Marx, Renner, and Sinzheimer. In a capitalist economic order, property gives power over objects and people; and the power over objects entails possession, direction, and utilization for profit: "Socialist legal theory considers it the task of economic law to decrease the discretionary powers of proprietors, with primary emphasis at present on regulating the directive powers of the proprietor" (Neumann 1929). Labor law has the special task of restricting proprietors' powers over their workers, as well as countering the powers of the one class over the other: "This development is by no means at an end; it is still under way and clearly aims at a further strengthening of the interventionary powers of state, trade unions, and works councils" (Neumann 1929:525).

During the liberal age, Neumann maintains, the theory of rights was more or less precise, because it was an ideology expressive of the actual situation (*Ausdrucksideologie*); but now "social relations have undergone fundamental change, and we proceed upon the optimistic assumption that they will shift ever more in favor of the working class" (Neumann 1929: 521). Under these conditions, the ideology of rights will take such forms as Rudolf Smend's (1928) theory of "integration," that allows almost anything to be construed as in accord with the fundamental will of the constituent people, because it has become nothing more than an ideology that obscures the actual situation (*Verdeckungsideologie*). If Parliament were to endorse the present tendency of the courts arbitrarily to impose their vague new theory of constitutional rights upon the law, it would seriously jeopardize the "further development of social law" (Neumann 1929:538) and the "further social forming of the law" (Neumann 1929:530).

Especially threatening to the socialist legislative program, in Neumann's view, would be judicial interventions governed by a substantive doctrine of the constitutional guarantee of equality before the law. Neumann is thinking of the American 14th Amendment jurisprudence that ruled out regulation deemed hostile to rights of property.[13] The potential conflicts he envisions include judicial challenges to trade unions' monopoly of workers' representation, attacks on measures that hollow out property rights by construing the guarantee of the institution very narrowly in reliance on constitutional deference to legislation, and judicial invalidation of proposals like Neumann's own for controlling monopolies and cartels by cutting off their right of appeal to the courts from regulatory decisions by administrative agencies. Neumann's strategic design is best indicated by his objection that judicial review might be used to perpetuate the established doctrine of parity between employers and workers in employment relations even after social development would allow further progress towards socialism.

The parity between workers and employers established by the postwar settlement between their organizations and registered in the constitution is provisional, a legal expression of a stage in dynamic relations between the contending social forces; while the democratic constitutional scheme, in its social as well as in its political dimensions is a framework for change. The rights generated by the constitution are valid organizing principles, to be vindicated in the courts as well as other agencies, but the interpreting and securing of those rights depends on political means, and thus ultimately on the contending social and political forces. Specialized courts, like the labor, tax, and economic courts, can play an important, partly independent role in this process, because their closeness to the social functions at issue and to the major social actors involved makes it unlikely that they would place arbitrary, ideologically grounded obstacles in the way of social development and the corresponding play of social forces. But a high court endowed with constitutional powers, remote from the social matters at issue, might be led to such antisocial excesses of the American courts. The constitution must be kept dynamic, able to recognize the periodic renegotiations that punctuate social development. In rare moments of general speculation, Neumann grounds his argument on a Rousseauist vision of an all-powerful democratic general will bent upon socialist transformation, an optimal but utopian alternative, always put aside, if always only for the present. In the context of his juristic discourse, this abstraction has no analytical consequences. The aspiration for a transcendent synthesis must be put off, while detailed work proceeds on the arrangements producing "syntheses" that cannot claim ultimate validity or achieve definitive resolutions, though they do sustain a vital movement.

That Karl Mannheim's use of the concept "synthesis" has a similar range of alternative meanings is evident. *Ideologie und Utopie*, it will be recalled, opens with a discussion of the political crisis caused by every party unmasking the positions advanced by the others as nothing but interest-bound ideology, destroying confidence in the objectivity of all political perceptions and claims. This is the impasse that the sociology of knowledge is to help overcome, at first by reassuring all parties that political knowledge is inherently perspectival. The intervention is meant to constitute a medium in which exchanges are possible, although these cannot correspond to the rationalistic "free exchange of ideas" projected by liberalism (Mannheim [1929] 1952: 108ff.).[14]

Mannheim's expectations about these exchanges are decisively influenced by his confrontation with revolutionary Marxism. In treating and implicitly criticizing the socialist-communist conception of the relationship between theory and practice, a central theme in the book's most important essay, Mannheim characterizes the Marxian conception of politics as a *Realdialektik*. Actors representing real social factors take one another's measure and cumulatively develop a sequence of "real" situations, each of which in turn provides the starting point for the next phase of development. Leaving Marxism aside, Mannheim contends, we know that this is a more adequate account of parliamentary political institutions than liberalism offers. Carl Schmitt has exposed the liberal illusion that parliaments are societies for the discovery of truth through discussion. But Mannheim is no more inclined to Schmitt's decisionism than to Marx's revolutionism. A politics brought beyond critical impasse through the intervention of the sociology of knowledge manifests itself as a regularization of the "real" process. The intelligentsia provides the essential catalyst for synthesis, not its constitutive elements or ruling force. Synthesis is more nearly a process than an achieved state, dynamic constitution, not revolution.

Despite the structural parallels between Mannheim's conception of mediation and Neumann's conception of the constitution, two fundamental differences limited Mannheim's ability to gain more than a fascinated surface hearing from the influential socialist jurists. The first difference concerns the direction of the "dynamism" within the mediated structures. For Mannheim, every "situation" is charged with a potential towards a "next step," but to judge whether participants comprehend their situation adequately can only be done by an imprecise negative standard that condemns manifestly irrational practices. For socialist jurists, the socialist telos is a given, if only in what they take to be the concrete aspirations of the working class movement and its accumulated and growing organizational power. The second difference concerns the constitution of the structures. Notwithstanding the ontological status he ascribes to the historical social existence that grounds conflicting ideologies, Mannheim derives practice not from the state of material factors, but from the public interpretation of reality. The integrative structure must be a knowledge, a science, a mode of consciousness. The legal advocates, in contrast, are looking at a complex of organized political practices, formalized through legal modalities and institutions (Luthardt 1984).

Neumann and Mannheim both identify the old legal order with capitalism, liberalism, and a theory of universal natural law. Both find important hints and premonitions in conservative critiques of natural law. It is both striking and puzzling that Mannheim worked so brilliantly on the conservative jurists he studied but never addressed the fact that they were working away at the law and not simply engaged in an ideological defense against the Enlightenment. Mannheim assumes that legal discourse is inherently bound up with the rationalized, static, finished dimension of things, while Neumann proposes a changed and transformative legal mode. Neumann's juridical discourse has political consequences, in coordination with social organizations in the political field, even when its strategic aims are not fulfilled. But Mannheim's ambition of introducing a self-reflective moment into political contestations to hold them in bounds, miscommunicates as a power claim by intellectuals. From the perspective of the older Russian debates about the intelligentsia, the contrast between Mannheim and Neumann recalls the question whether the intelligentsia best serves social salvation by acting in its own capacity or by going to the people. Mannheim and Neumann are nearly on the same side of that dispute. Mannheim's intelligentsia function as sociologists and Neumann's as jurists, and both leave to others the leadership of the popular groups whose activities shape substantive outcomes. Their aim is to reconstitute the forms available for action.[15]

With the growing crisis of the Weimar Republic, and especially after its collapse, both projects for dynamic mediation appeared hopelessly misconceived. After 1930, even Sinzheimer abandoned his belief in the transformative capabilities of labor law and thus in its character as paradigm for social and political reconstitution; and Neumann's writings in exile charge the reformist labor movement of Weimar with having operated on conceptions of law and state not only useless for their professed objectives but contributing to the destruction of the minimum of rationality the liberal order had provided. Mannheim, in turn, increasingly shifted the function of sociology of knowledge from therapeutically containing political conflict to preparing for the scientific management of society.

Notes

1. Mannheim appears in prosecutorial records as subjected to "disciplinary procedures" and as dismissed from the Institute of Pedagogy without pay (Gábor 1983). He was also among those denounced for their contributions to the Hungarian Soviet Republic, primarily because of his preferment by Lukács (Congdon 1991). Karl Polanyi remembers a visit from Mannheim and Lesznai (1985) during the days of the Commune, when they urged Mannheim to join them in reconstituting the Sunday Circle on the old, nonpolitical lines (AA). The project failed because they would not respect Polanyi's religious convictions. Arnold Hauser confirms Polanyi's report of Mannheim's personal convictions and conduct during the Soviet period (AA).

2. Éva Gábor (1983) reports that Mannheim conceived the review as a "gesture of farewell" to Lukács, in recognition of their estrangement. The public and private aspects of the gesture are complementary.

3. *Berliner Tageblatt*, December 11, 1919; cited in Benseler (1965:16). The statement concludes: "Lukács' rescue is not a partisan matter. It is the duty of all those who have, through personal acquaintance, experienced his purity, and all those who admire the lofty spirituality of his philosophical-aesthetic books, to protest against extradition."

4. The remark placing the Lukács group "East" of the other intellectuals stems from John Erös (AA), cp. Kettler 1971: 59–60. In an interview (June 14, 1963) Ilona Ducynska Polanyi emphasized the Russian influence on the radical Budapest intelligentsia, and especially on the youth. For the political among them, the general mystique of the Russian revolutionary movement and the propaganda of the deed were even more important than fascination with Dostoyevsky (AA). On Lukács and Russian students, see Congdon 1983 and Kadarkay 1991.

5. In 1934, Mannheim urged Fritz Borinski, a political refugee who came to study with him at the London School of Economics, to write a sociologically informed dissertation comparing the work of the legal theorists Carl Schmitt and Hermann Heller during the crisis of 1930-1933, cp. Fritz Borinski (1984). Harold Laski was the director of the LSE dissertation of the Weimar labor lawyer, Franz L. Neumann (1936) which deals with the relationship between the legal order and the competitive society and reviews the legal thought of the Weimar years; but Neumann credits Mannheim with major assistance, an acknowledgment edited out of the published version (Neumann 1986), and he quotes him at important points. In short, there is reason to think that Mannheim followed legal thought in Weimar more closely than appears from his published writings.

6. Report of the faculty of philosophy at the University of Heidelberg to the "Inner Senate" (April 8, 1926) in Mannheim's *Habilitationsakten* (UH).

7. For the Socialization Commission, see Miller (1978:143-61). Emil Lederer was very important to Mannheim in Heidelberg. The connection was personal as well as professional. Lederer's wife was Hungarian and had been connected with Georg Lukács; and they looked after Mannheim upon his arrival. He lived next door to them, and, according to Gábor, they helped to establish his "private seminar." Basing her claims on a letter from Adolf Löwe, she asserts that the seminar in 1920 was entitled "What is Sociology?" and had as "permanent members," thanks to the influence of Lederer, such distinguished figures as Alfred Weber, Marianne Weber, Heinrich Rickert, Karl Jaspers, Martin Buber, and others (Gábor 1983: 9). This seems unlikely, since Mannheim could not have secured such an audience on a regular basis. It is more likely that there was a single occasion to present the promising young man. In any case, Lederer played a major part in securing Mannheim's habilitation, writing a long, laudatory report (UH) on the (unfinished) *Habilitationsschrift*, and taking the lead in the campaign against the reservations of the "Inner Senate." Lederer's care for Mannheim did not stop there. When Lederer was offered the professorship at Frankfurt vacated by the retirement of Oppenheimer, he sought to assure Mannheim's position as well. A letter from the Prussian Ministry of Culture and Science to the social science faculty at Frankfurt (July 15, 1929) indicates that an offer to Lederer will also require a regular paid teaching position in sociology for Mannheim. At the same time, Lederer was negotiating with the corresponding ministry in Baden, who were

seeking to keep him at Heidelberg, and here too he made a settled position for Mannheim a part of his own terms. A letter from the ministry to Lederer on July 29, 1929 includes a commitment to Mannheim for three years, and a letter of September 13, 1929 promises to increase Mannheim's pay from 1000 to 1500 marks per semester (UH). The Frankfurt faculty, on the other hand, refused to agree to the appointment of Mannheim, insisting that they already had more than enough sociologists (UH).

8. See Pels (1993) on Hans Zehrer and *Die Tat*. We discuss Mannheim's reception by segments of the intellectual right further below.

9. The reviews in *Die Gesellschaft,* as well as others, are collected in Meja and Stehr, 1982, 1990. The last quotation is from a review by Julius Kraft (1929:413) not included there.

10. Radbruch was professor of law at Heidelberg, Social Democratic member of Parliament between 1920 and 1924, and twice minister of justice.

11. In the dissertation, the substantive issue is overshadowed by a methodological discussion, culminating in a plea for an evaluative philosophy of law somehow grounded upon philosophy of history. When Neumann (1936) refers to the earlier work in the introduction to the Ph.D. dissertation he wrote under the supervision of Harold Laski (and Karl Mannheim) at the London School of Economics, he characterizes it exclusively in terms of the substantive sociological thesis about the linkages between different legal theories, especially natural law theories, and different socially grounded ideologies, ignoring the labored philosophical efforts which occupy most of the 113 pages of typescript. See Franz Neumann (1986:7–8). Mannheim was not formally qualified to supervise dissertations at the LSE. Internal evidence reinforces the impression created by Neumann's acknowledgment of Mannheim's assistance in the preface. Mannheim's influence is far from negligible.

12. Even more fundamental, in some respects, is an article by Neumann's law partner, Ernst Fraenkel, appearing in the same issue. Fraenkel (1929) writes "Collective democracy...is a new mode of forming the political will, such that a direct influence upon the formation of the will of the state and upon the actualization of the state's designs is transferred to organizations. Recognition of the autonomy of organizations is the principal norm...in the unwritten constitutional law of collective democracy.... Collective democracy will not represent an independent social constitution alongside of the constitution of state; rather, it will insinuate itself directly into the latter."

13. Neumann's fears were stimulated by the debates and resolutions on Article 109 of the Weimar Constitution conducted at the 1927 meetings of the authoritative association of German teachers of public law (Deutsche Staatsrechtslehrer 1927).

14. Mannheim (1936a) omits the introductory discussion of the Weimar political context.

15. Mannheim's position is directly continuous with his conception of his generation's mission in "Soul and Culture" (Mannheim [1918] 1964). His generation had to carry out their critical, analytical work; the resurrection of the soul would follow, embodied in creative others.

5

Religion, Politics, and Education: Reassessing Civilization

During the summer semester of 1919, the last weeks of the Soviet regime in Hungary, Mannheim lectured on the sociology of culture in the Institute of Pedagogy, a new subdivision of Budapest University mandated by Lukács to retrain undergraduates for service in a mass literacy campaign. The notes for these lectures show unexpected continuities between the novice teacher, earnestly marking out the only choices he supposes to be open to humanists in a revolution, and the established professor a dozen years later, delineating the place of sociology in the crisis of Weimar. With epigrammatic intensity, the young Mannheim asks his students to consider three "forms of life" and he confesses his own choice. After weighing a life as saint or politician, he opts for the educator. This tense drama never loses its fascination for Mannheim. Much divides the educator as cultural philosopher from the educator as academic sociologist, especially Mannheim's reconsideration of his earlier flamboyant championing of "culture" against "civilization." Civilization and culture later appear sociologically interdependent, with civilization even given priority. The educator's task belongs to the rationalization achievable through sociology and not, as earlier, to the cultivation of artistic sensibility. Nevertheless, Mannheim's conception of his educational work remains surprisingly oriented to the choices stated in Budapest. Especially revealing is a consistency in the structure of his ambivalence about the politician.

In his 1919 lectures, Mannheim approaches political issues through a distinction between the state as an instrument for advancing the interests of individuals and the state as "entrusted with a cultural mission." The state can be either a mechanism of civilization catering to the physi-

cal wants of physical beings or an agency of cultivation, unifying ethics
and law. Mannheim finds the former view epitomized in Alexander von
Humboldt, and the latter in a tradition originated by Friedrich von Schiller.
In either case, however, the politician cannot avoid coercive means.
Politics entails institutions and revolutions; and both kill human beings.
To be justified before culture, politics must work towards its own de-
mise since it remains inescapably an institute of civilization. Mannheim
credits the Bolshevik regime with censoring and regulating only for the
sake of promoting moral and aesthetic education. But he provocatively
urges the present necessity of preparing for the next revolution because
revolutionary institutions are almost certain to become autonomous and
self-serving, as all institutions tend to do.[1]

Mannheim's qualified endorsement of Soviet rule is conditional upon
the validity of the philosophy of history invoked by politicians like
Lukács. But in the peroration of the lecture, Mannheim ([1919a]
1985:230-31) calls the extent of his acceptance of this premise into question. He distances himself from the politician:

> The politician does not believe in God; he believes in history. The saint believes in
> God, but says that his kingdom is not of this world. The educator believes in nei-
> ther God nor history, but in culture.
>
> The saint believes that only the straight way—the power of an exemplary life—can
> heal the world. Evil erupts. The politician sees evil and suffers from it. Because he
> believes in history, he fights for humanity through institutions.
>
> The educator does not believe in these two ways, but he thinks that there is a means
> of fighting against institutions: cultivation, the inherently tranformative effects of
> culture. He cannot disregard history; and he cannot simply follow the saint, be-
> cause he does not believe in the power of the exemplary soul to accomplish total
> transformations.... The educator is resigned. He cannot touch people with the
> immediacy of the saint because he knows that the gesture would be false. He knows
> that art, valuable as it may be, is not a cure, yet he hopes that the music of the soul
> somehow breaks through by its means. The susceptibility to art is the only thing
> given unto us all. And if the educator also knows and accepts that he cannot reach
> the infinite, he does as much as Charon: he guides across the dark water.

Similar uncertainties haunt Mannheim's late Weimar work.

Christianity and the Irrational

Disillusionment with rationality pervaded the Frankfurt university
milieu in the early 1930s. A transcript of a discussion registers both

continuities and changes in Mannheim's views of the confrontation between civilization and soul (Tillich 1983: 314–69). On June 27, 1931, the theologian Paul Tillich, recently appointed professor of theology and social philosophy in the innovative philosophy department in Frankfurt, organized a daylong meeting between his regular partners in intense discussions of political questions and several Protestant theologians, icluding critics of Tillich's secular involvements and social-philosophical theology. The immediate occasion was soul-searching about the Christian mission in a secularized world, an inquiry made urgent by perplexity about the role of Protestantism in the worldwide depression. Interestingly enough, the impetus for the discussion, both in Frankfurt and in the Protestant churches at large, arose from the Foreign Missions, an international religious community organized through regular conferences and congresses, that had been ever more pressed to justify, especially in England, the social and political role that it was playing worldwide, under imperial auspices and in the face of rising resistance.[2] In addition to "dialectical theologians" interested in Tillich, the participants included not only Karl Mannheim but also the classical humanist philosopher and university curator, Kurt Riezler, who had brought most of these leftist thinkers to Frankfurt, and the three principals in the new *Institut für Sozialforschung*: Friedrich Pollock, Max Horkheimer, and Theodor Wiesengrund-Adorno (Wiggershaus 1986; Jay 1973; Schivelbusch 1982; Tillich 1973; Krohn 1987). Adorno and Mannheim were close friends of Paul and Hannah Tillich, with "Teddy" the petted philosophical protégé and family pianist and the Mannheims companions in the Tillichs' occasional explorations of nightlife on the fringe. The other Frankfurt participants, to judge by the informal vehemence of the discussion, were also connected by more than the proceedings of that day.

In his introduction, Tillich defines the general situation as one in which the autonomization of culture and the rise of the proletariat critically challenge Christian thought and action. He separates those he has invited to encounter the Protestant theologians into three groups, each of which can contribute, he maintains, by frankly displaying its own position: a group that seeks contemporary orientation from philosophical traditions originating with the Greeks (referring to Riezler); a group of those who "take their point of departure from...the common experience of the proletarian situation and socialism, and who make this fact central to all of their work" (referring to the *Institut* trio); and finally, using language clearly endorsing Mannheim's self-characterization, a group "that begins by disinterestedly analyzing the situation, linking each of us in our diverse groups with our actual situation, and whose critique of what is going on in the other groups has gained decisive importance for me" (Tillich 1983: 32).

As the transcript indicates and memoirs confirm, the participants in such talks knew they were sheltered within a magic circle, and most of them suspected it could not last. But they still hoped to find the healing spell. At the time of these conversations, Germany's unemployment rate had been on an unparalleled steep climb for two years, a situation devastating for the unions that had been principal actors in the "collectivist democracy"—the pluralist constitutionalism analyzed by Neumann. Communists and the hard right consisting of National Socialists and Hugenberg's DNVP had paralyzed Parliament since their triumphs in the elections of 1930; the government had been ruling by use of blanket delegations of legislative power and presidential decrees; and furious assaults on the "Weimar system" dominated almost all media of public expression, including, increasingly, the streets. Universities and their graduates were not secure against these massive disturbances, and radical rightist tendencies swept student organizations and not a few lecterns. In his classroom lectures Mannheim paid some attention to these developments. He diagnosed a crisis of social orientation among decisive collective social actors, due largely to breakdowns in processes of social selection and social mobility, that is, malfunctionings in the rational order.[3] But in the Tillich discussions, for all the talk about crisis, questions of the day are addressed only by the *Institut* participants, and then provocatively, to justify overconfident assertions about external movements that expose the futility of the group's talk.[4] "The crisis of rationality" provides the theoretical context, especially as Mannheim and Tillich define it.

In his forceful statements, attuned to the inclination to paradox in Tillich's own thought, Mannheim dramatizes the insufficiencies of a secularized and rationalized worldview, even while he identifies his own discipline with it. Mingling metasociological theorizing with personal statements, he presents himself as one of those who would have to be converted, if Christianity had a valid claim to a contemporary mission. Yet no one has given him reason to believe that this tradition can meet his needs. He is aware of certain primordial religious stirrings in himself and among contemporaries everywhere, but these experiences are isolated within individuals, and there are no signs of a collective religious movement. From a sociological point of view, Mannheim muses, much renewed religiosity can be understood as a manifestation of reactionary polarization against the "progressive current that we designate as the leftist movement in politics, enlightenment or industrialization"; but he treats the developments subject to such sociological interpretation as an uninteresting distraction. In its reactionary guise, the religious tendency must clearly be opposed by all those "who desire a different world" (Tillich 1983: 232–25). The only issue worth discussing is a primordial religiosity that springs from an altogether different source. It emerges in individuals like himself, "who are not looking for anything politically retrograde from [it], no restoration of a lost haven, but rather want it for apprehending the newly emerging kind of human being." The old religion cannot articulate this religiosity, Mannheim announces, and he must consequently search for ways of expressing it in terms of his own situation: "Every human being who has been radically involved in rationalization as I have been, in my capacity as sociologist, tends to act like the vintner who smashed and demolished all about him as his vineyard was being destroyed by hail: 'we'll soon see who first finishes it off.' He wants to pursue rationality to its end, and he wants to get to the end as quickly as possible." To be sure, forms of experience, encounter, and self-awareness disappear with the rise of "this industrial, rational, sociological world." "But humans are more than this rationalized world," Mannheim continues, "and these repressed elements remain latently present in us, in search of their proper form. There is nothing about modern humankind, moreover, that compels them to repress these elements." Although the old mythologized language cannot give it voice, the existential reality of primordial religiosity is still there after rationalization has gone as far as it can. Mannheim explains the indefatigable yearning to go beyond rationality by a teleological dynamism in all formgiving. Only utopian anticipation, not the past, can actualize the new religious impulse (cp. Mannheim [1919b] 1985). Protestant churchmen, he fears, represent a mortal danger to him because they offer nothing but words to estrange him from his own situation. Someone like himself, Mannheim says twice, should "stammer" rather than stop struggling with his errors.

Mannheim uses the language of the medieval mystics to characterize the "ecstatic" source of his own religious experience, but he insists that his modernity obliges him to be accurate and admit there is no personal God speaking in him. No other kind of God makes any sense; the spiritualized divinities of the philosophers cannot appease his religious yearnings. But he thinks there is also something wrong with his disbelief, and his modern intelligence lacks the authority to impose the conclusion that there is nothing behind his experiences. "That is why I am ashamed," he says, "to speak of it." The religious impulse thrusts itself upon him when he (like the vintner in his analogy) has been duly pounding away, competing with the hail: "As I serve the cause of the hail ever more radically and explicate the world in rational-function terms, it is an exciting game to gain an immanent and sociological understanding of the world. But I find that as I progressively drive the devil—or God—out of the world, I am also expelling humankind."

The impetus to religion comes with the recognition that his sociological analysis is concerned only with the response mechanisms (*Reaktionsapparatur*) operative in the world. "Modern man needs that," because he has no time for anything beyond superficial transactions. "This has something to do with industrialization," Mannheim adds casually. While sociological method makes things transparent, it also represses the varieties of encounter richly present in the world of religion. He cannot accept prevailing religious formulations of this world, Mannheim avers, but he also will not accede to the impoverishment of human encounters, their reduction to functional responses. Modernity, rationality, and sociology belong together, and Mannheim will not deny his vocation for them. Yet the conscientious practice of this compound vocation brings the recognition that something is missing. Religion knows about this something else, but no known religion can make good on its promise in the present situation. Mannheim wants to show that sociology is indispensable to that which sociology teaches the sociologist it cannot do, just as, more generally, the most thorough rationality is indispensible to moderns who cannot live by rationality alone.

Such paradoxical complexities—reminiscent of the mysteries expounded in Lukács' Sunday Circle during Mannheim's Budapest years and anticipatory of his more sober appeals to Christian thinkers during his years as a member of the "Moot" in English emigration—were bound to repel at least two of the other nontheologians present. Max Horkheimer speaks early in the discussion and does not address his remarks directly to Mannheim, whose *Ideologie und Utopie* he had denounced in his first published article (Horkheimer [1931] 1990). But he scorns all this talk of crisis, spiritual need, and primordial religiosity. Capitalism knows full well what it is doing as it enters a new phase, and the need that causes suffering is much more real than all talk of the profanation of culture. It is necessary to take sides in the struggle against this suffering so that it can be overcome, so far as humanly possible. Since natural scarcity has been proven a fallacy, the real question concerns the forms of human organization. Adorno's direct rejection of Mannheim on this occasion is less harsh in tone but no less impatient. Although Mannheim introduced his vineyard hailstorm ironically, to model "the conduct of us awful rationalists and modernists," Adorno maintains, the image was subsequently taken seriously and it has obfuscated the whole discussion. The operations of this supposedly destructive rationality must be more carefully examined. Then it may well become evident that the functions Mannheim is ready to abandon to the demonic are actually taken up and preserved in this rationality. Between them, Horkheimer and Adorno, supported weakly by Pollock, propound a straightforward Marxist position, "brutally" (says Horkheimer) dismissive of the meeting's central questions and premises. But they nevertheless consider the discussion worth attending, and in this sense show their orientation to the constitutive themes of the Tillich circle. Their subsequent development, in the direction of what has retroactively been labelled the Critical Theory of the Frankfurt School, can be illuminated by contrast with their certainties during Tillich's "Frankfurt Discussion."[5] But however far they eventually distanced themselves from this political point of departure, they could never feel sympathy for Mannheim's experimental "stammerings" about the interdependence and irreconcilability between the rational and irrational. Neither would they acknowledge his recurrent idea of an autonomous sociological discipline vindicating itself by its contribution as a systematic whole to thought beyond scientific method. Mannheim's expression of just this hope in the "Frankfurt Discussions" offers a valuable guide to his design as he moves ever further from the boundary towards the center of sociology as discipline.

Fascism and History

Mannheim increasingly equated sociology and civilizational rationality, reconsidering his hopes for a sociology that would be cultural or political in a novel sense, not least because the successful National Socialist movement cruelly parodied the function that Mannheim had designed for the synthetic science of politics. It provided a comprehensive worldview (*Weltanschauung*) that gave millions a sense of having regained orientation, and it effectively dissolved the ideological impasse Mannheim presupposed in *Ideologie und Utopie*. The ideologically informed political contestation, in which sociology of knowledge had been supposed to intervene transformatively, was increasingly replaced by cultural and political forms in which great masses are swept by emotions to accept barbarously misleading but uniform myths about social realities and prospects. Under such conditions, the notion of the sociology of knowledge as an organon for a science of politics appeared increasingly irrelevant to Mannheim. It can serve only as an aid to thinkers trying to stay free of the tide and attempting, by their insight into the compulsions at work within themselves as well, to gain a clear understanding of what is happening.

Fascism is analyzed in *Ideologie und Utopie*, but Mannheim treats it in 1929 as a limiting case, plausible only to outcast social groups desperate in their isolation. At most, the ideology can guide such a group, as in Italy, to a momentary success because of a transitory crisis of obstructed social change. Fascism is the most intellectually impoverished of all ideologies. All thinking is for it arbitrary mythmaking, and the deed is all. Mannheim explains:

> When attacked from this purely intuitionist point of view, every kind of political and historical knowledge dissolves into nothingness, as far as its cognitive worth is concerned. Only its ideological, mythmaking attributes can be grasped. For this activist intuitionism, thinking can have no function except to expose the illusory character of these futile theories and to unmask them as self-deceptions. Thinking is experienced as nothing but preparation for the pure deed. The superior person, the leader, knows that all political and historical views are mere myths. He is free of them himself, but he prizes them—and that is the other side of this insight— because they are enthusiastic "derivations" (in Pareto's sense) that move the feelings, the irrational "residues" which alone can bring about any political deed. (Mannheim [1929] 1952: 120; cp. Mannheim 1936a: 122-23)

The only knowledge that counts is a knowledge of the laws of social mechanics and social psychology, comprehending the deepest motivational levels common to all humans. "Acquaintance with these laws serves the leaders as a purely technical knowledge: they must know how the masses can be moved" (Mannheim [1929] 1952: 121). In fascism, rational knowledge of the most narrow sort is put in the service of an unreasoning putschism. Fascism is not open to rationalization because it breaks with the common determination to find meaning in history that opens liberalism, conservatism and socialism to synthesis through mediation by the sociology of knowledge (Mannheim 1936a: 107–8). Fascists are an anomaly, when judged by Mannheim's 1919 aphorisms about forms of life: they are politicians who do not believe in history. Neither the project of politics as a science nor the conception of sociology of knowledge as an organon for this science is at first disturbed by Mannheim's recognition of fascism as a presence in the ideological field.

Mannheim consistently distanced himself from irrationalist extensions of the existentialist phenomenology that intrigued him and originally inspired his conception of the sociology of knowledge as organon. When making his case for a social knowledge capable of orienting conduct, he emphasizes the admixture of rational calculability and "irrational" volitions in the concepts and logical design of all such knowledge, as well as the historicity and partiality of what is discernable from even the most synoptic and comprehensive perspective. A concept like "capitalism," if subjected to Mannheim's analysis, would gain its analytical and even its descriptive force from a socially rooted design to understand human relationships through different and transitory modes of property, the point being, as Marx had said, to change those modes. The concept is ultimately "at home" within socialist ideology. The availability and bearing of the concept, moreover, depend on a certain historical constellation. But Mannheim denies that such analysis involves relativist undermining of its own claims because the analysis works out of a structure of knowledge appropriate to the historical reality towards which it is directed and because it yields findings pertinent to the attitudes shaping knowing in this domain. The contrast model of universally valid knowledge that gives meaning to the concept of relativism, he maintains, simply has no relevance. Accordingly, he insists that the knowledge he is seeking is susceptible to orderly formulations whose logic can be extrapolated and applied critically to appropriate knowledge claims in the same domain, even if comprehension might require a receptivity that is existentially grounded and not universally accessible.

With the explosive rise of the right after 1930, Mannheim wavers. Assertions that ideologies expressing a national or racial will to power are immune to challenge and sufficiently vindicated by the achievement of power appear not only in the propaganda of fascist movements but also in the academic work of colleagues with intellectual antecedents similar to his own. A burgeoning periodical of the right, *Die Tat*, praising *Ideologie und Utopie*, promoted its own "synthesis of the ideologies of the radical Left and radical Right" and, by 1932 had, fostered "a veritable archipelago of local discussion clubs" (Pels 1993). But an intelligentsia that abandons the search for rational meaning in history is a horror to Mannheim. In response to Hans Freyer and the editors of *Die Tat*, Mannheim emphasizes the sharp differences between a view that vaunts its volitionalist irrationality and one that acknowledges a residue of social purposiveness in all social knowledge only after having struggled to eliminate volition from its structure. Volitional elements no longer appear as a cognitive asset to Mannheim. This growing defensiveness about a notion central to the idea of sociology of knowledge as organon implies a change in Mannheim's methodological aspirations, bringing him closer to the rhetoric of empirical social science. He reconstrues the sociology of knowledge as simply recording the perspectivism and historicity of social knowledge manifest in social science, registering empirical patterns in that knowledge, and leaving questions about the philosophical ramifications of these findings to professional philosophers. Not objections to relativism but resistance to the hyperactivist Fascist threat to rationality lead Mannheim away from his political conception of synthesis.

Once Mannheim had decided that the conduct of everyday life is oriented by destructive delusions, at least in certain historical epochs, then the vocation of the seeker after knowledge once more appeared simply and perhaps hopelessly as the task of Enlightenment. And the "stammering" he could confess to when talking about ultimate religious questions with his most trusted associates was impermissible in responsible public utterance. Increasingly, in his courses and publications, he narrowed the political task of sociology of knowledge, likening it more to Bacon's attempts to shatter the idols impeding access to rationally grounded systematic knowledge and less to Socratic therapy for dialogue. In 1932, addressing university teachers of sociology, he warned:

> Interesting as we may find the attempts to extend our argument about the existential connectedness of thinking by tendencies employing the doctrine to legitimate their ever more questionable principles, we also consider certain conclusions that have been drawn from it to be dangerous. And when this theory goes so far as to give rise

to the exaggerated assertion that "a will that is true warrants true knowledge" (*"Wahres Wollen fundiert wahre Erkenntnis"*), the door has been opened to every kind of arbitrariness in theory. Who would not step into the intellectual arena armed with the conviction or pretense of "a correct will"? And who in such a situation would not be pleased to be excused in future from having to make a properly substantiated case and to be permitted, instead, to invoke his inspiration and genuine conviction? Taken this way, the task imposed by insight into the reality of the existential connectedness of thinking is misdirected, because the insight no longer serves self-criticism and distanciation from existential bonds, as originally intended. Instead, it legitimates every conceivable kind of partisanship. (Mannheim 1932a: 40)

The "Present Tasks of Sociology" (*Gegenwartsaufgaben der Soziologie*) laid out in Mannheim's extensive talk comprise an academic curriculum respectful of disciplinary traditions and wary of political exploitation. The meaning of history is not on the agenda. Mannheim appears as educator.

Mannheim as Educator

Mannheim's attempt to establish himself as a recognized member of the academic profession had always been a matter of principle as well as ambition. The popularity of such authors as Oswald Spengler and the disdain for them among the serious writers Mannheim respected, as well as the excited manifestoes against Weber's scientific ethos by such young writers as Erich von Kahler, close to the Stefan George circle, and the avuncular condescension accorded that kind of criticism by Ernst Troeltsch, for example, made it important for Mannheim to choose sides.[6] When Mannheim turns from philosophy to sociology in the early 1920s, he first stakes out a position for himself on the boundary between the two disciplines. And as philosophical commentator on sociology, he criticizes Weber's inductive "general sociological" method, especially when applied to cultural sociology. But in his surveys of possibilities in the field, he always treats the approaches he criticizes with respect, never challenging the scientific ethos Weber had struggled to establish in the profession.

Yet from his first entry into the field of sociology, many established sociologists resisted Mannheim as a suspect and overambitious figure, aggressively challenging the tenuously settled constitution of the new academic enterprise. This uneasiness among social scientists was not unreasonable. Like his debut at the Congress of German Sociologists in Zurich in 1928, his academic efforts were moves in the intellectual competition that is conjured up brilliantly by his provocative presentation "Competition as a Cultural Phenomenon" (Mannheim [1929] 1993). Mannheim's characteristic contention that sociologists are the intelligentsia come to self-consciousness—and not, for example, scientists addressing collective human phenomena—epitomizes the issues that many sociologists thought were at stake. Mannheim was an adroit competitor, however. The name of his objective was "synthesis," and his strategy centered on transmuting the contest among competing disciplinary currents into a complex negotiation, with himself as rapporteur—and ultimately arbitrator.

Mannheim's attitude to political and intellectual alternatives also frustrated radical thinkers eager to welcome him as ally against the sociological establishment. A commentator generally enthusiastic about his efforts in Zurich complained that "Mannheim is conciliatory toward other tendencies of thought because of his intellectual liberality. While this strengthens his striving for synthesis, it also undermines his courage for drawing lines" (Meusel [1928] 1982:403). However great the value of Mannheim's catholic sensibilities, he objects, we must nevertheless commit ourselves to "some one particular course," when cases require decision. A participant in the discussion following Mannheim's Zurich talk sought to sharpen the distinction between the norms appropriate to their own academic disagreements and the conflictual logic of world-constitutive spiritual struggles that he took to be Mannheim's topic. Applying a conceptual distinction made by Franz Oppenheimer, Robert Wilbrandt suggests that the contrasting views promoted by paid professors in academic settings exemplify "peaceful rivalry" (*friedlicher Wettbewerb*)," while the "intellectual attitudes referred to by Mr. Mannheim" must be locked in "hostile contest" (*feindlicher Wettkampf*):" "The two can never peacefully coexist. Just as businesses must ruin one another (to let one gain at the expense of the other), so it is with intellectual attitudes (Wilbrandt [1928] 1990:93)." When the speaker asks Mannheim whether he has captured his meaning, Mannheim sidesteps with an answer applying to all the conflicts at issue: "Some situations call for compromise."

Mannheim's attempts to design compromises between political and scientific discourses, as well as between sociological and philosophical discourses, made his work attractive to the intellectuals whose responses typically appeared in journals of opinion rather than academic periodicals—whose criticisms of *Ideologie und Utopie* constitute the German

"Sociology of Knowledge Dispute" (Meja and Stehr 1982, 1990). In contrast, the more senior sociologists, who were striving to establish the profession disagreed markedly about the status of Mannheim's work. The influential Alfred Vierkandt invited Mannheim to contribute an essay on the sociology of knowledge (*Wissenssoziologie*) to the institutionally important *Handwörterbuch der Soziologie* (Vierkandt 1932) and included him among the sociologists of knowledge whose work he reviewed in a short article in a pedagogical journal (Vierkandt 1931). The leaders of the two "schools" contending for leadership in the organized profession, however, viewed Mannheim as an admittedly brilliant but borderline figure.

The characterization of sociology as a struggle between a Frankfurt School and a Cologne School was offered by Franz Oppenheimer, speaking in 1928, on "Tendencies in Recent German Sociology" at the London School of Economics (Oppenheimer [1928] 1932): 256-57). While accepting Oppenheimer's mapping of the sociological field slights important questions about his eccentricities (Haselbach 1990), his position in the profession as well as his continuing influence in the university where Mannheim was proposed as Oppenheimer's successor adds weight to his judgment. Oppenheimer's talk antedates Mannheim's performance in Zurich, not to speak of *Ideologie und Utopie*. Yet his statements about his own "Frankfurt School" may explain Frankfurt misgivings about Mannheim's candidacy. "Ours is a sociology solely of civilization," he announced, "and neither of culture, which we leave to the historians, nor still less of social philosophy, which we leave to the philosophers" (Oppenheimer [1928] 1932:256). Oppenheimer's dictum reverberates in remarks about Mannheim by the Frankfurt Dean of Social Sciences in 1929. Pressed repeatedly by the Prussian Ministry of Culture to appoint Karl Mannheim to a vacant professorship—after the Ministry had rejected the plea that sociology was already adequately served by Oppenheimer's protege Albert Salomon,—the Dean insists that while he does not challenge Mannheim's high standing: "Professor Mannheim represents a tendency in sociology that is of little real value to our students. Our students need a sociologist with a background in political economy or legal studies. Professor Mannheim's orientation, however, is philosophical. His language, moreover, is hard to understand for people without the necessary philosophical education" (UF, letter of Dean Hellauer to the Ministry of Science, Art, and Education in Berlin, November 27, 1929).[7]

Less indirect is the evidence about Leopold von Wiese, whom Oppenheimer identifies as the head of the only alternative school and whose schematic explication of competition was overshadowed by Mannheim's tour de force in Zurich. In his introduction to the Proceedings of the Sixth Congress of German Sociologists, von Wiese magnanimously quotes at length from Mannheim's newspaper report on the Congress (Mannheim 1928), highlighting Mannheim's contention that the Congress demonstrated the cooperation and complementarity among different approaches to sociology, specifically the formal, empirical, and intellectual-historical-philosophic types (Wiese 1929a). Yet von Wiese, having noted in the same introduction that the succession of congresses traces the "progressive development" of sociology, monopolized the 1930 program, leaving Mannheim out. Käsler reports:

> Speaking of the Sixth Congress, we could confirm Mannheim's presentation of the state of German sociology as a pluralistic division of labor among diverse tendencies. But the Seventh Congress presents a different picture: The "establishment" of the association, Tönnies and von Wiese, regains full mastery over the Congress and its session on theory.... As Tönnies himself reports, preparation and execution are altogether in the hands of the "first secretary [von Wiese]." At the same time, he appears as the head of the Cologne School,...and surrounds himself with a circle of his students. His attractiveness, especially for younger sociologists, consists not only in his offering a unified—and easy—conceptual framework but also in his role as guardian of the discipline's borders. (Käsler 1981: 237)

Several recent commentators have argued that Mannheim was emerging as the founder of a new generation of professional sociologists in Germany, offering a third alternative after his "star" performance in Zurich, his widely discussed book, and his initiatives while at Frankfurt (Mathiesen 1990; Lepsius 1979, 1981; König 1987; Habermas 1992). Such promise was not allowed the time to unfold, however. According to Käsler, a principal task of one of the two keynote speakers at the Seventh Congress was to denounce Mannheim's work as nothing more than a type of "historical materialism": "At least this label was to be hung on the 'star' of the previous Congress, who was not there" (Käsler 1981: 234). A year later, von Wiese's standard survey of the discipline (Wiese 1931) firmly consigns Mannheim's sociology of knowledge to the category of "metaphysical and epistemological" studies classified as sociology only by mistake. Without denying the importance of "cultural sociology" or the "sociology of knowledge," von Wiese concludes that the use of the same-word "sociology" for such diverse undertakings is dangerous. Von Wiese's 1928 definition of compromise takes on new meaning: "[Competition] is primarily to be assessed by its function, which consists in consigning individuals or groups to their sphere of operations and to delimiting these operations" (Wiese 1929b:15). At the time of Mannheim's ouster from Germany, von Wiese was winning the competition; Mannheim never achieved the compromise he sought.

Mannheim and his Students: the "Mission"

A core of faithful students, in contrast, admired the breadth of Mannheim's sociological conception, but became restive at his aloofness from their immediate political concerns. Their involvement with him and his project was intense, lasting, and multidimensional. Yet there is ample testimony, as well, that those most fascinated by him resisted being altogether "placed" in the sociocultural net as Mannheim saw it woven. Perhaps his design was at once too slack and too entangling. Mannheim's experimental strategy towards the contradictions confronting intellectuals in politics was idiosyncratic and paradoxical: his students eventually sought clearer choices. For women, there was the added complication that Mannheim had little to say about strategies for remaking their relations to the world made by men. The pedagogue Mannheim may have been gratified by his adherents' independence because he prided himself on offering tuition that enabled his students to make choices. But the sociologist Mannheim also hoped to initiate a collaborative research program, and this aspiration was thwarted by the gap between his powers to inspire and his capacity to transmit an intellectual style. He had a devoted personal following among the young intellectuals, but he founded no school.

Two documents, both preserved by former students, are revealing. The first is a fulsome letter of thanks for some flowers sent to Mannheim in 1930 during an illness. Mannheim addresses it to the "Mannheimer from Heidelberg," playing on a geographic pun originating with the students who accompanied him to Frankfurt. He claims that the gorgeous flowers propel him to recovery and inspire a resolve to have them all "ascend with him to a comparably exalted harmony [of nature and culture], quitting our discordant phase of skepticism." Below his signature, he announces that the teacher and sociologist in him cannot rest without assigning some questions about the distinctive qualities, historical precedents, and functions of groups like the "Mannheimer from Heidelberg." He exhorts them, "We shall have to transform the sociology of function (*Funktionssoziologie*) ever more into a sociology of mission" (*Missionssoziologie*). "Each of you is to write three pages on this," he demands (NR: "Den Mannheimern aus Heidelberg," May 15, 1930.) We can guess at the Mannheimer's reaction to this professorial excess from a parody of Aristophanes' Clouds several of them had produced a few months earlier, to honor Mannheim on his call to Frankfurt.

"'The Clouds' or 'Politics as Science'" caricatures Mannheim's equivocations between progressive and conservative political conceptions, his hope that exposé can pacify conflicts, and his exhortational assurances that intellectuals can rise in society by practicing their vocation. One of the authors was a prime mover in communist sectarian politics and two others were active Mensheviks (NRI; RL; Foitzik 1985.) But the Mannheim-oriented friendship circle in Heidelberg and Frankfurt was not political, especially since its leading spirit was Mannheim's assistant, Norbert Elias, himself only slightly engaged. They enjoyed their comradely sense of intellectual adventures in Mannheim's courses, but their political or scientific commitments distanced them from Mannheim's ideal of the intellectual in their time, however genuine their appreciation for his teaching.

The subtitle of the parody answers Mannheim's title-question in the central essay of *Ideology and Utopia* (1929, 1936a): "Is Politics as Science Possible?" The skit mocks up the "platform" that Mannheim desiderates in that essay, the "free space" mentioned in his Frankfurt lectures, where new social formations constitute themselves. At its heart is Socrates suspended (*schwebend*) in a hammock, archetype of the "socially unattached intellectuals" (*freischwebende Intelligenz*) of Mannheim's theory. In a twist on Aristophanes' story, this mentor promises success (*Erfolg*) and upward mobility (*Aufstieg*) through mastery of scientific politics, invoking three more Mannheimian motifs suspect to his admirers. Such mastery presupposes a regenerative insight (*Umbruch*) into the universality of partisanship. A despondent father brings his failed son for instruction, and the novice gains instant elevation above ideology. The story ends in burlesque confusion, set off by the telephone as deus ex machina, literally calling Socrates away. Apart from the principals and antiphonal choruses—the deracinated intellectuals and the rooted existences—the cast features a twosome named for the most leftist stu-

dents in the group, Richard Löwenthal and Boris Goldenberg. Five qua-
trains rehearse their experiences as "Socrates' products, the heirs of his
spiritual force." No one, they declaim, could have been more willing to
swallow "politics as science." They honored Socrates and attended his
school so he might teach them the dialectics "that gives power over the
masses." To strengthen them in debate, they say, Socrates taught them
"above all, the newest terminology." They learned about political
perspectivism: "Shamed, the layman must keep still, when we teach
him how he thinks." Their conclusion teasingly anticipates the ultimate
doubt that haunts the memoirs later written by several of the student
intellectuals on whom Mannheim had counted most (Elias 1990:
138–143; Speier 1989: 35–49): "Once this wisdom has dissolved science as well as religion," they rhyme in witty German jingles, "dissolution also gently overtakes the master's own design." While the mockery
is loving and the tribute sincere, biting disquiet about Mannheim's seductive conceptualization and diffuse message is unmistakable. The
mission that Mannheim offered students who defined themselves as intellectuals and experienced their relationship to politics or science as
their central problem ultimately enlisted very few.

Mannheim restated his conception of education for politics at the end
of his Frankfurt years, on an occasion laden with multiple pathos. Writing to the Communist son of Oscar Jászi two weeks before Hitler's designation as Chancellor, Mannheim describes the political dimension of
the education he designed:

> What we can offer you is a rather intensive study group, close contact with the
> lecturers, but little dogmatic commitment. We do not think of ourselves as a politi-
> cal party but must act as if we had a lot of time and could calmly discuss the pros
> and cons of every matter. In addition, I think it is very important not merely to
> continually discuss dialectics but to look at things carefully, to observe individual
> problems and aspects of social reality rather than merely talking about them.
> (Mannheim to G. Jászi, April 16, 1933, CUL).

The promise of Mannheim's sociological education looked different
to women than it looked to men. They were less tied to partisan political
identities than most of the men, and less attracted to stringent social
science alternatives than Elias. While male students, under prevailing
patterns of university recruitment and political socialization, were more
likely than women to recognize their kinship with Mannheim's old project
of bridging the gap between Max Weber's two incommensurable "voca-

tions"—science and politics—they were also more likely to be skeptical about the results he achieved.[8] Women were a major presence in Frankfurt sociology between 1930 and 1933, with degree candidacies at least equal in number to men. Mannheim himself, in his three years in Frankfurt, could carry only two candidates to completion, one a woman; but five other women sociologists completed dissertations originated in Mannheim's courses and research seminars (Honegger 1994).

The intellectual relationship between Mannheim and his women students epitomizes his conception of sociologist as educator, while his lectures on women and the family exemplify his conception of empirical sociology.

Sociological Education: The Sociology of Women

In Mannheim's university lectures in Frankfurt in 1931 and 1932, he outlined an approach to sociology as a "science for living" (*lebenswissenschaftliche Methode*). Little remains of Mannheim's initial assumption in *Conservatism*, that all social meanings are encapsulated in political ideologies linked to political parties. Women, for example, must cope with different mythologies, beginning with those they encounter in the institution of the family. The knowledge of everyday life, Mannheim insists, is wholly misleading, distorted by mythologies that make individuals incapable of comprehending their situations or of acting appropriately in them. This represents a break with the line of thinking that had generated the view of sociology of knowledge as organon, since that line followed Dilthey in distinguishing between the specialized knowledge achievable by scientific disciplines and the richness available to the "whole person": the perspicacious actor not only in political situations but also in everyday life. Mannheim is moving back towards a more conventional academic contrast between scientifically grounded social knowledge and ordinary opinion.

Mannheim's principal lecture courses in Frankfurt included important segments on the sociology of women. Like all his courses, these sought to combine a chapter in historical sociology with an introduction to a major theme in sociological analysis, oriented to current issues. His basic course on social institutions, for example, focused on the sociology of the family as the example best calculated to illustrate the sociological approach to institutions. In choosing this focus, Mannheim demonstratively turns his back on the traditional "splitting of sociology into general theory of society, concerning men, and a special, separate family sociology, concerning women," a tradition exposed in the dissertation on his student Frieda Haussig (Honegger 1994: 76; Haussig 1934; Honegger 1991: 182). He justifies the choice of central theme by the urgency of understanding the family when the institution is in bewildering flux:

> Everyone knows—because everyone talks about it—that the family is in crisis; that sexual morality is in crisis; that the frequency of divorce is a problem; that there is talk of an uprising of women, an uprising of youth;...that one can speak of a reproductive strike; that widespread psychic emiseration is being traced to the family (psychoanalysis); that there is hope of forming an altogether new human being. To be entitled to talk about these issues and form a judgment requires much knowledge: one must be able to distinguish the essential from the accidental, and, in general, one must have given the matter much thought. (KMP)

The sociological method, he argues, starts out from experienced problems, not a system; and it seeks to apprehend essences (*Wesensschau*) by examining historical changes.

Mannheim situates the family in a distinct and autonomous human domain, centered on the erotic relations between men and women. Distinguishing it from the complex of activities addressing economic needs and the need to impart meaning to the world, he claims that "the economy provides the framework, but the erotic problem, as asceticism shows, is the one most central to humankind." The family in its various forms, as well as such institutions as celibacy and prostitution, represent solutions to this central problem, and "every solution creates its distinctive sense of the body [*Körpergefühl*]" (KMP). Interpretations of the world, in turn, are vitally influenced by such feelings. An example of decisive changes originating in this domain, is the eroticization introduced by the minnesinger of the eleventh century: "This attitude towards woman had revolutionary effects upon the whole of social life." At a more general level, Mannheim introduces the analytical figure that is a recurrent feature of his lectures on women: "According to Marx, crisis arises out of a discrepancy within the development of social forces of production. In the development of the situations of men and women [as in Greece]...a discrepancy emerges in the development of psychic productive forces. Like all such disproportionalities, this leads to a crisis" (KMP). Mannheim's diagnosis of the contemporary form of that crisis becomes clearer in the next course, where he again subjects an analytical theme from Marxism to a basic change in theoretical function. The principal element in social destabilization and transformation, he contends, is the upward movement of social group formations. As in the Amsterdam lecture on intellectuals in 1932, the Marxist account of class shifts is presupposed, but the rise of women and intellectuals provides the subject matter.

The crisis of the family, according to Mannheim, begins with the dissolution of its patriarchal type. More specifically, however, problems are centered in difficulties afflicting women in their rise from patriarchal domination. The heading for Mannheim's first lecture—and thus the overarching theme he announced at the beginning of the course—is "Woman as a Problem in Upward Mobility" (*Die Frau als Aufstiegsproblem*). Women's conflicts generated by these changes affect the family so profoundly, Mannheim believes, because they manifest themselves in frigidity and inferiority complexes that vitally damage the capacity of the family to solve the "central human problem" of the erotic. Applying the quasi-Marxist paradigm of disproportionality, Mannheim diagnoses a crisis and traces it to a discrepancy between women's actual situations and the ideology of domesticity that still governs their orientations. Amid profound social changes, women have moved into the work force or they have simply been made functionless in the home and left to devote themselves to self-cultivation or empty pursuits. But they continue to accept a model of womanliness derived from a time when the household was a center of production, providing full-time occupation for wives and other females. Women belong in the home, according to these persistent norms; they justify themselves by founding intimacy; they cling to the everyday; and they relinquish all claims to public recognition or competition with men. Such doctrines persist in part because the everyday worldview is itself a product of the home, where women are enclosed in the domain of consumption and largely shut off from rationalization. "Unworldly preachers and teachers" broadcast the ideology, and those who benefit from keeping women in confusion inculcate it less innocently. Yet women cannot fulfill themselves in the domestic sphere. They are victimized by the stresses attending their rise, but they cannot and will not be left behind.

To analyze the constituents, causes, and consequences of upward social mobility, Mannheim traces the rise of "woman" from classical antiquity to the High Middle Ages, devoting several lectures to a detailed review of Tacitus on the Germanic tribes to insist, like Marianne Weber (1907), on the patriarchal nature of their family regime against fashionable claims about supposed matriarchal origins. Summarizing his analysis, he focuses on a distinction between fixed social arrangements and free space, which he finds variously combined in different phases of different societies. In the free spaces, he says, "social restratification takes place—this is where individuals detached from various strata meet one another... to consolidate into a stratum" (KMP). The sociological generalization about openings created when institutional constraints are loosened clearly applies to Mannheim's theory of the intellectuals (see especially Mannheim [1922-24] 1982: 256, 265-72), but in the present context it also identifies the locus of a new dynamic force among women. Although Mannheim's historical survey does not extend beyond the Middle Ages, he extrapolates from his discussion of the lady of the manor to a characterization of the "lady" (*die Dame*), in the sense in which this type figures importantly in moderate feminist writings since the beginning of the century. According to Mannheim, the lady emerges as a new type among legally married women. She is "increasingly without functions in the social process of production" and by utilizes "her leisure for the cultivation of her personality, as well as the cultivation of manners and the erotic sphere" (KMP). For Mannheim, the lady encapsulates both the dilemma and the promise of woman's situation.[9]

In the historical lectures, Mannheim analyzes the effects of social differentiation upon the family. In the preceding semester, too, Mannheim had ascribed "revolutionary"—and paradigmatic—significance to redefinitions of women's identities during the High Middle Ages. Then he focused on the role of the minnesinger in the genealogy of erotic consciousness. Now he cites new accumulations of power in the hands of nobility to explain the emergence of new patterns of division of labor in new household forms in the castle and the socage holding. Mannheim notes: "This division of labor deprives the household, originally the site of production for all its needs, of ever more functions. The wife is first transformed into nothing more than the manager of production, then deprived of every function. She either seeks new functions or creates a new form for the free time now available. This... produced two new types of women: the abbess and the lady of the manor. These are at once new social and new cultural types" (KMP). Mannheim's shift from his discussion of the wife to the example of the presumably unmarried abbess is facilitated by the ambiguity of the German word for woman and wife, but primarily derives from his fluctuations between historical and structural analyses in the lectures: the changed status of upper-class wives helps to explain the choice of alternative lives by women who might otherwise marry. Mannheim's method allows use of historical figurations as prototypes for the formations that interest him in his own time, the insight into essences through historical study. He is implicitly alluding to the origins of the women's movement among women in new occupations and new forms of cultural activity. Except for his psychoanalytic reasonings and a more general emphasis on erotic dimensions of marriage, Mannheim starts with the woman question as defined by Marianne Weber and others speaking for the moderate middle-class women's movement (Marianne Weber 1919; Greven-Aschoff 1981; Roth 1988). In concentrating on "sociological" variables, however, Mannheim sacrifices the political awareness that enters Weber's analysis through legal issues of property and power, replicating in this context the contrast between his analysis of the political process and the conceptions of social democratic lawyers like Franz Neumann.

Expounding his notion of sociology as a "science for living" accessible only to persons who require its knowledge for the sake of their lives, Mannheim claims, "Those who have not yet despaired of their situation cannot really find their way to sociology and should give it up" (KMP). He then challenges his listeners in their various characters as young people, women, and intellectuals. Young people who have not realized their parents' loss of authority and have thus missed the youth movement experience, he maintains, are not ripe for the sociological problem of generations. Women are addressed twice, and significantly each time anomalously associated with the supposedly anachronistic type of "the lady":

> Any woman or girl who fails to face up to the fact that modern society...gives her enlightenment and culture, while denying her a field of action, falls prey to melancholy and the other psychic ailments that we will later encounter in the history of the lady. Only someone who has, as woman, confronted the experience of being alternately shunned as a "lady" (a throwback to the past) and shouldered aside as a competitor, can begin to see that a social situation is not a matter of anatomical destiny. (KMP)

Mannheim closes with the group whose dilemma immediately concerns himself:

Only someone who has, as intellectual, taken notice of the fact that he is esteemed above all others as cultivated person but counts for nothing in the world of bourgeois and proletarian, that he knows everything and can do nothing, that everyone needs him and that he is nevertheless rejected—only such a person is able not only to arrive at a general theory of the spirit's impotence but also to see it as the fate of a social stratum, and thus to understand himself as a product of a social situation. (KMP)

In sum, Mannheim posits a crisis experienced in the inquirer's life situation as the point of departure for sociological method.

The first methodological step requires the sociologist to expose both her situation and her identity as socially constituted events, to shake inherited misinterpretations which obscure changed circumstances, as when an employed woman orients herself to her situation by principles of domestic morality. But the initial recasting of situation and self is still partial and abstract; it only opens the way to the sociological work to be done. Even when we correctly place ourselves in society, we see from too limited a perspective. We neglect diverse historical points of view, differences of social standpoints, and the variability of the process whose moment we recognize. Social events are compound and interwoven; sociological method must comprehend these qualities. To illustrate the approach, Mannheim lays out a sequence of social dimensions requiring systematic study if a woman student is to move beyond her methodological starting point in sociology, her penetration of the disorienting domestic ideology.

As in his 1931 course on the family as representative social institution, he begins with the connections between family and prostitution: they are complementary, since historically prostitution solves the erotic problems left unsolved by marriage. The situation of the married woman cannot be illuminated without recognizing prostitution as corollary. The female family member stands in similar interdependencies with historical social formations of power and law, economy and education. She must understand her situation as a function not only of the institutions that include her, but also of those that keep her out. Beyond the institutional framework of society, Mannheim distinguishes variability of human types, forms of experience, and values—all for the sake of a more nuanced and more historically specific contextualizing of the social phenomena under review. As diverse but interlinked human types, he lists housewife, concubine, whore, hetæra, crone, working woman, and lady. He maps the erotic and cultural spheres by projecting reciprocal relationships among sensuous, sublimated, and repressed experiences, and he invites refinement in understanding the constitution and reconstitution of the instincts. Values are a function of differentiated moral codes, and male ideology appears as a distinct factor. The study that begins with an effort at self-clarification motivated by an experience of impasse, in sum, should eventuate in a structured view of a differentiated, interwoven and changing social universe.

Mannheim's methodology retains the historical and contextual approach of sociology of knowledge as organon, but the research objective is less focused on the institutionally defined political domain. When sociology as a science for living addresses the reflexive returns from the knowledge it generates, it grasps the diverse ways in which individuals can "own" themselves. The personal starting point is not merely a pedagogical heuristic; sociology is to be a self-transformative experience. This was Mannheim's promise and challenge to the students he addressed as youths, as intellectuals, and as women. Sociological education inherits the mission of cultivation (*Bildung*) Mannheim originally had claimed for the new cultural studies of Lukács' Sunday Circle.

Mannheim's conception of educator as guide extended beyond the formal lecture. His supervision of dissertations, strongly seconded by Norbert Elias, directed students to topics bearing on their individual situations.[10] Four dissertations completed by his woman students represent women's studies in the present sense: Frieda Elisabeth Haussig's (1934) sociology of knowledge investigation of Wilhelm Heinrich Riehl, a conservative, antifeminist founder of family sociology in Germany, Käthe Truhel's (1934) "analysis of the gradual emergence of bureaucratically regulated state welfare agencies out of the institutions of the woman's movement and volunteer women's social work" (Honegger 1994: 78), Margarete Freudenthal's ([1934] 1986) historical study of domestic economies, and Natalie Halperin's (1935) sociological analysis of "sentimental" female literary intellectuals in the later eighteenth century. The dissertation by Gisèle Freund (1936)—like that on German actors' associations thwarted by Ilse Seglow's forced emigration—arises out of the artistic backgrounds of these students, while Nina Rubinstein ([1933] 1989) examines political emigrations, a social formation of intimate concern to a person raised at the center of the Menshevik emigration, translating the émigrés she studied from the sociological category of political intelligentsia to the family. Rubinstein moves beyond Mannheim in taking distance from politics, but she has his support in exploring her own tacit knowledge (Kettler and Meja 1993).

Rubinstein was on the point of completion when Mannheim was forced into uncompensated retirement on April 13, 1933. An undated letter from Mannheim to Rubinstein (NR), written just before his abrupt departure for Amsterdam about a week later, illuminates his relationship with his students. He writes:

> I have not written you until now because I knew nothing certain about the status of the dissertation. Even today, I know nothing definite, but I do know a bit more. At the Ministry, I was requested to continue accepting dissertations prepared under me. But this goes against the general rule that suspended professors are not allowed to carry out anything of an official nature. The Philosophical Faculty is supposed to confer about this at the beginning of the Semester. Until then, you will simply have to wait. But basically I do not think that anything untoward can happen to you. If worst comes to worst, you will submit your work under [someone else]. But I believe that, as a student so nearly finished, you have a right to bring your studies to their conclusion.

> Besides, you must not complain. As a sociologist, you are called upon to understand what is happening and to allow events to run their course. Relinquish the habit of thinking about the long run. That is no longer timely. One merely feels aggrieved and neglects the most urgent things. These considerations explain my inability to answer your question about my own plans. For the moment, I remain at my post as a Prussian official. No running away, certainly not yet. After one has worked so long on emigration, one is duty-bound to a certain sense of proportion. Noblesse oblige. My advice, in short, complete the work, await the beginning of the semester, and hand in whatever they will accept.

Mannheim did not forget his other students either. The *Revue Internationale de Sociologie* (1932: 1932: 3) announces Professor Karl Mannheim of the Sociological Institute in Frankfurt as a contributor to the section on "*l'habitat humaine*" at the 1933 Congress of the Institut International de Sociologie in Geneva, with a presentation on "the human habitat from the perspective of the social role of women and the domestic economy." By the time of the meetings, however, Mannheim no longer had an institute or a home. His name appears in the official 1934 report of the Congress, with his new London affiliation, but he was not himself present in Geneva. Two of his degree candidates from Frankfurt appeared in his place: Margarete Freudenthal, whose dissertation research provided the topic Mannheim had originally announced (Freudenthal [1934] 1986), and Norbert Elias, who drew on the just-completed but never-to-be officially recognized *Habilitation* he wrote under Mannheim (Elias [1933] 1983). Their talks, so far as can be judged from the brief report in the *Revue* (Duprat 1934: 143–44), brilliantly illustrate how shared beginnings with Mannheim could be developed in quite different, strikingly distinctive directions.

Both undertake to explain "correlations between types of homes and levels of social existence" of their inhabitants. While Elias focuses on the houses of French courtiers in the seventeenth and eighteenth centuries, and concludes that "the residence represented the rank and function of its owner; it corresponded, moreover, to the nobility's manner of life: their relations of reciprocal hospitality, the requirements of luxury, of staff, of domesticity," Freudenthal contrasts proletarian and bourgeois homes by reference to the respective domestic economies, arguing specifically that "the mode of material existence varies with the economic role—inside as well as outside the home—of the woman." The differences between these two representatives of Mannheim's Frankfurt institute—the one stressing the proprietor's rank and function and the other the household role of women—are not explainable simply by the different historical and social milieux they examine. They typify the diversity of work—and common empirical commitments—generated by studying with Mannheim in Frankfurt.

Mannheim as Weberian Sociologist

In addition to his undergraduate lectures, Mannheim's primary interest at Frankfurt was a postgraduate seminar on the social and intellectual history of early German liberalism, intended as "an empirically oriented...interdisciplinary project, similar to his earlier empirical work on 'das konservative Denken'" (NS), according to one of its participants. The seminar, given jointly with the young economist Adolf Löwe and attended by other colleagues, addressed itself to questions about modern and classical liberal economics as well as to more general political themes. Mannheim's chances of establishing a university career as researcher and teacher depended, first, on his distancing himself from excited literary and political discussions of the very themes he had popularized and, second, on more nearly adjusting his scholarly program to the specialized manner and matter of colleagues struggling to overcome the distrust of the new discipline among university mandarins. Mannheim accepted the need to give his newly established but virtually unfunded

"Sociological Seminar" an empiricist face. If nothing else, Mannheim had to make his peace with colleagues and students imbued with the empirical traditions of Franz Oppenheimer's "Frankfurt School" (Oppenheimer [1928] 1932; Käsler 1981).

Karl Mannheim's "scientific secretary" in the seminar, Greta Kuckhoff, writes in her memoirs that she applied for the position when she learned that he "was interested in becoming acquainted with the new techniques of social research that had established and proved themselves in the United States." Kuckhoff was uniquely qualified, since she had just returned from two years with Edward A. Ross in Wisconsin, the last as his assistant. She lacked a degree, however, having interrupted her studies with Sombart in Berlin (concentrating on Max Weber) during the 1920s, where she had been admitted without academic high school qualifications. Mannheim agreed to inquire about a special dispensation if she proved herself "an independent scientific personality," a reply she resented because she had already passed her preliminary doctoral examinations at Wisconsin. She speaks of her difficulties sorting the library, most of whose topics were unfamiliar, "except for the few American books on behaviorism, pragmatism, and ecology—words that were barely known at the time" (Kuckhoff 1972: 106).

Following the successful example of the Heidelberg Institute for Social and Political Science directed by the triumvirate who had sponsored his *Habilitation*, Mannheim sought funding from the European social science program of the Rockefeller Foundation.[11] Mannheim attempted to impress the foundation's representatives with consonances between the approaches they sought to promote and the direction of his Sociological Seminar. Two primary motifs in Rockefeller program statements were the shifting of social studies from "philosophical" to "inductive" methods and the elevation of problems above disciplines (Bulmer and Bulmer 1981; Craver 1986). In a report for the Paris office of the Rockefeller Foundation in 1931, Mannheim accordingly emphasizes three primary activities of his seminar:

i.   The preparation of a problem-centered bibliography cutting across disciplines and summarizing the present state of research on selected problems;
ii. Inductive research into contemporary social problems such as
     a) the mechanism for selecting leaders in political parties, in trade unions and in the catholic church.
     b) women in politics

    c)   sociology of the immigrant
    d)   influence of education on social position
iii.   Historical philosophical investigations such as
    a)   German and English liberalism
    b)   Sociological analysis of changes in Germany's economic structure from 1750–1850
    c)   Nietzsche and his influence—a sociological study. (RF/RG2-1932/ 717/77/617)[12]

The Foundation's German representative praises Mannheim and rec-ommends "a small grant to permit him to acquire some statistical appa-ratus and to undertake more thoroughly inductive research and field work," but the Paris official appears skeptical, concluding "an examina-tion of the research under way and the types of students doing the work gives the impression that M's most advanced students go in for the his-torical-philosophical investigations." This appraisal must be seen in the context of a conviction that "any large aid [in Frankfurt] just now would be badly received by German public opinion," although "Frankfurt is of first importance from the point of view of research." The problem is that "the atmosphere is international and Jewish" and "many Jews are on the faculty." This proved an all too remediable problem, as Mannheim and the other "non-Aryans" were dismissed by the Hitler regime.

    In September, 1934, Mannheim and Löwe, building on their disrupted Frankfurt work, offered a five-day seminar in the Netherlands on "Economy and Man in the Age of Planning." The notice of the event states that they are "long accustomed to scientific collaboration with one another," and, indeed, the printed articles which are, by internal evidence, the outgrowth of the contribution of each, attest to mutual indebtedness and agreement. Löwe's elaboration appears in *Economics and Sociology*, also given as lectures in 1935 at the London School of Economics. Strikingly, he opens the lecture with a vehement attack on the "popular prejudice" that sociological method consists of "interpreta-tion based on inner understanding and comparative description, but not causal analysis." German sociology, he observes, has distracted itself too long with unproductive self-reflections and worries about differing modes of knowledge. Causal explanations based on empirical evidence are the goal in the social sciences, as in any other, and interpretive meth-ods are nothing more than suggestive aids in generating hypotheses and first approximations, to give direction to work that is properly scientific in character. His talk ends with the claim that "the main field and true justification" of the sociology of knowledge, professed above all by Karl Mannheim in his handbook article on the sociology of knowledge, is to contrast the "obscure fallacies and prejudices" of common sense with the "scientific results of the competent specialisms." Löwe's suggestion that he and Mannheim shared common ground builds quite properly on one of Mannheim's experimental postures and indicates one of Mannheim's sources of support and encouragement in this direction, but it treats as settled the basic issue Mannheim never finally resolved.

Sociology and the Irrational

After seven years in exile, however, Mannheim had moved far from trust in a complex interplay of the rational and irrational through the intermediation of sociology of knowledge. Now he writes:

> But one can only learn if one has belief in the power of reason. For a time it was healthy to see the limitations of *ratio*, especially in social affairs. It was healthy to realize that thinking is not powerful if it is severed from the social context and ideas are only strong if they have their social backing, that it is useless to spread ideas which have no real function and are not woven into the social fabric. But this sociological interpretation of ideas may also lead to complete despair, discouraging the individual from thinking about issues which will definitely become the concerns of the day. This discouragement of the intelligentsia may lead them to too quick a resignation of their proper function as the thinkers and forerunners of the new society, may become even more disastrous where more depends on what the leading elites have in mind than in other periods of history. (Mannheim 1940: 365)[14]

In the original and shorter German version, published five years earlier, Mannheim (1935a) did not go so far in disparaging his original claims about the synthesizing consequences of insight into the social grounding of thought. But he was already categorical in his argument that social-scientific intelligence now had to provide the capacity for rational planning that alone could overcome a systemwide crisis of out-of-control irrationalities. The spontaneous mechanisms of modern society—its various platforms for rationalizing the irrational (Mannheim 1936a)—could no longer manage their integrative and organizational tasks. The place of cultivation in the cultural structure and the attendant search for historical meaning, on which the hopes for sociology of knowledge as organon had rested, have been definitively undermined by German events, he concludes. Irrationalities cannot be dialectically or ironically acknowledged and transcended, it now appears; they must be subjected to planned social control through the newest social technology. And social science must direct itself towards diagnosis, prognosis, and cure, not fearing comparison with medicine or even engineering.

Mannheim's most poignant justification for his new approach to rationalizing the irrational is to be found in an unpublished exchange of letters with an intimate member of the Frankfurt Tillich circle, also in exile. After the publication of *Mensch und Gesellschaft im Zeitalter des Umbaus* (1935), Mannheim had sent it to several old discussion partners, and he quickly received a searching and fundamental critique from Eduard Heimann, a prominent theorist of the Weimar welfare state whose intimacy with Tillich and his circle dated to the first years after the war. In the first years of exile, several key members of the Tillich circle maintained an extensive round-robin correspondence, aiming at eventual periodical publication of the articles and mutual criticisms circulated in multiple copies.[15] The reply to Heimann was a serious occasion for Mannheim. What Heimann and the others thought about his work clearly mattered as much as it had had four years before, at the time of the Frankfurt Discussion. Eight months elapsed between Heimann's letter and Mannheim's carefully calculated article-length reply.

Heimann's principal charge is that Mannheim has abandoned the insights he had earlier shared with Heimann and other religious thinkers. A rationalism without adequate grounding in the irrational is empty of meaning, they had agreed, and cannot prevent its own demonization or defend against eruptions of irrationality in truly destructive forms. Mannheim had known this during his association with Tillich, Heimann contends, and he had presupposed it in his sociology of knowledge; now he was abandoning this knowledge, equating everything rational with the salutary and everything irrational with the destructive. This move, he charges, puts Mannheim on the side of the impoverished, merely instrumental forms of rationalization that had undermined Weimar socialism and Weimar democracy. He concludes: "Your rationalism is not contradictory to fascism but politically neutral and therefore supportive of whatever powers may be, because it reductively refers only to social techniques" (Heimann to Mannheim, January 31, 1935, PT). Heimann makes almost the same reproach on the grounds of a religious anthropology, as Lukács does reasoning from the rather mechanical Marxism he then professed (Lukács [1933] 1982).

Interestingly enough, Mannheim also had to defend his new position, some months after his letter to Heimann, against the sad but firm reproaches of Oscar Jászi, the liberal publicist and historian who had provided the counterpoint to Lukács in Mannheim's formative Hungarian years. Jászi, too, faults Mannheim's reliance on purely rationalist thought and techniques for the comprehension and management of the modern crisis, passionately pleading the humanist liberal case for the spiritually grounded, creative individual against the impersonal sociological perspective. Like Heimann, Jászi acknowledges that his position may be outdated, but he defiantly vows to remain at the post dictated by principle beyond pragmatic calculation (CUL).[16] Thus, when Mannheim tried to defend himself against the charge of hyperrationalism immediately after the publication of *Mensch und Gesellschaft*, he was pleading in the court of his own past, as well as before the more impersonal historical tribunal of sociological theory.

Two points in Mannheim's rejoinder to Heimann are particularly noteworthy in the light of the "Frankfurt Discussions." First, he denies that the concept of the irrational refers to anything specific enough to be respected as an entity with meaning or value as a whole, and, second, he insists that instrumental reason is a uniquely necessary form of thinking that must be given priority in the crisis of social thought signaled by the rise of fascism. Both points are clearly continuous with Mannheim's lifelong search for a comprehensive and differentiated account of rationality and its effects, a search in which Hegel's accomplishment long served him as ideal, but they also mark Mannheim's attempt to break with the dramatic imagery and essayistic subtlety of a thinking formulated in dialectical antitheses and paradoxical reversals. He tried to go beyond the discourse characteristic of the Weimar intellectual culture that had celebrated him, a culture hopelessly compromised by its ineffectual resistance to Nazism and by parodies of its themes in the more pretentious aspects of Nazi culture.

Mannheim sought to break the spell of the quintessential Weimar issue of a dialectic between the rational and the irrational by denying that the many things intended by the term irrational constitute a unity. The rational, he asserts, makes sense as a whole. It refers to thought and to organization congruent with thought. But the irrational, strictly speaking, refers to a wild diversity unified by nothing except the absence of thought or conscious organization. "It is a puzzle to me what the value in this heterogeneous category is supposed to be," he comments to Heimann, "in pursuit of which youth movements, philosophies, and so forth are set into motion." But he thinks that he does know after all what "religious people, romantics, the *Jugendbewegung*" have in mind when they affirm the irrational. They think that certain things are spoiled if they are thought through, that it is nicer to experience them without reflection. Mannheim now declares himself an unqualified enemy of such enthusiasm for the irrational, no less in its "higher forms" than in its most servile, where the Nazis have raised the submissive inability to think to the dignity of a program. To Heimann's plea for an irrational grounding of convictions and constitutions, he replies that spiritual contents are not devalued by being thought about, not even in ultimate, religious matters: "I have always found that genuine thinking enhances our capacity for experience and that the courage to think can only intensify convictions.... I believe that thinking is one of the supreme gifts of the human race, the most profound faculty for penetrating the world, whether directed towards the outer world or to the world of inner experience. Things are emptied of meaning not because man thinks but because empty men think." Set against thinking in all its forms, the irrational loses its coeval status as a legitimate power alternative to the rational, to be sounded and respected if not worshipped. Mannheim puts aside the ambiguous, dialectical conception of reason.

But, left there, the reponse is evasive, because Mannheim gives his concept of the rational a scope as wide as the uses of the words thinking and organizing. He speaks of the "capacity to provide a mental description, a causal explanation, a structural analysis or a synthetic reconstruction for anything experienced, encountered, or having existence." But Heimann's complaints about Mannheim's rationalist method are obviously not directed against the complex modes of reflection circumscribed by three of those four formulations. As Mannheim is fully aware, Heimann's question about the irrational is inseparable from his objection to Mannheim's focus on knowledge that consists of causal or functional explanations designed to be instrumental for planning. In fact, Mannheim conciliatorily suggests in passing that existential reflections on goals and purposes like Heimann's are a second valuable type of thinking, and he briefly implies that the differences between him and Heimann may be mere differences in current interests. Yet Mannheim also accepts the challenge.

The resistance to instrumental reason and especially to the kinds of generalizations on which it depends, he maintains, manifests "the besetting sin of German intellectuals," and it stems from an irresponsible indifference to outward action and results. Things are out of control in society, he insists, and they stand in need of planned management, not self-reflective inwardness. Such management will be provided ruthlessly by oppressors if cultivated people disdain the knowledge that such planning requires. Principles and designs uninformed by instrumental reason are mere "ideology," lacking integral effects. Moreover, reflection on principles itself is actually most searching and inspired when it runs in intimate parallel with active inquiry into causes and instrumentalities. The two are logically distinct forms of thinking, but they work best side by side.

Mannheim concludes his defense of instrumental rationality with an argument paradoxically rich in associations with Lukács:

> Or have you never been struck by the strange paradox that the materialist-determinist worldview is upheld by those who want to get rid of such determinations, while the ruling strata, for whom it is not a vital necessity to get rid of the existing social order, speak much more than the oppressed about the freedom of humankind? Only those who desire freedom bind themselves to the task of uncovering existing determinations. Those comfortable with those determinations, on the other hand, interpret the world as already free. When the will to freedom is in actualization, it ruthlessly exposes the chains. Those in whom the artistic is an actual presence do not speak about art (which they cannot do without, in any case), but about the means by which they can bring it forth.

Mannheim denies that his turn toward pragmatist instrumental thinking entails disloyalty to the high ethical mission of the intellectual represented by his Weimar work and characteristic of the Budapest groups in which he had intellectually come of age. Not only are the historical materialist formulations in the opening phrases of the passage quoted above reminiscent of Mannheim's encounter with Marxism through Lukács, but the concluding analogy to art also recalls Mannheim's apprenticeship to him. But his uses of these themes have the effect of a declaration of independence; the themes are reconstituted on Mannheim's own terms.

In a diary of his youth, there is a detailed account by Mannheim of his first visit to Lukács, on June 23, 1911, when Mannheim was eighteen years old. He reports himself as saying, "Socialism, and particularly the elements of historical materialism in socialism, did have a soul destroying effect, and the soul must emerge again. I told Lukács how little I trusted socialism. He said that lately he had regained his trust in socialism, because it had a branch going back to spiritual origins, the one originating from Hegel. If we read Marx, we could see the affinities. I should not forget, he told me, that this was the first movement since the mystics that really penetrated deeply and mobilized everything. We could be witnessing a unique process. In the old days there was the Bible and this had created sociology; now it would turn out the other way: sociology would create a new faith for humanity." Earlier, the talk had been about art and thinking about art. "Lukács on principle never takes into account what creative artists may say about themselves.... Lukács saw it as natural that artists tended to talk about their technical problems, because the transcendent and metaphysical elements were hidden within the soul, so only the fight with matter caused them problems" (Sárközi 1986:436–37).

Marxism and the talk of artists are themes familiar from this and many other discussions between Lukács and Mannheim in the early days, but, in his defense of his English writings, Mannheim not so much reversed the valences between the spiritual and material poles as he sought to surge beyond these disjunctions. "Talk about technical problems," he now implies, is more urgent and perhaps also more fundamental than discovering "a new faith for humanity." Civilization seems to have displaced culture.

But this reversal is not consistently sustained. The fate of one passage in his writings signals part of the problem. Heimann singles it out in his letter, as an encouraging indication that Mannheim has not wholly given up his earlier views, although he complains that Mannheim fails to develop the point. The same passage is quoted by Theodor W. Adorno in a critical assessment of Mannheim's "new value-free sociology" written in 1937. But he notices only the echoes of the Mannheim of the Frankfurt Discussion and takes it as representative for Mannheim's general position in *Mensch und Gesellschaft* (Adorno 1986).[17] Mannheim had written: "We must, moreover, realize, that the irrational is not always harmful but that, on the contrary, it is among the most valuable powers in man's possession when it acts as a driving force towards rational and objective ends or when it creates cultural values through sublimation, or, when, as pure élan, it heightens the joy of living without planlessly destroying social life" (Mannheim 1940: 62–63).[18]

According to Adorno, Mannheim's sociological conjectures about a crisis in culture and elite formation, as well as his projection of an omnipotent remedial planning reason, all go back to distortions characteristic of the ideologies that upheld the prevailing order in Weimar and continued to do so after its fall. Like Horkheimer in 1931, Adorno insists that ruling culture and elites are as strong as they have to be to preserve their domination; techniques of control do not lack effectiveness. Mannheim's failure in the passage quoted to make qualitative distinctions between generative libidinal energies and the irrational energies of repression is symptomatic of a method that also fails to make such distinctions between emancipatory and oppressive elements in culture, elite, and reason. The old ideologies cannot be displaced unless the social contradictions that they disguise are set free, and this emancipation is ultimately a conflictual political process. It is not enough to attempt, as Mannheim does, to criticize them from the standpoint of the *juste milieu*, denouncing them as interest-generated distortions of a disinterested social knowledge. Mannheim senses the ineffectuality of his passive rationalizing, Adorno contends, and he "corrects" for it by invoking themes from the old "irrationalism" to give vitalistic heightening and intensification to his sterile argument. Adorno might have accused Heimann ironically of an injustice to Mannheim. Mannheim never supposed that "instrumental rationality" can provide the pathos that rule and resistance alike require; he is simply unable, according to Adorno, to link it coherently to his analysis. The reinsertion of irrationality, Adorno concludes, "reveals the bias in Mannheim's theory towards the interests of the existing order...despite all his intentions towards enlightenment." (Adorno 1986: 41)

Mannheim's abandonment of the subtler aspects of the sociology of knowledge and his didactic insistence on a depoliticized planning dependent on the manipulative adaptation of old faiths open him to Adorno's scathing attack, although the new work could be read more sympathetically and had productive influence on a postwar planning-oriented readership. By the standards of the Weimar debates, however, it was shockingly unreflective, with its popularized periodizations of rationalities and its forced optimism about the old elites. The unpublished letter to Heimann is more interesting about the key issues than anything Mannheim published for his English-speaking audiences.

It is in fact tempting to close this discussion by showing how far Mannheim's subsequent career appears to vindicate Adorno's harsh critique, unperceptive as this may have been about the aspects of his earlier work examined above, and unwarranted as its own politico-philosophical presuppositions may have soon proved. As Adorno might have expected, Mannheim eventually aligned himself, as in Frankfurt, with a group of Christian thinkers. But this time they were mostly establishment figures, to whom he offered his own sociological rationalism as an instrument for taking charge of a reality that would supplement not only their irrationally grounded doctrine but their social beings as an elite of Englishmen having the special qualities that Mannheim, like many central European sociologists of his generation, ascribed to the social category of "the gentleman." It is hard to imagine that the leading and characteristic lay figure of that group, T.S. Eliot, would ever have been moved to praise Mannheim (or anyone) by saying about him what Tillich had said in the Frankfurt Discussion, that is, that he exemplifies the non-Protestant layman who nevertheless performs the distinctively Protestant task of asking the most radical question and risking himself on the outermost boundary situation. Mannheim became more publicist and pedagogue than theorist, and he failed to develop his thought. His mobilization strategy could do justice to neither the rational nor the irrational. The emancipation from Weimar culture turned into a barren exile.

There is truth in such exaggerations, but, nevertheless, they would make a misleading conclusion to this story of Mannheim's encounters with the theme of the irrational. Although Mannheim prided himself on his status as an outsider in Weimar and on the unique critical insights he thought this provided, he was in fact an exceptionally representative figure among the younger Weimar intellectuals, as evidenced by the brilliant success of *Ideologie und Utopie* in 1929. The destruction of the Weimar Republic devastated and scattered this vital community. Some, like Adorno, continued to ground their work in the conviction that "the essentially transformative effects of culture," gave them a "means of fighting against institutions," to use Mannheim's 1919 language; but Mannheim considered that project dangerously obsolete. Deprived simultaneously of the faith in history that empowers the politician and of the position that legitimates the educator, Mannheim faced a difficult rehabilitation.

Notes

1. Mannheim writes, "As long as individuals have not become wholly ethical and free, cultural institutions that force their subjects to become cultural beings by using means that resemble violence, are unavoidable. As long as we do not achieve the paradisaical condition where there are no institutions, there will always be revolutions—to destroy, not humans, but the institutions that have become an end in themselves, in order to create new ones. The tragedy of revolution is that people must be killed" (Mannheim [1919a] 1985: 226).

2. The "Frankfurt Discussion" was opened by Heinrich Frick, active in the Foreign Mission Movement, not by Tillich, and he cites as inspiration for his reflections a number of American Quakers and above all the English church activist and organizer, James H. Oldham. There are direct lines of continuity that led Mannheim to center the last eight years of his English stay on the activities of a Christian discussion circle, called "The Moot," organized and led by Oldham and generated by the same series of ecumenical church meetings that stimulated Tillich and his associates on this occasion.

3. See Mannheim's notes for his Frankfurt lectures in 1932 (KMP). A contemporary published essay by Mannheim is "On the Nature of Economic Ambition and Its Significance for the Social Education of Man" (Mannheim [1930] 1952: 230-75).

4. The tactic has sound Marxist antecedents, although its clearest explanation by Marx and Engels sheds a curious light on the later course of *Institut*—and Marxist—thought: "One of the chief pursuits of Absolute Criticism consists in first bringing all questions of the day into the right setting. For it does not answer the real questions—it substitutes quite different ones. As it makes everything, it must also first make the 'questions of the day,' make them its own questions, the questions of Critical Criticism. If it were a question of the Napoleonic Code, it would prove that it is properly a question of the Pentateuch. Its setting of 'questions of the day' is Critical distortion and misplacement of them…. This method, like all Absolute Criticim's originalities, is the repetition of a speculative witticism. Speculative philosophy…must transpose all questions from the form of healthy common sense to the form of speculative reason and change the real question into a speculative one to be able to answer it. Having distorted my question on my lips and put its own question on my lips like the catechism, it could naturally have a ready answer to my question, also like the catechism" (Marx and Engels 1956: 121).

5. "I cannot free myself of the impression," Adorno is recorded as saying, "that wherever the dimension of paradox enters it appears in fact to have the function of dulling the edge of social theory" (Tillich 1983: 364). That is a long way from *Minima Moralia*.

6. See, for example, the special issue of *Logos*, previously discussed, devoted to refutations of Spengler, as well as Troeltsch ([1921] 1925).

7. In the absence of detailed records, the reasons for the faculty's opposition to Mannheim must be a matter of conjecture. Yet the question is important for understanding his professional standing. Moreover, a long standard American survey of sociological theory misleadingly maintains that, "Mannheim…is said to have owed his appointment at the University of Frankfort not to his Jewish ancestry but to the fact that he had done much to make Marxism *salonfähig*, i.e., socially and intellectually respectable" (Becker and Barnes [1938, III:924]).

Mannheim's personnel file at the Johann-Wolfgang-Goethe University (UF) has only been made available to us in small part, but from the available correspondence it seems clear that the Prussian ministry, initially on the urgings of Emil Lederer, vigorously pushed the case for offering the professorship to Mannheim over the strong and repeated objections of the faculty. On September 7, 1929, the head of the faculty writes to Professor Windelband, the competent official at the Ministry, to say that the faculty had agreed that they would want a legal sociologist if the economic historian Lederer is unavailable, and reaffirmed their earlier decision about rejecting Mannheim and Adolf Löwe, whom Lederer had nominated as his associates. The reply from Windelband says that Lederer has indeed declined, and that the head of the division in the Ministry wants to discuss the situation with Arndt in person (September 28, 1929). Before the date set for the meeting, however, the ministry official preemptorily asked the faculty "to express itself" as soon as possible on the question of calling Mannheim to the professorship. A letter from the faculty's representative on November 27, 1929, alludes to a verbal conversation and to an enclosed copy of a formal reply to the letter concerning Mannheim. This copy was not released to us by the university archivist, but its point can be inferred from the closing remarks in the covering letter: "I will only add, if I may, that we have in the meantime heard from a South-German colleague, who was recently present at a lecture by Professor (sic) Mannheim, that this lecture was simply incomprehensible to him. That is also what would happen to our students."

It is known that the faculty was then allowed to offer the position to Hans Kelsen before finally making the offer to Mannheim. There is also reliable evidence that Mannheim secured support other than that of the Ministry. An undated page in Mannheim's handwriting included in his personnel file, apparently from a letter seeking to improve his pension after his forced "retirement" in 1933 (or, possibly, towards the end of his life in connection with claims for reparations), indignantly rejects the implication that his appointment was in any sense a political one. He presses the Rector to find the passage in the minutes of the faculty where he is proposed as first choice, after the "list of jurists is turned down." He also claims that, as far as he knows, the Minister proposed him because he was put ahead of all other candidates in a recommendation from the German Sociological Society. "In this time of rumors," he concludes, "I must emphatically insist on the elimination of all the irresponsibly broadcast talk, that my appointment could be considered as a political one." There is nothing discreditable to

Mannheim in having earned the confidence of officials in the two state government(s) most consistently faithful to the democratic constitution. Carl Heinrich Becker, the Prussian Minister of Culture was a powerful personality, generally close to the labor movement. At first a high official and then the Minister, he played a leading role in establishing the *Akademie der Arbeit*—a university-level training institute for trade union functionaries originally proposed by the Social Democratic labor lawyer, Hugo Sinzheimer—and in that case too it was necessary to put a good deal of pressure on the University of Frankfurt to make it possible. See Antrick (1966:147). Becker is also known as the only one of the state ministers to have attempted to counter the National Socialist takeover of the university student organizations. See Bracher (1960:147). On the evidence available, however, we cannot question the good faith of the Frankfurt faculty's initial opposition to Mannheim, especially since their eagerness to appoint either

Lederer on Kelsen shows that they did not object to him on political or ethnic grounds.

8. Hans Gerth is a principal exception. Described by Löwenthal as "perhaps the most intelligent" of the Heidelberg circle, he followed Mannheim to Frankfurt, developed his dissertation faithfully out of Mannheim's "Liberalism" seminar, and then in 1937 followed him into exile, although himself neither Jewish nor politically exposed (Greffrath 1979; Gerth [1935] 1976).

9. In partial analogy, manifesting another aspect of Mannheim's competition with Marxism, the "gentleman" assumes importance in Mannheim's English writings as both obstacle to and surrogate for the rise of an intelligentsia to socially strategic positions.

10. The list includes dissertations formally completed under Mannheim's successors but indisputably products of Mannheim's seminar. See Honegger 1994: 74–80. Honegger's research was first reported in an internal publication of the Frankfurt Social Science Faculty (Honegger 1990).

11. The Heidelberg Institute for Social and Political Science, co-directed by Alfred Weber, Emil Lederer, and Carl Brinkmann, initially received $2500 from the Laura Spelman Rockefeller Memorial in 1926 to build up a library that the Fund's German representative described, in a 1928 letter endorsing a preliminary inquiry about major funding, as "the best library in Germany for the fields of social sciences (LSRM/III/6/54/580)." The Institute's subsequent prospectus for a "research program aiming at a multilateral analysis of the economic future of Europe," incidentally listing Mannheim among the teachers of the Institute, earned it a massive $60,000 for five years (LSRM/III/6/54), an award that was continued and slightly supplemented when the social science program was transferred to the Rockefeller Foundation. The second principal German beneficiary of Rockefeller support was the Institute of Economics at Kiel, where Mannheim's close friend Adolf Löwe was active before his call to Frankfurt. Mannheim accordingly must have been familiar with the Foundation's preferences and practices by the time he headed the Sociological Seminar at Frankfurt.

12. The passage is quoted from "Suggestions for a German Trip" prepared by the head of the Paris office for a New York officer on May 31, 1932. Van Sickles reports that he is summarizing a "long report" he received from Mannheim, after missing him during a Frankfurt visit the preceding year. Describing the *Institut für Sozialforschung* in the same document, by the way, the author says, "Originally its research program was confined to a study of the labour movement. With the coming of Horkheimer, however, the program has been broadened and a promising start has been made in inductive research as opposed to philosophical speculation." See also "Social Sciences in Germany" (RF/1.1/717/20/186: 19).

13. The account of the Frankfurt seminar is from a letter by W.Baldamus, November 22, 1979 (WB); see also the preface by Ulrich Hermann to Gerth [1935] 1976: 9. The quotation is from Löwe 1935: 33, 152.

14. This passage is from one of the sections added after the publication of the earlier German edition, to be discussed below.

15. Heimann and Mannheim's letters are in the Tillich Archives (PT), and both evidently intended that they should go to him and to the others. Heimann assumes that Mannheim is familiar with some of the exchanges, but there is no evidence of other direct participation by Mannheim in this correspondence, whose regular participants were, in addition to Heimann, Gerhardt Colm, Arnold Wolfers,

Alexander Rüstow, and Adolf Löwe, who was Mannheim's friend and collaborator in the last years in Germany and the prewar years in England.

16. Jászi's original letter is not available. Mannheim's reply is dated November 8, 1936 and Jászi elaborates his position in a response, undated but identified as written at the beginning of the Christmas vacation, presumably in 1936 (CUL). Jászi's critique of Mannheim belongs in the context of Jászi's active participation since the late 1920s in the campaign against the commonplace American correlation of liberalism, science, and relativism (Gunnell 1993: 103, 135, 164-5).

17. Leo Lowenthal cites the editorial decision not to print this essay at the time in the *Zeitschrift für Sozialforschung* as proof that Horkheimer and Adorno did not run the journal as a purely personal vehicle (Lowenthal 1987: 209).

18. The last phrase has been retranslated, to conform more closely to the German text available to Heimann and Adorno. The later English version concludes, "breaking up the social order by lack of planning," rendering the meaning of the whole mysterious indeed. Cp.Mannheim 1935: 40

6

Diagnosis of Crisis

Mannheim's dismissal from Frankfurt and flight from Germany gave new urgency to the changes in his social thought underway since 1930. When he had come to Germany in 1919, he was disturbed by his emigration from Hungary, but he was a connoisseur of German philosophy and culture, at home in the language, well-connected, and quickly appreciated in Heidelberg. In England, Mannheim arrived as a refugee bearing unwelcome news of a catastrophic crisis, expressed in an idiom that appeared alien and overwrought to an academic community prepared, at most, to offer him asylum. To convey his urgency and legitimate his claim to speak, Mannheim turned to a medical image. In a note for his files, he lists himself along with other social thinkers, including Freud, Durkheim, Ortega y Gasset, Max and Alfred Weber, and John Dewey, under the key words, "Diagnostic Sociology, Diagnosis, eine Prognosis, eine Cure, Education" (KMP). The sociology of knowledge ceases to be central to his methodology. Mannheim reconceptualizes his mission. No longer a mediator who orients politically creative actors and fosters tendencies towards synthesis, the social thinker becomes a sociotherapist, who clinically analyzes social disorders, devises therapeutic regimes, and overcomes the inhibitions and distortions that hamper remedial action.

In a lecture reacting to the shock of political events and personal exile, given in September 1933 in the Netherlands, Mannheim introduces the concept of "socioanalysis" as a method for coping with the massive irrationalities symptomized by the Nazi triumph:

> This should be viewed as a complement to psychoanalysis. While the latter breaks the whole field of phenomena down into elements which it then studies, socioanalysis, in contrast, attempts to uncover the connection between phenomena and their contexts, the structure of the situation. Its objective is not only education

147

> but also therapy, especially for social pathologies. It seeks to achieve this by analysis and illumination of the situation. While psychoanalysis penetrates to the unconscious and subconscious, socioanalysis is concerned with the semiconscious, where there are also processes that profoundly affect people. (Mannheim 1934a:39)[1]

This conception, with its implicit distinction between pathological and healthy states of societies as well as individuals, epitomizes Mannheim's growing conviction that ordinary thinking has proved incapable of providing orientation in the current situation and that extraordinary, methodically acquired knowledge is needed to offer enlightenment and restore rationality to social conduct. The new belief also entails a standard of judgment more discriminating than historical success or a people's gratified sense of unity in dynamic movement. Mannheim moves closer to the liberal appeal to reason and liberal standards of individual personality and responsibility. More reminiscent of Durkheim than Max Weber, however, he treats these liberal themes as *sociological* problems and *collective* tasks. And, in express agreement with Freud, he postulates direct therapeutic effects for the acquisition of knowledge. In a Dutch university lecture program in 1934 jointly designed by the two friends, Löwe lectured on "the reconstruction of the *economy*," while Mannheim envisioned "the reconstruction of *man*."[2]

This ambitious objective introduces a new ambiguity into his theory. Mannheim was not only shaken by Hitler's success, but impressed. He felt compelled to revise his earlier contention that fascist social psychological mastery is a trick without lasting effects. Hitler had seen something right, after all, and his knowledge gave him control. Mannheim sought to crack the mystery of Hitler's success. Accordingly, he asks, first, how far the desires of "mass-man" can be reconstructed by propaganda and, second, whether there are individualizing forces in society that can be therapeutically enlisted against the sway of "mass-man." In moving toward his new emphasis on "planning," Mannheim shifts from a conception of knowledge with a catalytic function towards a knowledge instrumental for control. This knowledge is not designed, as before, to inform a revitalized political process; it belongs to members of a planning elite and must be deliberately applied by them. The healing of society, it now appears, requires supercession of politics by a novel mode of coordinating human conduct in spheres not yet rationalized, a mode that dispenses with conflict and competition. Mannheim shows no confidence in the recuperative powers of the social process, as it has functioned in history. "Reconstruction," in short, requires a way of knowing that will show how to manipulate mass populations before attempting to transmute them into more rational actors (Mannheim 1940:223).

Mannheim characterizes this new type of knowledge as product of an evolutionary scheme, "thought at the level of planning" coming latest in a series that had earlier moved from "the level of chance discovery" to "the level of invention." Reflecting the cooperation between himself and Löwe, he takes Adam Smith's economic theory as a model of thought at the level of invention. Smith, Mannheim maintains, abstracts an autonomous cycle of causes from the complexity of historical social life and subsumes each of the elements to principles of the highest generality. This type of thinking, he claims, is appropriate to a stage of historical development in which rational conduct requires mastery of the various internal requirements of diverse subsystems comprising a society that leaves several spheres unrationalized. The social system is integrated by automatic social processes.

But when increased "density" of social events makes the subsystems interdependent at decisive points, Mannheim contends, thought at the level of invention becomes anachronistic. Economic processes, for example, are intimately affected by political processes when workers demand "political wages," industry organizes in government-supported cartels, and the psychology of social expectations undergoes changes that render assumptions of *ceteris paribus* in classical economics hopelessly misleading. Correspondingly, the controls exercised in one subsystem directly influence processes assigned by the older thinking to another. The leaders of trade unions or the directors of cartels, for example, control institutions whose actions can render the decisions and designs of government irrelevant. Under these changed conditions, thinking must be able to comprehend interdependences if it is to perform its function of expanding the "radius of foresight" to the full extent of the "radius of action," enabling actors to understand the consequences of their actions and to take responsibility for them.

Weimar Germany illustrates the inadequacies Mannheim saw in linear methods. Economists projected consequences from relations among borrowing, capital formation, investment, wages, and prices; jurists analyzed transformations in the character and uses of law; political scientists explored patterns of interest group alliance and contestation; political sociologists grasped structural shifts in political belief and loyalty; and cultural sociologists observed changes in the social organization of cultural life. But the ensemble of changes produced novel, clashing mass political movements: towards proletarian revolution; towards regroupment of rational social forces imbued with a new realism; and towards fascist exploitation of mass disorientation, social uncertainty and fanatical determination among minorities with nothing to lose. Only an integrative "social" psychology, Mannheim thought, could have comprehended the whole. As with "cultural" and "political" sociology in earlier phases of his work, Mannheim attempts to transmute the familiar labels for a disciplinary subcategory into an adjective identifying a qualitatively new pursuit. To be "social," psychology must achieve a novel cognitive relationship to a subject matter it recognizes as novel. It is a new way of knowing.

"Thought at the level of planning" grasps what Mannheim called "*principia media*," that is, the interacting causes constituting a "situation" that, in its entirety, conditions the effects of any causal chain comprehensible by "thought at the level of invention." No such conjuncture of causes permits of unequivocal interpretation or prediction. *Principia media* are too complex, and their constituent interaction of factors can generate unprecedented novelties. Planning, then, must be satisfied with discerning "trends" and even accept the likelihood of conflicting trend lines. Narrative history also looks at a multiplicity of factors and possible outcomes, but "thought at the level of planning" is different in kind. Instead of an epic drama in which individual actors struggle with one another against a fixed backdrop, it reveals a structure of alternative emerging possibilities and comprehends the variables determining the relative probabilities among them.

Mannheim links the mode of thinking that can read *principia media* to planning because he treats all knowledge as a function of conduct and links the new level to new social capabilities for strategic interventions in situations. The capabilities already exist, but they are misunderstood and misapplied. In the last years of Weimar, for example, government and business pursued orthodox economic policies, expecting natural social forces to adjust the economic subsystem. They persisted in specialized thinking, along lines of separate social subsystems. They failed to realize that their actions would have consequences on noneconomic processes and that the reactions of the latter would prevent the economic adjustments expected. An economically orthodox decision to close factories, for example, made by the management of cartelized industries dependent on the state for supplies and markets, weakened the trade unions collaborating with them in the neocorporatist processes typical of Weimar and strengthened communist and fascist competitors of those organizations. No economic theory can comprehend the interplay of forces in postliberal society. In the event, Mannheim notes, such effects rendered the designs of key actors vain and created the opening for a strategy of social conquest, ruthlessly executed by mobile outsider groups.

Mannheim was convinced that the Nazis won power in 1933 because they had planned and because they had sensed the potency of a "group strategy" based on social psychology. An alternative to their domination requires effective competition for those intellectual weapons. Social psychology is so essential for grasping the *principia media* of the present age because the situation is defined, above all, by the unexpected breakdown of structures of rationality, the explosive eruption of mass irrationalities in a setting of social indecision. No design for economic planning can proceed without intermeshing with the present state of group-expectations and motivations. Reconstructing the economy requires reconstructing the human actors who operate it, and this requires planful therapeutic encounters with them, in their social identities and locations.

There is no alternative, Mannheim believes: people are bound to be planned in a world where there is too little social space for learning by trial and error, too little distance for spontaneity, too much crowding among masses and events. The only question is whether they will be planned for irrational feelings, mindless obedience, and destructive actions, or whether it will prove possible to put a collective social capacity for realistic judgment and measured conduct in place of individualized rationalities gone forever.

In discussing the achievability of such planning, Mannheim returns to the expositional device familiar from his earlier work. He presents the design he is propounding as already implicit in the work of contemporaries. He claims for himself the vision to see what they are about:

Apart from the cloistered systems of philosophy which merely sum up the results of past ages, there has always been another type, that of the pioneer who produced principles which at the next stage of social development were to become important tools of research, and set up the frame of reference into which specialists were later to insert the details. Seeking to follow this example, it seems to be our task to pick out the factors unconsciously at work in the empirical researches now under way, i.e., to demonstrate that in the scattered and apparently isolated philosophical, psychological, and educational tendencies of recent years, the will to plan is everywhere at work, though in most cases it has not yet become conscious. (Mannheim 1940: 223)

The three intellectual tendencies reviewed by Mannheim are pragmatism, behaviorism, and psychoanalysis. Reserving John Dewey for subtler appreciation, he concludes that pragmatist instrumentalism offers insight into connections between thought and action but fails to distinguish the diverse social forms of action that require thought. Accordingly, pragmatism fails to understand the thinking at work in planning. Thought at the level of planning orients groups for actions of many kinds. It differs fundamentally from the self-understanding of individual actors calculating the most efficient means of achieving discrete tasks in the complex division of labor. Rootedness in the considerations affecting group actions, including problems of style, identity, and cohesiveness, is essential if the thinking is to grasp the effects of the interdependent activities.

Mannheim's argument recalls his earlier political conception of the sociology of knowledge. But he adds remarkable new claims about the transformation to be achieved by transcending the limits of individual social locations:

> [Comprehensive thinking] only becomes possible if a new type of self-observation corresponding to the level of planning is developed. This new attitude consists in the fact that...the individual is able to perceive not only all the relevant facts and all the relevant ways of looking at things (ultimately he must perceive them if he is to avoid destruction), but he also becomes capable of seeing his special position in the social process, and of understanding that his thought is shaped by his position. New possibilities of planning now arise which hitherto were difficult to conceive, even theoretically. The individual not only attains a knowledge of himself but he can learn to understand the factors that determine his conduct, and can thus even attempt to regulate them.... His understanding still remains a product of the historical process which arose independently of him. But through his understanding of this determination the individual for the first time raises himself above the historical process—which now, more than ever before, becomes subject to his own power. (Mannheim 1940:212-13)

It is difficult to assess such utopian projections, since much is left unclear. Does this promised omniscience and omnipotence, for example, belong to an elite of reflective planners or equally to all individuals or to the human race? The passage can only be read as rhetorical invocation of the ancient vision of reason commanding the world of accident and change, revealing the memories and aspirations Mannheim hopes to enlist in his case for social reconstruction. He is using the conception of a sociology of knowledge, originally shaped by recognition that the self-certainties of Enlightenment rationalism cannot be sustained, to imagine just such omnicompetent consciousness. The intellectual exercises he had earlier proposed as a method for gaining entrance to the reason immanent in history postulated by the regulative ideal of his historicism, are now supposed to achieve a rational transcendence of history. But it may be misleading to characterize Mannheim's rhetorical turns in the language of philosophical idealism. More to the point is the Baconian conception of a state of mind that has overcome the "idols" obstructing knowledge and is prepared to use the correct scientific method: "planning" and not the sociology of knowledge now is to serve as "organon." Notwithstanding declamations reminiscent of *New Atlantis*, Mannheim's strategies for planned change depend less on total transfigurations of consciousness than on the application of mundane psychological theories, suitably modified to render them more nearly "social."

Mannheim treats behaviorism with marked ambivalence. While he criticizes its indifference to aspects of human personality that can be grasped only by "sympathetic understanding," he respects its power over "external individual behavior." He finds that fascist successes depend on such knowledge and he indicates that planning for the masses newly generated by the disintegration of the old social order must in any case begin with mastery of this type.

To complete the human transformation demanded by the age of planning, however, psychoanalysis is the most promising intellectual current. Yet while it probes deeply enough to get at the structure of personality, it betrays its liberal individualist origins by its indifference to social constituents of identity. The possibilities for incorporating greater social awareness in the approach Mannheim finds prefigured in Erich Fromm and Karen Horney, and, on the strength of their therapeutic innovations, he projects depth-educational work to create the pioneers of the new, planned social design. In this context, Mannheim calls for a reassessment of the achievements of the Enlightenment. What is often dismissed as a naive confidence in "Reason," he now maintains, is better understood as a pathbreaking effort to create a "new social economy in the control of impulses and a new self-conscious guidance of the restraints which are still necessary" (cp. Elias [1939] 1978–82). But these representatives of the effort now underway among the more socially aware psychoanalysts and in "the subtler forms of pragmatism," like that of Dewey, are only precursors (Mannheim 1940:222). The intellectual development must be understood as still unsettled and barely cognizant of the new comprehensive functions needed.

Mannheim admits that behaviorism and psychoanalysis involve radically different scientific methods, theoretical doctrines, and modes of practical application, but he insists that the differences are not decisive:

> Here we can be helped only by interdependent action and thought which make use of both the internal and external approaches in the sense that they combine at every step the transformation of society with the transformation of individual personality. Moreover, as with most theoretical paradoxes, the problem is insoluble [merely] on the level of abstract thinking. The exaggerated consistency of one-sided logical systems of thought tears out of their context things which, if reconciled in action, can be gradually united into a more and more appropriate pattern of conduct. The solution of these theoretical paradoxes is always possible in practice if the carefully thought-out alternatives are used not as final formulae, but as signposts to indicate the possible trends of events. (Mannheim 1940:227–28)

Pragmatism, behaviorism, and psychoanalysis, in short, appear as alternate approximations of the planning appropriate to the present human situation, and they lend themselves to theoretical elaboration and practical experimentation in the struggle against both irrational disruption and its brutal totalitarian social nemesis.

The structure of "planning," taken as a mode of thinking, is thus left indeterminate. Despite his characterization of specialized scientific disciplines as products of a superceded "thought at the level of invention," Mannheim leaves planning dependent on these sciences. "Thought at the level of planning" is a distinctive way of interrelating the lines of analysis generated by the sciences, a way of grasping trends concretely underway in the situations requiring action. His proposal remains programmatic. A method must be developed, he asserts,

> a scientific technique for describing the developing historical process must be worked out. This technique should serve those who are trying to discover existing trends and who are determined to deal with future events in terms of open alternatives, i.e., to approach ambiguous facts with an open mind. (Mannheim 1940:188)

This is a disappointing conclusion, yet Mannheim's perplexities and aporia are not due to idiosyncratic failings. And the project he defines is stronger than his tentative formulations.

Restoring Rationality

Mannheim's attempt to characterize this new way of thinking testifies to continuities in his project. His complex relationship to key texts in the liberal canon is evident in his use of John Stuart Mill's "Logic of the Moral Sciences" as a source of ideas for interrelating the requirements of scientific theory and political practice, universality and history, knowledge and character formation. Mannheim indicates that he is following Mill when he designates the regularities to be comprehended by planning knowledge as *principia media*. Mannheim's contemporary at the London School of Economics, the Austrian refugee economist, Friedrich Hayek, treats Mannheim's work as "one of the best illustrations" of a tendency fatally antithetical to the inherently individualist and universalist moral sciences (Hayek [1941] 1952: 218), but Hayek arrives at his polemical conclusion by disregarding inner conflicts afflicting Liberalism from Mill to Mannheim.[3] The structure of knowledge appropriate to political guidance is a major theoretical site of unresolved difficulties.

Like Mannheim's *principia media*, Mill's "intermediate principles" also designate scientific laws that grasp the tendencies operative in concrete situations, the elements of a "science of human nature in the concrete, and for practical purposes," as well as "the immediate...laws according to which social states generate one another as society advances" (Mill 1881: 599, 640).[4] Mill speaks of "*axiomata media*" or intermediate principles. For Mill, however, there is no question why these principles are termed intermediate. On the one side are the universal principles of the general science of human nature or psychology. Like all genuine sciences, according to Mill, the science of human nature is a deductive system of propositions verified by experiment or observation. Empirical laws derived from experience and relied on by common sense, although untestable by rigorous standards, limit intermediate principles from the other side. The intermediate principles are thus, strictly speaking, corollaries of the universal science. They postulate typical patterns of interaction of factors severally governed by general psychological laws, and are in turn subject to confirmation by empirical laws.

Mannheim lacks Mill's distinction between ethology and the general science of society, both sciences of intermediate principles, but one covering individual character formation and the other inquiring "into the laws of succession and coexistence of the great facts constituting the state of society and civilization at any time." Yet the distinction is unstable in Mill. Ethology proves the more general of the two and serves as the basis of the social science. Mill and Mannheim meet on the common ground of a social psychology that gives, in Mill's words, "a scientific character to the study of politics." Mannheim's convictions are foreshadowed by the criticisms, aspirations, and central metaphor in Mill's statement:

> Students in politics thus attempted to study the pathology and therapeutics of the social body before they had laid the necessary foundations for its physiology; to cure disease without understanding the laws of health...A large proportion of those who have laid claim to the character of philosophic politicians have attempted...to frame universal precepts...a pretension well meriting the ridicule with which it is treated by practitioners, and wholly unsupported by the art to which from the nature of its subject, that of politics must be the most nearly allied. No one now supposes that it is possible that one remedy can cure all diseases, or even the same disease in all constitutions and habits of body. (Mill 1881: 606-7)

Mill's political economy lays claim to be a social-scientific system possessing general validity and grounding universal precepts, thus epitomizing the conception attacked by Löwe and Mannheim in the 1934 Dutch workshops indebted to their Frankfurt Liberalism seminar. But the contrast can be exaggerated. Mill makes it clear that the underlying theory of motives for enrichment and labor holds only under specific limiting conditions. Drastic variations in these conditions require major adjustments in the theory and thus in the political economy grounded on it; and specifiable emergency states of the social organism as a whole render the theory of the economic organ beside the point. When Mannheim and Löwe claim that society has entered a new age in which such an emergency is the norm, they are making a substantive claim Mill never considered, but it is a claim that would not have been methodologically incomprehensible to him.[5] A deeper difference between Mannheim and Mill arises from Mill's methodological individualism, according to which all social phenomena must ultimately be traceable to principles of individual psychology, however compounded those principles are by ethological and sociological *axiomata media*. Mannheim, in contrast, upholds the methodological collectivism of Marx and Durkheim. Sociological relations are analytically irreducible realities. This difference too is less material in theoretical practice than in the respective programs. The logic of the social sciences is complicated for Mill by his fascination with the work of the Saint-Simonians, and especially with August Comte. While he continued to insist on the logical priority of the universal science of human nature, he conceded to Comte that the laws of social statics and dynamics could be uncovered only by refining the "empirical laws" derived from comparative and historical study. In matters of such complexity, the normal order of investigation must be inverted: the universal and individualistic principles of psychology in effect serve only to validate generalizations formulated in terms of the holistic concepts of observed experience. Mill's methodological proposals are closer to Mannheim's practice than are his philosophical principles of logic. Mannheim's interest in Mill's conception of social science is clearly more methodological than philosophical. But the affinities are real and consequential.

This conclusion is challenged by another difficulty uncovered by the comparison between Mill and Mannheim. The concept of intermediate principles is contested between Mill and Comte, and Mannheim conflates the two senses. The suspicion that Mannheim may be using Mill as a surrogate for Comte profoundly affects the political interpretation of Mannheim's project as oriented to constitutive problems of liberalism. The issue must be explored. Mill and Mannnheim both seek to understand the constitution and transformation of "the spirit of the age," as the young Mill called it; and both think such understanding vital to political diagnosis and therapy. Both classify the understanding of historical tendencies as knowledge of intermediate principles. And in practice they also agree in stating these principles as propositions about a socially constituted human nature. Mannheim, however, is far from clear about his reasons for designating these principles as intermediate. Usually he characterizes them not as corollaries of a basic science in Mill's sense but as products of interdisciplinary study, generated by inquiry into a complex of problems from the perspective of planning, the most comprehensive practice. But Mannheim's account comes close to the use of "intermediate principles" Mill ascribes to Comte, when he moves from the logic of science to the logic of art.

Mill distinguishes, as Mannheim does more perfunctorily, between art and science. Art adds an "original major premise, which asserts that the attainment of a given end is desirable" (Mill 1881: 654) to scientific conclusions appropriate to its aims. When combined with this premise, the findings of the science in question become reasons that justify precepts; the mood changes from indicative to imperative. Despite the intimate connection between art and science, the two differ markedly in method (in the old sense of mode of presentation):

> Art in general consists of the truths of science, arranged in the most convenient order for practice, instead of the order which is most convenient for thought... Art, though it must assume the same general laws (as science), follows them only into such of their detailed consequences as have led to the formation of rules of conduct; and brings together from parts of the field of science most remote from one another, the truths, relating to the production of the different and heterogeneous conditions necessary to each effect which the exigencies of practical life require to be produced. Science, therefore, following one cause to its various effects, while art traces one effect to its multiplied and diversified causes and conditions, there is need of a set of intermediate scientific truths, derived from the higher generalities of science, and destined to serve as the generalia or first principles of the various arts. (Mill 1881: 656)

Mill remarks that Comte had called these "intermediate principles" and had set their attainment as the highest objective of science, to be achieved only in the future. Mill too looks forward to laying out "the general scientific theory of the art, from which its practical methods will follow as corollaries" (Mill 1881: 656), especially in education and politics.

Mannheim's conception of *principia media* combines—or, perhaps, confuses—elements of Mill's two uses, yielding claims about a science of concrete tendencies that will function as a general scientific theory of the art of politics. Alternatively, Mannheim might simply be classed with Comte, as in seminal works by Mannheim's fellow-refugees and contemporaries at the London School of Economics, Friedrich Hayek ([1941] 1952) and Karl Popper [1944] 1951. Much in Mannheim's planning writings approaches a Comtean scheme of a naturalistic developmental theory as grounds for scientific social policy and political judgment. Yet Mannheim had deep reasons for avoiding Comte's closed and powerful system, resistance to which had initiated his intellectual career. The dilemmas and the drama of Mannheim's work are missed if the positivist admixture is taken for the basic design. Liberal themes of freedom, development of personality, and responsible choice are not propagandistic coating, even if they are not successfully integrated into the analysis of "planning for freedom." When examined in the context of constitutive liberal dilemmas, Mannheim's encounter with Mill's *Logic* points to nonscientistic elements in his conception of planned thinking. Mannheim has not wholly abandoned his practice of negotiated mediations.

Mannheim's distance from Comte is evident in his method. To account for knowledge of *principia media*, Mannheim retains from his earlier thinking the idea that the model for adequate practical understanding is thinking "in terms of situations as wholes," and he recalls his earlier use of humanist notions in his elaboration of this concept:

> The distinction between the accumulation of factual knowledge and the capacity for independent judgment, between the mere arrangement of details and their interpretation in terms of a situation, has long been clear in everyday life. This distinction is now becoming the concern of the theorists. A new type of scientific accuracy has taken the problem in hand. At the level of planned thinking, it is for the first time really scientifically possible to "grasp a situation," to be "master of a situation," as the common-sense expression puts it. (Mannheim 1940:236)

Mannheim's invocation of science in this text does not convey the sense present in *Ideology and Utopia,* that the concept "science" gains new meaning when applied in the political domain because political knowledge is unique in structure, ontological base, and function. But the correlative emphasis on "situation" distances Mannheim from positivism. He retains a link between political knowledge and responsible, rational acts of judgment. In principle, at least, the importance Mannheim assigns to "everyday life" and "common-sense knowledge" recalls and promises an egalitarian possibility, beyond the cleavage between elite and mass that he considers central to understanding the crisis of the times. That is ultimately a connection between the notion of sociology as the "basic discipline of the social sciences" and master-science of political practice, and liberal ideas of equality and universal reason.

Mill never bridged the discrepancy between his admiration for Saint-Simon and Comte's uses of historical theories and his commitment to a structure of moral sciences founded on a universal science of individual psychology (Cumming 1969). Mannheim's comparable difficulties implicitly pervade his discussions of *principia media.* He uses a sequence of historical stages to present his case for planning, and he treats his central problem as a function of a distinctive historical constellation. Moreover, he acknowledges parallels between his uses of *principia media* and the conceptions of historicist writers. But he dissociates himself from them. "Superficial insight into [the] character [of *principia media*]," he writes, "has led many thinkers to speak of a special historical logic and has misled them into believing that the individual destiny of each historical epoch is entirely independent of the general laws of events" (Mannheim 1940:177). Dialectical thinkers are not as arbitrary as romantic ones, he maintains, but they are "also inclined to use unscientific methods. In its concrete form, [the dialectic] is mainly inspired by a philosophy of history, which draws its vision of the course of history from the particular aims of certain groups" (Mannheim 1940: 178).

This implicit renewed critique of Marxism does not mean that Mannheim has solved the puzzle whose dialectical treatment by Lukács he once admired. When interrelating *principia media* and generalizing sciences, he draws on the work of his Marxist student, the refugee labor lawyer, Franz L. Neumann. He credits Neumann, along with other jurists writing in the late Weimar years, with having shown that the juristic model Max Weber considers integral to capitalist rationalization "obtains only for the liberal-competitive phase of capitalism." Surprisingly, Mannheim argues that Neumann's thesis illustrates the superimposition of *principia media* knowledge over a universal scientific theory which nevertheless retains its general validity. Mannheim treats the limits of formal rationality in law as a specification of the limiting conditions under which a universally valid theoretical generalization holds, and not, as Mill suggests in his treatment of similar themes in *Representative Government*, using Neumann's counter-examples as evidence that the theory Weber (allegedly) presents as universal is in fact merely an empirical theory, generalized from immediate and limited experience. Mannheim leaves his conception of universal scientific theory opaque.

Mannheim's treatment of Neumann on law would have been clearer if he had construed Weber's theory of formal rationality as a universal solution to the constitutive problems of law in society, in analogy to his collaborator Löwe's reconciliation between classical economic theory and the intermediate principles specifying the social historical conditions under which the universal economic relations appear. Löwe argued that the valid economic laws are empirically predictive only under conditions of an individualist liberal society. Economic analysis must work out, on the other hand, rigorous special theories corresponding to the intermediate principles regulating the contemporary social world, as those principles are supplied by the sociologist (Löwe 1935: 73). If Mannheim means anything comparable by his treatment of Weber's legal theory, he is granting liberal claims that the liberal legal order corresponds to scientific norms, as Löwe does for the economic system. But Mannheim's position remains in fact unresolved.

With his defense of universal theories against historicist challenges, Mannheim wanted to revise his earlier criticisms of Weberian "general sociology," but he had not finished rethinking the relations among the three types of sociology he distinguished. He remained constant in his determination to interpret "situations" as configurations pregnant with alternative historical possibilities, but he sought to enhance the legitimacy of his diagnostic interpretations by construing them also as composites of findings grounded in scientific disciplines. Equally clear is Mannheim's growing command of the sociological literature and his interest in utilizing the professional literature, while avoiding philosophically grounded complications. This attitude has less in common with Mill than it has with Mill's predecessors in the Scottish School of Common Sense (Kettler 1967; Davie 1991: 105).

And quite in the tradition of that school, it is Mannheim's concern with achieving changes in the way people understand and act in public contexts that gives direction to his multiple readings of the situation of his time. Underlying his reassessment of Enlightenment is a new emphasis on the demoralizing and brutalizing effects of disorientation and a corollary conception of the ethical regeneration to be achieved by fostering a conviction that knowledge of the way things are and where they are tending is possible and can be made effective in everyday life. This requires more than a transmission of information. It requires cultivation of the appropriate state of mind. Mannheim's thesis and his written and oral presentations on planning are both conditioned by the rhetorical tasks of creating his audience and giving its members the incentive to listen and the ability to hear. Structurally, his experiments in theory keep returning to the humanistic, Ciceronian designs Mannheim hoped to restore in modern life. The ideal of humanistic cultivation does not disappear from Mannheim's conception of Enlightenment when he turns to sociology. It assumes a new guise.[6]

Mannheim is therefore caught in a modern version of the ancient vicious circle. If the need for planning arises out of the breakdown of the personality type capable of substantive rationality—responsible judgment grounded on balanced reading of the situation—the case for planning requires an audience of just this type. Only the already enlightened, it follows, can be enlightened. Moreover, the personality required must have a public identity, responsibility, and role, since planning comprehends social relations and institutions and not the conduct of personal life alone. Older theorists have developed several strategies for escaping the circle. An attempt may be made to recall members of the audience to a deeper level of their "nature"; or it may be argued that the progress of "history" will bring the appropriate personality structure into being. It is also possible to rely on an analytical move radically distinguishing the logic of inquiry into the rational order of things from the logic of inquiry into practical choice. But Mannheim challenged such theories all of his life. He was drawn instead to theories of "dialectical" transformation of "consciousness" that incorporate and transcend theories of natural order, historical progress, or logical pluralism. Much of Mannheim's work in Germany is informed by experimentation with such theories. Now this strategy too has come under pressure by events, as Mannheim understands them. He does not claim to have solved the dilemma about the interdependence of knowledge and moral development, that had already troubled Mill. Mannheim undertakes to manage the problem by appealing to the urgency of the crisis.

Three Dimensions of Crisis

Adapted from the language of astrology and medicine, the concept of "crisis" becomes influential in the social-diagnostic literature of the late nineteenth and early twentieth centuries. Mannheim's recourse to the *topos* derives from Marxist usage. Seen from this historical perspective, what are ordinarily called "economic" crises, and particularly the culminating "universal" crisis, spell the doom of the social system afflicted by them, but by no means the death of the social organism. The accumulation of crises disrupts established patterns and uses of power, disturbing institutionalized order. Crises engender revolutionary class consciousness, and the final, decisive, universal crisis provides the occasion for the ultimate revolution that will forever purge social life of the affliction attended by crises. Crisis, as it mounts, renders the old constraining grammar of action without effect and facilitates revolutionary renewal. Confusion has a creative side. The disturbances that symptomize the crisis prove themselves indispensible for recovery—as the high fever during the crisis of a disease was thought to "burn out" the disorder. In this Marxist usage, then, crises are understood as harbingers of a new order, radically different from the crisis-ridden one, but they gain this character only when the diagnosis is received as a call to action by forces at once products of the process in crisis and independent of it.

To diagnose a situation as a crisis in this sense conveys a set of meanings: the notion that individual crises prefigure, entail, or symptomize crises in the system as a whole; the idea that crisis threatens catastrophe but also promises salvation; the indication that fulifilment of the promise requires something like death and transfiguration; and the proposition that the crisis must be met by vigorous response. As in all uses of the term, crisis here obviates questions about political choices or "value judgments." The decision of what to work or hope for is implicit in the acceptance of the diagnosis, although there may be disagreements about methods. Whether in an illness, a political venture, an economic process, or the transformation of society, crisis demands immediate, complete, and unambiguous response.

Diagnoses of crisis are a recurrent feature of Mannheim's cultural and sociological writings, and elements taken from the Marxist conception, stripped of economic and revolutionary emphases, occur in his earliest work. But the concept first becomes central in *Ideologie und Utopie*, where the project is defined by the claim that political ideology is in crisis. Mannheim argues that the spread among all groups and parties of the insight that all political knowledge is relative to social location—its character as a congeries of particularistic ideologies—and the disorienting effect of that insight for all groups and parties—as their doctrines are exposed and self-doubt is added to mistrust of all others—creates a crisis that breeds violence and passivity in place of practical political action. But when the knowledge initiated by insight into ideology is taken up by increasingly self-conscious intellectuals, it becomes sociology of knowledge and fosters a science of politics. The sobering effects of the crisis-process itself prepare the groups and parties to renew their dialectical political contestations at a higher level, informed by a reading of the situation provided by the new science. In *Ideologie und Utopie*, Mannheim adopts a military term to epitomize the linkage between his concepts of "situation" and "crisis." The ultimate objective of the sociology of knowledge as organon for a science of politics, he says, is to provide a "situation-briefing" on the crisis (Mannheim [1929] 1952:93).

To see the crisis as situation is to specify its historical place and to recognize its constructive powers. One month before Hitler came to power, Mannheim published a short newspaper article on "The Spiritual Crisis in the Light of Sociology" (Mannheim 1932b). In it, he rejects the "incorrect attitude" of those who interpret the crisis as a purely mental phenomenon and find in it nothing but the "destruction of values." Crises in personal and social life "should not be put under a magic ban or suppressed," he writes. The vital forces they generate must be grasped. It is first necessary to recognize that crises are not a product of thoughts alone but of disorienting changes in people's lives. A survey organized by Mannheim has found that only respondents who report a change in circumstances find themselves in crisis. Vital spiritual processes, he maintains, are decisively influenced by "our attitude...towards them, towards the crisis in our immediate environment and in our society as a whole." False attitudes bring about the "deformations" and "convulsions" that threaten to become habitual and irremediable. Where an incorrect, excessively intellectualistic attitude sees only "decline," Mannheim concludes, perhaps "a new human being" is painfully emerging out of innumerable "petty, exhausting struggles."

The most striking feature of Mannheim's thinking after the Nazi seizure of power is the reality and immediacy of "chaos"; and this changes the meaning of "crisis." In a paper based on his 1933 talks in Holland, "The Crisis of Culture in the Age of Mass-Democracies and Autarchies," Mannheim speaks repeatedly of the prospect of "cultural disintegration," "destruction," and even of "cultural decline" in the sense made notorious by Oswald Spengler (Mannheim 1934b). His later papers do not have such intensity of concern, but they also raise the possibility, unknown in the earlier writings, that the crisis will fuel regressive forces destructive of human civilization and culture. The situation may be resolved through oppressive and dehumanizing forms of totalitarianism. The "crisis" is now not so much a crisis of transformation as a crisis of survival.

This shift, by no means complete, brings Mannheim closer to a conservative use of the term. Mannheim himself once flatly asserted that "the reaction usually plays on fears of chaos" in their social strategy (SP). From this perspective, the crisis is a disruption and threat, and the diagnosis of crisis is a warning addressed to authority and a call to restore order. The disease metaphor points to infected parts to be surgically removed. When Mannheim warns the "elite" against the rise of the "masses," he comes close to such authoritarian themes. But his argument is almost never purely of this kind: progressive and conservative connotations of crisis are compounded, while Mannheim experiments with one or the other emphasis. The insistence on crisis as a pervasive feature of the times is in any case all-embracing.

In *Man and Society in an Age of Reconstruction*, Mannheim finds crisis in three dimensions. Each diagnosis depends on distinct *principia media*, and the situation in the "age of reconstruction" is a structured conjuncture of all three crises, its dynamics further complicated by the fact that some of the trends conducive to crisis counteract one another. Mannheim's concept of planning is correspondingly multilayered and charged with tensions.

There is first the crisis of personality manifested in the loss of substantive rationality. In this dimension mass irrationality must first be countered by external manipulation based on behaviorist social psychology. Qualitative changes leading to a restoration of full personal responsibility are reserved for the exceptions still capable of benefiting from socioanalysis and socially positioned for action able to earn the recognition that renders advances in consciousness more than ephemeral insights. Eventually, Mannheim hopes, organic therapeutic planning will everywhere supercede the mechanical.

Substantive rationality and responsibility are undermined by instrumental rationalization, organizational as well as technical. Among products of this process are instruments of mental control, especially through mass communications, effectively wielded by irrational and irresponsible people. Those who want to reconstitute a responsible personality must overcome powerful opponents also called to *their* mission by the crisis. The planners, although they aspire to more elevating means, must fight these opponents for control of the baser, manipulative means of mental control, and they must themselves refine those means in their struggle for support by the masses. Mannheim is aware of the paradox. Replying respectfully to Oscar Jászi's disapproving review of *Mensch und Gesellschaft*, Mannheim pleads that he is making a final effort to turn the techniques increasingly controlling the world into instruments for salvaging as much as he can for the liberal values he and Jászi share. But soon, he expects, he will join Jászi in Stoic despair (Mannheim to Jászi, November 8, 1936, CUL).

"Who plans the planner?" Mannheim asks at the end of his presentation of the planners' tasks. His treatment of this question is revealing about his adaptation of the crisis model and evocative of the Christian audience he increasingly has in view. He classifies it as a "religious" problem, an expression of the fatalistic thought that our powers are finite, and that events depend on forces that "are beyond our reach and dominate us." Without further comment, he turns to the "realistic and political sense" of the question, "that no one has planned the planners" and that, accordingly, "the planners can recruit themselves only from already existing groups.... Everything will...depend on which of these groups with their existing outlooks will produce the energy, the decisiveness, and the capacity to master the vast social machinery of modern life." His subsequent characterization of the groups is remarkably bare in social reference: "Is it to be those groups in which traces of primitiveness...operate without restraint or those which have, through gradual education, developed their rational and moral capacities so far that they can act not only for a limited group, but also for the whole of society, and bear the responsibility for it?" (Mannheim 1940:74–75). Although only "small minorities" today possess the latter qualities, "the masses always take the form which the creative minorities controlling societies choose to give them." Unlike his theory of the crisis of ideology, which contains a sociological explanation for the intelligentsia called to overcome the impasse, Mannheim's theory of the crisis of substantive rationality has no explanation for the "creative minority." Mannheim concludes with an "open question" and an appeal to the reader to "decide for himself." The crisis of reason is met by an appeal to reason.

While the conception of personality that informs the diagnosis of crisis in the first of the three overlapping and partly conflicting readings of the situation is expressly liberal in antecedents, the central theme of the second diagnosis is closer to a "progressive" conception of crisis. In the crisis attending the obsolescence of liberal social institutions, the forces irreversibly disrupting the liberal order are capable of constituting a new, higher order; and the crisis itself creates the conditions for bringing that reversal about.

According to Mannheim, the distinguishing feature of liberal society is the predominance of "automatic" mechanisms for social integration. The equilibrium automatically reestablished by competition in the market is paradigmatic for similar processes of unplanned order in other social domains, like the balance of powers in internal and international relations, division of labor as a mode of uncoerced cooperation, a balance between status and achievement as criteria for social advancement, and increasing satisfaction of social wants as a function of rising social productivity. The cumulative effect of these mechanisms, however, creates concentrations of power, as well as novel means for participating in the processes, that render the mechanisms ineffective or even destructive. Viewed differently, these positions and aptitudes appear as implicit constituents of a new social order integrated by planning, although they remain uncoordinated or blindly misdirected. The situation manifests too much planning for the liberal order and not enough for the planned society, except where (as in England) some local situation has retarded or (as in Germany) forced the pace of development in symptomatic but inherently unsustainable ways. The capability and the function are already present; their reality puts the social order in crisis; once this reality is recognized and consciously acted on, the crisis will be transcended and a new order can be established.

Because Mannheim's conception does not envision revolutionary conflict and assigns decisive importance to scientific understanding, this crisis of transition has more in common with Comtean positivism than with Marxism. It neglects the fears about mounting irrationality and the disqualification for judgment that preoccupy Mannheim's reflections on the crisis in personality. Totalitarianism loses its unique meaning as a threat, a warning to all modern societies. Instead, it appears as a series of localized events, national societies driven to crude planning experiments by particular circumstances. In this dimension, Mannheim appears complacent.

Mannheim's third characterization of the crisis, in contrast, is his most pessimistic. The crisis in culture threatens the life of the spirit, on which Mannheim had grounded his dialectical readings of crisis during the Weimar years. He had already warned, in 1932, that "democracy of intelligence" may turn into a "democracy of feelings"; now he speaks of the change from a "democracy of the few" to "mass democracy." Mass democratization destroys the social conditions requisite to the work of intellectual elites and thus jeopardizes the ability to generate the knowledge and sensibility needed for cultural renovation. Although the practical coordination of social actors' diverse wills is carried on by political and organizational elites, social and political understanding ultimately depend, according to Mannheim, on the public interpretations created by intellectuals. A crisis in culture therefore ramifies beyond the cultural sphere in the narrow sense. Mannheim distinguishes four processes of "negative democracy" or "negative liberalism" rooted in the cultural sphere.

He maintains that the sheer multiplication of "elites," in numbers and types, cumulatively weakens the leadership function of the elite. Instead of some leading voices in each of the limited number of subsystems in the compartmentalized liberal society, the individual hears diffuse and unmanageably varied signals from many sources. Furthermore, elites are deprived of the distance and exclusiveness needed to give them time and space to work out fully developed conceptions. The tempo of demands and opportunities characteristic of liberal society undergoing negative democratization means that distinctive styles or authoritative models cannot be created. There are only passing fashions. Finally, according to Mannheim, the process of social selection has moved beyond the phase in which the democratic principle of achievement displaced the older principles of aristocratic breeding and wealth—a change that was unsettling but invigorating—and has entered a new phase marked by blindly egalitarian principles like racism, a parody of the old aristocratic principle of blood. This development threatens to destroy the very possibility of culture. Such an unwarranted extension of the struggle against privilege comes about when democratization reaches the hitherto passive lower middle classes. The enfranchisement of the working class had escaped these consequences. The difference is that the lower middle class cannot comprehend the rational development of modern society and bitterly resents the harsh truths revealed by the cultural elites attuned to historical change.

The makeup of the elite is also transformed by the expulsion of the "mobile" and cosmopolitan elements that have provided the dynamic force behind the distinctively modern cultural development since the scholastic renaissance of the Middle Ages. Mannheim gets no closer to an examination of anti-Semitism. Autochthonous elements have been a valuable counterbalance within the cultural elites,[7] but giving them monopoly control is socially regressive, allied to autarchic tendencies in other social spheres, and hostile to culture. Finally, Mannheim contends that the work of cultural elites requires stable cultivated publics to mediate between cultural creators and the general population. He finds, however, that such "organic" publics are dissolved by the fluidity of mass society and that cultural creators become dependent on their ability to agglomerate temporary audiences. This can be done only by creating sensations, or by otherwise appealing to a low common denominator. Mannheim brings this point around to the crucial political domain, to account for the breakdown of the political competition on which his earlier comparatively hopeful prognosis for the crisis of ideology had depended.

In the political sphere:

> there was at the stage of the democracy of the few an intermediate body between
> the broad masses and the elites, as represented, for example, by the more or less
> constant electoral following and the different parties defined by the press. In the
> stage where democracy broadens into mass democracy, the role of those who have
> hitherto been non-voters, and of the younger generation which has not as yet made
> up its mind, becomes much more decisive as a fulcrum in [the] more or less defi-
> nite, political, intermediate groups.... The parties which in liberal mass democ-
> racy strive to attain some importance, turn, for these very reasons, towards these as
> yet unorganized masses and seek by appealing to emotional, irrational symbols, as
> these are understood by social psychology, to influence them in the desired direc-
> tion. (Mannheim 1940:97–98)

Mannheim insists that his reading of the situation is not antidemo-
cratic. The way out of the crisis must not be at the expense of the masses,
by the entrenchment of an irresponsible power. He desiderates some
forms of "organization" that will achieve through planning what earlier
"organic" phases of culture had achieved by tradition or spontaneous
social process. He cites two anticipations of the new development, oddly
juxtaposed: the shift towards organized audiences associated with trade
union-sponsored workers' theater; and the strict organization of its following instituted by the totalitarian parties after their attraction of voluntary adherents brought them to power. Yet Mannheim's theory of the
crisis itself gives little reason to expect such innovations.

The three diagnoses of crises converge on the need for "planning,"
that is, strategic intervention in the situation based on a grasp of its structured interconnections. The trend towards planning apparent in
liberalism's decadence must overcome the trends towards catastrophic
irrationality and the dissolution of culture. In one sense, Mannheim is
convinced that planning is destined to succeed: integrative planning is
inevitable. But the planning may take a perverse form that merely sus-
pends the worst effects of the other two trends, while inadvertently
strengthening their underlying causes. Totalitarian planning has this character, according to Mannheim. The question is how genuinely therapeutic planning can come about.

In the liberal age, spontaneous integrative social mechanisms had
been supplemented by the coordinative effects of parliamentary politics and law. And in his essay on politics as a science, Mannheim had
proposed an alternative conception of politics, as the practical domain
in which novelties are created to address situations not amenable to

the rational analyses of liberalism or to the predictabilities of administration. Neither of these conceptions can explain how the crisis might give way to planning.

Planning is like politics in addressing "situations." But far from treating the similarity as a promise of dynamism in society, Mannheim greets planning as a transition to universal administration. Sounding like one of the bureaucratic conservative ideologists he classified (and implicitly dismissed) in *Ideology and Utopia*, Mannheims asserts that such an administered world "emerges as soon as the social structure passes from the stage of planning into a completely organized state, and as soon as all or most of the historical forces, which have arisen in the struggle, have been brought under control through strategy" (Mannheim 1940:193). History itself appears as the enemy:

> It is also possible that at a later stage all that we now call history, namely the unforeseeable, fateful dominance of uncontrolled social forces, will come to an end. As contrasted with administration, planning is thus a form of conduct still operating within the framework of history. As we understand it, planning is foresight deliberately applied to human affairs, so that the social process is no longer merely the product of conflict and competition. (Mannheim 1940:193)

Mannheim's ideal has become the universal pacification he had once derided as a liberal delusion and as the end of all human striving, and thus of human knowledge as well. It appears as an antiutopian utopia.

In a brief speculation, responding to the challenge from the rightist sociologist Hans Freyer, that there must be a political "will to planning" somewhere if the intellectual conception is to have any effect, Mannheim finds a revealing historical precedent of an end to conflictual politics in the early modern period in Europe. Is it not possible, he wonders, that "there should now emerge, following this great tide of irrationalism, a new readiness to listen to reason," as happened "after the Wars of Religion" in the sixteenth century "when religious fanaticism and irrationality in general were in a certain sense transcended." He concedes that only small elites achieved statesmanlike insights and Machiavellian realpolitik in the earlier case, but he asks whether the masses, destined for disillusionment when their present experiences of communal ecstasy prove false, may not as a result collectively gain such political education. "It should not be forgotten," he adds, "that the labor movement, which is typically rational in its attitude towards the social process, began as a machine-wrecking movement" (Mannheim 1940:198-99).

But this echo of Marxist analysis, implausibly associated with a concept of "masses" expressly designed as an alternative to Marxist expectations about classes as coherent social actors, is little more than a wish. In any case, there is nothing to suggest that the "masses" can initiate political action. At best, they may listen to reason, as directed by postpolitical planners. Mannheim sees no hope in the Marxist model of social transformation through class conflict. He denies that classes are the sole or even primary social actors under condition of mass society, and he rejects the thought that conflict can overcome the crisis. In marked contrast to his earlier thought, competition and conflict now imply chaos.

In *Ideologie und Utopie*, Mannheim's conception of politics is not obsessed by fear of social disintegration. There, without faith in Marxist visions of revolution, he nevertheless emphasizes the value of class conflict. He denies that "progressive" political and social development involve, as romantic critics of liberal progressivism had contended, a mechanical rationalization of the world, abstracted from the deeper authenticities of prerational human experience and hostile to emotion, unpredictability, birth, and creativity. He calls for a new knowledge and synthesis, but he sees these rising from the *Realdialektik* of political conflict, once politics regains spiritual balance through mediation by sociologically aware intellectuals.

Mannheim's diagnosis of a triple crisis in mass society, as it appear to him in exile, vitiates his earlier solution of his central political problem. Spirit, social knowledge, and politics do not work—or no longer work—as he expected. Theory and practice do not mesh. Mannheim had hedged his commitment to the approach he expounded in his essay on politics as a science, as we have seen, and he had cultivated alternative conceptions more modest in their speculative sweep and more narrowly oriented to the academic discipline of sociology. In the mid 1930s, he draws on sociological literature to construct a strategy at least as sweeping in scope as his earlier philosophy of history.

Planning is a concept that interrelates theory and practice, and it is offered as an alternative to merely technological conceptions of applied science. As a comprehensive understanding of "situations," this thinking has an inherent practical capacity, in Mannheim's view, with the knowledge of *principia media* approximating to the science of the political art of which Mill and Comte had spoken. But the theory of planning as a way of thinking fails to explain how theory can turn into practice, how planning can become a way of governing. It is too paradoxical to count on "enlightenment" in any simple sense, when the theoretical explanation for the necessity of change depends so heavily on the experience of mounting irrationality. Mannheim works with the analogy of psychotherapy to explain a knowledge with inherent transformative effects, and he repeatedly invokes the parallel of Socratic questioning, the paradigm of another sort of therapy for another sort of soul. But all these approaches leave unanswered the questions, who plans the planners, who legitimates and installs them as planners? The diagnosis of crisis is not so much meant to answer these questions as it is to avoid them being asked.

Mannheim puts his case frankly, in an essay written just before the war:

> It has often been said that...planning would be possible in the democratic states [only] in the case of war.... [I]n a time of crisis with victory as the goal it would be easy to obtain public recognition of a single purpose and an ultimate value. The question is: Cannot a planned society, especially in the present period of transition, work out a number of vital purposes that are clearly determined by necessity, without the need for war? Thus a problem which may be quite insoluble on the theoretical plane, where all values—at least at the present moment—seem to be relative, can be instantly solved in practice. The philosophical dilemma is considerably simplified by the fact that our whole society finds itself in an almost military state of emergency. (Mannheim 1940:346–47)

Mannheim speaks of the "plane" as "theoretical" and the "dilemma" as "philosophical," like the theoretical inconsistencies between the premises underlying behavioral and psychoanalytical approaches he sought to bypass by the pragmatic injunction to get on with the practical work. But the cases are dissimilar. Here the question is inescapably political as well, since Mannheim's "relativism of values" refers to conflicts among social actors with incompatible demands, not, as in the earlier case, to problems of philosophical method.

Mannheim is well aware that such agreement on common purposes does not in fact exist. The diagnosis of crisis must rhetorically forge the unity presupposed by the thesis of the planned society. The crisis takes the place of revolution in the Marxist approach, objectively as well as subjectively. In its supposed historical reality, it breaks the social resistance to change, and once recognized, it constitutes the actors—the "creative minority"—to bring the change about. The planners, in short, comprise the persons conversant with the crisis. Agreement on the diagnosis of crisis implies agreement on what is necessary, agreement that the emergency is too great for the luxury of disagreement. Crisis sets the priorities of inquiry and the standards for action. It mobilizes the key actors and legitimizes their counsel. If the creation of a synthesis to orient the politics envisioned in *Ideologie und Utopie* requires an intelligentsia to serve as prophetic watchmen, the realization of planning depends on a self-fulfilling prophecy.

Problems of History

As Mannheim moved away from historicism, he increasingly objectified his conception of crisis. His seminal essay on the concept of "thought at the level of planning," *"principia media, "* and the "problem of transforming man" opens with the proposition that "man" has "taken a new step forward, when he can live his own history in the spirit of experiment and create out of the emergent forces of the social process the knowledge and will to shape history itself" (Mannheim 1940:147). This new relationship between human actors and the events of their past and present experience is expounded first through a contrast with the view of history exemplified in "the older epic form of historiography" that "placed the individual man and individual events in the foreground." The "sociological view," in contrast, "sees history as a field of experiment and reform." Corresponding to this view is a new mode of "self-observation" documented in autobiographies. Mannheim contends that the "modern observer...is concerned" with himself mainly insofar as he can use his knowledge of the origins of his psychological defects as a universal remedy for society as a whole." "This form of self-analysis," he maintains, "has a leveling tendency and disregards individual differences because it is concerned with the general aspects of the human personality and its capacity for transformation." Mannheim cites as paradigm the "experimental" life of Saint-Simon, perhaps a model for J.S. Mill's autobiography (Mannheim 1940:148).[8]

In his introduction to *Man and Society in an Age of Reconstruction*, Mannheim drives home the contrast between "epic" and "sociological" readings of self and history. He distinguishes between the "function" of his book in its original German and in the revised English version: in German, it was "an attempt at self-enlightenment, made for the benefit of those who have actually lived through these experiences" and who consequently see "the collapse of liberalism and democracy and the adoption of a totalitarian system" as political developments that entail "a change in the very structure of modern society." Now the book must communicate with a readership "which has only hearsay knowledge of such changes and is still wrapped in an illusion of traditional stability." Such readers are inclined to localize the crisis, to see it as part of the aftermath of the Great War and as similar to the many instances in history when dictatorships have been established "as temporary solutions in an emergency." But if they are to take steps to avoid "the negative aspects of the process" that "were often only bewildered attempts to deal with the concrete difficulties in which these countries were suddenly involved," they must recognize that what is happening in the "danger zone" or the "crisis zone" is a "phase of disintegration" whose symptoms are only postponed in the "countries which still enjoy comparative peace." Timing and intensity belong to history; the process inheres in the structure (Mannheim 1940:3–6). To comprehend the process, it is necessary to move out of historical space and time defined by subjective experience, and to live in the crisis, in the world of social structures in dissolution and reconstruction, and in the objective temporality of phases, transitions, and ages.

Mannheim is aware of the perplexing nature of the interplay of disembodied yet anthropomorphized "forces" and acting "men." He writes:

> Processes are at work...which can only find fulfillment in a new form of planning. As long as the social forces are left to themselves, conflict breaks out just when they are on the point of reaching a solution. But it is due to human inadequacy, and not merely to the social forces themselves, that men fail at the eleventh hour to build these latent tendencies into a workable system. At a certain stage of development it is not enough to leave external trends to themselves; we need a new type of man who can see the right thing to do, and new political groups which will do it.... [Today] there are indications that if the groups engaged in politics still refuse to look beyond their own immediate interests, society will be doomed. At the present stage of events we need a new kind of foresight, a new technique for managing conflicts, together with a psychology, morality, and plan of action in many ways completely different from those which have obtained in the past. It is only by remaking man himself that the reconstruction of society is possible. (Mannheim 1940:14–15)

Since Mannheim also argues that "remaking man" requires the insight and actions of a "new type of man," the problem appears insoluble.

As so often, Mannheim turns to sincere and disarming personal statement. "The writer feels it is better to confess," he says, "that he is only groping his way."

A time will probably come when it will be easy to describe the events in our own lives or in the life of the community, not in narrative form, but in a series of sociological problems and conflicts. To try to translate them into these terms today is like exploring a new country.... This incompleteness...has influenced the form of this book. It is a series of essays.... [H]ere and there contradictory statements have not been reconciled where they seem to express the genuine predicament of our thought.... [If] there is to be a science of politics and of society there must be no obligation to find a definite solution before the time is ripe. (Mannheim 1940:32-33)

Mannheim's apology follows an excuse for the speculative character of his inquiry, which he expects to be criticized by the learned community. He insists that theoretical models are essential in the social sciences and criticizes the emphasis on measurement and the accumulation of facts. "[T]he established sciences unconsciously try to belittle the newcomer," he observes. "[E]very branch of science is expert...at creating inhibitions and defense mechanisms which bar the way to a complete and adequate knowledge of society" (Mannheim 1940:27-28).

The structural discontinuities in Mannheim's work in emigration are not limited to those engendered by the abrupt and shocking turn in German political life, rendering the historical calculation of contesting forces and the projection of a "next step" irrelevant. Nor are they only a question of the disorienting break in cultural life, as the shared cultivation and Weimar spiritual community proved ephemeral, and fellow intellectuals and academic colleagues enthusiastically fell in with the marching ranks. Mannheim also suffered from the requirement of communicating his thoughts in an alien language to people he considered closed to the mode of knowledge he had to offer. In time, he came to pride himself on his success as mediator between cultural traditions and on his acceptance by the community of English scholars and gentlemen, but his method was profoundly affected by the effort at adjustment. While attempting to break through all historical particularism of speaker and audience to a shared condition as social function in a specifiable state of the social system (that is, a crisis), Mannheim also attempted to establish living contact with an English audience in a shared historical setting (that is, the Nazi threat). His works are conditioned by these contradictory responses to the problem of historicity and theory.

Mannheim and British Social Science: Translation Problems

Mannheim's sensitivity to inner connections between cultural variations and the modes of theoretical discourse appropriate to social theory
is already evident in 1917 in his review of *Freiheit und Form* by Ernst
Cassirer. Despite skepticism about some of Cassirer's claims, Mannheim
agrees that the link between "national character" and "intellectual mission" will manifest itself more precisely in the forms than in the contents of intellectual productions. "We come closer to the solution [of this
problem] through style analyses in art and literary history and by examining the distinctive dialectics, the capacity for systems construction,
and the incidence of thought patterns in cognitive acts," he writes
(Mannheim 1917: 409).

Questions about varieties of knowing and about the ways new knowledge depends on authentic grounding in contexts of existing knowledge,
on coparticipation in social projects of knowing, are the stuff of much of
his subsequent work. Sometimes those contexts are conceived as "systematizations," related to, though not identical with, disciplinary frames
of reference, and sometimes they appear as various sociohistorical entities—experiential communities, social classes, generations, groups bound
to a location in the social and historical process. In his ambitious methodological treatise of the mid-1920s, "A sociological theory of culture and
its knowability," Mannheim ([1922–24] 1982:144–288) had distinguished
between abstract and technical knowledge that is universally communicable, translated from language to language and place to place, and the
interpretive identity-defining and action-constituting knowledge rooted
in mutual connectedness and contagion. But the model provides for inter-
communal synthesis, mediated by special strata, open to diverse currents
and able to initiate interactions; and Mannheim's subsequent move towards sociology of knowledge further distances him from the conservative limitation of authentic meanings to "communities," as distinct from
"societies." But there is never any doubt that social knowledge has a deep
rhetorical dimension, and that its validity depends on the resonances and
associations it generates in those addressed. Mannheim's position in his
German work is carefully developed with sympathetic reference to the
present state of the intellectual domain, presenting itself as a reflection on
what is going on, a "following after" and experimental extrapolation, and
ultimately as an offer in a continuing negotiation.

When in 1930 he sent *Ideologie und Utopie* to the American sociologist, Louis Wirth, who had requested the book during a short visit with
Mannheim and eventually oversaw its English translation, Mannheim
writes:

> Since I have experienced in my own case and in that of others how difficult it is for
> a mere examination to do full justice to an investigation which emerges in a differ-
> ent setting, I would ask you, in the spirit of our conversation, not to take a final
> position on our sociological efforts until you have a chance of living with us for a
> while and seeing how we pose scientific problems in the immediate problem con-
> text of our life here. (Mannheim to Wirth, November 17, 1930, LWP/7:11)

For a short time and on rare occasions after his arrival in Germany in
1919, Mannheim had spoken of himself as a Hungarian exile, using his
observations of Germany to clarify his own sense of national identity,
but the self-classification as exile was never more than one of his brief
experiments, altogether replaced—as far as his public and literary per-
sonae are concerned—by complete identification with German cultural
life. In England, however, he presented himself as the refugee, the outsider seeking a haven and bringing in return the wisdom earned by his
sufferings. This mode mixed oddly with the presentation of himself as
the sociologist who commands by profession a knowledge transcending
the surface particularity of historical events. Yet it is the mixture of these
two modes that shapes both manner and matter of his English work.

In Germany, he was satisfied that he could show that the sociology he
represented grew out of and entered into the spirit of intellectual and
political life. His work on conservative thought had that as one of its
major theses, and his vigorous defense of the sociology of knowledge
against charges of "sociologism," as enunciated, for example, by the
influential German Romanist, Ernst Robert Curtius, was precisely its
continuity with the philosophical tradition of the German classics (Curtius
[1929] 1990). His contrasting expectations in England are captured in a
letter to Wirth, July 26, 1933 (LWP/7:11), announcing his acceptance of
a temporary post at the London School of Economics.

Mannheim explains his reasons for not awaiting the outcome of his
discussions with representatives of the "University in Exile," to be associated with the New School of Social Research in New York, before
accepting the opportunity offered in London:[9]

> What was morally and psychologically decisive for me was [Harold] Laski's state-
> ment that it would be my task, in collaboration with [Morris] Ginsberg and him-

self, finally and truly to establish sociology in England. It really is inconceivable that, in a time that can move forward only on the basis of sociological knowledge, a world power like England still rejects this study. You will understand that one would rather go where one has the feeling or the illusion of being needed, and that one is not called simply out of pity for one's troubles.

He fears that Laski is too optimistic. The chances for success are slight. "To me England seems too self-assured a country," he writes, "and the intellectuals too little unsettled, to question their academic philosophical, historical, and aesthetic conventions and to see that life is urgently forcing us to confront novel questions."

Mannheim writes Wirth that while an immediate move to the United States might enable him to resume his interrupted work, he feels obliged to stay in England for a while. He speaks of a "task I consider a mission: to study, together with younger scholars, the forces that have already ruined Germany and that will destroy the entire world, if we do not rise to them." But that these efforts will be received as contributions to social science is doubtful, he concludes, because the English academic atmosphere is thick with smugness and very few recognize that only immeasurable effort can preserve the cultured world from destruction.

Before Mannheim arrived in England he had initiated a strategy to regain a measure of independent standing.[10] He had asked the Rockefeller Foundation to finance a research project that would put him at the head of a team of prominent exiled social scientists, assisted by his best Frankfurt students. Mannheim requested $50,000 to fund an interdisciplinary collaborative study of "The Sociological Causes of the Cultural Crisis in the Era of Mass-Democracies and Autarchies" (RF/RG1.1/401S/73/969). Two comparisons indicate the audacious scale of Mannheim's request. In November 1933, John Van Sickle of the Paris office of the Rockefeller Foundation recommended a three-year grant of $10,000 to permit Alfred Weber and Arnold Bergsträsser to complete extensive research begun at the Heidelberg *Institut für Sozial-und Staatswissenschaften* in 1928 with a Laura Spelman Rockefeller Memorial grant. Fifteen or more monographs would be supported (RF/LSRM III/6/54). The Rockefeller Foundation considered an award of $100,000 to the London School of Economics in 1938, to help the new director, Carr-Saunders, initiate changes they strongly endorsed (RF/1.1/401/71/945). Mannheim sought a formidable, institution-building, amount of money.

The urgent occasion for study, he writes to the Rockefeller Foundation, is the conjunction between an "era of the most highly perfected technical rationalization and planning" and social-political forces that will, if unchecked, "lead to the dissolution of all forms of culture and a universal reversion to barbarism." His "sociological investigation into the social conditions for the growth and existence of 'culture'" is designed to uncover "the clue to the remedial measures needed" to direct the unavertable shift to the planning of culture not "according to the preconceived patterns of the various political groups" but according to knowledge capable of halting the abandonment of the "common Christian-humanitarian basis of Western society." The central analytical figures are the distinctions between unplanned and planned sectors of society and the correlate conceptions of elite and mass; and Mannheim's leading idea, as in his subsequent published writings, is that developments in the unplanned sector have led to destructive changes in function of liberal nonintervention, undermining the structured reproduction of cultural elites and their publics in favor of a vicious symbiosis of leaders and masses. What emerges perhaps more clearly here than in some of Mannheim's later writings is that his distinctive contribution to the widespread confident advocacy of planning was intended to be the planned reconstitution of an intellectual elite dedicated to high culture, albeit democratic in recruitment. This engagement with the central problem in John Stuart Mill's *On Liberty*, subjecting Mill's response to new tests of "time and place," helps explain Mannheim's subsequent relations with continuators of the culturally conservative strand in English liberalism. The research aims to integrate historical, comparative, and empirical studies of social mechanisms of elite (de)formation, with the sociologist functioning as coordinator of an interdisciplinary team.

The proposal was discussed several times with Rockefeller Foundation officers in Paris and submitted in several drafts. The version preserved in the Rockefeller Foundation archives is the subject of correspondence between Paris and New York in May 1934, but Mannheim already tells Siegfried Kracauer on June 30, 1933 about a possible trip to Paris "in a few days" to discuss implementation of a "plan" likely to provide employment to emigré social researchers like him (DL). The Paris officer of the Social Science Division forwarded an extensive and generally favorable report to New York on the project almost a year later (RF/RG1.1/401S/73/969), triggered by a Mannheim

visit in May 1934, and based on a twenty-one-page draft that he describes as already "in our files." A letter from Mannheim to Van Sickle
on May 10, 1934 a few days later implies prior negotiations by pointedly referring to "our most recent conversation" about the scheme. To
increase prospects, Mannheim reshapes his proposal:

> I have thought over the various possibilities of the design again and have con-
> cluded that if one wants to achieve an objective that one can stand behind with full
> responsibility, this must perhaps start out at an intermediate level. A radically
> shrunken minimum would make it impossible to enlist valuable forces, and too
> broad an attack runs the risk of over-organization. I feel that the healthiest would
> be to enter the project in stages, so that semester by semester I could promote and
> supervise its growth organically, always subject to your critique. (RF/RG1.1/401S/
> 73/969)

Despite the cautionary concessions in this letter, Mannheim was encouraged by his exchanges with Van Sickle. Writing to Wirth two weeks
later, he takes him into his confidence and diplomatically solicits his
support:

> I have proposed to the Rockefeller Foundation a research plan to bring together
> German, American and English sociologists in a joint task. As I gather from him
> but also from third parties, the head of the European Section of the Rockefeller
> Foundation, Mr. Van Sickle, strongly supports the proposal. If I am not mistaken,
> everything will depend on Mr. Day, the American head of the Rockefeller Founda-
> tion and a Board there. Although I do not think that one should promote one's own
> projects too strenuously, I consider the research so important and urgent that I
> should be sorry to see the undertaking fail because of insufficient understanding. It
> is a matter of analyzing empirically the causes of the crisis of culture and the col-
> lapse of a greater part of international intellectual linkages in the present state of
> society. The problem of the possibilities and modalities of cultural planning is
> touched, as well as the spiritual and psychological construction of the authoritarian
> state, etc.... The question is whether you think it right to enlist some influential
> person close to Day or the Board, or would it be better to let things run their
> course.... I believe I can leave it to your discretion to decide what should be done,
> who might be the right man for such a task, who occupies the key position with
> regard to Day or the Board. It is my quiet hope that this plan will lead me to coop-
> eration with you. (LWP/7:11)

Mannheim was not altogether mistaken. Van Sickle speaks respectfully
of "a proposal of very considerable importance." "I have a feeling," he
writes, after conceding the extraordinary cost, "that Mannheim is on the
track of a problem that is fundamental to any understanding of the international relations of today." The strongest argument in favor of the
project, however, is that Mannheim's staffing scheme "would provide

an excellent type of training for younger [refugee] scholars and help to salvage some of the exceptionally able younger German scholars who have not yet been taken care of." For the interdisciplinary senior staff, Mannheim proposed the psychologist Theodor Reik, the social historian Alfred von Martin, the political scientist Sigmund Neumann, and the legal sociologist, Franz L. Neumann. Mannheim also asked for five "young social scientists," as well as two "observers" in Germany and Russia. Another source adds Ernest K. Bramstedt, Norbert Elias, W. Falk, Hans Gerth, Svend Riemer, and Albert Salomon—all but one former Mannheim students—presumably to fill the junior roles (Woldring 1987: 40). Van Sickle suggests as first step, if New York finds the plan "worthy of further consideration," the selection of a "Consultation Committee" from the LSE faculty members nominated by Mannheim: Bronislaw Malinowski, Eileen Power, Harold Laski, and Morris Ginsberg. But New York was not persuaded.

A minute by Van Sickle dated November 19, 1934 records a decision of the director and assistant director not to "revive" Mannheim's proposal "at this time," indicating that it was rejected earlier. Notwithstanding Mannheim's claims about team research, Day and Walker characterize the project as "an individual piece of research, even though a number of people cooperate in subordinate capacities." Van Sickle draws his own conclusions: "I judge that if it did get under way, Foundation support would not be definitely excluded. Our support, however, would depend upon clear evidence that the undertaking, if more amply financed, would exercise a constructive influence upon the general development of British historical research. It would probably have to come as an institutional proposal. In the meantime no encouragement should be given, and no indication of even this remote possibility" (cp. Greenberg 1985). The casual conduct of the Paris office is evident from a memorandum to Van Sickle from his subordinate, Tracy Kittredge, a month later. Replying to an appeal by Malinowski supporting Mannheim's project, Kittredge ventures, "if a British institution were to become interested in the program and were to present it as part of a general project for development of research in the social sciences, some assistance might later be envisaged." Malinowski responds that he is "particularly interested in Mannheim's proposal" precisely because he thinks that "the whole of the sociological program of the London School of Economics needs reconstruction," and that Mannheim's proposal might provide a focus for research (RF/RG1.1/401S/73/969).[11]

Malinowski was unique among LSE social scientists in his consistent support of Mannheim. After a promising beginning, with a warm welcome from Harold Laski and Morris Ginsberg, Mannheim's attempts to secure recognition of his work from colleagues in his academic discipline faced greater difficulties in England than in Germany. He judged his peers to be unapproachable by his familiar continental philosophical means. Despite some efforts to cast his theoretical design in terms continuous with traditions of political character study and social psychology deriving from John Stuart Mill, he encountered academic resistance or indifference.[12] Mannheim's appeals to the crisis and to the urgency of strategic experimentation found little resonance in university departments.

One connection Mannheim made early was with a mixed group of university teachers and publicists influenced by British positivist traditions, and Mannheim contributed to an anthology called *Human Affairs* published by them (Cattell 1937).[13] In the autobiographical sketch appended to the volume, Mannheim introduces himself as follows:

> Professor Mannheim's studies commenced with History, Literature, and Philosophy. During the post-war period he gradually realized that a satisfactory explanation of changes in human culture could only be obtained through an exhaustive study of society. For this study of society he took as his guide the sociologist Max Weber.... Professor Mannheim's stay in this country has brought home to him at once the urgent need and the great difficulty of translating one culture in terms of another. The best elements in English and German culture, he holds, need to be synthesized. Neither the purely factual approach of the former nor the purely theoretical approach of the latter is in the long run fruitful; the requirement is an integration of both. (Cattell 1937:355)

Mannheim's conviction that British sociology was devoid of theoretical traditions irritated colleagues and signaled his misunderstanding of the discipline's history and controversies. This misunderstanding is especially puzzling since it brought him into direct and avoidable conflict with his colleague, Morris Ginsberg, whose opposition destroyed Mannheim's hopes of helping to "establish sociology" in Britain. Mannheim enjoyed popularity as lecturer among students and publics of socially concerned professionals, but, as he wrote Wirth in 1938, he failed to get "intellectual support" from his peers:

> Here [unlike the USA], it is necessary to quarrel too much with those who are afraid to look new knowledge in the face and to re-learn. This applies above all to my colleague [Morris Ginsberg]...who even wanted to get rid of me, out of fear

for his way of pursuing a sociology distant from life. (Mannheim to Wirth, August 13, 1938, LWP/7:11)

Ginsberg's objections to Mannheim's work, however, add up to the contention that Mannheim repeated the worst faults of the vague, speculative, and moralizing sociologism that had historically ruled sociology in Britain until Ginsberg began a campaign to reclaim the discipline from the LePlay House group.[14]

The tensions between Mannheim and Ginsberg are unmistakable in the published record of several conferences held in the mid-1930s to elevate the academic level of British sociology. The British Sociological Society was the first such society in the world, having been founded in 1903 at a conference addressed by Emile Durkheim, but the discipline had been resisted by the universities. Among the founders were Leonard Hobhouse, Patrick Geddes, and Victor Branford—the first two, ingenious innovators with primary interest in the theory and practice of progress, and the latter, a wealthy enthusiast. Institutional continuity derived from the Chair of Sociology, originally endowed for Hobhouse at the heterodox London School of Economics, and from the Institute of Sociology and the *Sociological Review*, subsidized and virtually controlled by Victor and Sybella Branford.

By the time Mannheim came to England, the Branfords had been succeeded by Alexander Farquharson and his wife. "They were passionate admirers of Geddes and Branford," T.H. Marshall has recalled, "and yet anxious to stand well with the 'academics' of London University" (interview, September 1976, AA). The tradition of Geddes and Branford now appeared as a practice of field work and social surveys, initiated by Geddes in implementation of the speculative design he derived from Frederic LePlay, a follower of Auguste Comte. Mannheim criticized the emphasis on local social descriptions in British sociology, equating it with the untheoretical empiricism he presumed to be the core of American sociology, but he appeared unaware of the theoretical antecedents in both cases. Yet Mannheim's own theoretical conceptions must have sounded uncomfortably familiar to social scientists raised up on Branford's call for a "third party" or "third alternative" between capitalism and socialism, with the "town planning" of Geddes as a central feature. Despite the dated language of "spirit" and "evolution," every page of Branford brings anticipations of Mannheim even to a casual reader. Given Mannheim's links to the prewar progressivism of Jászi, this should

occasion no surprise, since most of the early British sociologists belonged to the same general movement of "the new sociology and the
new liberalism" (Abrams 1968:60; cp. Branford 1927).

Neither Geddes nor Branford is mentioned in *Man and Society* or in
Diagnosis of Our Time, and Hobhouse appears only twice, as an after-
thought in footnotes devoted to continental thinkers. Mannheim never
became aware of the difficulty and the consequent need to distinguish his
own position from the tradition Ginsberg and his associates were striving
to supercede. A key opportunity would have been the conferences on the
social sciences held in 1935 and the next two years. Marshall reports:

> After Hobhouse's death [the Farquharsons] won effective control of the Institute
> of Sociology and its Journal and were also running the LePlay Society and its field
> studies (which had also been endowed by Branford). So they had important facili-
> ties to offer to those who wanted to restore the quality enjoyed by the early Socio-
> logical Society and its Papers. Consequently the "academics" made their move to
> gain control of the Journal and to dominate the academic activities of the Institute
> without ousting the Farquharsons. The three Conferences of 1935-7 were an im-
> portant part of this campaign. (Interview, September 1976, AA)

The first of these conferences took place in September of 1935. It was
called, "The Social Sciences: Their Relations in Theory and Teaching,"
and it was opened by an address on "Sociology Today" by the elderly J.A.
Hobson and by a revealing survey on the state of social science, social
studies, or sociology as a field of study in British universities, delivered
by T.H. Marshall. There is a major in sociology at London University and
a field of specialization within the London School Economics degree,
Marshall observes, but that is all, as far as degree-level study is concerned.
Interdisciplinary social science study is distrusted by most specialists and
prevalent only in pre-degree programmes preparing for social work.

> We also notice that the most ambitious schemes of comprehensive social study
> flourish where the general standard of scholarship is elementary. The prevalence
> of this policy suggests that experience has confirmed the view that the best educa-
> tion for the less scholarly minds is found in a stimulating contact with a wide range
> of general ideas. (Marshall 1936)

But such popularization was clearly not what Ginsberg and the other
"academic" sociologists had in mind.

Mannheim's talk, on "The Place of Sociology" (Mannheim 1936b),
pleads for recognition of sociology as "the basic discipline of the social
sciences," aggressively insists on an analogy with the place of biology

in the medical sciences, and characterizes the aim of sociology as "a complete theory of the totality of the social process." Early thinkers speculated prematurely, and modern writers fail if they do not have a "methodological basis," clear concepts, and "the picture of the totality of the social process constantly before us." Max Weber's accomplishments show that the time for sociology is ripe. Mannheim then distinguishes among three "functions" of sociology, the "systematic," "comparative," and "structural." The distinction between the first two is not clearly drawn, as he associates the phenomenological methods that had originally attracted him to systematic sociology with the empirical generalizations that had in earlier years made him skeptical of Weber's comparativism. The account of structural sociology divides it into social statics and social dynamics, quite in the manner of Comte and John Stuart Mill. His examples are conservative: he illustrates social statics by an account of elite controls over passive masses, and social dynamics by the disruptive effects of excessive individualistic striving for advancement, as a function of competition.

Ginsberg's remarks on the same subject (Ginsberg 1936) are not expressly critical of Mannheim. His only substantial reference to him, in fact, is correct and even complimentary. But his presentation is nevertheless a reproach to Mannheim. He begins by distinguishing between ideal statements about sociology and an empirical account of what sociologists do. While both have their uses, he maintains, the former sometimes leads to needless confusion. When general statements are made about tendencies towards sociology in other social sciences, for example, it is worth recalling that both Hobhouse and Westermarck had already spoken of political science as a branch of sociology in their inaugural addresses in 1907. Ginsberg wants to specify the domain of the discipline, while rejecting Simmel and Vierkandt's a priori systems of social relations. The "systematic sociology" discussed by Mannheim can be nothing more than some general statements of findings in comparative sociology; claims about the "direct inspection" characteristic of the "phenomenological method" simply testify to the backward state of social psychology. Although Ginsberg cannot see how anyone can resist Mannheim's "illuminating" case for a synthetic structural sociology, he remarks drily that such learned commentators as Marshall and Sidgwick have nevertheless recently raised interesting questions, as did others when Hobhouse and Durkheim were first making such claims, based on Comte, in 1903. Ginsberg applies only the second of the two tests which Sidgwick proposes, inquiring whether there is a sufficient measure of "consensus" between sociologists as different as Hobhouse and Durkheim to warrant the contention that they are at work on a common enterprise. He concludes:

> [At] bottom the trend towards the organic types of society with the pathological deviations from it which Durkheim describes has much in common with the trends towards harmony which Hobhouse seeks to establish with great caution and with many qualifications. Both are concerned with the problem of reconciling individual autonomy and social order and both find the root difficulty in the imperfection of the organic relation so far achieved. (Ginsberg 1936:205)

Notwithstanding these similarities, Ginsberg finds an important difference. Unlike Hobhouse, Durkheim had claimed that sociology has its own laws *sui generis*. Without express reference to Mannheim's version of this thesis, Ginsberg cooly urges that any such conclusion be withheld until the study of physiology and psychology is much further advanced.

Any doubts remaining that such statements are to remind audiences that the issues so dramatically promulgated by Mannheim as novelties are in fact long-standing problems, well known in England and more carefully developed by others, are dispelled by Ginsberg's contribution to a conference a year later under the same auspices. Lecturing on "Psychology and Sociology" (Ginsberg 1937), he announces his theme as "rational and irrational elements in human behavior," an obvious allusion to Mannheim's just-published Hobhouse Lecture, and opens provocatively with the observation that "the terms 'rational' and 'irrational' are used in a bewildering variety of senses, due probably to the lack of any generally accepted theory of the nature of value judgments." For Ginsberg, the concepts themselves belong to social philosophy, with "rational action" ultimately equivalent to "right action." Rational action is "action which is likely on the best available knowledge to satisfy human needs when these are brought clearly to consciousness, and examined fairly and impartially with reference to all relevant claims and to the means available for their realization" (Ginsberg 1937: 121). Social science presupposes these philosophical analyses when it addresses its own proper subjects, the "psychology of moral life," especially "the reality of moral progress and the part played by reason in it" (Ginsberg 1937:123). The contrast with Mannheim's sociological theses about the crisis of "substantive rationality" engendered by the uncontrolled advance of "instrumental rationality" is stark.

Mannheim had not been scheduled to speak. He remarks, however, that he was asked "on the eve of the last session to take up some of the threads of the discussion," an assignment he shared with T.H. Marshall. Mannheim offers "a few concrete examples concerning the sociological nature of human valuations, with some theoretical remarks on the difference between the psychological and sociological approach" (Mannheim 1937:171). This time, it is his turn to comment on the "illuminating remarks" of his colleague. But Mannheim does not address Ginsberg's distinction between the philosophical and sociological aspects of the problem, although this issue is especially important to Ginsberg and other English thinkers of the time. He turns instead to reflections on consistent differences between the values of fighting and sedentary groups, citing research by Ginsberg, among others. He stops for one of his homilies on method, superfluous and perhaps provocative under the circumstances, since the issues addressed in that research were theoretical, and he notes that while "field observation" is a welcome improvement on "empty armchair speculation," there is, lamentably,

> in this country a tendency to put a premium on pure description, surveys, collections of statistical data, to the exclusion of theoretical and historical analysis of society.... [To] learn from history, we must be able to theorise; otherwise the historical facts mean nothing and cannot even be compared or adequately related. (Mannheim 1937:180)

After listing several vague hypotheses about the relationships between valuations and social factors, Mannheim closes with a reflection on the contrasts between psychological and sociological approaches. He concludes that psychology studies spontaneous expressions of individual drives, and sociology the counteracting constraints structured by "established relationships," understood in terms of their objective functions for society. Instead of explaining why he thinks it mistaken to view the actions constituting the counteracting constraints as expressions of the subjective impulses of the actors, he closes with an example that testifies, even over the distance of six decades, to the strained atmosphere in the hall. A psychologist, he says, would study "the subjective motives which have induced me to waste so much of your time," and he would doubtless come upon "the subjective urge to self-display." The sociologist, in contrast, would emphasize the restraining influence of the chairman, who embodies institutionalized arrangements to meet the needs arising out of a scarcity of time (Mannheim 1937:190). Before an audience of English academics, that disarming gesture, coming at the end of a very long impromptu intervention, undoubtedly failed to be helpful.

According to T.H. Marshall, a colleague of Mannheim at the LSE, the conflict with Ginsberg was so intense because Mannheim never appreciated that his appointment was partly funded by a special collection among the faculty, organized by Lionel Robbins and Lord Beveridge, and consequently not considered permanent or entitling the holders to full participation in collegial academic decisions (interview 1976, AA; cp. Beveridge 1960:236). Until 1938, while Beveridge was director of the London School of Economics, Rockefeller money was willingly used to support Mannheim, first from windfall discretionary funds from the institutional grant to the School and later express allocation (RF/RG1.1/401S/73/969). After a comprehensive review of the School's program initiated by Carr-Saunders as new director, however, the Foundation was repeatedly asked whether it considered the School bound to retain Mannheim and requested to assist in his relocation. The Paris officer of the Rockefeller Foundation summarizes Carr-Saunders' rationale: "The School is more interested now in developing empirical sociology in England and Mannheim has not the particular qualifications necessary for this new orientation.... As indicated by Carr-Saunders, they would certainly carry him for a year or two until he has an opportunity of obtaining another position. They wish, however, to give notice immediately to Mannheim that he cannot expect his position at the school to be indefinitely maintained" (March 31, 1938). The situation was undoubtedly complicated by the conflict between Mannheim and Ginsberg, but Carr-Saunders' attempt to get Rockefeller Foundation help in removing Mannheim to the United States in September 1939, casts doubt on Mannheim's certainty in August 1938 that the matter had been purely a matter of personalities and that his retention meant that his colleagues supported him against Ginsberg because of their "desire for the development of 'up-to-date sociology' in England" (LWP/7:11). Mannheim never achieved a satisfactory settlement at the London School of Economics.

Notes

1. For Mannheim's concept of socio-analysis see also "Mass Education and Group Analysis" (in Mannheim 1943:87).

2. The "Universitaire Leergang" of the "International School for Wijsbegeerte" took place in Amersfoort from September 22-30, 1934. See the announcement in *Amersfoortsche Stemmen* (June 1934:30).Neither the text nor a detailed report of this material has been located, but the descriptive paragraphs in German, printed in the course announcement and probably drafted by the lecturers themselves (AA), make it highly likely that Mannheim's lecture was a preliminary version of the material published as Part III of *Mensch und Gesellschaft im Zeitalter des Umbaus*.

3. Hayek quotes Mannheim on "functionalism" to portray him as an unqualified proponent of a "doctrine of technical supremacy," but he fails to acknowledge that the scattered passages he knits together are excerpted from Mannheim's recapitulation of Romantic, Anti-technicist objections to functionalism, which he credits with offering a criticism that "will preserve its value in the future (Mannheim 1940: 242)." Hayek's critique remains important, but his Manichean intellectual history obscures constitutive problems of modern Liberalism.

4. It should be noted that Mill never uses the Latin expression that Mannheim favors, "*principia media*"; he says "*axiomata media*" or uses the English. But Mannheim's citation of Mill leaves no doubt that he is referring to at least the former of these passages.

5. 4. cp. Löwe 1935:35ff. Compare J.S. Mill on the political choice of "the stationary state": "If the earth must lose that great portion of its pleasantness which it owes to things that the unlimited increase of wealth and population would extirpate from it, for the mere purpose of enabling it to support a larger, but not better or happier population, I sincerely hope, for the sake of posterity, that they will be content to be stationary, long before necessity compels them to it.... Only when, in addition to just institutions, the increase of mankind shall be under the *deliberate guidance of judicious foresight*, can the conquests made from the powers of nature by the intellect and energy of scientific discoverers, become the common property of the species, and the means of improving and elevating the universal lot" (Mill [1844] 1965).

6. Mannheim's hope of peruading proponents of humanistic education that his sociology represents a timely adaptation of the older idea of *Bildung* is documented in his occasional correspondence with Eduard Spranger (BK; Loader 1985: 19, 234-35). Spranger's "humanistic psychology" was an important point of reference for Mannheim's cultural sociology, although Mannheim always reserved his objections to Spranger's "platonizing tendencies" (Mannheim [1921] 1993: 144 n.1). In January 1929, Mannheim visited Spranger to solicit a book for Mannheim's new series. Mannheim wrote Spranger a few months later, having earlier thanked him for his promise of cooperation, to urge Spranger to read the forthcoming *Ideologie und Utopie*. Contrary to the denigration of the spirit in naturalistic sociology, he assures Spranger, his own work is designed to complement the understanding of the spiritual development that is provided by the cultural studies Spranger exemplifies. The social is a mode of the spiritual, Mannheim argues, and a sociological view is not identical with Marxism: "It is not Marxism but a thoroughgoing sociological approach that alone is capable of bringing to full consciousness the situation which breeds the crisis—I would say, with you, the generative crisis—which you have so brilliantly characterized at the level of worldviews" (BK). Mannheim concludes by invoking their close, even fraternal, affinities, and he throws himself on Spranger's judgment, however stern. Unpersuaded, Spranger harshly denounces the "sociologism" of Mannheim's thought when he reviews *Ideologie und Utopie* a year later (Meja and Stehr 1990: 239-40).

7. Mannheim's analysis is reminiscent of his Heidelberg teachings, parodied by his students in "The Clouds" through the antiphonal choruses of "rooted existences" and "deracinated" intellectuals.

8. Mannheim (1940:147–48) draws on Lorenz von Stein. On crisis in Saint-Simon and Comte, see Sombart (1955:55ff). On Mill's *Autobiography* see Cumming (1969).

9. Mannheim's long-time patron, Emil Lederer, among Alvin Johnson's first candidates for the new "University in Exile," came to New York in April 1933. "In New York, Johnson and Lederer quickly came to terms and settled on a preliminary list of faculty. In late June, Johnson accompanied Lederer to London, where they spent nearly a month interviewing prospective faculty members. Besides Lederer, Johnson hoped to appoint Lowe, Marschak and Karl Mannheim.... Marschak and Lowe, who believed that the regime would crumble in a relatively short time, preferred to find positions in England...Karl Mannheim likewise preferred to remain in England. Johnson seemed almost relieved at Mannheim's decision, since Mannheim had insisted that the New School create a school of social thought that revolved around his own ideas. In Johnson's words, Mannheim wanted to be 'the whole show.' Johnson clearly disliked this attitude, but he could not resist someone of Mannheim's prestige" (Rutkoff and Scott 1986: 99–100; cp. Krohn 1987: 74f). Rutkoff and Scott (1986: 276n70) add that "Johnson is polite on this his Pioneer's Progress, but elsewhere the facts are quite clear." Mannheim's defection was costly to him, and he felt he had to find others to take Mannheim's place. See Johnson to MacIver (April 10, 1957, AJP).

10. In an unexplained episode that may represent an effort at negotiating the terms of a London appointment, Mannheim gave his Frankfurt "scientific secretary" leave in March, 1933, to attend the London School of Economics (Kuckhoff 1972). A GDR biographical reference work asserts that she "prepared the way for Karl Mannheim's emigration." Her memoir says only that she returned to Germany in May, surrendering to an ultimatum from her lover. She had drawn close to the Communist party in the last months before Hitler's accession to power and spent most of the Nazi period as a translator—including work on *Mein Kampf*. She was arrested in 1942, sentenced to death but reprieved, and lived to occupy various governmental offices in the GDR, the last as president of the German Bank of Issue [Deutsche Notenbank].

11. As with the social science faculty in Frankfurt in 1929, Mannheim's approaches to the Rockefeller Foundation and other American agencies of the institutionalized discipline were burdened by his reputation as insufficiently inductive in method. Joseph A. Schumpeter included him in the select list of nine exiles he urged the Rockefeller Foundation to bring to the United States, the first plea of that kind received by the Foundation in April 1933, but he too characterizes him as "the leading exponent of that typically German kind of sociology which verges towards philosophy" and tinges his recommendation with reservations: "whatever one's opinion about the value of this line of thought, it may be useful and interesting to have that exponent of it in the country" (RF/RG2-1933/717/91/724). Mannheim's cultural crisis research proposal, like his earlier communications with Rockefeller representatives in Germany, stressed his determination to incorporate the "empirical verification" methods "admirably worked out in America," but he may well have dissipated some of the effect of his avowals when adding that "their full value, however, can be realised only if one possesses the theoretical ability of interpreting the data which they provide as a functional unity, and when the significance of the historical-locational value has been worked

out." While there is no documentary evidence that misgivings about Mannheim's qualifications as empiricist figured in the rejection of a proposal that was in any case unlike anything the Rockefeller Foundation was prepared to do for the social science emigration, the theme is prominent in subsequent correspondence between the London School of Economics and the Foundation about plans to reallocate funds the Foundation had let the school use to subsidize Mannheim.

12. Mannheim was given material recognition during his first year by the opportunity to deliver the Hobhouse Memorial Lecture at the London School of Economics (Mannheim 1934c). The following year, his collaborator, Adolf Löwe, gave a series of lectures at the LSE, published as *Economics and Sociology. A Plea for Cooperation in the Social Sciences* (Löwe 1935). Ginsberg wrote an introduction, welcoming the extension of "ethology" in J.S. Mill's sense to political economy, where Mill had not thought in necessary. Löwe dedicated the work to Karl Mannheim and Franz Oppenheimer. Having cited Mannheim's Hobhouse Lecture together with Max Weber's posthumous political writings published in 1921, Löwe writes: "We have to realize that there is only the choice between an unconscious conception of the whole on the basis of common sense with all its obscure fallacies and prejudices, and a scientific working hypothesis with its obvious insufficiencies which are at least accessible to correction in the face of new and inconsistent facts. Here the synthetic work of sociology has its place. In this task, which is not merely scientific but positively ethical, no substitute for it is possible. Among other things it brings into the light of rational criticism the infinity of traditional preconceptions which ebb and flow about the nature of man, the destiny of mankind.... Contrasting these prejudices with each other and with the scientific results of the competent specialisms, sociology could achieve a work of enlightenment comparable only to the great victory over superstition with regard to nature." In a footnote, Löwe adds: "Here is the main field and true justification of the work the sociology of knowledge has started in recent work. Compare above all the work of Karl Mannheim, in particular his article 'Wissenssoziologie'" (Löwe 1935: 152). Building on the planning concepts he and Mannheim had been developing, Löwe also notes that all signs point to "the time" when "economics will be replaced in its advanced post, perhaps by political science," as "key positions" shift from acquisition to management.

13. Mannnheim's contribution is a draft of what was to become Part V of *Man and Society*, here called "Present Trends in the Building of Society," (Cattell et al. 1937: 278–300). The contributors include J.B.S.Haldane, Lord Raglan, Havelock Ellis, B. Malinowski, William McDougall, and Morris Ginsberg.

14. If the violence of his responses in an interview twenty-five years after the events is any guide, Ginsberg became very hostile to Mannheim. In his later recollections (Interview with Morris Ginsberg, July 1963, AA), he put special emphasis on Mannheim's "facile popularizations," which attracted many undergraduate students, overstimulated them with vast and portentous questions, and left them with no analytical method for doing social research or engaging in philosophical reflection, especially since Mannheim failed to distinguish between sociology and social philosophy. To the credit of both eminent sociologists, their students had no idea of the conflict between them, according to the authoritative testimony of Jean Floud, who was a student of Ginsberg as well as Mannheim's unpaid assistant during the revision of *Ideology and Utopia* and who assisted him on *Man and Society* as well (Interview with Jean Floud, March 1976, AA).

7

American Hopes: The Dispute
over *Ideology and Utopia*

From his first days in London exile, Karl Mannheim maintained that he could continue the work begun in *Ideologie und Utopie* only in the United States. In his letters to Louis Wirth, Mannheim spoke of his planned research on the German catastrophe as an interlude in his work, a crisis-hastened application to current issues of the unfinished sociology of knowledge program (Mannheim to Wirth, May 23, 1934, LWP/ 7:11). His hopes for an American career paralleled his initial skepticism about British prospects:

> I feel confirmed in my views by my conversation with [the American colleague to whom you referred me], who repeatedly said that my concerns speak directly to the American situation, and that I could count on the liveliest interest in both academic and non-academic circles there. Although it is too soon for me to be certain, I consider it highly likely that in an American environment I could simply pick up the work I was forced to abandon in Frankfurt.... I therefore must look at my London appointment in the spirit that governs plans for the [New School for Social Research], viz., as a stepping stone toward something more permanent.... I want to reiterate, even at the risk of sounding immodest, that I am strongly convinced that contact between American sociology and the sociology I am trying to develop will yield something truly productive. (Mannheim to Wirth, June 24, 1933, LWP/7:11)

And he was clearly thinking of the sociology of knowledge as the element in his Frankfurt work to ground his American career. Mannheim promises Wirth that the next mail will include a draft translation of *Ideologie und Utopie* by Paul Kecskemeti, and he indicates in surprise that his German publisher is still prepared to publish his just completed "Sociology of the Spirit [*Geist*]," notwithstanding his status as Jewish outcast.[1] Mannheim's failure to seek later publication for this text or for the two treatises posthumously published as *Structures of Thinking*

(Mannheim [1922–24] 1982) signals his conviction that he could not devote himself to a systematic development of the sociology of knowledge in England.

Mannheim's judgment of his English difficulties affects his treatment of the sociology of knowledge. At times, he seems to have put the study altogether behind him. Just before the war he writes about the need to learn "a new experimental attitude in social affairs," in view of the "practical deterioration of the ideals of Liberalism, Communism, and Fascism." He continues:

> But one can only learn if one has belief in the power of reason. For a time it was healthy to see the limitations of ratio, especially in social affairs. It was healthy to realize that thinking is not powerful if it is severed from the social context and ideas are only strong if they have their social backing, that it is useless to spread ideas which have no real function and are not woven into the social fabric. But this sociological interpretation of ideas may also lead to complete despair, discouraging the individual from thinking about issues which will definitely become the concern of the day. This discouragement of the intelligentsia may lead them to too quick a resignation of their proper function as the thinkers and forerunners of the new society, may become even more disastrous in a social setting where more depends on what the leading elites have in mind than in other periods of history (Mannheim 1940: 365).

The theory of the social determination of ideas properly applied to the present age, Mannheim continues, shows that everything depends on "whether or not sound thinking goes on today and whether it reaches the ruling elites." Elsewhere, of course, his criterion of "healthiness" does yield a function for the sociology of knowledge: it has the therapeutic function of freeing the mind for "sound thinking" from misleading, ideological notions dictated by group egoisms.

The ambivalence and drift of Mannheim's thinking about the sociology of knowledge are manifest in a textual alteration between *Mensch und Gesellschaft* (1935a) and *Man and Society* (1940). In January of 1935, while *Ideology and Utopia* is in preparation, Mannheim solicits Wirth's soliciting his opinion about *Mensch und Gesellschaft*, "and especially about the third part of the book, 'Thought at the Level of Planning,' which is, I feel, a further application of the sociology of knowledge." In the book, Mannheim makes the claim explicit in his exposition of a socially aware psychology. He argues that such psychology cannot take its departure from a theory of universal human nature, but must instead see individual human beings as a function of their situations (*situationsbezogen*). A footnote expands the point: "This is the novelty in our approach, also in the field of logic and in the analysis of concrete human thinking. The point of departure of the 'sociology of knowledge' is the 'connectedness to existence (*Seinsverbundenheit*),' the 'situational determination' (*Situationsgebundenheit*) of thinking— and not 'thinking in general'" (1935a: 164–65). Mannheim refers the reader to his 1931 handbook article on the sociology of knowledge. In the English edition, the footnote is gone, and the text avoids terminology from *Ideology and Utopia*, content with viewing "individual facts and individual human beings in their particular social context as it reflects itself in their character" (1940: 201).

But uncertainties about the sociology of knowledge are balanced by counter-considerations in Mannheim's deliberations about *Ideology and Utopia*. First, even in England his standing as a sociologist and thus his legitimacy as diagnostician of the crisis were founded on the fame of *Ideologie und Utopie* and his sociology of knowledge. In February 1933, Ginsberg had brought Mannheim's article on "Wissenssoziologie" in Vierkandt's *Handwörterbuch der Soziologie* to special notice in a review of several textbooks and handbooks in sociology. Aligning the sociology of knowledge with Max Weber's "work on the relation between religious systems and economic development," he hoped it would be "helpful" in making less vague the musings by Robert MacIver and Leonard Hobhouse on relations between "the growth of mind and society"—a key problem in Ginsberg's evolutionary theory (Ginsberg [1932] 1948: 121). Ginsberg's disappointed hopes undoubtedly effected the subsequent unhappy relationship between him and Mannheim. Mannheim's original sponsor at the London School of Economics, Harold Laski, moreover, favored the social interpretation of political ideas, although he inclined towards a Marxist approach to political theory. Speaking at a conference on the social sciences in 1935, Laski remarks: "Theories...have an ancestry and its investigation alone gives us the clue to its understanding. More than that. It gives us a clue to the validity of ideas. For they emerge always as a statement of the thinker's idea of a good to be realized; and this is born of...the environment to which he belongs...no more than a magisterial summary of certain tendencies of his time" (Laski 1936: 125). Laski's political activism limited his LSE influence. Mannheim arrived at the LSE just after the director, Lord Beveridge, had reprimanded Laski for compromising the institution by his militant electioneering. Laski denounced the attacks as truckling to the Rockefeller Foundation, but he was profoundly hurt and withdrew from college affairs for several years.[2] Nevertheless, Mannheim could not ignore him.

A dissertation directed by Laski evidences cross-fertilization between Mannheim and Laski and hints at the terms on which they communicated. The evidence is admittedly tainted, since the writer is Franz Neumann (1936), who knew *Ideologie und Utopie* in the Weimar context. But Neumann's attempt to integrate *Mensch und Gesellschaft* in an analysis indebted to the earlier work shows engagement with Mannheim in London, verified by the acknowledgment in the dissertation. As in Heidelberg and Frankfurt, Marxist students were attracted to Mannheim, albeit with reservations, and at the LSE such students worked under Laski. Neumann is addressing the "existential determination of the judicial process," and he announces, "since Karl Mannheim raised the sociology of knowledge to the rank of science, we have been in possession of a technique, even if not fully developed, enabling us to distinguish the existential determination of thought" (Neumann 1986:232). After translating the pertinent passage from Mannheim's "Wissenssoziologie" article, Neumann rejects Jerome Frank's "realist" legal sociology as excessively individualistic in its psychoanalytical method and unable to account for the structure of rules operative in decisions:

Far more important...is that social structure conditions mentality. The manner in which [the judge] regards a thing, what he grasps, and how he mentally transforms it, is determined basically by his social position. The existential determination of thought differs in the various stages of the judicial process. We follow Mannheim's distinction between the various stages of thought [Karl Mannheim in *Mensch und Gesellschaft im Zeitalter des Umbaus*, p.93.] The first stage is that of intuition (*Finden*). Here the judge waits for the intuition, the "hunch." It is the most primitive stage of thought, and is realized in the Kadi justice or in the activity of the jury. In this stage, the part played by thinking is relatively small, or is non-existent. The decision is mainly an unconscious reaction. But the judge does not stop short at this stage. He ascends to the stage of inventive thought (*Erfinden*). The process of subsumption begins. The judge is not allowed to be satisfied with an intuition; he is compelled to produce arguments, that is, to rationalise the intuition. At this stage of inventive thought, the share of thought is large, but the existence determines the thought. If the judge now begins to think sociologically, he ascends to the third stage, that of planned thought (*planendes Denken*). Sociologically this means—from the judge's point of view—that he makes himself conscious of the fact that his thinking is existentially determined. This sociological self-analysis is in my view the first task of the judge.... "Planned thought" means materially—according to its function—the fitting of the judge's decision not only into a logical system of rules, but into a social system which is determined by the constitution.(Neumann 1986:234-35)

Neumann continues, "Marxism fills materially this methodological conclusion of the sociology of knowledge, by the assertion that the attitude of the judge towards the law is conditioned by the class relationship upon which it is dependent (Neumann 1986:235). While Neumann thanks Mannheim and Ginsberg in the preface for "invaluable suggestions," he credits Laski's influence with pervading "the structure of the book" (Neumann 1936). After Neumann came to the Institute of Social Research in New York, he disavowed Mannheim. He was so vehemently against Mannheim's friends at the New School—Löwe, Lederer, and Speier—that Horkheimer cautioned him against resorting to an "Anti-Dühring style" in professional exchanges (Krohn 1987: 217-19). By 1941, Neumann uses Mannheim as an insult in his battles with F. Pollock. One of Pollock's essays, he writes Horkheimer, "contradicts, from beginning to end, the theory of the Institute, and it is in fact nothing but a reformulation of Mannheim's sociology, especially as presented in his most recent book, *Mensch und Gesellschaft im Zeitalter des Umbaus*" (Neumann to Horkheimer, July 23, 1941. Erd 1985: 135). Neumann's adaptation of Mannheim's distinctions is forced, but his effort to link the two books echoes a position Mannheim was clearly reserving, notwithstanding his tone in the correspondence with Heimann, as witness his letter to Wirth about *Mensch und Gesellschaft*.

Second, his principal link with American sociology is Louis Wirth, professor in the prestigious Chicago department and since 1931 managing editor of the *American Journal of Sociology*. After Wirth's original visit to him in 1930, their correspondence had led to an agreement for Wirth to arrange for a translation of *Ideologie und Utopie* and to write "an interpretive introduction that will introduce the average American reader to the problem area and show him the right way to get into it." Wirth suggests inclusion of the *Handwörterbuch* article as well. Mannheim's insecure position in 1933 and his hope that Wirth could find him an American appointment added to the importance he attached to the translation project.

Third, Mannheim hoped to orchestrate his own reception in America. He recognized his intellectual project could not survive without gaining understanding in an intellectual world remote from the cultural context in which his work originally prospered. He saw the transfer of his sociology of knowledge to English-speaking sociologists as a test of the extent to which the cultivated stratum of intellectuals (*Bildungsschicht*) can develop a discourse subtle enough to avoid the formalism of the merely communicative yet sufficiently independent of localized linguistic and stylistic idiosyncrasy to be truly transcultural. A discussion of Mannheim's reception should therefore include his understanding of the new cultural requirements, as well as his adaptive strategies. In this respect, at least, his reception cannot be understood as a unidirectional process. It was a negotiated reception.

Mannheim trusted that the response among American sociologists to the book that had propelled his extraordinary career in Germany would produce a comparable effect in the United States. In view of his own sense that the sociology of knowledge was more program than accomplishment, Mannheim was not so much interested in making American converts to *Ideology and Utopia* as in securing recognition from the institutions that determined professional standing and employment. Having refused an offer to join peers among refugee scholars in founding the Graduate Faculty of the New School for Social Research in 1933, not least because he mistakenly feared it would become a segregated charity ward hindering integration into American sociology, he writes Louis Wirth in high expectation that the translation of *Ideologie und Utopie* will bring him the long-sought offer from Chicago or some similarly highly regarded sociology department.

Although Wirth encouraged Mannheim in these beliefs, they were disappointed. In 1933, Wirth speaks with confidence: "If we can bring out your volume in English, the stage will be set for your coming to America" (Wirth to Mannheim, August 31, 1933, LWP/7:11; Wirth to Mannheim, February 2, 1936, LWP/7:11). Yet by 1940, when Mannheim's position at the London School of Economics seemed untenable, at least for the duration of the war, he was offered no alternative but to join the second wave of similarly displaced refugees to the New School. When Wirth's influential colleague, Herbert Blumer, was solicited on Mannheim's behalf by T.B. Kittredge of the Rockefeller Foundation, after the Foundation had turned down a plea from the director of the London School of Economics to fund an extended Mannheim stay in America, he coolly replied: "I rather feel that Prof. Mannheim would be successful as a teacher primarily along the line of seminar instruction. He probably would not be suitable to any job requiring the instruction of a large undergraduate class. And I fear that the only jobs available at the present time are of the latter sort" (Herbert Blumer to T.B. Kittredge, January 9, 1940. RF/RG1.1/401S/73/969). Seeking an alternative solution, a joint effort by Wirth and Bronislaw Malinowski—Mannheim's London ally, now established at Harvard—managed no more than a scattering of invitations for a lecture tour by Mannheim. Before Mannheim announced he would not come because he feared to jeopardize his unaccountably delayed British naturalization, Malinowski and Wirth had received lecture invitations from Columbia (two or three weeks) and Wisconsin, and inquiries from Swarthmore and the University of California. Wirth was unable to secure the summer term appointment at Chicago he had led Mannheim to think probable.[3] In a letter to Malinowski, Wirth lists the failures: "I have not heard from Harvard, nor from Fisk, nor have I had any word from Duke, Pennsylvania, New York, Smith, Amherst or Vassar" (February 23, 1940, LWP/7:11). The results are strikingly poor, especially under prevailing conditions of controversy and enthusiasm over the war and Britain. Mannheim's *Ideology and Utopia* had been a principal topic at meetings of the profession only two years before.

The outcome of the American version of the earlier German dispute on the sociology of knowledge (Meja and Stehr 1982, 1990) was the virtual exclusion of *Ideology and Utopia* from the *scientific* enterprise of sociology and its relegation to the uses of a minor "classic" in the discipline's *instructional* routines. The work joined other books in the "antiquarian enumeration of names, terms and paraphrased summaries unrelated to crucial problems of human judgment and action" (Shils 1948: 56–57) that comprises courses on the history of sociological theory. As textbook matter, Mannheim's sociology of knowledge was reduced to a stereotyped collection of clichés, fit for beginners' exercises in refutation.

The contrast between the German and American versions of the dispute about *Ideology and Utopia* corresponds importantly to the difference between two types of bargaining. Recent work distinguishes between bargaining in a mode designed to yield win-win outcomes, even where parties are unequal in many respects, and haggling from fixed positions (Fisher, Ury, and Patton 1991). Compromise takes two correspondingly distinct forms, with the first generating more fertile connections. We think that reception theory can be enriched by appreciating the role of bargaining between publics and "authors" (actual and imputed). The contrasting types of settlement are paralleled by the differences between the outcomes in Weimar Germany and America. In the one case, an undifferentiated political-literary authorship addresses a "cultivated" general audience and strikes various mutually beneficial deals with Mannheim's provocative essays. In the other, Mannheim's recognition depends far more on a disciplinary public, caught up in processes of self-differentiation and closure against unscientific and unsociological speculations. The latter preoccupations make for greater rigidity in setting conditions for acceptance and yield a settlement deeply disappointing to Mannheim and impoverishing for American social thought.

German Sociologists and American Sociological Theory

Why did the publication of *Ideology and Utopia* fail to bring Mannheim the American opportunities he expected? What happened to thwart the hopes he had expressed to Wirth in the first days of his forced "retirement," writing still from Frankfurt:

> I am confident, because you and many other visitors (both professors and students) have told me on earlier occasions that the tendency I represent (sociology of knowledge, empirical-historical research, etc.) would be desirable for American sociology—that the renewal of our science would emerge precisely out of the blending of my own research tendency with the American. (Mannheim to Wirth, April 18, 1933, LWP/7:11)

A preliminary answer might begin with Mannheim's provocative overconfidence. Mannheim asserted his claim not only in private letters but also in two publications in English, before and after his emigration. In an invited contribution to a colloquium on Stuart Rice's *Methods in Social Sciences*, published in the *American Journal of Sociology* in 1931, Mannheim announces that "there were hardly every two different styles so fit to supplement each other's shortcomings as are the American and German types of sociology.... We must learn from American sociology that science must remain in contact with real life and its exigencies." He concludes, "on the other hand, American sociology may gain if its studies on questions of practical detail are alive to the great theoretical problems which pervade and coordinate with each other all the scattered empirical facts" (Mannheim [1931] 1953: 193–94). Three years later, in his first publication in England, his essay on "German Sociology," he lays claim to a special place for his own work in the development he describes as uniquely qualified to enrich the universal discipline:

> The most surprising event in the recent development of sociology has, perhaps, been the way in which *Wissenssoziologie* (the sociology of knowledge) has described the differences in human thought among different groups and at different times.... Thus the recent appreciation of the significance of those social forces, that up to a certain point influence all sciences, places the new problem of the theory of knowledge, on the one hand, and new tasks that have to be disposed of in the search of objectivity, on the other, on a higher plane. The merit of recent German sociologists lies, perhaps, in the fact that they have freed themselves from that exaggerated "methodological asceticism" for which nothing that is not susceptible of measurement can be deemed to be exact, and, further, that they have successfully shown that the spiritual sphere has its own peculiar criteria of exactness which have hitherto not been noticed. (Mannheim [1934] 1953: 220–22)

While claims for German sociology as theoretical mentor to American (and English) social researchers had a long history and many cosponsors in America as well as Germany, Mannheim's special claim to personify the most advanced of this advanced species of study—notwithstanding his accompanying disarming praise of American empirical interests—invited exacting scrutiny of his *Ideology and Utopia* when it eventually appeared.

Mannheim's closes his essay on "German Sociology" with an attempt "to suggest sociological reasons for the differences that exist between American, English, and German sociology." A representative sample of that analysis alleges that American sociology is pervaded by an "isolating empiricism" that veils the "constructive bases of social life... behind the mass of secondary details" because "the most difficult and vital problems crop up one by one... in any colonizing society that spreads itself over an expansive territory, and has to develop its social institutions in a relatively short span of time" (Mannheim [1934] 1953:224–25). Wirth thanks Mannheim for an offprint of the article because "it helps me to clear up a few points in the translation of your manuscript which were rather obscure to me" (Wirth to Mannheim, May 12, 1934. LWP/7:11), but it is not likely that he found Mannheim's improvised illustration among the helpful features. A Chicago loyalist like Wirth could scarcely admire Mannheim's rendering of efforts led by his own department.

Wirth himself, applying in 1934 for funds to continue Edward Shils' assistantship for his project on German sociology, indicates the test American sociologists would apply to Mannheim. "For the past eight years," he writes, "I have been engaged in a study of the developments in German sociology during the period from about nineteen-ten on—a period which corresponds to the turn in the United States from speculation and philosophizing to empirical research." Although the Germans "by virtue of their traditional interest in philosophy" should have been "methodologically better prepared to embark upon scientific social research than the Americans," they "failed to produce anything aside from uninspired historically or philosophically oriented elaborations of existing systems" while "the relatively novel and fresh contributions by American sociologists during this period have given to American sociology a position of world leadership." There are "a few exceptions" among the Germans, he contends, and his research hopes to draw on these, including Mannheim, to remedy the comparative weakness of American "theoretical foundations."

But Wirth had not always been convinced that Mannheim should be numbered among the saving exceptions. After their original meeting in Frankfurt in 1930, Mannheim cautioned him "to postpone a final judgment of our sociological efforts," implying skepticism from Wirth during their talk (Mannheim to Wirth, November 17, 1930, LWP/7:11). By 1934, Wirth was persuaded. Among theoretical treatments of "the presuppositions, the implications, [and] the historical setting of their problems and methods," Mannheim's work "represents the most thoroughgoing analysis yet made of the problem of objectivity in the social sciences" (Wirth to Donald Slesinger, April 20, 1934, LWP/65:4). Clearly, the crux for Wirth is whether a theoretical contribution reverts to "speculation and philosophizing" or whether it bears directly on problems of methodology. Despite Wirth's confidence, the question he raised was not simple, when asked about Mannheim's *Ideology and Utopia*; and there was far from unanimity about the answer among the German sociologists who agreed with Wirth's test for accepting Mannheim's credentials as a sociologist.

Mannheim's most influential German critic and competitor was Leopold von Wiese, and his word carried weight among the minority of American sociologists who shared the general German view that American sociology needed theory. He was widely recognized. Although Howard Becker's rendition of von Wiese's *Systematic Sociology* (Becker 1932) was greeted with reserve by a reviewer for the *American Journal of Sociology* (House 1933), the objections were aimed partly at Becker's confusing "clarifications," soon known by insiders to have infuriated von Wiese (von Wiese to Wirth, March 8, 1932, LWP/66:8; von Wiese 1960: 86n.1; cp. Mannheim to Wirth, July 22, 1932, LWP/7:11), while the book was recognized as an important reference on an urgent problem: "The problems of the logic and grammar of sociology cannot be permanently evaded; hence these contributions to their solution should be welcome to all thoughtful students of the subject." Theodore Abel put von Wiese on a par with Max Weber, Simmel, and Vierkandt as the principal theorists whose works embody "the efforts made...to establish sociology as an autonomous and specialized science" (Abel [1929] 1965:6). Four years later, Abel (1933:212) called von Wiese's *System der allgemeinen Soziologie* "the most important theoretical treatise in contemporary sociology." Connections were personal as well as literary. Louis Wirth's original project on American adaptations of German sociological theory had brought Wirth into contact with von Wiese before he ever met Mannheim; they corresponded until the late 1930s (LWP/66:8). Moreover, von Wiese was present in the United States as visiting professor in the 1934-35 academic year, first at Wisconsin, through Robert Park's intervention with E.A. Ross, and afterwards at Harvard, thanks to Pitirim Sorokin.

Von Wiese addressed the December 1935 meetings of the American Sociological Society on "Social Theory and Social Practice," reasserting the program with which he and his followers had won organizational supremacy in German sociology (Käsler 1981), that is, that progress in sociology is blocked by "too much uncertainty about the principal and essential task of sociology, and about the fundamental difference between the questions it addresses and those of other disciplines," and that his doctrine of relations (*Beziehungslehre*) opens the way forward (Wiese 1936; See Wiese 1935).[4] Von Wiese accepts the basic premise of the conference, that social planning is of vital contemporary interest to sociologists, but caricatures German thinkers, who take up sociological themes in a "transitory" and "dilettante fashion" when they encounter a gap in their philosophical or political reasonings, as well as Americans who dissipate sociology by narrow practice in special applied domains. "Theoretical sociology" alone, von Wiese asserts, can provide social practice with a "wealth of insight and general rules." He concludes, "We are confronted, then, by the seeming paradox that systematic sociology which has been decried as an abstract discipline, is the most concrete and realistic instrument aiming at an adequate solution of the urgent problems of the present" (Wiese 1935: 59).

Yet in a German essay written immediately after his American stay, which includes a paraphrase of his American remarks in the context of an international survey of sociology, von Wiese writes in a different spirit when he addresses the prospects for sociology in Germany:

> Even if it remains theoretical and unpolitical, sociology must do justice to a shift in the times towards socialism (no matter what kind). The students—destined to be public officials, leaders of industry, and so forth—are invariably taught to explore the importance of interpersonal linkages for social structures. Because this approach—in contrast to the [atomistic] conceptions dominant in the nineteenth century—is congenial to all influential schools of thought, whatever their differences, the years before the great overturn in Germany were favorable to sociology. None of this need change today. Quite the contrary. Once socialism is freed from ties to economic materialism, the principle of class struggle, and anti-national excrescences—as has happened—, the ideal of community stands forth. While this ideal is a matter of ethics and belief, it is fostered scientifically by the study of interpersonal linkage. (Wiese 1936: 15-16)

A balancing act pervades the 1936 publication. Speaking of the state of English sociology, he reports courageously, "in London, Ginsberg and German emigrants, K. Mannheim above all, are heard with great interest by students." In qualification, he adds: "The ultimate flaw of these London efforts is soon evident. It is uncertainty about the essential task [of sociology] and its delimitation from other studies. The danger of degenerating into a mere syllabus of social reform has not been overcome." Von Wiese, moreover, wrote a harsh review of Mannheim's 1935 book on planning, portraying it as epitome of a hypersociology proposed by writers consumed by a desire to make humankind dependent on them (Wiese 1935a). Writing Wirth about it from Germany, he says: "I strongly object to the idea of total planning. It is precisely in America (*sic!*) that this principle could initiate a dangerous development" (September 9, 1935, LWP/ 66:8). A passage in a later letter shows that Mannheim minded very much, but it also reveals the complexity of their relations. Writing Wirth (March 28, 1937) about a guest lecture in London, von Wiese reports: "I saw Mannheim and his wife frequently. When we had last talked 1-1/2 years ago in Brussels, my response to his most recent book had unfortunately alienated him. I was therefore pleased that he had in the meantime changed his mind about my criticism. He agreed with me more now than I could have expected. We got along quite nicely once again."[5]

Von Wiese's attitude towards Mannheim remained throughout his long life a mixture of marvel and misgivings, not free of racial stereotyping. His Mannheim obituary does not make pleasant reading:

> Thinking was a weapon for him in the struggle against ruling elites, a means of transforming the world and for demolishing the social structure for the sake of objectives he deemed just, free, and human. I argued with him about the essence of freedom. I do not believe I am mistaken when I say that his idea of freedom was different from anything imagined by anyone whose ancestors do not come from the ghetto. As it seems to me, he wanted to replace the elite position of those who have hitherto led society with another elite, for whom he wanted to secure no less sweeping rights of domination: the elite of the clever. The only question is whether their rule would not in practice lead to the tyranny of the sly. (Wiese 1948: 99)

Von Wiese's perception of Hitler's academic victims in general was strikingly insensitive. Recalling his American visit in his memoirs, he explains with disgruntlement that his intercourse with colleagues in 1934 was made difficult by the fact that it "took place at a time...when distrust was first growing in America against Germany and its National Socialist Party." "The first Jewish emigrants and other political refugees," he adds, "had started to surface" (Wiese 1957: 68). The attitudes and assumptions he reports as having shaped his decision to return to Germany in 1935 reveal the same touch of resentment:

> Should I become an emigrant myself? My acquaintances among the emigre scholars were in a situation very different from my own. As Jews or political opponents they would not be allowed back to Germany. When one or the other declaimed with false pathos, "Never again will I set foot on that soil," he was not being completely honest. He was in banishment. What was important and even decisive is that almost all of them had salvaged some part and possibly all of their assets or had other secure income. (Wiese 1957: 71)

Von Wiese remained professor in Cologne, though ousted as director of the sociological institute. He was trusted enough, moreover, to be chosen for a team detailed to search French archives in 1941 for documents supporting German propaganda about the causes of the first war. In his memoirs he contends that he neutralized the effort since he used the opportunity only for disinterested scholarship. But the memoirs also still curiously resent the attacks against him by "sycophants" of the regime who maliciously portrayed him as hostile to it. He instances their selective quotations from his *Allgemeine Soziologie*: "They were slyly chosen and always stopped short of a passage less offensive to national socialist eyes." Although he had indeed refused a *Volk* the status of "social substantiality," as charged, he had also written that a *Volk* was something even more basic, namely a living entity; and his opponents suppressed this (Wiese 1957: 73).

Von Wiese sought accommodation with the regime, but avoided major concessions to Nazi ideology in his sociological writings. Utilizing mostly Austrian outlets before 1938, he campaigned to show that a nonpolitical sociology would harm no one's politics—not even that of the Nazi government. To promote his case, he argued against those who demanded partisan commitment—firm, if cautious, against such influential converts to National Socialism as Werner Sombart (Wiese 1936a), but no less cool to opponents of the regime. Von Wiese's ambivalence and his complex maneuvering to reconcile the National Socialist regime to his conception of sociology (Zinn 1992) merit closer examination because of the widespread misconception that relations between American and German sociology between 1933 and 1948 concern nothing but the integration of anti-Nazi refugee thought. Influential American sociologists, resisting the "politicization" of the American discipline, felt more comfortable with von Wiese, who denied that he was compelled to take sides for or against the German regime.

Wirth's high opinion of von Wiese is made clear by his help in arranging the visiting year, although von Wiese made some ambiguous comments in his letters to Wirth during the first months of Nazi rule. Writing in 1933, von Wiese sounds awed rather than dismayed by the changes under way. He chides Americans who do not appreciate the magnitude of the shift and the extent to which liberalism has become obsolete; he remarks that they have a "false impression" because they "judge according to the stereotypes of an age that is for us now forever in the past" (June 7, 1933, LWP/13:2; cp. von Wiese to Wirth, October 30, 1933, LWP/13:2). Wirth's response is polite but testy (August 7, 1933, LWP/13:2). Then, however, von Wiese's New Year's letter for 1934 summarizes the events of the year, casting himself as helpless victim more than present research considers justified (Klingemann 1986, 1992). He reports that he and Tönnies have been ousted from the leadership of the German Sociological Society, that his journal has been eliminated, and that he fears he will not be allowed to attend international congresses and will thus be prevented from taking up his position as president of the International Institute of Sociology.

Wirth went into action. In February, he writes von Wiese, "I spoke to Dr. Park about you when we met in Philadelphia last Christmas, and he said that on his trip East he was making it one of his main objectives to see what he might discover that might interest you" (LWP/66:8). These interventions led to funds for a semester at Wisconsin, granted by the Carl Schurz Memorial Foundation, which Becker had earlier enlisted to subsidize American subscriptions to von Wiese's sociological quarterly (LWP/68:8).

Wirth and his Chicago colleagues went further, however. Von Wiese writes Wirth in grateful delight:

> Today I received a letter from Prof. Park, who writes, "I expect that you will receive in the course of time an invitation from the University of Chicago to deliver a course of lectures on German sociology in the Spring quarter 1935. Prof. Wirth, who ordinarily gives that course at that time, informs me that he will be engaged at that time in a special piece of research for the university and will recommend that you be invited to give the course in his stead." (LWP/66:8)

Wirth never made such a recommendation on Mannheim's behalf.

Wirth's regard for von Wiese is symptomatic of the reservations in Wirth's championing of *Ideology and Utopia*. He drew the line at Mannheim's philosophical ambitions. Perhaps equally to the point, however, is a fundamental agreement between Wirth and von Wiese that sociology must become, as von Wiese (1928) puts it, a "cooperative" and not a "solitary" study. While preparing his 1937 recommendations for revamping the strategy of the Social Science Research Council, Wirth jotted this note: "In Europe social science is still in the handicraft stage.... In America we have entered the stage of organization for mass production. We know what the others are doing" (LWP/44:11). Wirth and von Wiese shared a commitment to the interdependence of the institutionalization and the advancement of scientific knowledge. Wirth could not support Mannheim as isolated thinker, however profound. The extent of Mannheim's acceptance by organized sociology would be the measure of his worth.

Mannheim's Nemesis: Alexander von Schelting

Von Wiese's appeal to key American sociologists active in the discipline's controversies about its institutional definition in the mid-1930s is only one warning against disregarding the earlier history of relations between German and American sociologists when studying the shocks that attend the introduction of refugee academic intellectuals. On the one hand, no one was willing to accept without critical scrutiny

Mannheim's claims to represent German sociology or his bid to serve as arbitrator of differences between it and American sociology. On the other, the contention that the relationship to German sociology was important to the discipline was itself controversial. Mannheim was correct in thinking that the relationship between ideology and social science was a lively topic among Americal social scientists, but neither he nor Wirth anticipated the surge among leading sociologists towards intellectual strategies to insulate sociology from political contamination. The rise of Marxism was a factor among its opponents, but no less important was the spreading belief that confusion in the face of fascism disproved earlier faith in the harmony of social science, relativistic experimentalism and American democracy (Gunnell 1993). The American sociology under construction would be immune from the philosophical issues that open the way to politics. Its empirical methodology would be philosophically warranted as scientific, and its findings would be philosophically divorced from conflicting ethical claims. Viennese positivists and the professionally sanctioned interpreters of Max Weber's metamethodological writings received a surprisingly friendly welcome. They sanctioned the inclination to limit critical debates about the design of sociology to questions of method.

A few months before the publication of *Ideology and Utopia*, the *American Sociological Review* published an eleven-page review of *Ideologie und Utopie* by Alexander von Schelting (1936), another non-Jewish visitor from Germany—and a visitor, incidentally, strongly approved by von Wiese (May 13, 1935, LWP/66:8). Howard Becker, the assistant editor in charge of the book review section, explains in a note that the journal is deviating from its policies by reviewing such an old book because it is "among the dozen...most important sociological works that have appeared since 1930" but nevertheless has never been "adequately reviewed" in the United States. Moreover, Becker gives notice of the forthcoming translation: "We await *Ideology and Utopia* with interest; in the meantime we can prepare ourselves with *Ideologie und Utopie*" (Schelting 1936:664, n.1).

In his review, von Schelting takes up criticisms he had already developed in Germany. After crediting Mannheim with raising some important questions, he concentrates on Mannheim's speculations about the epistemological implications of his concept of total ideology. He begins magisterially: "Mannheim's fundamental views on the problems of ideology and the sociology of knowledge cannot be accepted, because of basic lack of logical and epistemological consistency and their incompatibility with empirical facts" (Schelting 1936: 664). He plows grimly through the text in search of an epistemological theory that can meet the formal standards of his own neo-Kantianism, and concludes—after crediting the empirical suggestiveness of some of Mannheim's concrete observations—that Mannheim's distinctive approach is marred decisively by the "nonsense" (Schelting 1936: 674) of his philosophical claims.

As the review appears, after undergoing the 30 percent abridgement and revision for which Becker takes responsibility, it is a polemic. Becker was well-known for his sharpness of tongue and his defiance of the discipline's gentility. These are probably the qualities that led him to align himself for a while with the rebellion in the American Sociological Society against the hegemony of the Chicago seniors, the rebellion that spawned the *American Sociological Review*. He soon disappointed his allies, however, especially by his attention to high theory—and specifically German theory—in the book review section. A leading member of the rebel group attacked the editor of the journal in January 1937 for his willingness "'to publish anything and everything of German origin,' which he attributed to the influence of 'that Nazi Becker'" (Bannister 1987: 219-20). In short, Becker's publication of this extraordinary review damaged Mannheim's prospects in the discipline.

It stigmatized Mannheim for one group as a theorist in the German mode; and for another, as a theorist in the bad philosophical mode. Mannheim's reputation as an excessively "philosophical" sociologist also followed him from Germany at the crucial confidential level of opinion at the Rockefeller Foundation, whose officers contributed to the institutional formation of sociology as discipline, notably in the endowment of Chicago's social science program (Bulmer and Bulmer 1981). Despite repeated tries, Mannheim never gained the disciplinary legitimation that came with a public award from the Rockefeller Foundation.[6] Success would have made his prospects for an American career much less dependent on the reception of *Ideology and Utopia*.

In the profession, von Schelting's preemptive review defined the terms of debate to an extraordinary extent. In Becker's own brief review of *Ideology and Utopia*, Becker (1938) contends that there is little to add to von Schelting, while praising Wirth's introduction and conceding to Mannheim some contribution to the discussion of scientific objectivity.

He introduces a political innuendo, reminiscent of Mannheim's condemnation as historical materialist at the 1930 Congress of German Sociologists, and self-assuredly offers a preposterous version of Mannheim's intellectual biography: "In order adequately to understand Mannheim, one must remember that he began as a scholarly Marxist, developed discontent with the revisionist interpretations current in German Social Democracy, and became uneasy about the validity of his doctrine when confronted with Max Weber's trenchant critique" (Becker 1938: 261). Becker spins his fiction further in his later, long-standard history of sociological thought, where he mixes it with a decoction of vile German academic gossip about Mannheim: "Mannheim... was for a long time identified with German Social Democracy, and is said to have owed his appointment at the University of Frankfort not to his Jewish ancestry (*sic!*) but to the fact that he had done much to make Marxism *salonfähig*, i.e., socially and intellectually respectable." He again recapitulates von Schelting's critique, treating it as definitive (Becker and Barnes 1938, 3:924ff.). As late as February 1940, the Mexican publisher of Mannheim's book urges Mannheim to write a special introduction, telling "what would be your answer to the main objections made by... von Schelting." Mannheim ignored the request.

To Wirth, however, Mannheim wrote immediately about von Schelting's article, at length and in anger (December 28, 1936, LWP/7:11). Mannheim warned that "it may be necessary for us to be concerned about the immediate effects" on the prospects of the book, which had just appeared. His urgent appeal has two parts. First, he presses Wirth about the disciplinary politics of the publication, suspecting a link to the conflict that culminates in the displacement of Wirth's *American Journal of Sociology* by the *American Sociological Review* as the official journal of the American Sociological Society. Mannheim's letter in fact is occasioned by a standard request from the *American Journal of Sociology* to become a contributor. He wants especially to consent, he says, "because I feel myself part of your tradition, since the appearance of the *American Sociological Review*, and called upon to show my colors." He has just seen the August number of the *American Sociological Review* and was astounded to find "that almost the entire book review section is organized as a maneuver against me, or at least against a tendency that identifies with me." He claims to be amused by "how, to this end, poor Schelting has been inflated into a 'commanding figure,' thanks to Parsons." Schelting, he maintains, was viewed as a perpetual student in Germany; his overblown dissertation on Weber's method was accepted as his habilitation thesis because of faculty manipulations in which he was a mere pawn. After further disparagement of von Schelting, Mannheim returns to his original question, "What is going on behind the scenes?"

Wirth never addresses Mannheim's political question. He consistently refuses to treat the changes in the American Sociological Society as products of clashes among disciplinary partisans, and he reiterates his public position on the new official journal in his correspondence with von Wiese (February 28, 1936, LWP/66:8). The sole disadvantage, Wirth maintains, is a possible loss of a few subscribers; the advantage is freedom from organizational interference, so they can "make it as independent, as scientific and as effective as we can." Von Wiese has been following the issue, and assures Wirth that he agrees "that your journal can only gain scientifically by becoming independent" (March 15, 1936, LWP/66:8). This statement does not contradict the central importance that von Wiese attaches to the "cooperative" and organizational character of science: he likens the circumstances in Chicago to his own case before his journal was shut down. Control over a journal provides an additional organizational sphere for constituting the discipline. In a reply to Mannheim written eight months after the original letter, Wirth's casual remarks about von Schelting consequently ignore Mannheim's suspicions: "As to von Schelting," he writes, "I have never entertained any notions that he knew what it was all about. His interest is primarily an epistemological one and he fails to see the important sociological implications of your work" (August 18, 1937, LWP/7:11).

Wirth's dismissal of von Schelting's epistemological preoccupations implies a response to Mannheim's second question. Mannheim asks whether he should answer von Schelting, or whether it would be better to let someone else express "what one thinks about Schelting and about Becker's maneuver as a whole." Wirth's evasion on this point signals a key difference between him and Mannheim about the aspects of *Ideology and Utopia* worth disputing. Although a distinction between the sociological core and the epistemological periphery of sociology of knowledge is not alien to Mannheim, his outline of points for a rejoinder show that he takes von Schelting's philosophical criticisms to heart. It would be simple to demolish von Schelting's stale old line, Mannheim says. Von Schelting suppresses all the newer arguments against neo-Kantianism (*die*

212   Karl Mannheim and the Crisis of Liberalism

Geltungsphilosophie); he deliberately misinterprets in order to invent contradictions; and he abuses a tired formula that any thought that does not presuppose its own truth is self-contradictory. Especially interesting is Mannheim's insistence on the experimental character of his work: "[von Schelting] suppresses the fact that the author expressly states that he is on a search and that several systems are at work in the same person, and that this is why—with the new methodology of 'experimental thinking'—he does not touch upon the contradictions that consequently come into view" (December 28, 1936, LWP/7:11).

Mannheim's frustration is bitter because he had urged the need to make just this point unmistakably clear when Wirth and Shils had objected to the last-minute addition of Mannheim's "Preliminary Approach to the Problem" to the text of *Ideology and Utopia*. To "spare himself the experience of having critics (perhaps von Schelting)...busy themselves with exposing contradictions," disregarding his own insistence that he is "deliberately letting the contradictions stand because they are given in the situation of our thinking and must be made transparent rather than reasoned out of existence." Mannheim considered it crucial to emphasize at length "that these inquiries must be taken as essays, as a search" (February 15, 1936, LWP/7:11).

An increasingly self-conscious academic sociology was not interested in "essays" in Mannheim's sense (Rohner 1966; Lukács [1911] 1971; Kadarkay 1991; Mannheim [1918] 1985). The reviewer in the English *Sociological Review*, Charles H. Wilson (1937), takes up Mannheim's presentation of the work as a collection of essays. He attacks the disclaimer. It puts criticism "out of court," he protests, and imposes a major and unfair "disability" on the critic, "for it inevitably makes the critic feel that he may be in error, and unjust, in imputing to the author this or that fundamental omission, this or that inadequacy of information, this or that contradiction." "In fact," he concludes, "by this method the author has all the best of it; he all but removes the ground from the reviewer's feet." But Wilson, a student of Ginsberg, does not appear to have been much cowed. He credits Mannheim with having raised interesting questions about historical relativism and with proposing a useful undertaking, in the analysis of social myths, but he denies that Mannheim has initiated a properly scientific approach to his problems and charges him with eclecticism and inconsistency on the key issues of relativism. Mannheim offers attractive "speculative generalizations" of the sort which enhance the aesthetic and philosophic interest of the past, he maintains, but nothing to encourage belief that the knowledge of his intellectuals can provide "scientific, exact, precise diagnosis of cultures." Both British and American sociologists were blind or hostile to Mannheim's characterization of the genre to which he assigned *Ideology and Utopia*. This point is especially important because the essayistic mode provides the medium for Mannheim's explorations of the philosophical borderland. Wirth was not prepared to build his case for Mannheim among his fellow sociologists on such paradoxical grounds: they had little to do with the "sociological implications" he wanted to see explored.

From *Ideologie und Utopie* to *Ideology and Utopia*

The English book, *Ideology and Utopia* (1936a), differs far more from the German *Ideologie und Utopie* (1929) than can be explained by the normal friction of translation. A dramatic contrast between the two versions concerns the starting point. The German work begins with the crisis of mutual distrust: all social actors denounce the statements of all the others as mere ideology, exposing their roots in the particular volitions of the groups concerned. It is the presumed experience of this crisis that forms the existential presupposition for the sociology of knowledge. The knowledge creating this crisis, the ways in which each social group adapts the originally Marxist insight to its own ideology, opens the groups to the synthesizing intervention of the intellectuals and their organon. Now none of this can any longer be presupposed.

When Mannheim and Wirth first discussed a possible translation in 1930, Mannheim urged Wirth, much his junior in standing, to write an introduction to break the path for a precise translation, instead of issuing a misleading loose adaptation, like that later inflicted by Howard Becker on Leopold von Wiese's book. The project languished. In one of his first letters from exile, however, Mannheim reopened the question of an English translation addressed primarily to American audiences and enclosed some partial drafts attempted by his relations, Paul Kecskemeti and Ernest Mannheim. Wirth assumed responsibility for the translation, although his assistant, Edward Shils, eventually did most of the work. Notwithstanding his earlier opposition to textual adaptations, Mannheim now insisted on thoroughly reworking the literal translation prepared by Shils, drawing on the help of a native English undergraduate. The original book was revised by three recontextualizing additions. At Wirth's urgings, Mannheim's included his encyclopedia article on sociology of knowledge (Mannheim [1931] 1952). While *Ideologie und Utopie* had appeared in a series of which Mannheim was the general editor and that he had heralded, in a publisher's announcement, as striving for a boundary position between philosophy and sociology, "Wissenssoziologie" was designed for a disciplinary audience. In turn, it was at Mannheim's request that Wirth prepared a twenty-page "Preface" to build a bridge between the sociology of knowledge and comparable developments in American sociology. Finally, Mannheim insisted on inserting a "Preliminary Approach to the Problem" after the preface, to Wirth's dismay. Mannheim's added chapter closes with the extraordinary contention that the three chapters of the widely recognized original book should be read as essays in exploring the scientific program outlined in the systematic encyclopedia article at the end of the enlarged book.

While Mannheim rushed through the writing of the "Preliminary Approach" and had no time to revise the translation, he spent several months on the main body of the text. The effect of the work is changed, first, by the transformation of the theoretical vocabulary, moving it from the universe of philosophical discourse of the post-Hegelian German *Geisteswissenschaften* towards the psychological frames of reference of English post-utilitarian philosophy of mind, with its characteristic emphasis on distinctions between judgments of facts and judgments of values, or American pragmatism. "Spirit" (*Geist*) becomes "mind" or "intellect"; "consciousness" (*Bewußtsein*) becomes "mental activity" or "evaluation"; the various terms for the objective directedness of the will, its tendency towards one or another state of things, become "interests," "purposes," "norms," or "values"; "primaeval structures of mind" become "irrational mechanisms"; and "false consciousness" is divided between "erroneous knowledge" and "invalid ethical attitude." Cumulatively, the distinctive claims about the inner connections among social location, practical design, and social knowledge characteristic of sociology of knowledge as organon become difficult to grasp.

In the German version, Mannheim says that the "evaluative concept of ideology" "*makes* judgments about the reality of ideas and structures of consciousness"; according to the English version, it "presupposes" such judgments (Mannheim [1929] 1952:85; Mannheim 1936a:86). More broadly, if "evaluations" based on "interests" introduce "bias" into "thinking," creating "erroneous knowledge" and "invalid ethical attitudes" lacking in "objectivity," there is little reason for giving the resultant "ideologies" the measure of credence implied in all the talk about "relationism." The structure of social knowledge no longer appears as ontologically grounded, as knowledge in its social and historical nexus. Its constitutive stylistic principle is no longer conceived as an "ontological decision," with the difficulties about the interworking of rational and irrational elements this implies; ideologies appear more nearly as divisible compounds of empirical "ontology" and "value judgment."

A slight terminological emendation in the subtitle of the central essay signals the important shifts underway. The title in German is a question, "Is Politics as a Science Possible?". The English equivalent, "The Prospects of Scientific Politics," loses the two allusions in the German title— first, to Weber's essays (Gerth and Mills 1958), "Politics as a Vocation" and "Science as a Vocation," and, second, to the Kantian question about the "possibility" of one or another kind of knowledge, so important to Mannheim's own epistemological and methodological reflections. Moreover, the change from "politics as science" to "scientific politics" reduces the multiple possibilities left open by the German terms to one. The German could mean that politics itself becomes a mode of "scientific" inquiry, interrogating reality to achieve orientation and mastery; it could mean the opposite, that a political science comes into being that studies scientifically the partially irrational activity of politics; or it could mean what the English does. Mannheim's essayistic approach in German is designed to play these possibilities off against one another without settling on any one. His design in the English version is different.

A change in the chapter's subtitle confirms that the other changes noted are not simply victims of translation losses. The German subtitle refers to "Theory and Practice," and corresponds to the substantive problem for which the sociology of knowledge exercise is proposed as "organon." The English subtitle becomes "The Relationship between Social Theory and Political Practice." Theoretical and practical activities are assigned to separate domains, as in *Man and Society*, and the way is opened to the possibility of "scientific politics" superceding "political practice," in the sense worked out in the chapter. Of course, the chapter does arrive at such supercession; it remains a translation of the German essay. But the argument becomes less coherent, and the special role of "intellectuals," increasingly portrayed as possessing a governing knowledge, dramatically overshadows the recourse to the "practical dialectics" (*Realdialektik*) of political life.

These conceptual modifications and other methodological changes amount to a substantial adjustment in the theoretical structure. In a footnote to the discussion of the "school" that is the practical outcome of the inquiry into theory and practice, Mannheim extrapolates from his immediate argument. He contends that the text has come upon the "correct" answer to the question about the schooling needed, and that it has done so by nothing more than the "concrete analysis of situations" characteristic of sociology of knowledge. The goal of his whole inquiry would be achieved, Mannheim avers, if he were able to formulate the logic according to which the result was attained. He concludes: "A genuine situational analysis of a style of thought would have to be able to specify the measure of its validity." Mannheim eliminates the footnote from the English version (Mannheim [1929] 1952: 159).

More generally, then, the sociology of knowledge is moved farther from a mode in which Mannheim, as essayist, participates reflectively in the common spiritual life present in politics and towards a science providing its practitioners with causal explanations for a class of political phenomena. The author does not offer himself to the political reader as someone engaged in a shared project, engaged in self-clarification, and hoping that thinking the critical situation through will itself bring about a turning towards realistic practice. Although the contents remain rich in ambiguities, the form moves from the sophisticated, reflective essay towards the scientific treatise. And the latter form makes demands on the rigor, precision, and economy of the presentation that the work cannot meet. In sum, the English version of *Ideology and Utopia* shows marks of tacit negotiations between Mannheim and Wirth's putative constituency.

Wirth's Offer and Mannheim's Counter: Two Introductions

As a participant in the Chicago "social science" approach to sociology, as well as an influential mainstay of the professional association in which this sociology had been challenged, Wirth—building on drafts by his assistant, Edward Shils—presents Mannheim as bridge to a new unity in the discipline.[7] In his "Preface" to *Ideology and Utopia* he views Mannheim's work above all as a contribution to the methodology of what Wirth significantly still calls "the social science," recalling the American ideal of an altruistic technology (Gunnell 1993). Wirth considers this social science to be in crisis, both because the value consensus underlying the earlier confident use of "social" has been displaced by a reciprocal debunking of the clashing interests promoted by various "social" designs, and because the hopes for a powerful scientific method derived from the physical sciences have been widely abandoned in recognition of intractably subjective factors in the interpretation of human relations. Mannheim's sociology of knowledge, Wirth maintains, points the way toward a procedure for reestablishing the only reliable consensus. Once the rootedness of all social judgments in interests is systematically exposed, as the sociology of knowledge promises to do, a tentative universe of discourse among social scientists can arise from working agreements about the facts involved in an issue.

Mannheim, according to Wirth, also complements the attempts by American social scientists to devise an objective method for the scientific study of phenomena that cannot be understood without empathy with the human actors under examination. This does not entail an abandonment of the determinism that is integral to a usable science, but merely the elaboration of disciplinary techniques appropriate to the comprehension of a determinism through motives. There is no need to despair of rationality and objectivity in human affairs if the factors that lead to disillusionment can themselves be mastered scientifically. Mannheim, writes Wirth, shows the way towards a methodological propaedeutic that reinterprets past social science achievements and plans its future design. His sociology of knowledge is nevertheless little more than an illustrated program and a sketch. It lacks a social psychology to comprehend the link between experience and thought; it also has to pay more detailed attention to the institutional factors that govern the production and distribution of knowledge. Once stripped of extraneous matter and informed by recent American sociological approaches to education and politics, Wirth concludes, Mannheim's new subdiscipline will make a major contribution to the renewal of a problem-solving social science on a grand scale.

Mannheim sent Wirth an exultant letter about the introduction in 1935, when he received the draft:

> I have read [your preface] twice, with great attentiveness and dedication, and I can say that it gave me great joy. That came not only from your profound understand-

ing of the time and circumstances out of which the book arose, but also from your interpretation of the thoughts I sought to develop—the like of which I have never met with, despite the extensive literature on the subject. I never would have thought that individuals from wholly different worlds, with differing scientific traditions, could have approached one another so closely. The consciousness of this is much more important to me than any external success: it is a guarantee for spiritual cooperation among the intellectuals in the contemporary world. (December 24, 1935, LWP/7:11)

Mannheim then announces calmly that nevertheless he will soon send a new opening for the book.

Immediately after receiving Mannheim's unexpected manuscript titled "Preliminary Approach to the Problem," a dumbfounded Wirth, speaking for Shils as well as himself, urges him to save the new article for a different occasion. He states a list of objections and inducements, none of them substantive, except that it "might actually obscure the burden of the book itself." Wirth expresses his confidence that after publication of *Ideology and Utopia* "there will be an insistent demand for the type of studies that your work has opened up and that we will see a great awakening of interest in the field in the English-speaking world" (February 2, 1936, LWP/7:11). Wirth's strategic objectives for the book suggests reasons for his dismay more substantial than the eight points neatly numbered in the letter. The didactic urgency of the writing, expressly addressing a nonprofessional audience, leads Mannheim to proclaim his hopes for the wider ethical and epistemological implications of the sociology of knowledge—the "philosophy distrusted by Wirth"—more openly in the "Preliminary Approach" than in the main body of the text.

Mannheim begins with Socrates. He places him in the "great surge of skepticism" that accompanies democratization in Athens and asks rhetorically, "Was it not...the great virtue of Socrates that he had the courage to descend into the abyss of this skepticism?...And did he not overcome the crisis by questioning even more radically than the Sophists and thus arrive at an intellectual resting point which, at least for the mentality of that epoch, showed itself to be a reliable foundation?" Mysteriously Mannheim adds, "It is interesting to observe that thereby the world of norms and of being came to occupy the central place in his inquiry" (Mannheim 1936a: 9). The mystery soon is solved because this passage is only the first of several indications of Mannheim's belief that the radical doubt engendered by the crisis of universal distrust will, paradoxically, generate a new historical ontology and perhaps even a new foundational science of being. From this point of view, the sociology of knowledge is not a positive discipline with consequences for methodology: it is philosophy carried on by more appropriate means. To Wirth, Mannheim justifies his extended introduction by citing difficulties in communicating with the classically educated English reader; but he is also implicitly surveying the scope of bargaining between himself and American sociologists, testing American receptivity for the more philosophical dimensions of his sociology of knowledge.

Having thus balanced his larger claims against Wirth's narrower conception while preparing the English-language edition, Mannheim can do little more than to leave the American case for his book to Wirth. Wirth, in his capacity as journal editor, surprisingly contributed to Mannheim's distress about the original reception of *Ideology and Utopia* in the journals of the American profession. Hans Speier's respectful but unfavorable review in the *American Journal of Sociology* (Speier [1937] 1985) was no less disappointing to Mannheim than von Schelting's polemic, and an ironic result of Mannheim's own attempt to do what Becker's publication of von Schelting achieved, that is, to define the terms of the American discussion of *Ideology and Utopia*. Mannheim first called Speier to Wirth's attention in mid-1934. Speier would be glad to write an article on the sociology of knowledge in Germany. "He is a former student of mine, and a chap you will like. I leave it to your discretion to decide whether it would be better to wait until after the appearance of your introduction to my book before encouraging the discussion of the sociology of knowledge in the journals through Speier's article" (August 25, 1934, LWP/7:11). Wirth eventually invited Speier to review the book.

After promising Wirth to avoid von Schelting's concentration on epistemological issues, out of respect for Mannheim's courageous confrontation with the crisis in thought (November 26, 1936, LWP/11:10), Speier shortly announces that he must nevertheless voice his "doubts and questions concerning the implications of Mannheim's system" (December 4, 1936, LWP/11:10). Speier is aware of the delicacy of his situation. He twice writes Wirth offering to withdraw the manuscript (November 8, 1936, LWP/11:10 and January 4, 1937, LWP/11:10), and, in a letter to Mannheim, he apologizes for his failure to show his former teacher the manuscript before its publication (Speier to Wirth, March 19, 1937, LWP/11:10). In his review, Speier makes philosophical objections no less biting than von Schelting's, charging confusion between truth and rhetorical effectiveness, as well as a lack of sociological realism about the role of intellectuals (Speier [1937] 1985). Mannheim's reaction is personal and bitter: "It keeps happening these days...that the next generation is glad to be lifted into the saddle by us, live by our inspiration, and then, for careerist reasons, will know nothing more of it and deny a person at the next best opportunity. I can't help thinking of Speier and Schelting in this connection."[8] Disregarding Mannheim's construction of the situation as a competition, Wirth soothes him: "It is the longest review we have ever printed, [but] since in so many respects it is a negative review I cannot be accused of favoritism in giving it so much space.... I felt it best not to take issue with his opinion since as editor I wish to be perfectly neutral. I do believe, however, that the review nevertheless assigns a significant position to the book and in the long run will aid it to become better known" (August 17, 1937, LWP/7:11). Mannheim makes one more attempt to influence his reception through an erstwhile student, the dispatch of Hans Gerth in December 1937. But he had counted heavily on what he thought were deep affinities between his work and current developments in American sociology. His relegation to dismissive treatment by fellow refugees must have been deeply painful.

Dispute 1: Refugee Conversations in Atlantic City

If Mannheim was right in supposing that much depended on the first professional responses to *Ideology and Utopia*, Wirth's—and Mannheim's—hopes underwent a decisive test in December 1937, when the American Sociological Society met in Atlantic City. In an evening session on "the relation of ideas to social action," organized by Talcott Parsons, Parsons' more general paper, "The Role of Ideas in Social Action," was preceded by two papers on Mannheim's book. After Hans Speier, under the title "The Social Determination of Ideas" (Speier 1938), expanded the arguments earlier adumbrated in his review (Speier [1937] 1985), Hans Gerth, another student of Mannheim, read a rejoinder based largely on the published review (Gerth [1937] 1985). Wirth had persuaded Parsons at the last moment to include Gerth (November 13, 1937, LWP/9:9), after receiving an urgent request from Mannheim: "Dr. Gerth...is exceptionally well versed in the theory and method of sociology of knowledge, as well as cultural sociology.... If you think it a good idea, you might recommend him for the planned discussion of sociology of knowledge, in which I hear Parsons, von Schelting, et al. are to take part. He can be of great help in defending our point of view" (November 4, 1937, LWP/7:11).

Gerth had followed Mannheim from Heidelberg to Frankfurt in 1930. He wrote a dissertation based on Mannheim's "Liberalism" seminar, completing it after Mannheim's expulsion. Gerth, though not Jewish, was politically too far compromised for an academic career in Germany. Mannheim's letter to Wirth, in fact, reinforces the message in a correspondence initiated by Gerth himself two years earlier, when he solicited Wirth's help in establishing himself in the United States.[9] Mannheim's 1937 intervention, however, is above all another attempt to shift the debate on *Ideology and Utopia*. Gerth does not travel to New York until days before the Atlantic City meetings in December; he comes directly from Mannheim in London; and he quotes recent conversations with him to validate his own claims about Mannheim's adherence to Dewey's philosophy. In short, Gerth is dispatched as personal advocate for his teacher. Counter to Mannheim's expectations, his principal opponent is neither Talcott Parsons nor Alexander von Schelting, but his fellow refugee and fellow Mannheim student, Hans Speier.

Parsons opens and closes his talk by complimenting Speier on having shown, first, that the "battle of the implications of rival philosophical and other extra-scientific points of view" has interfered with the "positive empirical analysis of the role of ideas," and, second, that it is necessary to develop a theory without reference to "objectionably metaphysical" prejudgments (TP:12,1). He speaks of Speier's talk as a "prolegomenon" to his own conceptual exercise in distinguishing normative from existential ideas and the further subdivision of the latter into empirical and nonempirical for the sake of clarifying Max Weber's achievement in the sociology of religion and assisting further empirical inquiry. Without mentioning that Speier is talking about Mannheim, Parsons anticipates his own much later assertion that Mannheim's "epistemological relativism was a last-ditch defense of the basic historical relativism which increasingly emerged from the general idealistic tradition, at the same time becoming involved in mounting difficulties. Mannheim's relativism,... if taken in a radical epistemological sense, leads to an untenable position completely incompatible with the foundations of science in the fields of human action" (Parsons 1961: 989).

Parsons' implied concession that Mannheim may be taken as other than a epistemological relativist goes with recognition of contributions by Mannheim to the study of intellectuals and ideology, all qualified by the contention that Mannheim himself could not develop—or perhaps even grasp—his contributions because of his theoretical vacillation and confusions; the "classic discussion" of Mannheim remains that of Alexander von Schelting (Parsons 1961: 991-92, 989n.). Parsons' 1937 role on a panel devoted largely to Mannheim's book is best understood in the context of his move to seize the leadership in interpreting German sociology to Americans, most recently through the publication of *The Structure of Social Action*. Neither the philosophical nor the historical constituents of Mannheim's work fit the formalistic model of theory that Parsons imputed to Max Weber and successfully promoted in the American profession (Zaret 1994).[10]

Notwithstanding Parsons' cooptative praise, Speier's approach in his Atlantic City paper is far from that of Parsons or von Schelting. Speier sees Mannheim's relativism not merely as a distraction from scientific sociology but as a threat to the philosophical pursuit of truth. Mannheim's attempt to distill workable truths about society from the contest among ideologies, he charges, reflects the fundamental mistake of confounding philosophical (or scientific) truth with rhetorical persuasiveness. Mannheim has been victimized by the historicist fallacy that genuine thinking can be evaluated by standards of historical efficacy or suitability. Sociological interpretation may be instructive and even salutary when applied to ideas deployed as weapons in the Hobbesian struggle for advantage and power—"promotional ideas"—, but it can have no bearing on mental activities governed by the need to uncover truth, whose reality is presupposed by the very enterprise of inquiry. At most, sociology of knowledge can show when valuations rooted in interests corrupt intellectual productions purported to derive from disinterested applications of autonomous reason.

Accordingly, instead of arguing from norms of scientific method, Speier builds on the morally charged conceptions of New School philosophers, notably Hans Jonas and Leo Strauss, to accuse Mannheim of abandoning rational truth. The search for truth, he maintains, must be distinguished sharply from the "distrustful" [sic] activities of men in their selfishness; it must be recognized as integral to the "non-distrustful actions" that culminate, as the classics insisted, in the *vita contemplativa*. Although Speier's objective is clearly to safeguard the autonomy of sociology by blocking its overextension, his argument derives its legitimacy from the higher claims of a philosophy remote from social science.[11]

Speier's approach and objective abandon the standpoint of his 1930 German review of *Ideologie und Utopie*, which closed with the flourish, "the intelligentsia will no longer know the 'homelessness of the spirit' once it realizes" that its cooperation is valuable to the party of the working class, whose "practical politics...stands in a dialectical relationship to a comprehensive theoretical orientation" (Speier [1930] 1990: 220). In itself, there is nothing astonishing about Speier's decision to align himself, after consideration, with the critics who have denied since the first appearance of *Ideologie und Utopie* that Mannheim escapes the self-contradictory vicious circle of relativism. Yet there is something puzzling about Speier's realignment. Speier could have associated himself, for example, with von Schelting's arguments. That would have cleared the way for the unencumbered empirical sociological research he was readying himself to do. Speier's uncritical affirmation of universalistic rationalism is curious because Speier joins Strauss' attack on the "Hobbesian" modern mentality—a mentality that ostensibly sees and makes a world dedicated to the ceaseless pursuit of interest, ordered by nothing but temporal sequentiality—without attending to Strauss' claim that Weberian social science is the "historicist" epitome of this corruption. Moreover, Speier's program for a more narrowly empirical sociology of "promotive" intellectual productions—what Weber had termed language used as a weapon— disregards the issues most important to Strauss. In his sociological projects, Speier exemplifies what Strauss attacks.

Speier cannot be faulted for concluding that Mannheim failed in his search for a nonmetaphysical foundation for the distinction between rational knowledge and other types of intellectual structures. The problem posed by his "denial" of Mannheim so soon after a period of apparent discipleship is his sudden and sweeping rejection of the philosophical problem complex that had occupied his generation of liberal and socialist political thinkers. Speier's abrupt settling of accounts with Mannheim must be put into a wider and more compelling context than the dynamics of intergenerational exchanges alone. The dual shocks of failure in Germany and adjustment to the conditions of exile put past intellectual experiences into a dramatically different light. Speier himself, in an essay on "The Social Conditions of the Intellectual Exile" (Speier 1937), analyzes and reflects upon some of these factors. He finds that intellectual exiles, if they are not wholly cocooned by a community of fellow exiles or recognized members of a universal intellectual fellowship, are uniquely placed to learn the difference between thought shaped by national peculiarities and universal reason. Without debating Speier's claim that this distinction corresponds to diverse philosophical structures, it is instructive to apply a historical version of his scheme.

Many intellectual exiles from Germany experienced a revulsion against the sophisticated speculations they now thought had fatally undermined ethical and intellectual convictions whose integrity is asserted in the older humanistic language. The impulse manifested itself among social scientists in a turn to empirical research and philosophically unreflective political commentary, often perfunctorily dismissing the complexities of the "Weimar conversation."[12] Seen in this context, Speier's puzzling way of dispensing with his inheritance from Mannheim should be taken less as a case of careless philosophical reasoning than as a mark of impatience with disruptive philosophical issues, now recast as localized German preoccupations with dreadful consequences. Speier was content to postulate a secure and universal rational ground for social inquiries whose methods promised firm results. Conceding the division of academic labor, he reproached himself as well as his milieu and its guides for their past ventures in historicist metatheory, and he accepted the authority of congenial philosophers who could free him from these uncertainties and let him continue with what he now understood as his proper scientific work.

Gerth's ([1937] 1985) rejoinder turns the tables on Parsons' argument about the distortion of sociological science by the intrusion of arbitrary philosophical assertions. Gerth maintains that a sociology that denies itself the cultural artifact, philosophy, as subject matter accepts a dogmatic censorship. He dismisses portrayals of the philosopher as social, like all humans, but, unlike all others, disembodied in spirit. According to Gerth, such findings of the sociology of knowledge as the correlation between the ideas distinguishing Marx's interpretations of capitalism from Weber's and the different attitudes marking their respective social standpoints are established empirically and are therefore analytically independent of philosophical theses about knowledge. Perspectivism is as observable in the products of the greatest minds as in everyday opinion. Among empirical studies bearing out this point, Gerth deftly cites Speier's dissertation on Lasalle, along with Mannheim's ([1927] 1952) "Conservative Thought" and his own work on liberalism (Gerth [1935] 1976).[13] Gerth insists, "If thought is bound up with the total outlook of the group, just as all other activities are, then there cannot be an unbridgeable disjunction between thinking and the other activities of a social group." He denies that this condition leaves social knowledge worse off than quantum physics, where results of measurement have "validity only with reference to the measuring instrument in use" (Gerth [1937]:1985: 201-2). In a note echoing Mannheim's letter to Wirth, he adds, "It is a pity that Dr. von Schelting... did not discuss these problems of the sociology of knowledge in the form presented by Mannheim but rather discussed them only in their older form" (Gerth [1937]:1985:208n.6).[14]

Gerth heaps up arguments. He implausibly equates Mannheim's contention that objectivity is brought about by an effort to find "a formula for translating the results of one [perspective] into those of the other and to discover a common denominator for these varying perspectivistic insights" (Mannheim 1936a: 270) with Parsons' unrelated contention that valid conceptual schemes are intertranslatable (TP). Citing Mannheim's essay "Competition" (Mannheim [1929] 1993), Gerth states that perspectivism does not preclude discussion; it generates competition "resulting in a constant enrichment of knowledge and the improvement of methods." Moreover, the criterion is adequacy to the intellectual framework of our time. Gerth enlists Dewey and Mead against utilitarian or idealistic alternatives, and quotes an instruction from Mannheim that expressly authorizes Gerth to say that Mannheim accepts their instrumentalism as "the epistemological viewpoint of his system."

After this dazzling potpourri from diverse German and American intellectual controversies, Gerth concludes: "For this instrumental and pragmatic view, the tradition of German idealist philosophy is a serious handicap. Indeed, it was mainly due to the strength of this philosophy that sociological thinking won so little ground in Germany" (Gerth [1937] 1985:206). To complete the case, Gerth suddenly flourishes the debunking capabilities of psychoanalysis. Not surprisingly, Gerth reports to Wirth that, although he received compliments from Read Bain and other stalwarts of the profession, they clearly let him know that they would not support the sociology of knowledge (January 13, 1936, LWP/4:1).

Gerth leaves Atlantic City convinced that Mannheim himself must enter the debate. Mannheim informs Wirth: "Now Gerth also writes that I must publish a rebuttal, especially to von Schelting. It would give me pleasure to do it now, because it would be so easy to pour cold water on him, in his arrogance" (March 2, 1938, LWP/7:11). Reporting that he has already promised a rejoinder to Max Ascoli's critique in *Social Research*—a work worth taking seriously—he asks whether Wirth will give him space in the *American Journal of Sociology* to confront his critics, "especially von Schelting."

Wirth replies that he and his colleagues agree to give Mannheim twelve to fifteen pages for such an article, but he continues with symptomatic caution: "I hope you will deal less with the epistemological and more with the sociological aspects of the problem, although of course we recognize that some of the issues von Schelting has raised particularly have nothing to do with sociology and would have to be taken account of in your reply" (March 2, 1938, LWP/7:11). Wirth sounds uneasy about Mannheim's angry enthusiasm; he urges Mannheim to allow his "article to stand on its own feet as a clarifying argument" and to refuse to "stoop to answer every nonsensical question that is raised." Mannheim never answered his critics.

Wirth's manifest reservations may have helped to deter Mannheim.[15] For Wirth, as he wrote to Mannheim, the discussion between Speier and Gerth was not the interesting part of the Atlantic City conference. He did not even attend the panel organized by Parsons. In the United States, the site of the decisive "dispute" about Mannheim's *Ideology and Utopia* was the meeting of the Sociological Research Association (SRA), where Wirth himself defended *Ideology and Utopia* against Robert M. MacIver and Read Bain (March 2, 1938, LWP/7:11).[16] The level of discussion was not high. Both sides combined to deflate the brilliance of the book; the attackers relied on hostile American stereotypes of portentous German self-importance, and the defender on American idealizations of sober, craftsmanlike social science method. Yet by comparison, the debate between Gerth and Speier must have struck the Americans present as a typical refugee display. Speaking as they did, these contenders could not determine the reception of Mannheim's book in American sociology.[17] The debate held under the auspices of the Sociological Research Association was a different matter, however.

Dispute 2: The Principals at the Table

The Sociological Research Association has been puzzling to students of the history of American sociology because it arises from the controversies attending the "coup" in the American Sociological Society between 1932 and 1936, but its membership cuts across the conflicting sides. Its activities soon become so uncontroversial that, by 1951, the approved history of the discipline by a past president of the Society (and member of the SRA) dismisses it as "little more than a catalogue of self-elected members" (Odum 1951:381). The Association is a counterpart of the *American Sociological Review*, which also was founded in 1936. Both institutional innovations appear to have been of slight importance, but only in retrospect, because both furthered the evolution of a disciplinary community whose discourse is complex enough to internalize the disturbances they manifested and to render them harmless for a generation. In 1937, however, they betokened a "situation ripe for compromise" in Mannheim's 1928 sense, a situation that was absorbing as well as noisy. The profession's bargaining—and the preliminary bargaining about bargaining—left little flexibility for an encounter with an additional party as demanding as Karl Mannheim. Bargaining with *Ideology and Utopia* occurred from a fixed position.

When Mannheim represented himself in his publications and his correspondence with Wirth as fit arbitrator between "German" and "American" sociology (Mannheim [1931] 1953, [1934] 1953), he was recapitulating his efforts at integration after his establishment in Frankfurt. In his 1932 address to German sociology teachers, Mannheim promoted a plan of instruction and research that was supposed to integrate accepted German approaches with the Chicago model of "social science" (Mannheim 1932a). As Wirth's "Preface" to *Ideology and Utopia* shows, "social science" was the common ground between them.[18] By 1937, however, Chicago Social Science was urgently engaged in renegotiating its deal with an American sociology whose transformation had been announced by a coalition's "coup" against Chicago hegemony. At the same time, as a measure of the progress of these negotiations, the leaders of the electoral and constitutional rebellion initiated in 1932 found that they were virtually shut out of the new arrangements which their actions had precipitated. Luther L. Bernard, the insurgent president elected in 1932, whose committee spawned the new official journal, was relegated to a disappointing role on the editorial board of the *American Sociological Review*, although his nominal allies were in charge; also, he was excluded from the Sociological Research Association (Bannister 1987:215-22; cp. Faris 1967:121). The "political" outburst of 1932 had unanticipated consequences: sociology was reinstitutionalized on terms that militated against the implicit "liberal" politics of the older reformist social science (see Gunnell 1993).

The Sociological Research Association originated in 1936 from consultations among sociologists who were anxious to maintain an authoritative voice for the profession in its relations with principal research funding agencies (Bannister 1987: 217). According to Faris (1967: 121), the precipitating worry was the politicization of the Society's elections: "Such political activity caused some of the leading members of the Society, not all of whom were Chicago men, to feel that the integrity of the society was being threatened.... Such a concern led to the formation of the Sociological Research Association, an organization...originally envisioned as a fortress to which the objective scholar might retreat if the American Sociological Society were to be diverted from its traditional purpose by the new regime." Its character as a mediating forum is made clear by the fact that of the preliminary list of forty-nine members in 1938, "eight were at the University of Chicago...ten of the fourteen members of the the ASS executive committee belonged, as well as five of the nine members of the editorial board of the new ASR" (Bannister 1987: 218). The founders adopted a cooptative design for an organization with restricted membership, a plan rejected earlier for ASS, but they included influential sociologists from the methodological poles of the discipline.

Mannheim's two critics in December 1937 represented the extremes of the SRA. MacIver was derided by some empiricists as a "mystic" because of his concentration on conceptual and methodological problems. Bain, a late replacement for W.F. Ogburn (Wirth to Mannheim, August 17, 1937, LWP/7:11)—the most prominent sociologist to be rigorously "objectivistic" in his scientific ambitions—was a less than loyal follower of the original dissidents. Scoffing at the Sociological Research Association, even while retaining his membership, Bain said that the SRA incoherently combined "some who think research is solely quantitative, some who think sociology is repetitive mouthing of Wissenssoziologie and other Germanic maunderings, some who think sociology is social work, social survey, case studies, and God knows what" (Ban-

nister 1987: 218). Bain's polemical analysis indicates his lack of sociological subtlety: in its time, the organization was constituted by complex probes and exchanges, not homogeneity. Only later did become an
annual dinner party, with the participants as their own guests of honor.
When Mannheim's *Ideology and Utopia* was debated, the meeting was
serious and the invited audience comprised the most powerful members
of the organized profession. In this setting, Louis Wirth backed his investment in Mannheim, speaking strongly in support of *Ideology and
Utopia*, but he hedged it too.[19] Afterwards Wirth cut his losses and became increasingly comfortable with the bargain that was struck.

   In his confrontation with Bain, Wirth has to match his earnest discursive style against an overbearing cleverness, as epitomized in Bain's
word-juggling conclusion to the parodistic opening pages in which he
applies the categories of *Ideology and Utopia* to "the present disorganization of sociology, a possible flight of the Gadarene swine": "The remainder of my remarks will be more or less dogmatic. This has a certain
appropriateness since the temper of the book is essentially dogmatic and
ex cathedra. This method will have the additional value of presenting
my subjective reactions to the book and thereby revealing the ideological and possibly Utopian foundations of my mind to those who are skill-
ful in Mannheimian analysis" (RB:3).

   Bain's charge against Mannheim is that he could learn nothing from
Ideology and Utopia that he did not already know because "the exposition of simple matters is often pretentious, verbose and muddy as if the
author were struggling with ideas which have long been commonplace
to American sociologists" (RB:4). Presenting a philosophy of history,
not a sociology of knowledge—"whatever that is"—Mannheim (says
Bain) offers nothing but a wealth of "vague generalizations" cast in obscure and arbitrary language. Bain singles out the treatment of intellectuals, which he considers a conflation of two incompatible, equally
unsound analyses, as well as the distinction between biology and spirit.
Mannheim, he says mockingly, does not even have as good a method for
unveiling hidden motives as Freud. Bain rejects the ill-informed attacks
on "statistical, behavioristic investigations" that he finds in the book,
and he denies the contention that the nonrationalized sphere has been
diminished in any way.

   Although Bain's polemic on the last two points situates him clearly in
the immediate context of disagreements about the uses of German soci-

ology, his sarcastic conclusion indicates his more general impatience with the process of differentiation and reconstitution in the discipline: "Sociologists will become more understandable to each other when and if they develop a conceptual scheme as commonly accepted by them as is the case with the symbolic consensus of hyperspace-time mathematicians. However, when the sociologists get so they can understand each other better than they do now, it will be correspondingly difficult for anyone else to understand them. So I suppose there will always be work for sociologists of knowledge" (RB:10).

In reply, Wirth first complains that Bain's procedure of dogmatic assertion "necessarily makes any succeeding comments appear like a complete apologia," disrupting "the progressive clarification of central issues" (LWP/ 65:4). His first concern is with the constitution of the discussion. Bain's manner makes it much more difficult for Wirth to talk past him to explore possible compromises with the others. From the viewpoint of negotiation theory, Wirth faces a party firmly fixed in position; he has to counter his sweeping claims, even while trying to amend the rules of encounter.

Wirth takes his lead from Bain's contention that his own dogmatism simply mirrors Mannheim's. He argues for the openness, the reasonableness, the moderation, the profound preparation grounding the book. Repeatedly citing the opinion of the educated world against him, he also contends that Bain lacks the information needed to recognize Mannheim's allusions to empirical studies supporting his principal claims. If there is nothing to learn in the book, he asks, how does one explain "the immediate, continuous and intensive discussion... it has received by responsible scholars?" Bain thinks it a vague generalization to distinguish between European and American "realism" by the greater attention paid to class structure and historical periodization in the former. Wirth replies, implicitly asserting his own authority, "It is strange that Bain feels it possible to deny so dogmatically the validity of a comparison which became something of a commonplace, not merely among European students, but also among American sociologists who have compared the content of sociological analysis here and abroad or who in the post-war years personally visited European, and especially German, centers of sociological investigation,"—as did Wirth himself. Bain claims to be perplexed by Mannheim's uses of the terms *subjective* and *objective*, the expression *rationalization*. Wirth counters that "so little are Mannheim's uses of the [latter term] 'strange and unusual' that they are practically the only uses discussed in that very respectable source, the *Encyclopedia of the Social Sciences*," a disingenuous response in view of the prominence of refugee scholars, including Mannheim, among the contributors to that compilation. Wirth uses similar reasoning from authority to counter Bain's claims that Mannheim's distinction between fascism and communism or his concept of historicism are eccentric. Wirth admits that Mannheim's distinction between biological and transcendent factors "are apt to be puzzling to the American reader," but insists that "to those who are familiar with the intellectual tradition and terminology of the culture from which this book comes" they are no more puzzling than Bain's use of "societal" would be to a German social scientist familiar with American social scientific literature.

Mannheim's supposed indifference to empirical work evaporates, according to Wirth, when it is recognized that his analysis of intellectuals, to which Bain objects, is "simply taken…from the results of competent (and practically unanimous) judgment of specialized historical research." "If Bain wishes to convince anyone that this view is unsound, he will have to provide new data." Bain misquotes Mannheim on his doubts about the scope of statistical method, according to Wirth, because the full context shows him to be equally anxious to counter "reactionary" opinion that dismisses such methods. The distinction between "relative" and "relational" is novel indeed, Wirth concedes, but Mannheim expounds it at length, and the meaning he intends is clear. Wirth claims no more for it. Finally, Wirth denies that Mannheim is indifferent to method, citing his brief remarks and his reference to his own illustrative experiment in "Conservative Thought," but he concedes, in parentheses: "It may certainly be added that a precise and consciously contrived methodology for the sociology of knowledge does not yet exist in a satisfactory form." Methodology is presumably the point where Wirth wanted the discussion to begin.

MacIver, however, offers him scant relief.[20] His manner is earnest, but his judgment is no less harsh. Like Bain, MacIver implies that the critical encounter with *Ideology and Utopia* is mostly a matter of prophylaxis for sociological theory, the response that ultimately distinguishes the American from the German dispute about the work. MacIver charges Mannheim above all with promoting a "dangerous" philosophical doctrine that "might afford much comfort to our modern totalitarians," instead of analyzing "even a single case" to substantiate the claims of the

"much heralded 'sociology of knowledge'" (RM). Yet MacIver bore
Mannheim no ill will. In fact, he materially assisted him in 1940, when
Mannheim appeared in urgent need of an American refuge.[21] The SRA
meeting was not about personal matters, or about human decency to
recognized refugees scholars.

MacIver (RM) welcomes Mannheim's attention to a problem that
MacIver formulates as "whether [and] in how far the social derivation
of our thinking prevents it from discovering the reality or the truth of
things" (RM:1). But he calls Mannheim's handling of the problem "ambiguous, confusing, and wholly inadequate." He scoffs at Mannheim's
attempt to explain his concept of ideology as an uncompromising extension of Marxists' insight into their opponents' thinking and concludes
patronizingly: "Both parties had resorted to 'wishful thinking,' as it has
been less pretentiously called by one of our own sociologists" (RM: 1).
Despite the tone, however, MacIver professes eagerness to learn how
Mannheim proposes to overcome the consequences of social scientific
thought's being "tainted with relativity" by virtue of its unavoidable attention to "realities" that are not "value-free." Yet Mannheim merely
skirts the problem, he maintains. MacIver stigmatizes Mannheim's theses as a heaping-up of dubious opinions, and concludes that Mannheim's
formulations of both problem and solution rest on "the Hegelian element in Mannheim's own Marxism." "The integration of many errors
into one truth, dearly beloved in principle by our modern Hegelians," he
oraculates, "surely pertains to the realm of alchemy or magic."
Mannheim's sociology of knowledge is identified by its "pretenses" of
being not merely a "pathology of knowledge," but also a "new science"
able to uncover the truth hidden in ideologies. Mannheim, states MacIver,
proposes to "revise the thesis 'that the genesis of a proposition is under
all circumstances irrelevant to its truth'" (RM: 3).

The rest of MacIver's comments dwell on this ostensible philosophical core of Mannheim's book. The argument, says MacIver, rests on a
confusion between validity and meaning; it bewilders the reader by its
play with "existence"; it illegitimately relies on the very distinctions it
has called into question. "Has no water flowed under the bridge between the day of Hegel and the day of Max Weber?" MacIver expostu-
lates, further echoing von Schelting. "Surely, after the illuminating
analysis of the greatest of German sociologists there is less excuse for
the equation of 'understanding' as an intellectual process and 'judging'

as a normative one" (RM:8). MacIver concedes that Mannheim has done some "excellent work" in "characterizing a particular approach or set of attitudes," that MacIver assumes to have been the objective of a work that he oddly identifies as "his book, *Das Conservative Denken.*" He also praises Mannheim for inspiring beyond Marxist simplifications in studying "the relation between the social conditions of a group at a given time and its intellectual habits." This is a proper "scientific objective." Mannheim goes wrong, according to MacIver, because he also "proclaims the 'sociology of knowledge'...as a scientific instrument for the discovery of the realities which these approaches purport to interpret" (RM: 4). In this respect, MacIver believes, Mannheim's sociology of knowledge cannot bear fruit.

Wirth's rebuttal (LWP/ 65:4) covers many detailed points, but centers on the defense of the sociology of knowledge as a properly sociological enterprise: "The point is...that MacIver ought not to have identified his strictures on Mannheim's epistemological discussion as being strictures on the sociology of knowledge." In wholly identifying the subdiscipline with an adventurous speculation incidental to Mannheim's work, says Wirth, MacIver has neglected "the more purely sociological question of the social conditioning of knowledge" for the sake of his own special interest in epistemology; and this not only distorts Mannheim's contribution but also unjustly transfers "his critical animus against a particular writer...to a field of study." Wirth counters, quoting *Ideology and Utopia*, that for Mannheim the "principal problem" of the sociology of knowledge is "the purely empirical investigation through description and structural analysis of the ways in which social relationships, in fact, influence thought'" (Mannheim 1936a: 239).[22] The epistemological inquiry to which such study may lead, according to Mannheim, does not affect the findings of the sociological investigation. MacIver's narrow emphasis leads him to slight Mannheim's sociological achievements. The dismissive introduction of the homely "wishful thinking" into the discussion fails to acknowledge that Mannheim's contrast between particular and total concepts of ideology serves especially to distinguish sociological from psychological approaches.

MacIver ignores Mannheim diagnosis of the widely acknowledged crisis of political thought and disregards his "singularly penetrating analysis" of the contending "modes of thought." Wirth argues that Mannheim's concept of "synthesis" is far from an alchemistic "mystery." It rests on a detailed explanation of special circumstances under which "each of the thought systems which are contending centers around a different aspect of reality," which it brings into "sharp focus," at the cost of unwarranted "over-generalization." For reasons that Mannheim develops sociologically, Wirth thinks that contemporary intellectuals have a potential for "eliminating the overgeneralizations and allocating them to their restricted but legitimate spheres of application." While Mannheim does not in fact maintain that social conditioning leads to truth more frequently than to error, his insight into the possibility of such occurrences is borne out, for example, by the "consensus among specialists" about the beneficial impetus given to economic theory by the "apologetic function" it performs when it is stated in exaggerated form. Social factors are even more likely to be implicated in social sciences dependent on "Verstehen." Yet MacIver errs, says Wirth, in thinking that Mannheim is indifferent to the risks while uncovering the compensating "advantages that come from such a multiplicity of stimulations."

As in his preface to *Ideology and Utopia,* Wirth declines to explore philosophically the grounds supporting the truth claims of findings reached by adequate sociological method. His aim is to rescue sociology of knowledge as a special sociology for which apt methods have yet to be distilled from an abundance of applied efforts and speculation. Mannheim's book is to be welcomed as a profound stimulus to thought and a repository of brilliant illustrative investigations. Above all, Wirth hopes that Mannheim will be acknowledged as a collaborator in a "cooperative," continuing scholarly activity that is recognized as sociological by the profession.

Wirth's overriding objective in his dealings with fellow-sociologists, including Mannheim, is implicit in his criticism of the published volumes of the three Congresses of German Sociologists held during the 1920s:

> In the papers themselves, and more clearly, in the discussions, the sharp division into schools of thought in the ranks of German sociology is revealed. For the most part matters of opinion still hold the center of the stage, and one can only hope that the beginnings which are being made of stating problems in such a fashion that they can be proved or disproved by means of factual evidence rather than authoritative pronouncements will characterize the programs of our German colleagues in the future. (LWP/56:10)[23]

Wirth's commitment to an empirical and cumulative sociology, manifest as well in his consultant's report to the Social Science Research

Council in 1937, required him to prevent the formation of anything like a Mannheim "school"—or even to associate himself, in Mannheim's words, with "a tendency that identifies itself with me. (Mannheim to Wirth, December 28, 1936, LWP/7:11).

Wirth's late reply to the letter in which Mannheim uses this language of school formation quietly signals the direction in which he hoped to take the discussion. "During the coming year," he writes in mid-1937, I shall again give a course on the Sociology of Intellectual Life, which I am coming to think is a better translation of Wissenssoziologie than the Sociology of Knowledge" (August 17, 1937, LWP/7:11). Mannheim's appropriation of Scheler's coinage of the German term was carefully considered. In the 1929 prospectus for the publication series in which *Ideologie und Utopie* originally appeared, Mannheim writes about the relationship between philosophy and sociology in his designs:

> In the collaboration between the two disciplines, the aim is not to erase the boundary lines between them but to achieve mutual enrichment. Imposing sociology on intrinsically philosophical inquries is as little the objective as burying the empirical methods of the social sciences under vain speculation. Cooperation cannot hope for more than, on the one hand, showing philosophy its point of contact with this most recent stage in the world-orientation of science and life and, on the other, directing sociology's research drive, in its empirical penetration of the world, towards a [philosophically defined] unified objective. Philosophy loses itself if it becomes estranged from the world and fails to address the contemporary, and sociology, if its inquiries lose their [proper] focus.[24]

Wirth's shift from "knowledge" to "intellectual life" abandons a vital dimension of Mannheim's conception. The defensive posture to which Wirth is driven by the negotiation from fixed positions (common to both Bain and MacIver) apparently prevent him from offering this concession in Atlantic City. Although he does not announce this narrowing of implicit claims, his aim is clearly to negotiate recognition for a field of study within a common sociological discipline—in boundaries congenial to von Wiese or Parsons—rather than to serve as advocate for Mannheim's ambitious and unfinished theoretical project. Mannheim knew his own book, however. The risks he took in it—and the demands he makes through it—could not be justified without deeper reflections about sociology than Wirth was prepared to entertain.

Ideology and Utopia leaves Atlantic City as a book weighty enough to attract the attention of well-known sociologists but intellectually too unwieldy for production-minded professionals. In short, it is a book to stimulate undergraduates when coached by suitable teachers; and Wirth leaves it at that. The American destiny of *Ideology and Utopia* was a function of several simultaneous negotiations to which Louis Wirth was party, and the outcome left important aspects of the book needlessly opaque to sociology because the decisive negotiations approximated more nearly the zero-sum type of negotiating from fixed positions than the win-win model based on recognition of interdependence. Wirth is negotiating with Mannheim about the contents of the book in the context of his wanting an important voice in the relations between German and American sociology; he is active in the negotiations about relations between Park's Chicago sociology and the rest of the profession in several forums, especially the journals and the Social Science Research Council; and he is bargaining about the book with influential sociologists in the context of his larger concern about securing recognition for the sociology of knowledge—or the sociology of intellectual life—as a subfield of the discipline.[25] Mannheim's hopes are defeated by competing demands on Wirth.

Robert K. Merton ([1941] 1968) finished Wirth's work four years later, offering a detailed sociological insider's rereading of Mannheim's book. He extracts and recasts the issues that make sense within the wider disciplinary frame of reference he subsequently helped consolidate (Merton [1949] 1968). Merton thinks that Mannheim's excessive philosophizing exemplifies a European penchant for speculation and distracts him from the unfinished business of specifying the principal propositions of his suggestive sociology of knowledge so they can be tested and refined through a systematic research program. On the question of methodology as such, Mannheim suffers from his limited familiarity with psychologically and analytically more subtle American writings; on the question of values, he needlessly obscures his return to neo-Kantian findings about the value-relevance of topic choices. Mannheim merits recognition for intuitions, insights, and hunches, many of which can be restated to guide exact research; and he stands out for his imaginative projection of an impartial new inquiry. Merton appreciates Mannheim's exploratory studies, especially the study of conservative thought, but he finds it more useful to abstract a "paradigm" of central questions for a positive science in this field—extended to include mass communications data—than to dwell critically on Mannheim's pioneering ventures. Merton's conception of Mannheim as a deserving seer, earning respect for his courageous anticipation of problems and themes that others must now explore with scientific rigor, became canonical in sociology.

Sociological theory would have been better served if the profession had not been prevented by its internal preoccupations from sharing Kenneth Burke's fascination with Mannheim's contribution to exploring "the relation between politics and knowledge," especially the shifting boundaries between ideology, utopia, and political knowledge (Burke 1937). The possibilities of win-win bargaining with Mannheim's thought depend less on attitudes towards philosophy than on recognition of the crisis of liberalism and acceptance of Mannheim as contributor in the multisided dialogue about political understanding. The sociological profession was caught up in strivings to acquire "normal science" in Kuhn's sense; thus works were classified either as dead "heritage" or as scientific contribution (cp. Rüschemeyer 1981; Nelson 1990).

Wirth attempted to make the case that *Ideology and Utopia* was a genuine scientific contribution, but he could not rescue the book from relegation to the status of "classic." He accepted the logical consequences of this organizational judgment. In 1946 Wirth cooly refused when Kurt H. Wolff, a younger colleague he had mentored, sought his help in securing funds for writing a book solicited by Karl Mannheim for his International Library of Sociology and Social Reconstruction:

> As to your contemplated book on the Sociology of Knowledge...I hope that...you are attempting to develop the ideas...more or less systematically. The difficulty, I find, with the field is that there is so much talk and so little actual research that we tend to make the field a critique of one another's ideas, but I know mighty few people who are actually, modestly inquiring into some little phase of a problem and doing some empirical research on it. (June 12, 1946, LWP/13:8)

The bargain brokered by Wirth excluded much theory when it stigmatized philosophy.[26]

Edward Shils' preliminary memorandum (LWP) for Wirth's rejoinder to MacIver documents a different American encounter with *Ideology and Utopia*, still critical and in a bargaining mode, but more open to Mannheim's own priorities in the book, a competition premised on collaboration. As befits a good staff worker, Shils numbers objectionable points in the text and provides Wirth with most of the counterpoints he uses. In a curious reversal of normal relations between apprentice and master, however, Wirth prefers to quote Mannheim where Shils has more confidence in his own elegant and often more precise formulations. Where Wirth speaks generally of the "more purely sociological question of the social conditioning of knowledge," Shils poses "the sociological problem" untouched by MacIver as "what is the relationship between the goals, values, ideals and norms involved in social action and our perceptions and theoretical formulations of an analytical and ethical character?" Where Wirth quotes Mannheim to show why MacIver's reference to "wishful thinking" misses the distinction between psychological and sociological levels of analysis, Shils demonstrates working command of Mannheim's concepts of styles and structures of thinking. Shils repeatedly challenges the "objectivism" in MacIver's critique, contrasting it with MacIver's own instrumentalist strictures on other occasions, as well as the sociological thought of Sumner, Max Weber, Tönnies, Thomas, Park, and Cooley. "If one takes MacIver's point of view in a thoroughgoing way," Shils suggests, "one is forced into a behavioristic position." Wirth leaves this kind of criticism strictly alone, perhaps because it entails acknowledgment of historical divisions among sociological theorists, as well as an unconditional rejection of the view that Mannheim is only concerned to explain and undermine ideological intrusions into rational thinking, a rejection more sweeping than Wirth wants to put on record.[27]

While Wirth is content to cite agreement among economists as authority for the claim that economics has benefitted from contributions activitated by political objectives, Shils offers his own assessment of the analytical achievements of Marx, Burke, Savigny and Adam Smith, linking their economic theories to their "sharply-defined political ethical attitudes." Shils challenges MacIver: "Are we to assume then that all their errors were due to their ethical motivations and all their correct perceptions were due to their untrammelled free intelligences?" He apologizes for making what sounds like an *ad hominem* argument, but contends that "such a conclusion sounds too much like the *überholte Aufklärungs* [obsolete Enlightenment] doctrines of Helvetius and Condorcet—and that is the position into which MacIver is forced." Parenthetically, Shils notes that the *Wissenssoziologie* promoted by Speier in his review of *Ideology and Utopia* "must [also] fall into this position or else postulate some purely rationalized personality which makes some men into philosophers." He returns to Speier later in the memorandum. In their critiques, Speier and MacIver agree in deprecating Mannheim's claim of a connection between the sharpening of political conflict and the rising awareness of ideological mechanisms, Shils remarks. Yet Speier is implicitly singled out as someone whose conscientious scholarship and engagement in sociology of knowledge opens him to continuous reassessment: "Speier...tells me that he is now making some studies of *wissenssoziologische Ansätze* [moves towards sociology of knowledge] in the 18th Century, and discovers that the awareness of duplicity, feigning, 'ideology,' and self-delusion was most sharply pronounced among those writers who participated actively in court intrigues and duplicity. Certainly here is a discovery or a rediscovery of the first order which was made possible not merely by outside observation but by inner participation." By his example, Shils is urging Wirth to speak as an "insider" in sociology of knowledge (Wolff 1974:556–59), but Wirth insists on distance.

The specific differences between Shils and Wirth are less important than Shils' eagerness to engage challenges such as Mannheim's "dynamic synthesis," linkage between genesis and validity (where he works openly on an interpretation about which he is "not entirely clear"), and other difficult issues at the border between sociology and philosophy. Shils stresses the superiority of the work done by Mannheim and his students—especially the dissertations by Gerth and Speier—when compared to even the best Marxist efforts, citing Franz Mehring's *Zur Geschichte der Philosophie*, Karl Kautsky's studies, Otto Bauer's *Weltbild des Kapitalismus*, and Georg Lukács' *Geschichte und Klassenbewußtsein*—"of which the latter two are the very best works before Mannheim." He welcomes methodological constructs worth developing and lashes out at "negative bickering and complaining approaches instead of a collaborative attitude of desiring to begin where Mannheims stops and to clarify and carry the thing further." "The thing to emphasize," he advises, "is that *Ideology and Utopia* represents a rich field of concrete research possibilities of which MacIver doesn't seem to be aware." Shils was an unusually gifted postgraduate student steeped in the German theoretical literature, but his intense response to Mannheim's book is nevertheless of some general significance. He was already anti-Marxist. He was dedicated to empirical research. But he was not engaged in institutionalizing sociology, and thus free to get excited and to be troubled by a difficult and essayistic *tour de force*, at least for a while.[28]

As a discipline, sociology declined Mannheim's offer. John Gunnell (1993) maintains that American political theory, in contrast, was unable to cope with the philosophical complexities pressed by the refugees; the result was a damaging division between a behaviorist political science devoid of self-critical reflection and a segregated arena in which political theories do battle without sufficient reference to the experiences of American political life. For a generation, American sociology avoided such divisions. The discipline's resistance to Mannheim illustrates the mechanisms by which this result was achieved, as well as its intellectual costs. Karl Mannheim lacked the bargaining power (and the bargaining agent) to enter the American sociological profession on terms he could accept. It was as a stimulating political thinker that he gained recognition, and the ensuing opportunities most promising to him surprisingly arose in England.

Notes

1. Mannheim is referring to the work posthumously revised for publication as *Essays on the Sociology of Culture* by Ernst Manheim and Paul Kecskemeti. The lead essay is "Towards the Sociology of the Mind: An Introduction (Mannheim 1956a)."
2. Beveridge gained the support of the Professorial Council in 1934, censuring Laski for his columns in the *Daily Herald* (Beveridge 1960: 55). The new director, Carr-Saunders, returned Laski to influence and high morale, when he took over from Beveridge in 1938. Coincidentally, one of Carr-Saunders' first projects was to replace Mannheim. See Newman 1993.
3. The chairman of the department ultimately wrote Wirth in embarrassment: "Dean Redfield reports that he has been able to pry loose $100 for Mannheim if you think we could induce him to come out for that amount and visit us" (W.F. Ogburn to Wirth, January 24, 1940, LWP/7:11).
4. Von Wiese speaks after E.W. Burgess, Robert E. Park, William F. Ogburn, and Lewis L. Lorwin. Louis Wirth took responsibility for translating von Wiese's paper (Von Wiese to Wirth, November 20, 1934 LWP/ 66:8).
5. The unpublished research of the American sociologist, Earle E. Eubank (EEEP, Käsler 1991), further complicates the picture of von Wiese's relationship to Mannheim, as well as von Wiese's standing among German sociologists. In 1934, Eubank, an unremarkable professor at the University of Cincinnati and author of a textbook on sociological concepts, began a project on the "makers" of European sociology. Helped by several American sociologists, especially Howard Becker, he planned and conducted interviews with European sociologists, most during a field trip to Europe during the summer of 1934. His interview protocols record personal impressions (reinforced by snapshots), general conversations, and a research focus on the single reputational question about "makers" and "outstanding leaders" of sociology in the various countries. They conform to Eubank's characterization of the book he still hoped to produce seven years later (with

Antonin Obdrbik): "It will not deal with abstruse questions of sociological theory, but will be more of a chatty 'travelogue' sort of book" (EEEP:11,2). Dirk Käsler's tabular distillation of Eubank's interviews with German sociologists (Käsler 1991: 612) lists von Wiese as the only informant to include Mannheim on his list of "makers"; and Käsler thinks the reference is favorable enough to warrant his coding it with a double plus, his highest assessment. Eubank did not interview von Wiese in Germany but at home in Cincinnati, where he brought von Wiese for a guest lecture in the winter of von Wiese's visiting year in the United States. Despite the possible bias introduced by von Wiese's calculations about the fitting thing to say to a well-connected American sociologist under the circumstances of 1935, his assessment of Mannheim as the equal of only von Stein, Simmel, Max Weber on his own list of eighteen names, would be remarkable. Käsler's rating is only a rough approximation, however, since von Wiese said nothing more than that Mannheim "is one of the ablest of the younger men." In any case, Eubank's own reading of his interviews—and perhaps his other conversations with von Wiese—did not lead him to add Mannheim to the list of "makers" he planned to include in his book. In a 1937 master's thesis stored in Eubank's project files presumably because the author was his principal source of translations from the German, Eubank's student, Nellie Jane Rechenbach, dismisses Mannheim on the authority of von Wiese 1931: "Dr von Wiese lists [Mannheim] as a typical exponent of the metaphysical and epistemological sociology—sociology of knowledge" (EEEP: 9,6). Eubank's interviews in Germany, in Käsler's judgment, show von Wiese matched only by Oppenheimer as a "negative 'star'" (Käsler 1984:14). Of eight sociologists interviewed in Germany and Austria in the summer of 1934, Oppenheimer, Vierkandt, Tönnies, Spann, and Alfred Weber agree in a characterization of von Wiese that Käsler codes with a single minus. Only Sombart and Freyer gave him a positive rating. This odd assortment indicates, first, that von Wiese's German colleagues apparently failed to share the assessment of von Wiese current among influential American sociologists, and, second, that assumptions about politicization in the German profession in 1934 have to be subtle—Freyer and Spann were the sociologists on the list closest to the National Socialists, but they disagreed about von Wiese—and that von Wiese's accounts of his professional difficulties in his letters to Wirth and his memoirs must thus also be treated with care. Eubank is an intriguing source, but lightweight. He knew no German, about German sociology he knew little more than what he gathered from a brief preliminary draft of a chapter lent him by Becker, and he was asking politically loaded questions in the summer of Hitler's great purge without any apparent understanding of the context. His only public report of his research was a cursory survey prepared for the International Institute of Sociology in 1935 (Duprat 1935).

6. Mannheim's 1931 request for Rockefeller research subsidy for his Sociological Institute in Frankfurt was rejected because the assessor found his students' work insufficiently empirical. See RF:RG2-1932/717/77/617 and cp. Craver 1986 for the ramifications. Schumpeter reinforced the "philosophical" label (RF:RG2-1933/ 717/91/724). The issue resurfaces in the Rockefeller Foundation's exchanges with the London School of Economics (RF/RG1.1/401S/73/969), and again a month before Mannheim's death (RF/RG1.2/200S/540/4616).

7. Shils not only translated *Ideology and Utopia* (Shils 1981), but also prepared memoranda for Wirth's preface. Archival evidence also indicates that Shils composed the lecture notes for Wirth's first course on the sociology of knowledge (LWP/66:2 and Shils interview, August 25, 1967, AA). The documentary record

is unequivocal. All in Shils' unmistakable handwriting: analytical reading notes on Mannheim, Grünwald, Plessner, and others; the analytical outline and the bulk of lecture notes for the first offering of Wirth's sociology of knowledge course in 1935 and lectures on intellectuals. Even after his departure from Chicago, Shils collaborated with Wirth on issues arising out of *Ideology and Utopia*. Wirth's 1937 rejoinder to Robert MacIver's critique of Mannheim in Atlantic City rests on a detailed memorandum from Shils (LWP/65:4; LWP/67:2).

8. Mannheim to Wirth on July 3, 1937. Although there is no detailed published information about Speier's interactions with Mannheim during the years together in Heidelberg, both close to Emil Lederer, there are clear indications that Mannheim's recollection of the facts is better founded than his bitter speculation about the reasons for change. In the earliest of his own works (Speier 1952), the two-part essay "From Hegel to Marx" originally published in 1929 in the *Archiv für Sozialwissenschaft und Sozialpolitik*, Speier's first footnote sweepingly cites Mannheim's writings as the source of his method. The second footnote credits Lukacs' *Geschichte und Klassenbewußtsein*, but adds reservations similar to Mannheim's: "Sociology cannot cede its right to examine Marxism, too, as an ideology" (Speier 1952:467). Speier's 1930 essay on one of Mannheim's major themes, in effect as a review of *Ideologie und Utopie*, disagrees with Mannheim on the social character and mission of intellectuals, as well as on the conception of "synthesis" as the decisive mode of adequate social knowledge, but is far from condemning Mannheim's project or approach. It is recognizably the work of an apprentice scholar "inspired" by a master, Mannheim (Speier [1930] 1990).

9. Gerth to Wirth, September 3, 1935; April 19, 1936; October 12, 1937. Wirth faithfully backed Gerth through 1939, until he was securely placed, including support for a rushed and poorly written SSRC project in January, 1938, all correspondence in LWP/4:1. Speier's personal backing helped overcome suspicion, especially in the exile community, that he was a German agent (Greffrath 1979).

10. Talcott Parsons wrote Louis Wirth an eight-page rejoinder to Wirth's review of the *Structure of Social Action*, in which he concentrates on criticisms of his abstractions from Weber's more historical contextualizing of the "rationality" theme (LWP/9:9).

11. Speier sent Wirth the text of "The Social Determination of Ideas" on November 22, 1937 (LWP/11:10). It does not differ in substance from the published version (Speier 1937).

12. This phenomenon complements the developments analyzed by John G. Gunnell (1993) in his stimulating book. "Weimar conversation" is Gunnell's coinage. Concentrating on political theory, Gunnell argues that Strauss and like minded antimodernist émigré thinkers radicalized the American academic reaction against the previously predominant liberal social science. Gunnell emphasizes the ensuing division between political theory and political science, with both sides assuming a philosophically fixed guise unknown to earlier American social science. The 1937 episode in Speier's career suggests another aspect of the situation. The American social scientists who called themselves behaviorists found opponents like Strauss more congenial than Marxists and other theorists who were in competition with them about the theoretical and methodological consequences of modernity. At another level of analysis, the odd coupling of behaviorism and antimodernist theory can be explained by their common opposition to leftist thought. As Gunnell makes plain, these developments belong to the crisis of liberalism. Mannheim's complex relations with Christian thought in the late 1930s

and 1940s manifest a comparable turn. After 1937 Mannheim never again made himself vulnerable to attacks like Speier's.

13. After first reading Speier's Mannheim review (Speier [1937] 1985), Gerth told Wirth he was astounded by the change in Speier's thinking since Heidelberg (October 12, 1937, LWP/4:1).

14. The posthumously published version (Gerth [1937] 1985) differs in small details from the Louis Wirth Papers copy, evidently edited by Shils after Gerth sent it to Wirth after the Atlantic City meetings (January 13 LWP/4:1). Mannheim asks Wirth about publication plans after receiving Gerth's report and expresses confidence that Gerth will be "a strong support in our intellectual struggles (February 13 LWP/7:11)." If there was a plan to publish Gerth's paper, it was abandoned.

15. Mannheim's failure to write the reply may have been influenced by a perception of incompatibility between controversy with sociologists and his promising effort to be accepted as authoritative and representative sociologist by a group of influential English policy thinkers (Ziffus 1988). He could not simultaneously engage in two such different negotiations. But there is also evidence that he was unsure of his philosophical ground. Generously responding to Kurt H. Wolff in 1946 after the latter had transmitted criticisms expressed in a seminar, Mannheim acknowledged that he did not think the epistemological riddle would be solved in his generation, although he had no doubt that he had posed it right (Wolff 1974: 557–59; see Kurt H. Wolff, *The Sociology of Knowledge. A History and a Theory* [Protocols of a Graduate Seminar, The Ohio State University, 1945–1946] unpublished. Partial copy in LWP/66:9. Full copy in AA.

16. Documentation for the S.R.A. debates is incomplete. While the talks by Bain and MacIver are available in clean typescript in Wirth's papers (LWP/65:4), the contents of Wirth's replies have to be taken as identical with rough-typed, single-spaced pages in the archives, corrected in Wirth's hand, although it is possible that Wirth subjected these to further editing. There is a further intriguing complication. The files contain a number-keyed copy of MacIver's remarks together with a corresponding point by point draft critique in Shils' hand. The absence of a comparable analysis of Bain's text does not mean that Shils did not supply one. Mannheim depended so much on Wirth's commitment to his cause that it would be worth knowing how far Wirth's public advocacy was a function of his dealings with his brilliant erstwhile assistant, by then establishing himself with Parsons at Harvard.

17. Edward Shils reports an additional treatment of *Ideology and Utopia* at the Atlantic City meetings. He writes that "[Robert] Lynd, under the guidance of Paul Lazarsfeld, presented a devastating critique.... He showed no sympathy for Mannheim's epistemological questioning of the prevailing belief in the possibility of an objective social science" (Shils 1980: 376). It is unclear whether this recollection refers to an intervention from the floor at the Parsons section or to a separate presentation. It would be surprising if two Columbia sociologists had delivered prepared papers on the subject, and it would be especially surprising if the prospective author of *Knowledge for What?* was one of them. If Shils' memory does not deceive him, the influence of refugee scholars in both cases is remarkable. Shils' memorandum to Wirth in preparation for the confrontation with MacIver repeatedly underlines MacIver's obvious reliance on von Schelting's coaching (RL:LWP/67:2). This parallelism, however, also heightens the likelihood that Shils mistakenly substituted Lynd for MacIver and Lazarsfeld for von Schelting. The session featuring the Speier and Parsons papers is reported in the

American Journal of Sociology 43 (July 1937–May 1938): 812. The Sociological Research Association program is not listed.

18. Wirth and Mannheim's assessments of affinities between *Ideology and Utopia* and Chicago social science are borne out by R.E. Park's enthusiastic letter to Wirth after he finished reading the book: "I was quite thrilled by it all. Now I know what sociology of knowledge is. I was surprised and interested to find a good many ideas of which I had given some intimation in my paper on Communication very much more clearly stated in this volume" (April 5, 1938, LWP 9:9).

19. Wirth's contribution to the 1934 plenary sessions of the ASS, when the translation of *Ideology and Utopia* was well under way, was a review and critique of five papers on "Regional Research and Regional Planning" (Wirth 1935: 107–114). Wirth received Mannheim's writings on planning shortly after the meetings, but he never answered Mannheim's repeated eager questions about his opinion of them, although Mannheim presses the claim that *Mensch und Gesellschaft* continues the sociology of knowledge (RL:LWP/January 8, 1935). There is certainly no sign of sociology of knowledge in Wirth's writings on planning. Wirth's principal target is Chicago's active antagonist within the ASS, L.L. Bernard, and he charges him with empiricism in the crassest sense, data-gathering without reflection on questions. Wirth's compartmentalization of his interests and approaches is striking.

20. MacIver published a slightly revised version of his comments as a review of *Ideology and Utopia* (MacIver 1938).

21. MacIver invited Mannheim for a two-week visit at Columbia in 1940 (Malinowski to Wirth, February 19, 1940, LWP/7:11) and later that year supported an application to the Rockefeller Foundation to fund Mannheim's appointment to the Graduate Faculty of the New School for Social Research (RF:RG1.1/401S/73/969).

22. The passage from *Ideology and Utopia* quoted by Wirth provides an excellent illustration of the adjustments Mannheim made in revising the English translation. In the German version, the empirical aspect of the sociology of knowledge is characterized as a matter of *phenomenological* description and the transition to epistemological inquiry is treated as a logical step that can be delayed or avoided but not called into question (Mannheim [1931] 1952:229).

23. Wirth singles out for praise Mannheim's "Competition" presentation in Zurich.

24. The programmatic statement can be found in Mannheim's "Announcement" (1929) written when he took over the editorship of the series *Schriften zur Philosophie und Soziologie*, originally founded by Max Scheler and published by Friedrich Cohen, Bonn (AA).

25. In an obituary notice, Leopold von Wiese recognizes the importance of disciplinary negotiations in Wirth's career, epitomizing Wirth's achievements with a recollection of Wirth's "adroit and clever management of negotiations" during the founding of the International Sociological Association in 1949. Von Wiese's characteristic susceptibility to anti-Semitic stereotyping mars his tribute: "His accomplishments were all the more surprising because Wirth's outward appearance suggested a crafty petty trader rather than a diplomat and scholar. Yet anyone who did not know him and formed this opinion after a hasty first impression soon found occasion to reconsider" (Wiese 1948: 578).

26. Kurt H. Wolff became the most devoted and original heir of Mannheim's sociological legacy (Wolff [1971] 1993; 1974, 1978; 1989; 1991). While recognized as a social theorist of standing, especially abroad, his position in the American profession has always been contested. In 1947, Louis Wirth responded to a sur-

vey of professional opinion about the state and prospects of sociology organized by the Carnegie Corporation (LWP 20:2). His meticulous answers to questions about "outstanding accomplishments in the social sciences...up to World War II" and "major gaps in the social sciences...great unanswered questions" disregard the "sociology of intellectual life" he once professed to see as an area of unique achievement and promise. In his only reference to the themes of that inquiry, he unconditionally reverses the constitutive base-superstructure relationship: "We have done very little...in making studies of the value systems of our society, and various segments thereof, and how their contradictions in values and our hierarchy of values affects our divisions into interest groups and parties which become organized around conflict, much of it unavoidable but some of which could be carried on more rationally if the issues were more clearly understood."

27. Shils expressly objects to MacIver's paraphrase that "Mannheim suggests [that]...relative or situational thinking *penetrates*..." He counters: "Mannheim does not say that situational thinking penetrates into the rest of our thinking (or into the whole structure of knowledge) as if the latter were a thing apart, preformed, with its whole categorical apparatus set up and which is then slowly colored by certain acts of situational thinking (again MacI[ver] exhibits a remnant of a crude objectivism). If Mannheim's statements mean anything at all, they mean that the 'whole structure of thought is situationally oriented,' i.e., oriented towards certain phases of the situation which our striving for the realization of our values have brought to our attention as problematic."

28. Shils quickly went through a repertoire of other roles within sociology, becoming an elder as precociously as he had become a scholar. But his deep encounter with *Ideology and Utopia* haunts his work, whether he cooly judges it a failure, as he has sometimes done, or puzzles over its unmerited neglect (Shils 1947, 1968, 1970). He was in England before the war, associated with Mannheim, and Mannheim acknowledged Shils as translator of *Mensch und Gesellschaft*, later incorporated in *Man and Society*. Shils, back in the United States in 1941, wrote an appreciative review of the book in *The Journal of Liberal Religion*, reserving objections to lack of detailed analyses, especially of economics. The entire issue (Vol.II, Winter 1941) is devoted to Mannheim and Freud, with an editor's introduction fully accepting Mannheim's diagnosis that "the present world crisis must be interpreted as the prelude either to a totalitarianism that will crush all individual freedom or to a new kind of society in which enclaves of freedom will be planned and brought into being in the teeth of an irrationalism that is equally destructive in its tendency, whether it comes from the conservatives or from the revolt of the masses." The issue also contains Merton's original essay on "Karl Mannheim and the Sociology of Knowledge" (Merton [1941] 1968). In a later issue, Shils published a letter from Mannheim thanking both Merton and Shils for their objectivity and attentiveness—contrasting Merton with von Schelting—and responding to a few points in Shils' review. Only six years later, in his short book on American sociology for an English audience, Shils (1948) finds the new locus of theorizing for democracy in Parsons' sociology and relegates Mannheim to a single, patronizing footnote, where he is noted as nothing more than a purveyor of information. Shils neutrally refers to Mannheim after he praises two publications that, as a matter of fact, single out Mannheim's method as the epitome of dangerous fallacies: "The best discussions of some of the methodological assumptions of German sociology are Karl Popper's "The Poverty of Historicism" [in *Economica* (Popper [1944] 1951)] and Talcott Parsons' *The Structure of So-*

cial Action. Karl Mannheim's "German Sociology" *Politica,* Vol. I (1934) presents a brief survey of the main topics covered in modern German sociology."
Shils continues, "There are no treatments of the French background comparable to Popper's and Parson's" (Shils 1948: 4–5n1), expressly slighting Mannheim's article. In 1948, Julia Mannheim was enraged by a critique of Mannheim that Shils showed her in advance of publication, characterizing his criticisms of Mannheim as "blind violence to somebody to whom you owe so much" (Julia Mannheim-Lang to Edward Shils, April 3, 1948). Later, she wrote her sister, the wife of Paul Kecskemeti, that despite her demands Shils had failed to return the full text of Mannheim's uncompleted "Essentials [of Democratic Planning],"—the manuscript commissioned by the Institute for World Affairs in the mid-1940s—although she had been able to thwart his plan "to publish an extremely nasty paper on Karl" (Julia Mannheim-Lang to Mr. and Mrs. Paul Kecskemeti, July 18, 1949). The missing portion, she contends, leaves "the book...a torso," presumably referring to the posthumous *Freedom, Power and Democratic Planning* (Mannheim 1950). Julia Mannheim offers various psychoanalytical explanations for Shils' rejection of Mannheim. Apart from false expectations she might have entertained of Shils as a candidate for discipleship, her disappointment had realistic grounds in Shils' abrupt shift. She was well informed about Mannheim's professional work. When Earle Eubank interviewed Karl and Julia Mannheim in 1934, he recorded that "much of their work is done together and a good deal of his writing must divide the credit with her" (EEEP, 3:15). In the absence of documentary evidence about Shils' reasons, the most promising speculation about Shils' disavowal of Mannheim's legacy is political rather than psychological. Mannheim did not live to make the Cold War "break" that became decisive for Shils and his intimate friend Michael Polanyi after 1946. (See below for relations between Polanyi and Mannheim). The management of Mannheim's papers and reputation was apparently a battleground for conflicting responses to the political situation after 1947. While Shils was relatively unaffected by the crisis of progressive liberalism within the profession of sociology, as manifested in the 1937 meetings, Shils' subsequent career was largely defined by the crisis of the same ideology in the context of international intellectual politics, where "progressive" meant soft on communism (or, in time, 1960s radicalism).

8

A Political Sociology: Mannheim and the Elite

Mannheim's sociological work—as writer as well as teacher—has a strong rhetorical dimension. His teaching and his texts evince throughout the sense of mission he emphasized in his descriptions of the sociological project after his arrival in England in 1933. "Competition," *Ideologie und Utopie*, and Mannheim's lectures as professor in Frankfurt are efforts to reconstruct "the intellectual" and "the sociologist" as terms of social discourse.[1] His truth claims are laced with demands that those who entertain them also enlist themselves in his intellectual undertaking, that they judge and counter his claims, so to speak, from his side of the argument. Mannheim demands recognition as practitioner of a discipline and method uniquely capable of giving voice to the consciousness of the groups comprising his audience. He not only wants to bring competing "definitions of the situation" to synthesis, as announced in his "Competition" essay (Mannheim [1929] 1993), but also to tell those who study his work who they are and even—as his Heidelberg students told Mannheim in their satirical tribute to him—"how they think" (*Soziologisches Kollektiv* [1930] 1986: 393). A confrontation with Mannheim's ideas appears to require surrender or rejection.

Mannheim's activism transgresses the bounds of Weber's scientific vocation, but he respects Weber's injunctions against deriving political value judgments from scientific work. The participants in the political schooling proposed in the chapter on the possibility of politics as a science in *Ideology and Utopia* (Mannheim [1929] 1952, 1936a) will make individual choices, as will both active and passive collaborators in the "planning for freedom" that is the centerpiece of his English campaigns (Mannheim 1940). But the choices are substantially conditioned by prior acceptance of an "empirical" reality they must first acknowledge as their own, and this reality incorporates Mannheim's image of their social identities and their constitutive problems. While such indirect but substantial control over choices appears to indicate an authoritarian relationship between Mannheim and his public, the absence of disciples among his admirers and the impressive variety of reputable thinkers who have reported learning from him suggest the need for a more subtle reading of Mannheim's rhetorical strategy. How is it possible to reconcile Mannheim's implicit hegemonic claims with a reality of varied and lasting influences on important thinkers?

One answer is that Mannheim made deals in his intellectual relations, though he lacked a theory of negotiated settlements. As Edward Shils (1973: 83) has noted, "Mannheim was extraordinarily sensitive to his national and continental environment and to his own time. He read widely; he had a lively curiosity and a quickly moving imagination which enabled him to respond to many kinds of events." Mannheim's rhetorical sensibilities include a sense for Cicero's rules of propriety, adapting speech to occasions, and, in the humanistic tradition, such adaptations are not equivalent to mastery of manipulative devices. The classical distinction between sophist and philosopher is internalized by humanistic rhetorical theory, and mutations of the distinction recur in Mannheim's conceptions of politician and educator. Without abandoning either his project of "rationalizing the irrational" or his demand to be accepted as a veritable voice of social reality, Mannheim recasts the terms of his discourse in response to actual or anticipated resistances. Rather than designating such moves manipulative adjustments in a hegemonic strategy, however, we prefer to speak of more or less tacit bargaining.

In theories of bargaining, the decisive conditions constituting a bargaining relationship between parties who hope to redistribute scarce and sought-after goods between themselves is a mutual awareness of interdependence, as well as recognition that neither can gain total control (Du Toit 1990; Bacharach and Lawler 1981). The interactive decision-making that comprises negotiations, moreover, need not be understood as a process of haggling from fixed positions. Contemporary approaches recognize that principled exchanges that adjust differences of interests can avoid much of the arbitrariness commonly associated with concepts of compromise (Fisher, Ury, and Patton 1991).

Mannheim's "mission" required him to reach accommodation with those from whom he sought to learn; this need is implicit in his unexpectedly qualified concept of synthesis, where contradictories may be transformed into complementarities rather than fully reconciled. His "mission" also required adherence from learners who contributed unique capabilities under their own control; this additional condition is evident from the record of his collaborations with both students and peers. Mannheim's "mission" implied collaborative relations, with implications of reciprocity. There are unresolved ambiguities about the alternatives between authoritarian imposition and mutuality in Mannheim's conduct as educator and there are ambiguities in his texts: resolutions come only in the diverse receptions. Some of Mannheim's listeners and readers find themselves confronted by intellectually protean—and thus unarguable—takeover bids, while others discount the occasional hyperbole and respond as if the terms were negotiable. The contrast between the receptions of *Ideologie und Utopie* by German intellectuals and *Ideology and Utopia* by American sociologists indicates that the differences in reactions—whether to reject or bargain—are not simply due to individual idiosyncracies. Some cultural environments—and problem constellations—foster willingness to benefit from openings in textures of thought, while others are hostile. Mannheim's work provides such openings because his thought is constituted by his own intellectual bargaining with others and because the settlements documented in his texts are often provisional.

Mannheim's writings are best characterized as a congeries of intellectual experiments centered on a basic theme that undergoes several striking modulations during his career. The goal is a rationality that comprehends and masters irrationalities not acknowledged by earlier formulations of the Enlightenment project. In addition to the widely noted shifts coincident with his relocations—from Hungary to Germany to England—, his thinking underwent discontinuities and reorientations in each of these places. Until his departure from Budapest in 1919, while mainly preoccupied with the nonrational creative forces that had such fascination for Georg Lukács' Sunday Circle (Karádi and Vezér 1985), Mannheim sympathized with the hopes of Jászi and other reformers that social evil was an anachronism that modern knowledge could overcome. His German studies begin with a philosophical search for a synthesis to transcend the reductionism and relativism attending the collapse of rationalism, and they end with a sociological project of diagnosis and sociotherapy to overcome the political incoherence due to universal distrust. In England, Mannheim's focus shifts to the fatal defects of elites supposedly swamped by mass-democratization and organizational technologies. Other important changes follow, however, as Mannheim moves from social science problems to problems of social education and to the public role of the elite. Since he rejected premature systematization, motifs from earlier phases of his work are never altogether absent in his later publications.[2] Yet the secular trend is clear (Loader 1985).

These transformations are best traced to Mannheim's ability to learn and to reconsider his views, as well as to his adjustments to changing external circumstances, to cultural discourses, and to practical imperatives. Mannheim moves through a sequence of settlements with key interlocutors, and the resulting successive resolutions rarely cancel one another (see Mannheim [1921] 1993). They define a series of places where Mannheim establishes his principal residence, so to speak, but they also constitute powerful memories he never wholly abandons. We can trace the main stages: Georg Lukács in Budapest, but Oscar Jászi too; Alfred Weber in Heidelberg superceded by Adolf Löwe in Frankfurt, within a more general framework defined by relations with Emil Lederer; the negotiation with American sociology epitomized for Mannheim by Louis Wirth, as well as Morris Ginsberg in London, subsequently displaced by A.D. Lindsay and T.S. Eliot.

The recasting of his sociology of knowledge project, both in Germany and in England, represents Mannheim's efforts to establish a basis not merely for recognition but also for collaboration. In decentering this aspect of his work when surveying sociology as academic discipline for university teachers (Mannheim 1932a), just as in redirecting *Ideology and Utopia* from dialectics to objectivity in the English translation, he hoped for specific and by no means narrowly self-interested returns. His adjustments pursued a strategy of going beyond disciplinary language— in Frankfurt it was aimed at anti-philosophical academic social scientists, and in London at sociologists distrustful of theorizing not informed by "psychological" terms of reference. Mannheim's sociological "mission" always included ideals of cooperation among social researchers, and his efforts to enlist those who studied him always entailed a call for a larger scholarly community. While most of his peers in British and American sociology failed to see the timeliness of his diagnosis and therapeutic proposals, Mannheim found collaborators elsewhere. His final design for a rational incorporation of irrational tendencies in social life reflects his new connections with English public life. Mannheim's trag-

edy was that his partners in these intellectual negotiations, while interested in his ideas, considered their dealings with him marginal to their
own intellectual and cultural projects. Only a few had enough at stake to
counter and criticize him. He made a contribution to their thought, but
they had little need to reciprocate, and they easily shifted from
Mannheim's work to other, incompatible sources of intellectual inspiration. Mannheim recurrently scolded his English interlocutors for their
lack of "seriousness about their common endeavors," but he underestimated the gap between them and him. While his marginality made him
interesting, it also excluded him from their practice designs. His greatest success in his new circle was with T.S. Eliot, and Eliot was no more
English or politically influential than Mannheim.

Mannheim and the Crisis of Christianity: the "Moot"

In the same 1938 letter to Wirth in which Mannheim reports on LSE
quarrels arising out of Ginsberg's presumed "fear" of looking "new
knowledge in the face" and his inability to "relearn," Mannheim also
writes: "There are symptoms that reveal that the way of comprehending
and interpreting culture which you and I represent has been taken note
of by very influential English circles. I do not view it as an illusion, that
in connection with the renaissance of democratic nations in the campaign against Fascism, this will play a role quite soon" (Mannheim to
Wirth, August 13, 1938, LWP/7:11). A few months later Mannheim is
elated: "Life in London is very delightful—the English are changing
rapidly. The dynamism of the time reminds me a little of the Weimar
Republic, as is also shown by the growth of my following among students and the general public. One has the feeling of having a 'mission'"
(Mannheim to Wirth, April 6, 1939, LWP/7:11). This theme of "mission," reminiscent of Mannheim's 1933 "feeling or illusion that one is
needed" for the task of establishing sociology, now refers to action on a
wider stage. He writes, just after the outbreak of war: "I feel, however
sad the happenings are, it is our hour, and our study of society which
formerly perhaps had been the satisfaction of scientific curiosity or pleasure in professional skill, must become the tool of the surgeon"
(Mannheim to Wirth, September 17, 1939, LWP/7:11).

Despite the tone of expectation, Mannheim's letter must also report
that the director of the London School of Economics has encouraged him

to go through with a planned trip to America and to use the opportunity to seek employment there, since he will not be needed in the reduced wartime program. Mannheim speculates that there may well be financial reasons for this advice, but that it undoubtedly also arises out of "the wish that the time of war should be used by those who, like me, have connections in America, for building bridges and making contacts between England and the USA." Later in the letter, having inquired about prospects for temporary employment, he escalates his speculations: "If I come to America it is very likely that I should be charged with the task of fostering cooperation between scholars and exponents of public opinion."

Nothing came of these American plans, and Mannheim spent the war years in various locations with the evacuated London School of Economics, working part-time, then with the Institute of Education of the University of London, where he received a professorship in 1945. He did in fact establish himself during those years as representative from one world to another, although not in the sense he had expected. His "mission," as it turned out, made him spokesman for secular, sociological thinking within the association of clerical and lay figures grouped around a prominent Christian publicist, organizer, and noted missionary, J.H. Oldham. In this setting, his legitimacy as sociologist was never challenged; but neither could it be tested and affirmed.

A close associate of William Temple, Archbishop of Canterbury, Oldham had become convinced, according to Temple's biographer, "that the most serious danger to the Christian Faith lay...in the secularism which was clearly defined by the trend of political organization and social thinking in the years between the two wars.... [T]otalitarianism and "scientific" humanism [now]...constituted the dominant creeds in State and Community. Here were two weapons pointed straight at the heart of the Christian Faith and the Christian Way of Life" (Iremonger 1948:409). To propagate the Christian social thought generated by the Oxford Conference on "Church, Community, and State," Oldham sought to found an "order" to advance the cause of a Christian society with more initiative and intensity than could be expected from formal Church organizations and with access to expert advice.

Mannheim was not present during the long weekend in April of 1938, when Oldham first brought together the group quaintly styled the "Moot." Mannheim joined at the next meeting, in September 1938,[3] and he was the only member except Oldham present on all eighteen occasions for which records were kept. There were twenty-four meetings in all, and the organization dissolved a few days after Mannheim's death on January 9, 1947. In addition to Oldham and Mannheim, the group included several clergymen prominent in the Oxford Movement, as well as T.S. Eliot, Adolph Lowe (until his move to Manchester in 1940), H.A. Hodges, John Middleton Murry, Sir Walter Moberly (head of the University Grants Committe), and Sir Fred Clarke (the director of the Institute of Education, whose professorial chair Mannheim eventually inherited). The formal activity of the Moot was limited to periodic meetings to discuss books or papers submitted by members or guests, usually after preliminary written exchanges among the most interested participants. But the group also generated the *Christian News-Letter* (which had a circulation of 10,000 and was edited by Oldham together with others in the group), *Christian News-Letter* books (mostly on education), and a series of lunches that brought a larger circle of public figures together with members of the group under the name of the "Christian Frontier Council." Through the Moot network, Mannheim became close to A.D. Lindsay, the master of Balliol, and other established university people in a variety of academic fields with a shared interest in social reform and adult education under Christian auspices. Mannheim was the most frequent contributor of papers to the Moot and the most regular circulator of memoranda, and virtually every of his publications after he became a member originated in a presentation to this group.

Mannheim's first contribution came at the second Moot meeting, when he read "Planning for Freedom," later revised as part five of *Man and Society in an Age of Reconstruction*. In this paper, Mannheim's elaborates the position towards which his first English essays were working. He succinctly reveals adaptations to his new audience, however, in a memorandum on the second topic of the weekend, Jacques Maritain's *Humanisme Integral*. Mannheim's criticisms of Maritain implicitly indicates his conception of the group and of his role within it. They also suggest an important readjustment in his own "way to knowledge." Claims of sweeping authority for science as the element of reason amidst the universal crisis of irrationality give way to the image of the sociologist as "practical thinker," as counsellor to an elite loyal to traditional values. Hinting at aspirations to full partnership, Mannheim speaks of "our problems" and "our philosophy" with new confidence and concreteness of reference; he sees himself allied with a real force against a

"concrete enemy." He is not simply an advisor on problems of implementation, however broadly conceived; he is proposing to become a
collaborator in the composition of a "'Summa' for our age." This can
only be done, he maintains, by "linking up the philosophical and ontological approach...with the empirical and instrumental one"; and this
requires, in turn, "a closer cooperation between the philosopher, the theologian, and the practical thinker."[4]

A letter to Oldham several years later indicates that the talk of a
"Summa" had not been merely a passing reference occasioned by
Maritain's devotion to St. Thomas Aquinas.[5] It also indicates what
Mannheim understood by the term:

> I am glad to see that my suggestion for working out a "Summa" has been supported
> by M. Murry and you. May I now add another suggestion? The discussion of a
> "Summa" as such may lead to an over abstract discussion of pure principles. Would
> it not be better, as it is our aim that our proposals should be in the spirit of Chris-
> tianity, that we should start with the discussion of...[the] surveys [I have pro-
> posed] concerning the recent changes in society. This would automatically lead us
> back to the discussion of the underlying principles of our proposals. Thus the mean-
> ing of the Christian attitude to the present world [the main content of a new
> "Summa"] would directly grow out of our discussion of the concrete details. (AA)

The "Summa" and the practical advice are inwardly connected. A
"Summa," Mannheim contends, serves "to bring our philosophy closer
to the world of everyday affairs and the outlook of the empirical thinker"
(AA). Empirical and instrumental thinking cannot itself create such a
comprehensive knowledge. They are, however the proper starting point.

Mannheim's comments on Maritain anticipate this view. Maritain's
humanism is too abstract, he objects, too much concerned with what
others have thought and not enough with what has happened and what
must be done: "Maritain's book would be even more topical and might
be a prelude to action if he had a concrete enemy such as the Communist, Fascist or Liberal in mind. . . . He could not in that case have avoided
a discussion of the strategy of action which would have led him to a
more thorough analysis both of the social setting and the actual psychology of the people to be changed" (AA).

Bonds between social thinking, social action, and "topicality"—that
is, belonging to a place—, are familiar elements in Mannheim's thinking, and there are clear similarities between this general approach and
what Mannheim had called "thinking out of a situation" in his early
work, and *"lebenswissenschaftliche Methode"* in his Frankfurt uni-

versity lectures. But it is nevertheless striking to see how earlier dialectical paradoxes of homelessness, relative social detachment, and unplanned planners give way to the security of shared English identity, mobilizing against "concrete enemies" under the traditional symbols of Church and State. Among Mannheim's earlier conceptions, it most resembles the productive conflict between socially mobile intellectuals and place-bound antimodern classes which Mannheim had examined years before in his work on German conservatism. As in that case, despite the seemingly harmonious adjustment, paradoxes abound. Mannheim is aware of himself as refugee among those at home: he remained a Jew among Christians; he was a secularist among the faithful; and he continued to aspire to a theoretical completeness belied by the regimen of topical and occasional pieces to which, despite all talk of a "Summa," he committed himself.

After Mannheim's death in 1947, the *Times* obituary said that "in a remarkably short time he penetrated to the essence of the English spirit, and became, in some ways, more English than the English themselves (*The Times*, January 11, 1947, 7)." It is neither a denial of the sincerity of the tribute nor an affront to Mannheim's deserved reputation to notice that these two clauses add up to an ironic awareness of Mannheim's strenuous effort to bridge what may not have been bridgeable. "Essence of the English spirit" is an expression after Mannheim himself; "more English than the English" is an English comment on it.

Like his turn towards sociological professionalism in the late 1920s, Mannheim's commitment to the network of English social Christianity had more than careerist purposes and did not imply abandonment of his own distinctive project. Here was another of his experiments, undertaken with that modern personal self-awareness which he found in such experimental lives as that of Saint-Simon. He was on a mission among these missionaries. Yet the experiment was not wholly successful. He had once memorialized Ernst Troeltsch as someone who sacrificed his inwardness to mediate between the academic and the public worlds. Mannheim paid a similarly heavy price during his late years. He suspended theoretical reflectivity, the main strength of his best work in Germany. The key problems of liberalism evaded him. When he finally formulated the "political creed" he regarded as the adequate contemporary expression of liberalism, he practically abandoned the claim to characterize and justify it as a structure of knowledge (Cumming 1969). The quest begun in the tension between Jászi and Lukács—mirroring the one which John Stuart Mill had begun three generations earlier, between Bentham and Coleridge—ended prematurely, in didactic exhortation.

This unfortunate aspect of Mannheim's position during the "Moot" years comes out especially clearly in two encounters with Michael Polanyi, immunized by his own qualifications from being impressed by Mannheim's legitimations as refugee or as scientist. Polanyi had been Karl Mannheim's contemporary in Budapest. He had been less active in the radical intellectual life than his brother, Karl, but both were Christian believers and attained scholarly prominence. In the 1930s, Polanyi was well established as a chemist in Britain, and gaining a reputation as philosopher and publicist. According to the recollection of a participant, Polanyi's visit to the Moot in 1944 occasioned "a ding-dong battle between Polanyi and Mannheim, the latter being taken by surprise at Polanyi's demonstration of the intuitive and traditional elements in all scientific discovery" (Kojecky 1972: 155). This report is amplified by an exchange of letters between Mannheim and Polanyi.

Polanyi thanks Mannheim for an evening's entertainment, their first long talk since Budapest, and he confirms plans for the book Mannheim wants for his "International Library of Sociology and Social Reconstruction" at Routledge & Kegan Paul. Polanyi expresses annoyance, however, that Mannheim has seen fit to cross-question him on the sources and origins of his religious convictions, as if they were some sort of pathological symptom. Polanyi rejects categorically that his beliefs could be explained as functions of psychological or sociological factors: "I reject all social analysis of history which makes social conditions anything more than *opportunities* for a development of thought. You seem inclined to consider moral judgments on history as ludicrous, believing apparently that thought is not merely conditioned, but determined by a social or technical situation. I cannot tell you how strongly I reject such a view" (Polanyi to Mannheim, April 19, 1944, MP/4:1). Mannheim replies soothingly, but expresses surprise that a scientist would make categorical judgments about something that is after all an empirical question, and he asks knowingly: "What would happen in science if one were still to go on and do what one did with Galileo, to reject factual statements because they were in contradiction with some religious or moral axiom one happened to hold" (Mannheim to Polanyi, April 26, 1944, MP/4:1).

Polanyi does not accept this commonplace. In a homely illustration of Kantian fundamentals, he says that every time he comes to his laboratory, he must draw on his reserves of categorical confidence in the logic of science, since the experiments left in the charge of his collaborators and assistants may all have failed: "Failures prevail overwhelmingly over successes, and the lack of reproducibility of phenomena is our daily bitter experience.... Still, from all this experience we do not draw the conclusion that natural events are governed by magic or by the devil—even though everything points in that direction." In the study of history too, he asserts, we must make assumptions if we are to understand anything, but in this case the assumptions are about freedom and responsibility, both moral and intellectual:

> No life can be without some conviction and the necessity to embrace one is as irresistible to the normal intelligence as it is to our normal moral instincts. So there is no way out. We must choose—and usually we have chosen already by implication. That is, we must choose in such a fashion that what we instinctively love in life, what we spontaneously admire, what we irresistibly aspire to, should make sense in the light of our convictions. When the prospect of such a solution opens up before our eyes, we undergo a conversion. Henceforth we do not doubt the faith to which we have been converted, but rather reject such evidence as many seem to contradict it. By exposing the fallaciousness of such evidence we fulfil our daily task and find ever renewed confirmation for our fundamental beliefs. (Polanyi to Mannheim, May 2, 1944, MP/15:3)

What is striking about the exchanges is, first, that Mannheim puts himself in a false dogmatic position about science, at variance with what he knows about its problems, and, second, that, speaking to his compatriot, he poses skeptical questions about religion he would never have raised at the Moot. Both points occasion misgivings about the extent to which Mannheim's experiments in identity jeopardized his critical powers and intellectual integrity. The question arises whether Mannheim made a "*sacrifice quotidien*" for the sake of securing what Marx once called "the this-sidedness of thinking," even as his erstwhile mentor Georg Lukács did within the Stalinist Communist Party.[6]

Such analogies are suggestive and troubling, but they are nevertheless misleading. The founders of the Moot shared a general orientation, including a missionary conviction that they should come closer to action, but they were hardly inclined to exercise overt intellectual control and they were little equipped for mass mobilization. At most, some dimly thought they ought to display more of these political qualities and a few occasionally had a regrettable weakness for expressing these vague aspirations by wishing for a Christian counterpart to *Mein Kampf* and for mastery of the successful techniques of the Nazi movement. For Mannheim, acceptance by the Moot represented not submission to a creed or organization but a tempting opportunity to act as a politician while remaining an educator.

Unlike the academic practitioners of social science disciplines, who were indifferent to Mannheim's warnings of systemic dissolution and projections of total regeneration, these Christians had a sense of "crisis." Yet they thought of the crisis as a spiritual one, in the senses common to well-established Christian churches, and Mannheim accordingly now opened his diagnoses with a "crisis in valuation" rather than a "crisis in rationality." In the sociological tradition, he drew closer to Durkheim and his characteristic problem of anomie; he turned from Max Weber's complex ambivalence about rationalization or Marx's developmental sequences. Yet his new audience simply helped crystalize a trend in Mannheim's work. Increasingly, he redefined the principal therapeutic task to be the generation of substitutes for the division of labor, professionalization, and legalization that Durkheim pictured as constituting organic integration. Mannheim considered these processes obsolete and insufficient in mass society, to be replaced by planning. In Mannheim's talks to the Moot, however, the functionally defined and thus sociologically abstract "planner" is transmuted into the English gentleman, whom Mannheim characterizes as a historical type accustomed for generations to combine theory and practice. Neither the intelligentsia of central Europe nor the professional social scientist, he concludes, has this necessary blend of qualifications.

The historical emergence of the gentleman in England, together with the professional man and civil servant had obviated the formation of an intelligentsia in the continental sense, Mannheim contends.[7] England does not know the dilemma of linking theory and practice. Although averse to abstruse speculation, the gentleman recognizes that knowledge is power, and accepts as his obligation to put his knowledge at the service of the public. In the terms of Mannheim's earlier diagnoses of the multiple crises of modernity, his analysis of the gentleman implies that the crisis of mass democratization has been muted in England by structural and not by accidental historical events: mass democracy has been resisted by an unusually successful democracy of the few.[8] The task Mannheim had earlier defined as bringing intellectuals to self-consciousness now appears as subjecting gentlemen to organization, revising the instrumental knowledge and forms of power at their disposal, while confident that they are in a position to recognize and utilize both. Bringing "gentlemen" to see themselves as destined for supervision of a planning elite, Mannheim thinks, entails none of the paradoxes of attempts to interlink intellectuals and power.

Mannheim contends that past performance and future prospects of this elite make it unnecessary to interfere with the conventionalized institutions of parliamentary democracy. Like the Crown, the forms of parliamentary rule lend legitimacy and continuity to the instrumentalities for social control, even while the substance of decision must be ever more clearly left to processes capable of determined realism, farsighted planning, universal coordination, and strategic sequential implementation.

The traditional values of England's liberal democracy, moreover, have substantive worth for the planning process, when properly interpreted. Mannheim finds similarities between traditional conceptions of freedom and his own notion that freedom is an element of spontaneous choice and decision within a structured framework of constraints essential to freedom (Lowe 1937). Without freedom in this sense planning will neither contain the pressures generated by excessive discipline nor retain the capacity for innovation. The new social knowledge, in other words, does not have to explode and displace all established social belief, as Saint-Simon and Comte had thought, and as Mannheim himself had earlier experimentally conjectured, but neither does it arise out of a dialectical interplay with contesting social doctrines, as the sociology of knowledge had once proclaimed. Sociology must inform, revitalize, and concretize the beliefs beyond knowledge upon which traditional values rest, and the reoriented elite must then point its control in new directions.

A critical point to which Mannheim keeps returning during the years of the Moot is the notion of an "order." The term arose in the group at its the beginning and undoubtedly persuaded Mannheim that these influential religious gentlemen might be serious about organizing for action, making the idea of joining them in forging a doctrinal "Summa" intimately connected with wide-ranging and long-term strategy seem so promising. Yet the "order" divided the group. Disagreements arose even at the first meeting. The Catholic historian, Christopher Dawson, spoke about the ultimate ideal of a "Christian totalitarian," and the Cambridge theologian, H.H. Farmer, set up the Nazi Party as a model for the order, stressing its closeness to everyday issues, its "transcendence" and its ingenious range of educational methods. T.S. Eliot and the founder, Oldham, cautioned that the order must be kept "informal" and "elastic," distinguished by "friendship" and "free discussion" (Kojecky 1972).

Mannheim, presumably working from the records of the first Moot, as was the custom, devoted several pages of his first Moot presentation to defining the "order" in the context of his "planning for freedom." "Half-way between the free lance existence [of planned sectors of freedom] and the organized one stands what we call the 'order.' Its task is to revitalize the social body and to spread the spirit" (LP). The order mediates between cumbersome organizations and irresponsible individuals—gathering information, innovating adjustments, and influencing the Church and Civil Service. Citing the Communist and National Socialist parties, Mannheim concludes: "A combatant order which forms an integral part of the social organism like its nervous system, coordinating its activities and spiritualising its aims, seems to be a necessary innovation in any modern, dynamic society." But unlike its contemporary analogues, the order "must desire not power but influence." Mannheim thus appropriates the distinction J.S. Mill uses to draw the boundary between his own conception of intellectual leadership and Comte's clerisy. But the change in the structure of public opinion since the time of Mill smudges the line between power and influence. Mannheim remains ensnared in the dilemma also manifest in his ambivalent attitude towards behaviorist techniques of propaganda. He mixes the language of technical control with humanist reservations: "Although they must have a highly developed technique for influencing society, it should never corrupt the mind or appeal to the lowest instincts of the masses." At the heart of the "order" Mannheim places "small consulting groups," neither "purely intellectual, like the Brain Trust in America, nor purely emotional like sects." Comprising clergy and representatives of secular thought, the groups are to be "the focus both of a new spirit and of a new thought." Stating his own claim for standing in the Moot—and drawing on memories of the "religious" quality of the Budapest Sunday Circle—Mannheim urges, "in spite of their intellectual differences the members should be capable of what we might call communion; for, sociologically speaking, a society whose mind is being deadened by large-scale organization has to find springs where the spirit of the community accumulates and spreads."[9]

In subsequent meetings, throughout the years of the Moot, Mannheim took the lead in urging concrete political tasks and a measure of political organization upon the members. At the beginning, the Moot agreed in principle to provide for "staff and cell groups." Mannheim next proposed that members use their specific institutes and other lines of connection to educate for change. Oldham was carried away to speak of founding "something analogous to 'The Party' (sic)," though also "wholly different" from the Nazi or Communist Party. These plans came to nothing and a reduced group eventually decided to restrict the Moot to the "body of friends who have established through common experience a certain relationship and common life."

The informality projected by this resolution did not dampen Mannheim's expectations or his campaign. In February 1940, he presses for "decisiveness" and an "active order," urging imitation of a "revolution from above." Two months later, he repents of the expression, but speaks with surprising enthusiasm and insensitivity: "The Germans, Russians and Italians are more advanced than we are in the techniques of managing modern society, but their purposes are wrong and even atavistic. We may look to elite groups in our society, e.g., the Moot, or enlightened Civil Servants, to use these techniques for different ends. The new techniques constitute a new opportunity and a new obligation" (Kojecky 1972: 175). By April 1940, when these remarks were made, the Moscow Trials and associated "techniques" cannot have been unknown to Mannheim and his audience, not to speak of the German administrative measures that had intensified in brutality since they had forced Mannheim to seek refuge. Mannheim was so fixed on the general message he wanted to convey and on the rhetorical opportunities provided by the situation that his judgment became at times perverse: "We are always waiting for means. But are not the means there? e.g., the Christian youth movement which is waiting for a lead, Oldham's access to people in key positions, the Christian News-Letter, the BBC, public schools, groups in the churches, etc. We are too lazy to move. Hitler started with six people" (Kojecky 1972: 175).

These were worrying times, and Mannheim undoubtedly spoke out of great anxiety, in a company he thought he knew well enough to stir up with his exasperation. Yet there is an extraordinary lack of political judgment in all this. During the Weimar years, Mannheim had shared the conventional dislike of parties and interest groups common to social liberals no less than revolutionaries and rightist authoritarians, but his conception of *Realdialektik* and his republican commitments required him to accept democratic politics. The talk of leadership and personalities prevalent among the heirs of Max Weber found no echo in Mannheim's German writings. The idea of Hitler as a model, even if a perverted one, is a shocking novelty in Mannheim's thinking. Mannheim spoke of it already in July 1934, when the American sociologist, Earle Edward Eubank, informally interviewed Karl and Julia Mannheim in London at the outset of his European field trip to research "masters of sociology" (EEEP, 3:15). Eubank records his delighted impression of the Mannheims' friendliness and grace, but emphasizes the strain due to the coincidence of their meeting only one day after "the terrible Nazi executions of the bloody June 30" and the Mannheims' uncertainty "as to the extent to which their friends might be involved in the executions and imprisonments." Eubank continues:

> Partly to make conversation and partly because I wanted to know, I asked them what was their opinion of Hitler. To my surprise, both of them replied instantly: "We like him." I was startled that such an opinion could come from members of the Jewish race whom he was persecuting and who, themselves, had been obliged to leave the country. When I asked why, they said: "Not because of his policies, of course, which seem very wrong to us. But because of the fact that he is an earnest, sincere man who is seeking nothing for himself, but who is wholeheartedly trying to build up a new Government. He is deeply sincere *(Einez Stuck)*, all of one piece, and we admire his honesty and devotion." (EEEP, 3:15. Also in Käsler 1991:28).

The report is not easy to assess, partly because it is difficult to know how the Mannheims assessed their interlocutor and interpreted the occasion. Refugees in need are never in casual conversations, especially when speaking to an American sociologist when they are eager for a "normal" American appointment. The Mannheims took other measures to avoid appearing as bitter, politically committed émigrés. Recalling a distinction Mannheim made in 1921 and that his student Nina Rubinstein elaborated in her dissertation, they impressed on Eubank that they were not "exiled or banished," but compelled to leave Germany by the circumstance of Karl Mannheim having been debarred from teaching. The Mannheims' avowals of admiration for Hitler must also be discounted by the extent to which they were using the trope of praising Hitler's moral integrity in order to assail the republican leadership he defeated, a nuance Eubank may have missed. In short, the report is unsettling, but it is unclear in political meaning. Mannheim's evocation of the National

Socialist model in the Moot six years later also serves a complex rhetorical function, but it occurs in a setting where he hoped to have continuous influence and where he consequently would be held responsible.

Mannheim is clearly politically unnerved: "We want to mobilize the intelligent people of goodwill in this country who are waiting for a lead. At the same time there must be a popular movement to back what the elites are doing. You cannot build up a great movement without the dynamism of social leadership. I am amazed by our lethargy" (Kojecky 1972: 175). One of the members was thereupon moved to produce a "Bill of Duties," which Mannheim delightedly proclaimed "a magnificent instrument for creating a popular movement." Nothing more was heard of it, although Mannheim reproaches Oldham with neglect of such initiatives for action, in a letter sent three years later.

In a memorandum solicited, evidently after prior discussions, by Sir Walter Moberly, fellow Moot member and chairman of the University Grants Committee, Mannheim proposes a different approach. He urges formation of a new social science faculty, preferably housed in the LSE but independent from sociology, to conduct research and reeducate educators, social workers, and pastors. It would also train leadership cadres for a youth movement. One of the "most urgent tasks" of the research would be to elaborate "our pattern of social reconstruction," which "would become the basis for our foreign and home propaganda." Mannheim opens the plea with a suprising revision of a metaphor he cannot have forgotten. Having asserted that "total war demands the total mobilization of our intellectual and spiritual resources," he contends that "we can afford to wage the battle in the intellectual field because we have, as a weapon, the social sciences."[10] Max Weber, of course, had thought that it was political ideology that was designed to serve as weapon. While social science education and research would encourage free discussion, the leadership training would be different:

> It is here that the great mistakes of our pre-war democracy must be corrected, namely that the intellect of our youth has been too much severed from action, and that freedom of discussion was misintegrated as a shameless anarchy of varying opinions on the basis of which no cooperation could exist. What should be established in these self-governing groups is the elaboration of a discipline, of a code of conduct, which make a pioneering attitude possible. (Kojecky 1972: 175)

The contrast to Mannheim's 1929 design in *Ideologie und Utopie* for political education is striking, although the teaching and research plan is reminiscent of the Berlin *Hochschule für Politik*, whose rationale Wirth considered equivalent to Mannheim's plan.[11] The principal difference is that the original conception aimed at informing partisan politics; the new one dismisses politicians and parties.

Mannheim's final statement on the proposed "order" concentrates his brief on the relationship between established elites and the Moot. He begins by praising the record of adaptability and innovation of the British "historical leadership," but finds that a tendency towards oligarchy has reduced their vitality: "The test... is whether in times of emergency they are capable of reorganising themselves from within, breaking traditional habits of mind, revitalising the dynamic elements in their own traditions, making the best use of outward stimuli and of personality types outside the boundaries of their own social groups." When vitality is lost, change by violent revolution is likely. Mannheim likens the youth of the day to the generation of 1914, stressing their "activism" and disdain for prudence. He invokes the powerful symbolism of Munich in a shocking way: "Opposed to the umbrella is the symbol of the trenchcoat which [Hitler] wore with such emphasis. In this struggle... what should be our decision? With whom should we side?" (RL:MP/15:3). "The need is to accept this activism and to see that it is directed to those issues which we feel to be constructive and creative." And: "There is only one organic way of preventing deterioration; it is regeneration from within. The regeneration of a group consists in a vital participation in a new spiritual movement by those members of the group who are the most alive" (MP/15:3). While isolated individuals have these capacities, they cannot be secure or effective in their exercises unless they reinforce one another: "The task of the 'Order' is exactly this: that it should draw together on terms of fellowship these pioneering minds who otherwise would remain inefficient in their isolation." Vitality depends on incorporation of individuals like himself. Mannheim likens the members of the Moot to the twelve just men of Jewish legend upon whom the world rests, adding only that they should organize.

From this Jewish analogy he moves abruptly to the inner circle of the Communist Party in Russia or the Nazi and Fascist elites. There are differences: "We can do without such rigid regimentation because the inner cohesion and solidarity of the leading groups in this country is strong enough to guarantee co-ordinated action in case of emergency.... As long as this country possesses a historical leadership which is elastic enough to give a lead to social reconstruction, there is no need for the creation of a new single-party system" (MP/15:3). He claims a functional equivalence between a "single-party system" and "historical leadership" and treats party competition as obsolete. "Right" and "Left" have been discredited by the Fascists and by Stalin and "nobody in the community who identifies himself with the historical situation in which we are fated to live" could follow the lead of either. The contrasting perspectives that offered reasonable grounds for the distinctions between parties have lost all relevance: "The strategic situation in terms of a historical setting prepares the ground for cooperation between all those who want both to maintain historical values and to bring about social reconstruction" (MP/15:3). Mannheim's extraordinary investment in the Moot was importantly linked to his hopes for the "order."   ⊩

A testy letter to Oldham in 1943 indicates a measure of disillusionment without acknowledging the effects of mutual misunderstanding. Oldham had circulated a memorandum on "The Fraternity of the Spirit," and Mannheim complains that the Moot was closer to a commitment to action in 1940. All this talk about pure inwardness and spirituality will "kill the spirit." "Nobody who really means business will join a fellowship in which he cannot know what his commitment will mean in the concrete situation." He continues: "I appreciate...the subtlety of this invisible social network as long as its task is the propogation of inner experience only. But I see no justification for this subtlety if our aim is the collection of men to whom ideas mean action."

Mannheim concludes with a valedictory to his disappointed hopes, characteristically ascribed to an objective process in which he simply participated:

> I may perhaps remind you of the fact that the idea of the order was originally conceived in strict connection with the assumption that it might one day become our mission to make this country aware of her opportunity to develop the new pattern of society, which is neither communist nor fascist, which is planned but still preserves the essential forms of freedom and all that on the basis of a pledge between the parties which could spare us the detrimental effect of a revolutionary upheaval. The idea was that if a religious group were to conceive and develop the image of a new order of society, its mediation between the parties would not only help them to overcome their partisan views but also to bring about the necessary sacrifice which is needed if the reconstruction is to be carried out to the benefit of the whole. At the same time it was felt that if ever there was a chance in history for the idea of Christianity really to influence our social institutions it was at the present juncture. (Mannheim to Oldham, MP/15:3)

Mannheim undoubtedly gained the assent of all or most of the Moot to all or most of these propositions at one time or another. But the Moot was not a center point for identity or action for most of the others. Sir Walter Moberly, chairman of the University Grants Commission from 1935 to 1949, said it strikingly, in an ingenuous idiom the sociologist Mannheim must have found very clear, when he confessed his discomfort about Mannheim's proposal for "revolution from above": "The Moot was in part composed of people who had cut themselves loose from ordinary standards of comfort, etc. (and who therefore had a reality of attack lacking in others), and in part of people like himself, who had comparatively large stipends and were consequently enmeshed in a certain range of social obligations" (Kojecky 1972: 174).

The Moot continued four years after Mannheim's solemn reproach to Oldham, and Mannheim remained active and respected. But his focus shifted to Chatham House, the International Library of Sociology and Social Reconstruction and the Institute of Education. And he never completed another substantial work for publication. Mannheim's disappointment with the Moot coincided with the rising influence of Michael Polanyi, whom he had introduced to the circle in 1944. Polanyi differed from Mannheim in substance and style. He was a liberal, a Christian, and his principal cause was the protection of science against proponents of planning. The Society for Freedom in Science was founded in May 1941, inspired by Polanyi's "Rights and Duties of Science" (Polanyi [1939] 1945). The group's manifesto announced that a new "threat to scientific freedom" stems not only from "the existing dictatorial powers but also from adherents to the philosophy of 'central planning'": "Those who would apply this doctrine to almost every detail of the social life represent an influential school of thought which makes a specially strong appeal to many of the more active-minded and socially conscious of the younger generation of scientists.... [I]n default of articulate and powerful opposition there is real danger of its success because of the enthusiasm it can evoke and its superficial appeal to the supposed interests of society" (MP/15:1). Deliberately mirroring organizational devices of popular front organizations, Polanyi's Society campaigned against the influence in the Academy of Science of the Communist-led Association of Scientific Workers, whose slogan was the "planning of science." In a confidential circular to members in November 1943, the secretary warns, "We have always thought the period of reconstruction as the most critical time for our cause" (MP/15:1). Although Mannheim and Polanyi corresponded on friendly terms until September 1945 and Mannheim solicited Polanyi's books for Routledge, there was more than merely a difference of views about science and religion between them. Polanyi better captured the changing interests of the Moot.

Differences between Mannheim and Polanyi are epitomized in contrasting comments on a paper on "Clerisy" presented by T.S. Eliot at the second Moot attended by Polanyi. Mannheim welcomes the concept, likens it to his own earlier "intelligentsia," but emphasizes the importance of the "elites in the elite" who "have the mental power to break the crust of convention in every sphere of life by penetrating into new possibilities of the mind and social living" (Moot Papers, November 20, 1944, LP). For Polanyi, the crux is the continuation of a "great heritage of the mind." Although "each generation of a living civilization must...exercise criticism and...make radical criticism...[it] must accept the overwhelming majority of thoughts as handed on to it." The clerisy is "a perfect example of a dedicated society"; and "where there is dedication there is faith.... This faith consists in the acceptance as good of certain traditional skills, values and insights forming together a traditional inspiration" (Polanyi to Oldham, October 16, 1944, MP/15:3). Strikingly, Polanyi reconciles his view with the subdivision of the clerisy into "specialist circles," while Mannheim, of course, presses the case for supraspecialist thinking to encompass situations.

Polanyi spoke for a revival of liberalism, not for its incorporation in a supervening design like Mannheim's "Planning for Freedom." In a short paper written for the Moot after the war, Polanyi reviewed the historical experience of "the men and women who came of age in 1918," the cohort common to himself and Mannheim. He recalls the faith in progress and its disruption, first, by Lenin's revolution and, second, by segments of the bourgeoisie who decided to adapt the Marxist "theory of politics as violence": "They took over its contempt of law and justice, of international obligations, and applied these principles in the first place to the suppression of Communism." In reaction to the rise of fascism, many turned to the communist alternative. Liberal principles were sneered at, as was Wilsonian idealism in international affairs. In the postwar period, however, Polanyi thinks liberalism can return. Even the Russians recognize the failure of their political conception, and the new weapons impel all nations to realize that destruction can only be avoided by mutual agreements, impossible, in turn, without trust founded on shared values (Moot Paper, January 6, 1947, MP/15:8). Cautiously optimistic, Polanyi breaks sharply with Mannheim's central topos of crisis. Assessing the Moot meeting during which his paper shared the floor with several papers by M. Middleton Murry, Polanyi writes Oldham, "I felt that we achieved a definite position which consolidated the gains of many years of preparation" (Polanyi to Oldham, March 13, 1947, MP/15:3). Coincidentally, Mannheim had unexpectedly died in London during that last Moot weekend.[12]

Towards a Practical Political Theory

From 1940 to his death seven years later, Mannheim's publications are dedicated to political sociology. The crisis of democracy, he contends, calls for a sociological theory of the changes undermining earlier conditions for the social effectiveness of democratic institutions and overtaxing the adaptability of existing institutional designs. Although dedication to democratic values is a necessary condition for resistance to dictatorship, it is not sufficient. Sociological awareness is integral to a political practice capable of steering society through the age of reconstruction. Mannheim's analysis in effect abandons his earlier distinction between technical and political actions. Governing comes close to applied sociology, a technology of social control. Yet Mannheim's fear of imminent chaos brings his underlying rationale closer to Hobbes than to Comte. The breakdown of controls over controls at the heart of the crisis has more in common with the war of all against all than with the dawn of a new scientific age of perfection. In the language of Hobbes' frequently overlooked contrast, Mannheim's political sociology is conceived as "counsel" for a responsible elite, not as "exhortation" for a scientific clerisy. The frayed connections between Mannheim's political sociology and the liberal project depend on the force of that distinction.

Like Hobbes' political philosophy, Mannheim's political sociology comprehends all "practices and agencies which have as their ultimate aim the molding of human behavior and of social relationships (Mannheim 1940:247)." From a twentieth-century sociological perspective, however, the state is no longer conceivable as an autonomous entity that constitutes not only a sovereign power but also private space for activity free of control. All human institutions now appear as "permanent elements in the political organization of society (Mannheim 1940:270)." In the absence of crisis, order is defined by the ensemble of social techniques exercising social control—that is, achieving the socialization of human beings in a particular space and time, integrating them in a system of social cooperation. Adapting Marxist ideas, Mannheim maintains that the progressive development of social techniques is the social process that has moved society through traditional and liberal stages toward planning. Crisis arises when new techniques render old ones ineffective without as yet gaining command; and the crisis threatens to explode, suddenly and unexpectedly, into chaos. The political imperative is to institute social techniques capable of subordinating the discordant newly powerful forces to stable and structured control.

Since government is the encompassing social technique for the control of controls, the discrepancies generating the crisis are manifest in deficiencies of government; and the resolution of the crisis requires a transformation of government. Liberal parliamentarianism had accomplished control by providing a forum in which interests could compete and by legitimating the ensuing compromises through legal formalization. The rational legality engendered by liberal government and the implementing mechanisms which it empowered depended on traditional beliefs, shared in the political community since the Middle Ages. Legislation and adjudication did not create these underlying beliefs. Liberal government, in short, presupposed traditions independent of government. The autonomous economic domain was similarly beyond its control; it served as an agency for social control over most members of society, as well as defining the interests whose conflicts and adjustments liberal governments oversaw. Nongovernmental controls as well as governmental controls of controls have been rendered perverse in their effects by innovations in the social techniques employed at both levels. Interests are now reorganized, Mannheim argues, to preclude the bargaining necessary for compromise; governments are bureaucratized and lack legitimacy; the system of justice is in crisis because it is too technical and opaque in its operations; and the slef-regulating economy does not work where economic organizations overpower the market. The control and coordination of the new techniques that overwhelm liberal government requires planning, and this in turn requires institutionalized agreement "on some basic values which are acceptable to everybody who shares the traditions of Western civilization," constituting a "militant democracy (Mannheim 1943: 7)."[13]

Democratic elections and parliamentary procedures should remain, unless political structures and traditions have been wholly disrupted. But the old forms must be given unfamiliar contents. Mannheim defines "politics" as "the struggle between the rival groups and authorities which determines the trend of development" (Mannheim 1940: 294), and he insists that "the reduction of the political element is essential for any form of planning" (Mannheim 1940: 360). Where controls are rationally coordinated, the control of controls must sooner or later be rationalized as well. Since the overgeneralized notion of irreconcilable class conflict is a principal source of conflictual politics, the social peace achieved through wartime collaboration will have to be extended through public policies of economic welfare and equalization. In any case, "elections may well be regarded as a guide only, as an ultimate indication to the consulting bodies who have to carry out the public's wishes" (Mannheim 1940: 360). Mannheim is not specific about the characteristics of democracy, except for emphasizing the need for proven rituals and for advocating openness to merit. Democracy is an ambiguous referent for Mannheim, oscillating between conceptions of institutional continuity and Rousseauist sovereignty.

Mannheim is more precise about the reorganization of governing after the abandonment of liberal reliance on compromise, law, and social processes beyond governmentat control. As valuable experiments with the new control over controls he first cites the effective if rigid techniques pioneered by absolutist armies, the brilliant psychological methods of "Americanization" pervading civic education in the United States, and the coordination of social forces by totalitarian regimes. But planning in the more nearly intact liberal communities will make extensive use of indirect techniques of control, using social psychological insights to manipulate the social contexts that most effectively constrain human emotions and conduct. Mannheim draws on various disciplines to identify several such agencies of indirect control, including communities, associations, politics, fields, and situations. Claiming Durkheim's *Division of Labor* as precursor, he finds social-psychological conceptions of "field" and "situation" insightful about the subtle methods of integration required in complex societies. Field structures constitute a world in which conduct is controlled by social and natural laws. To act intelligibly in any such world requires orientation to its norms, no matter what psychological motives may impel the actor. Conduct can thus be directed by regulating the norms. Mannheim defines "situation" more narrowly than in earlier writings, although the definition illuminates his broader uses as well. Situations are constraining contexts, like fields, but they are structured by concrete interactions rather than by norms. They lend themselves to "specific reconstruction and sociological readjustments" of the sort undertaken by social workers. Education and social work are important professional sites for the development of social techniques, but Mannheim does not exempt these agencies and practices from his general conclusion that innovative techniques of social control are socially disruptive until they are integrated within a plan.

"The ideal at which modern society is aiming," according to Mannheim, is the artificial replication of conditions prevailing in customary society by "intuitive consent," a state of affairs in which regulation is all-encompassing in its effects but experienced as self-regulation. Mannheim, following the casually provocative terminology of the time, speaks of the control as simultaneously totalitarian and democratic (Mannheim 1940: 328). Mannheim has in mind a situation in which cooperation, responsibility, and other minimal civilizational values are so effectively inculcated that they constitute a reliable foundation for autonomous decision and action. Because such values have been effectively destroyed by the emergence of "the mass," a phenomenon that Mannheim classifies as a powerful social technique with reductionist effect on human motivation, the inner constitution will have to be restored by field and situation control, along with more blatant techniques of mass education. Mannheim speaks of "articulating the mass," but apologetically assigns great importance to emotionalism and the manipulation of mass ecstacy. Social techniques of emotionalism are necessary to create the security and constitutional value-order that will free individuals—usually in articulated groups—from control by the mass, and restore them to rational autonomy (cp. Mannheim 1943).

Such coordinated totalitarian control is not antithetical to freedom in its modern sense. Planning will secure the social space within which spontaneity can have free play, and there will be no interference in individual preferences among the choices available. The norms of every field inevitably limit the range of choices. Planning will adjust norms by manipulation, but this does not differ in kind from earlier constitutions

of freedom. Freedom in this sense contributes to flexibility and ingenuity, especially among the elite, and it provides an outlet for irrational
drives, especially among the masses. Mannheim speaks of "mastering
the irrational." Instances of such mastering, in this puzzling anticlimax,
include the modern functions of sports as well as the uses of advertising
to counter the "chaos of consumer freedom," while allowing preferences
free play. Mannheim contends that indirect total social control is not
dehumanizing, but makes life more natural and less subject to instinc-
tual repression because it guarantees the conditions necessary for civil
life without direct—and punitive—social techniques of control. Social
techniques of control by field and situation, moreover, keep planners
close to the "creative tendencies in living material," and thus open to
change. Controllers in touch with situations are more likely to sense that
actions breaching norms that have been established by more formal
mechanisms may be appropriate and positive responses. Mannheim likens the social worker to the psychoanalyst, taking both as models for the
capacity of modern social control techniques to allow for the expression
of emotional needs. Rather than subjecting all conduct to rational supervision, such controllers achieve the detachment necessary to reinforce
limits while permitting even risky experimentation and expression.[14]

Mannheim admits that his political sociology sets forth a functional
approach suffused by technical thinking, and he acknowledges that romantic objections to such thinking are valid and justified—but only at
an abstract methodological level. The objections must be disregarded in
practice because the predominance of technical knowledge cannot be
prevented once the new social techniques are in operation. At the point
of crisis, possibilities of control must be ruthlessly explored and consci-
entiously applied: "Once the preliminary steps have been taken, we cannot escape the task of requiring sufficient technical skill to steer the
social machine instead of letting ourselves be crushed beneath its wheels"
(Mannheim 1940: 242). Mannheim had also used this image at the conclusion of his essay on politics as a science, when he referred to the
"party machine" as flattening everything before it. But then he had called
for resistance at the last moment. Ten years had changed his attitude
towards such machines.

Yet Mannheim also expresses sympathy with critics who counter his
advocacy of social technology with arguments based on principles that
Mannheim acknowledges as "valid" and "justified." He is thinking not

only about Jászi and Heimann's objections to *Mensch und Gesellschaft*, but also about his hopes for "communion" among members of the Moot. In an essay on social philosophy originally prepared for the Moot and expressly credited to the stimulus of that group when published (Mannheim 1943), Mannheim argues that the type of metaphysical thinking represented by Christian theology is a necessary complement to his sociological efforts. To perceive concrete, meaning-giving archetypes of human experience at the deepest level supplies a dramatization of existence essential to the constitution of commitment and action. While the theory of social control can neither generate nor test such truths, it must acknowledge that its own composition depends on a ground of moral energy beyond its ken. In a paradox reminiscent of his Budapest puzzling over saintliness and the soul, the essay on the utopian mentality (Mannheim 1929), as well as his interventions in the Tillich circle, Mannheim asserts that the experience of "presentness" integral to responsibility is impossible without a utopian vision, while responsibility in his time dictates the practice of a sociology destructive of utopianism. Despite these unresolved concessions to another universe of discourse. Mannheim returns to the functional mode of his political sociology. The social uses of religion are more urgent for him than the problems religion poses. Mannheim offers a token to his critics, but he does not qualify his theory of control.

As a political theory, Mannheim's design has major flaws. Mannheim fails to deal forthrightly with force and violence as aspects of political life or with coercion as an aspect of social control. A political theory that does not deal with the most signal political facts, a political history that leaps over the formative period of the modern state and moves from a stereotyped medievalism to a stereotyped liberalism, a conception of government that is uninformative about its form or processes—such a conception of social control is one-sided, ambiguous, undeveloped. There are remarkable suggestions, insights, reformulations and recombinations of earlier ideas, and there is an admirable display of energy in taking the planning theme out of the repertory of progressive thinking, and elaborating it into a comprehensive ideal type. In this capacity, the one-sided abstraction from the complexity of power relations is not simply a defect. By suggesting this wider context, Mannheim stimulated new thinking in such fields as education, social work, and economic planning. While he failed to produce a political theory of democracy, as he had hoped to do, he did generate a useful model for identifying new problems and possibilities.

Democracy and Planning Elites

Mannheim was not alone in elevating planning for reconstruction to a central political theme or in thinking that such planning required new institutions to link social scientific research and public policy. The London School of Economics interrupted its publication of *Politica* between 1942 and 1945, in favor of a "quarterly journal of reconstruction" named *Agenda*, a term still fresh enough to retain its original significance of distinguishing actions from matters of belief. Since the first months of the war, the heads of social science research in and out of government experimented with schemes for coordinating not only social science research but policy design, and *Agenda* offered surveys of this work and reflections on research coordination, as well as articles on specific reconstruction problems. Mannheim was not involved in the journal, and an opening programmatic article cautions against thinking that the war signals a "defect in our social order" or promises a new one. "This belief is vaguely held," the representative of the editorial group explains, "and it is a serious sort of concession to make to the Dictators. This is, also, a political democracy, in which each party will define a better order differently" (Macgregor 1942: 4). His concluding recommendation, however, comes closer to Mannheim's distrust of partisan democratic processes to plan and manage reconstruction. "In what sense do we contemplate a national policy of reconstruction?", the author asks. His answer suggests the uncertainties afflicting conventional political thought:

> There will still be political parties [after the war], who will wish to take different roads out of the actual post-war position. Each political party is, in fact, at work on its own plans. In addition, there are various bodies engaged on research into reconstruction, and the outlines of programmes have also been issued by persons of high authority. Will all this just be thrown into public debate, so that the path chosen will really depend on whichever party first obtains power? Or what is the alternative? There is a Ministry of Reconstruction, and its head is a party man, who is not likely to be neutralized. Ought we not to safeguard the position of the Ministry itself, and meet an unprecedented condition in an unprecedented way, by something in the nature of a Council of Reconstruction? How else will the position be straightened out.... Such a Council could not settle our affairs for us; but its authority could be such that no government could neglect its findings. We are prepar-

ing a great many plans, but who are to be the planners who will pass upon this mass of research and suggestions.... Reconstruction is being spoken of as in some way a policy of the nation. Then by what method is it to be made national? There is this and that which "we" are going to do. Either no promise is reliable, or "we" must have an organ for shaping policy. (Macgregor 1942: 12; cp. Clark 1942: 93-94)

Questions about the ability of the political system to generate or use plans captured the attention of Rockefeller Foundation officials dispatched to England at the beginning of the war to survey research needs. They were especially struck by representations from Political and Economic Planning (PEP), a group founded in 1938 by Julian Huxley. The most extensive report was prepared by D.P. O'Brien on October 5, 1939, after meetings with leading officials of the National Institute of Economic and Social Research, the London School of Economics, The Royal Institute of International Affairs (Chatham House), Oxford University, the University Grants Committee, as well as Political and Economic Planning. O'Brien reports: "The determination to carry on significant work will...overcome the present chaos and disorder. It would seem that an internal upheaval in certain governmental departments will occur and thus increase efficiency through the elimination of the intellectually unfit. It impressed me that some of the best brains of the nation are hard at work in attempting to bring about a peaceful revolution in England which will eventually eliminate some of the old inadequate systems of government." His concluding remarks refer to a planning document prepared by Max Nicholson and Julian Huxley of PEP, "which Huxley would like to place in the hands of President Roosevelt, the Rockefeller Foundation, the Carnegie Endowment, and important bodies such as the Social Science Research Council, [and which] has been read by significant groups such as the two secretaries of the Royal Society.... The document has been subjected to their corrections and approval, with an explanation that the matter was strictly confidential" (DPO'B to SMG. RF:RG6.1/281.1/40/471).[15] The PEP document, "What Are We Fighting For?", concentrates on defining issues for coordinated research "and propaganda," but the political implications are evident:

While I was given a copy of this document, I was counselled not to attempt to bring it to Paris because of the strict censorship which went into effect a few days before my departure. The document is in many ways charged with dynamite in so far as it would be a blast against some of the evidently inadequate policies of the present government in England. Clear acknowledgment is made of many of the significant and important advances realized by the Fascist and Socialist (*sic*) groups in Italy and Germany, and that certain of the aspects of these policies could well be introduced in England, while at the same time retaining the best of English life and methods. This would no doubt mean a great internal upheaval. The writers of the document are strongly in favor of such a re-arrangement of government and political service, which, it is strongly stressed, would be needed to meet the present problems of the world.

"In essence," O'Brien concludes, "the document is aimed at forming a government whose major policy would be to serve the people and would be fairly devoid of so-called politics."

Huxley, as spokesman for the group circulating "What Are We Fighting For?", wants the Foundation to discuss the contents of the document with other funding agencies, and if possible to have its contents edited for publication from an American point of view.[16] Speaking for a group of Commonwealth officials, the Australian High Commissioner, S.M. Bruce, independently agreed that research and plans for reconstruction require active support from American private and public agencies, and that this should be solicited through confidential soundings at nongovernmental levels facilitated and funded by the Rockefeller Foundation (TBK to SMG, October 21, 1939, RF:RG6.1/281.1/40/491).[17]

The intense discussions about the PEP proposals and more general issues of research coordination, in which the director of the LSE was a prominent participant, coincide with Mannheim's hints to Wirth that "if I come to America it is very likely that I should be charged with the task of fostering cooperation between scholars and exponents of public opinion" (Mannheim to Wirth, September 19, 1939, LWP/7:11). The correspondence between Carr-Saunders and the Rockefeller Foundation effectively excludes the possibility of the director having given Mannheim any encouragement for such speculation; Carr-Saunders thought that Mannheim failed to understand empirical research and he was concerned about Mannheim's lack of naturalization (Carr-Saunders to Kittredge, September 19, 1939, RF:RG1.1/401S/73/969). Julian Huxley of the Political and Economic Planning group, the principal force behind the idea, was selected as "a representative of the British groups" (Kittredge to Willits, November 20, 1939, RF: RG6.1/281.1/40/491). But there can be little doubt that Mannheim knew about the discussions, and he evidently hoped for an assignment connected with these plans despite the distance between himself and the most important interlocutors of the Rockefeller Foundation. One point of contact between Mannheim and the planners was Sir Walter Moberly, who had been so impressed by Mannheim's first Moot presentation that he invited him to write up a proposal for a special social science faculty in 1938.[18] The discordance between the language in which Mannheim's ideas were expressed and traditional patterns of English thought (Harris 1986: 241) did not wholly exclude him from political influence.

His most highly placed admirer was R.A. Butler, Minister of Education between 1941 and 1945. Mannheim's acquaintance with Butler dated from the summer of 1940, when they met and engaged "in a series of conversations…which 'cleared the ground for definite action in the field of planning.' They found that their views on reconstruction 'were in full accord'" (Harris 1986: 240).[19] Butler was the leader of Conservative Party reconstruction planning subcommittees charged with designing a strategic conception for the party's future. The circle of Conservative intellectuals he recruited shared his fascination with older Tory ideas about Christian organic community. Butler was simultaneously "a modern Peelite and supporter of empiricism and material progress," and the combination of these clashing aspirations explains his sympathy for Mannheim's attempted synthesis of similar elements. The draft of "Planning for Freedom" was circulated in Butler's group before Mannheim published it in *Man and Society*; and "draft outlines of a potential Conservative reconstruction program in 1941 and 1942" contained elements compatible with Mannheim's views, despite important differences in language. More direct were the connections between Mannheim's thinking and the work of the education subcommittee selected by Butler (Harris 1986: 242–46). In the end, neither the program nor the report of the subcommittee prevailed, but the appeal to Mannheim in these deliberations is an indication that Mannheim's voice had resonance in the political discourse of his time, notwithstanding its foreign tone. It would be a mistake, however, simply to identify Mannheim with the utopian streak in political conservatism.[20] A subtler insight into Mannheim's political place is provided by Mannheim's correspondence on political matters with his friend A.D. Lindsay, the Master of Balliol.

Lindsay was not only an important academic politician and Moot member, but also a widely recognized liberal democratic political theorist. Lindsay began his career in Scotland, gaining notice as a leading thinker of the Labour Party. In 1938, Lindsay ran as a radical anti-Tory candidate in a famous by-election. By the time Mannheim knew him, he was Master of Balliol and active in social Christian groups. Although he never agreed with Mannheim on some important issues, he eagerly engaged him in correspondence and conversations while composing *The Modern Democratic State* (1943). Against vigorous opposition, Lindsay attempted to make Mannheim the director of a major publication program on "Democracy and Its Working," planned by Chatham House in 1941 and funded by the Rockefeller Foundation. In notes prepared for an obituary broadcast, Lindsay describes his relations with Mannheim:

> I remember vividly the occasion when I first met Dr. Karl Mannheim. He had sent me a copy of his book *Ideology and Utopia*. We had some correspondence about it. I asked him to come and stay with me for a weekend. The matters of our discussion could not be dealt with satisfactorily in correspondence. He came. I had a fine weekend, and we talked to our hearts' content ranging over our whole social theories. I, while welcoming and interested in almost all he said, thought him too systematic, too elaborate, too much of a planner. He thought me too empirical, too intuitive. But I knew that each of us was interested in the other's views and wanted to hear more. But with this beginning of a warm friendship between us, he sent me his writings and I sent him mine and we continually interchanged ideas. (LP)

An example of these exchanges is a long letter from Mannheim in 1941 on an early draft of Lindsay's book. A remark on a specific chapter sets the tone for the whole: "[I]t is not only the great numbers which create new obstacles to democracy," Mannheim notes, nor is it only "the problem of 'discussion'" More important is the "emergence of new social techniques" which "hamper democratic institutions in their working" because they create "a chance for minority rule." For these reasons, Mannheim says, he "should rather like to see the constitutional discussion turned into one of social organisation in general." Mannheim welcomes Lindsay's dual emphasis on the aristocratic and religious roots of English democracy, underlining the importance of the latter in view of the decline of the former traditions. But he cautions against drawing mechanical egalitarian conclusions from the "equal priesthood of all believers": the religious emphasis implies an obligation to raise individuals to service. Characteristically, Mannheim relativizes distrust of the central state, citing his own experience in Republican Germany, where "for about a decade the spirit of progress was at work in the Ministry of Education whereas the spirit of semifeudal tradition barricaded itself in the semi-autonomous bodies of the universities" (Mannheim to Lindsay, November 19, 1940, LP). In a striking passage, Mannheim remarks parenthetically, having praised Lindsay's defense of "final causes" as a framework for values, "it is in this context that I understand more and more your emphasis on political science apart from descriptive sociology. You mean by political science the setting in which the element of purpose and value in political problems is not being neutralized." He expresses a revealing doubt about this, "whether the removing of the sociological problems into the purely technical field doesn't once more kill the spirit in them," but drops the question. The aim is to distinguish neutrality from tolerance, and to abandon the former while proclaiming the latter: "the belief in truth includes the belief in free thought and experiment. Politics, ethics and economics are heading for a new integration."

Mannheim is most vehement on the theme of elites. He poses problems of "qualitative" selection and emphasizes the need for newcomers who can revitalize elites tamed by established institutions. In this context, he expands on "the amazing vitality and efficiency of the Nazis," as well as Hitler's "new impetus which simply says 'it must be done' and doesn't care about the taboos of the old-fashioned economist or strategist." British elites are too rigid and the opening to talents is too conditioned on conformity: "what is lacking is both a progressive leadership of the middle classes which could prevent them from becoming fascist and the vitalizing new ferment in the historical leadership which as in the past made them able to adapt their minds to the requirement of new situations." This brings Mannheim back to his "order," which "should represent a *sect* within the old leadership, with its spiritual powers it should bring about the fermentation and reorganization which by methods of reform would gradually transform the traditional leadership groups into the new type of leadership."

In his broadcast after Mannheim's death, Lindsay explains how he understood Mannheim's elitist arguments:

There are those who regard "democratic planning" as a contradiction in terms. "Planning" seems to imply a "planner" or at most a committee of planners—in one way or another a few superior people imposing their ideas on a whole community. Mannheim's democratic planning implied the existence throughout a society of what he called "social awareness." He recognized that "democratic planning" meant the voluntary cooperation of many elements in society: it meant a habit of widespread discussion: it meant that the leaders of all the various sections of society— politicians, churchmen, industrialists, trade unionists and others—should have a genuine sense of common purpose and a belief in the same social values. His main business as a sociologist he considered to be to point out the factors in society which made possible this social discussion. His "plan" was as unlike as possible to a "blue print" or an elaborated scheme of legislation. It was more like a doctor's diagnosis than an engineer's drawing. He tried to discern the decisive factors which made for the health and vitality of society. This method of approaching political problems needed a rare combination of learning and wisdom. (LP)

Lindsay's liberal interpretation of Mannheim's challenge illustrates the cultural confidence that simultaneously delighted and provoked Mannheim. In discussion with an earnest, self-confident partner in the context of secure democratic institutions, Mannheim's sometimes scandalous indifference to democratic political norms appeared stimulating. Mannheim's description of their relations almost two years after his original comments on *The Modern Democratic State* also carry conviction, despite some polite exaggeration. Having traced their disagreement about state power— whether it should be understood as sovereignty in a sociologically realistic sense or as the workings of the constitution—to a difference between the German mind and the English mind, Mannheim writes: "[I]n my view much more important than whether one has a German or an English mind is that one should have both. I really think that the future of thinking rests with those of us who have got a bi-lingual mind...What I always enjoyed in my discussions with you was that they were a real 'Auseinandersetzung' where we could all of a sudden see that behind our personal differences stood the conflict and the possible synthesis of different worlds" (Mannheim to Lindsay, June 4, 1942, LP).

It was not the Mannheim of discussion and compromise who responded to the opportunity Lindsay opened for him at Chatham House in 1941. The Publications Committee sought to publish "a statement of the principles of democracy...an appraisal of [successes and failures], with a view to providing the facts necessary for an examination of how democracy as a form of society is to meet...the challenge of the totalitarian system of government and to convince others of its worth as a substitute" (May 5, 1941, LP). Mannheim was commissioned to prepare a plan of research and responded with fifteen single-spaced pages, "Studies in Democracy: A Research Plan" (LP), encompassing ten vast topics and a scheme for "an organic synthesis in which the group work as an entity and try to agree on the scope of the work, the methods to be used, and to watch the natural ramifications of the problems rather than their traditional departmental aspects." The topics ranged across functional, idealist, psychological, historical, structural, and cultural approaches, with a list of questions for each, and the plan ended with the theme of "democratic reconstruction." Lindsay's book was allotted a spot, taken as exemplification of idealism, and Mannheim's familiar planning theses unified the conception. Several of the committee's consultants were appalled.

The most hostile, G.M. Young, pleaded for an empirical approach, studying actual political systems before deciding whether there was any such thing as democracy, protesting that "under the domed and columned magnificence of [Mannheim's] enterprise any bricks and mortar would look like an Anderson Shelter set down in Santa Sophia." Classically fulfilling Mannheim's more dire prophecies about English reactions to his ideas, Young pleads: "With all humility, I hope the Publications Committee will before adopting the Mannheim scheme, consider very carefully whether this native method of inquiry... is to be ousted by a procedure which in every line betrays its continental inspiration, and is really a product of the political inexperience of the academic classes in Germany and Russia"(LP). R.C.K. Ensor is more subtle in assessing this "highly characteristic document." He would like to see it funded if wartime personnel problems can be solved, but only "if the proposal were that Dr. Mannheim should run a seminar of young research workers, who might fairly be regarded as his disciples, and whose function would be to enable him to paint a larger canvas than his individual brush could cover" (a relation something like that of Rubens' pupils to Rubens). Lindsay, speaking for Mannheim as well as himself, picks up Ensor's suggestion of several separate books, with Mannheim's only one among these, and apologizes for Mannheim's having smothered this original idea up in detail. Ensor suggests Mannheim for a book on the social dimensions of democracy, while Lindsay urges that he be assigned "The Breakdown of Continental Democracies." Neither of them suggest what eventually emerges as his assignment from the subcommittee that was struck, "The Essentials of Democratic Planning," a project that was resisted in the committee at every stage of deliberations and successfully defended by Lindsay, and that yielded no published results in Mannheim's lifetime.[21]

Theories and Ideas: Limits of Bilingualism

Many of those Mannheim addressed in England and America could not sympathize with his theoretical interest and took his systematizing statements as manifestations of a continental weakness for abstruse speculation. Others carried on their own theoretical discourse in modalities to which Mannheim was largely tone-deaf, and they avenged his seeming indifference to their accomplishments by their response to his efforts. The one group, exemplified by the Moot, humoured his weakness for system-building, but were satisfied to abstract the many ideas they found rewarding. The other, including some of his professional colleagues, finally "reacted furiously to him...and considered him a charlatan who confused young people" by posing "deep" but unanswerable questions "but couldn't teach them anything because he didn't have anything valuable to teach" (interview with Jean Floud, March 2, 1976, AA). Both kinds of responses worked back on Mannheim's theoretical efforts, to their marked detriment.

Mannheim was admired by a number of people of intellectual achievement and discernment during his years on the Moot. They secured him the position at the Institute of Education and they enabled him to found the International Library of Sociology and Social Reconstruction at Routledge & Kegan Paul. And they thanked him for suggestions and praised him for his ideas. But they did not take his theories seriously, as he wanted them taken. His admirers on the Moot—A.D. Lindsay, Sir Fred Clarke, T.S. Eliot—agreed with his general political search for a form of planning as compatible as possible with established values and institutions, and they were stimulated by his ideas.

But the distinctly English sense of "ideas," as separately reasoned opinions on discrete questions, stands opposed to Mannheim's lifelong search for philosophically grounded structures of knowledge, and, indeed, to John Stuart Mill's aspirations in his "Logic of the Moral Sciences" (Cumming 1973). A.D. Lindsay closes his review of Mannheim's posthumous *Freedom, Power and Democratic Planning* (Mannheim 1950) with the wish that "someone could write a short and popular book called 'The Wisdom of Mannheim' which might be widely read." This wisdom does not depend on Mannheim's conception of sociological theory as synthetical knowledge:

Doctor Mannheim knows so much, has such a proper consciousness of the altogetherness of everything, and the way in which any one factor in society may affect others, that it is very difficult for him to leave things alone. I remember dicussing with him and a group of friends containing H.H. Oldham how social reform ought best to come about, and I maintained that you must make up your mind as to what in society was of the most danger, and grapple with that, and assume that modern society was naturally healthy, and would somehow deal with other things that are rotten. Mannheim stoutly maintained that you could do nothing until you knew exactly what to do for everything...Mannheim always resisted very strongly any suggestion that legislation, like moral action, was partly a leap in the dark. One always felt that he had a sociological faith that all these blanks of ignorance about society could be overcome. (Lindsay 1952:85–86)

The good-natured skepticism about Mannheim's theoretical design is as interesting as Lindsay's turn to the biographical, in his and in similar reviews of Mannheim's later achievements. He had become a prominent personality—forceful, interesting, articulate—a presence in cultural and intellectual life, a lively and stimulating conversationalist.

That personality was not everywhere appreciated. Jean Floud recalls: "There was something in his conversational manner that appeared 'slippery.' He trimmed and adjusted what he was saying, in order to forestall objections and keep the flow. He sought thereby to create the impression of general agreement, even when his evasions left the point quite muddled and his partner in conversation often quite frustrated. What might have seemed fair to him appeared opportunistic and more preemptive than accommodating to others."[22] But other testimony, like that of T.S. Eliot, emphasizes Mannheim's brilliance. In his *Times* obituary, Eliot writes: "In informal discussion among a small group, he gained an ascendancy which he never sought, but which was, on the contrary, imposed upon him by the eagerness of others to listen to what he had to say…. His talk was always a stimulant to original thought" (Eliot 1947).[23]

It is quite in keeping with this high opinion, however, that Eliot took the lead among those who resisted Mannheim's attempts to unify the Moot in doctrine and action. For Eliot, the purpose of conversation was to study types, to seek knowledge about things, to get responses, to be stimulated. In a Moot paper, "On the Place and Function of the Clerisy" (MP/15:6), Eliot insists: "It is not the business of clerics to agree with each other; they are driven to each other's company by their common dissimilarity from everybody else, and by the fact that they find each other the most profitable people to disagree with" (MP/15: 6).

This conception was far from Mannheim's hopes for an organization of gentlemen intellectuals for common tasks of policy guidance and popular inspiration.

Another feature of the exchange of ideas that the English milieu cultivated and Mannheim sought in vain to coordinate is the ease with which one attractive idea is replaced by another. When A.D. Lindsay began planning the university that became Keele, for example, "Mannheim was one of the first people he wanted to consult…. He was very much impressed by Mannheim's stress on sociology and social awareness" (Scott 1971:344). On a subsequent occasion, however, he was struck by a remark by his wife that "we in England...get our Weltanschauung from...poetry" (Mountford 1972: 370). The latter conception had more effect on Keele's curriculum, and it was not until 1966 before a full professor of sociology was appointed at Keele.

Similarly, Fred Clarke (1940) opened his influential book, *Education and Social Change,* with a summary of Mannheim's thesis about the transition to planning and especially about the need to overcome the lack of self-awareness about ideology in English thinking, as well as the inability to work through comprehensive designs. But a year or two later, at a LePlay House Conference, Clarke rejected the idea of sociology in the school curriculum and pleaded for history, quoting R.G. Collingwood, "The idea of action as duty...is inevitable to a person who considers it historically" (Dymes 1944: 95). Even Mannheim's most ardent supporters, in short, equivocated about his style of thought.

There were successes and major achievements in the program of publications Mannheim initiated at Routledge & Kegan Paul. He attempted to cultivate the international community of intellectuals which—as in Hungary and Germany and the earlier years in England—he saw as already being everywhere at work. He made special efforts to naturalize some of the intellectual currents that had influenced his own earlier development, including a book on Dilthey by a Moot associate, publications by Lukács, and writings by German existentialist writers. Despite the influential standing presupposed by that work, however, an exchange of letters between his two closest collaborators documents the pattern of misunderstanding which haunts his later endeavours. There is an unpleasant undercurrent of shared assumptions in the brief correspondence between Lindsay, one of the four prestigious members of the Library's Advisory Board, and T. Murray Ragg, the responsible official at the publishing company. Lindsay writes about the manuscript of the book on Dilthey:

> I think it would be a much better book to publish than some of the stuff you have got in the library, but then I think the library is a mixture of very good stuff and some books the only justification for which was that they were written by distressed Germans. But Mannheim never consulted anyone. (RKP)

Ragg replies:

Your comment about books in the library interested me very much, and perhaps you will have some sympathy with me when I tell you that for every book accepted by us for the library at Mannheim's urgent request, we turned down at least a dozen equally urgently put before us. It was difficult indeed to keep him on any sort of leash. We are now, however, trying to maintain a much higher standard, though there are still many legacies from the Mannheim regime to appear. (RKP)

The question of Mannheim's relations with his special audience is important to an understanding of his thought, because he made the connection with a collective consciousness a constituent of his experimental theoretical structures. A crucial part of the experiment for him was the testing of resonance. In a sense, the conception is congruent with Lukács' conception of class consciousness, but the experience of connectedness and intersubjective grounding was to be more empirical in character: not the elucidation of objective interests and tendencies alone, but the acknowledged clarification of the practices actuating the real unit—a generation, an intelligentsia, a discipline, a spiritual elite—bringing it to itself and making it articulate. Mannheim's attempts to achieve such results were jeopardized by resistance in the groups addressed, who often did not recognize themselves in his account of them, and by his own weakness for self-deception, intensified by the sheer energy with which he embarked on his efforts and by the frustration at finding his means insufficient, especially in the resistant new cultural context. Without producing the experience of "insight" in the "patient"—to borrow Mannheim's favorite analogy—the diagnosis was "not valid" and the "therapy" without effect.

Much has been written about the contributions of the immigrant scholars to the cultural and social sciences in England and North America, and rightly so. But perhaps students of exile have not said enough about the personal costs to the émigrés. They found themselves forced to accept a role as alien and esoteric prophets, praised for the heuristic value of their work for the native scholarly enterprise, but too often not accepted as collaborators in the cooperative effort. Or they had to recast their thought into modes whose capacities for subtlety they could not easily master. Theodor W. Adorno, who opted for each of these alternatives in turn, wrote: "Every émigré intellectual, without exception, is damaged. And he better admit it, if he does not want to have the harsh lesson brought home to him behind the tightly closed doors of his self-esteem. He lives in surroundings that must remain incomprehensible to him, however well he may find his way among labor organizations or in traffic. He constantly dwells in confusion.... His language has been expropriated, and the historical dimension, that nourished his knowledge, has been sapped" (Adorno [1951] 1969:32).

While the intellectual communities in the host countries could often make productive use of the stimulation they received, this usefulness was not always good for the refugees themselves and for their intellectual development. The loss of a language rich with meanings and of a responsive audience may sometimes be a stimulus for new creativity. But it more commonly works harm. Authors may translate their thoughts into an idiom whose conceptual apparatus cannot easily bear it and which they do not fully command. Or they may coin new formulations in the new language, but find these stillborn—dead words in a ritualized vocabulary, reified and stylized as they are expounded and defended, and therefore antithetical to the movement of thought. Mannheim's theorizing was in fact so victimized, despite the fact that his earlier work on the context-dependency of concepts in the cultural sciences uniquely prepared him for the problems he faced.

Mannheim felt obliged to make a rapid contribution, to repay his reception as a refugee and to earn his due place. Accordingly, he did not follow the advice that he had himself given to Wirth in 1930, to live "there" for a while to see how "scientific problems" are posed from "within the immediate problem context there." His turn to John Stuart Mill was well-conceived; but he used it more as an opening to Saint-Simon and Comte than as a starting point for exploring the British line of social inquiry, back from Mill, through Stewart and Millar to Ferguson and Smith, and forward from Mill, to Geddes and Hobhouse. As a result, he sometimes appeared arrogant and ill-informed to important colleagues, and he lost important opportunities. Mannheim himself, it should be recalled, professed that the refugee condition provided a position of strategic marginality and a unique capacity for intermediation. He hoped to "serve as a living interpreter between different cultures and to create living communications between different worlds which so far have been kept apart" (Mannheim 1945). But even Mannheim underestimated the liabilities of this emigration.

Notes

1. In a letter to some of his students, for example, Mannheim (NR) exhorts them: "We shall have to transform the sociology of functions (*Funktionssoziologie*)

ever more into a sociology of mission (*Missionssoziologie*)." Six years later, Mannheim writes to Louis Wirth (LWP/7:11) that life in London is becoming ever more attractive, that the English are rapidly changing: "The dynamism of the time reminds me a little of the Weimar Republic, as is also shown by the growth of my following among students and general public. One has the feeling of having a 'mission.'" In his BBC obituary of Mannheim, his academic patron, A. D. Lindsay (LP), uses the same term: "Dr. Mannheim in the years he spent in this country was a man with a mission."

2. In his 1918 doctoral dissertation (Mannheim [1922] 1953), Mannheim distinguishes the cumulative and progressive elements in the histories of art, philosophy, and science. While the former does not know qualitative criteria of obsolescence and the latter is fully controlled by them, philosophy is intermediate, having to grant in principle the possibility of a supervening truth but also acknowledging the continuing merits of older efforts amid uncertainties.

3. Mannheim's admission in the exclusive Christian company of the Moot coincides with the forced expulsion from Germany of noncitizen *"Ostjuden."* Mannheim's academic career in Germany started after his sponsors certified that he did not fall in this category, and it was ended by a decree that the Nazis rationalized as purging *Ostjuden* from the civil service. Mannheim's association with Christian thinkers did not imply dishonorable denial of his ethnic identity. His origins were in the assimilated Jewish community of Budapest, and in Budapest as in Frankfurt he and his closest associates never looked to Jewish religious traditions in their occasional explorations of religious issues. Exceptionally, Georg Lukács (1986: 147ff) went through a period of enthusiasm for Buber's reconstruction of Hasidism during the years Mannheim knew him best, and Mannheim, during his Heidelberg years was a member of a seminar attended by Martin Buber (Woldring 1986: 21). In Mannheim's writings, however, Buber's religious ideas appear only once, and then only fleetingly in a posthumous book subjected to extensive revision by its editors (Mannheim 1950: 298). Despite Mannheim's lack of interest in Jewish traditions, he was known as a Jew to his students and colleagues. One of his Frankfurt students, Nina Rubinstein, interviewed in 1987, exclaimed in surprise when told about Mannheim's association with the Moot, "But he was always 'ein guter Jud' (a regular Jew)" (AA). He lived among Jews in London, and his home was a gathering place and communications center for Hungarian refugee intellectuals (Karl Polanyi to Michael Polanyi, undated [1938], MPP 17:13). Although Arnold Hauser complained that Mannheim kept his life with prominent English figures separate from his life in common with émigré intellectuals (AA), there is reason to think that the patronage by Herbert Read that made possible the publication of Hauser's *Social History of Art* came through Mannheim's good offices. T.S. Eliot, Mannheim and Read's mutual friend, wrote Read in 1943 that Mannheim "suffered rebuffs...from English Jews (Eliot to Read, April 3, 1943, AA)," but the context offers no clarification. After Mannheim's death, the Routledge & Kegan Paul director overseeing Mannheim's series bemoaned Mannheim's susceptibility to fellow-refugees (RKP). In short, Mannheim's interest in the Moot does not represent any attempt to change the sense in which he was Jewish. That he took distance from Eastern Jews and left no record of recognition of the Holocaust, let alone reflection on it, does not distinguish him from most members of his Budapest or Weimar era circles. His library went to the Hebrew University in Jerusalem at his death.

4. "Some Remarks on *Humanisme Integral* by Jacques Maritain," two-page mimeograph, circulated to "Moot" members prior to a dinner meeting with Maritain on May 11, 1939, AA. Partial collections of Moot papers in MP and LP. Oldham's complete records are in the care of Professor Duncan Forrester of the University of Edinburgh, the literary executor of Kathleen Bliss, a Moot member who was working on a biography of Oldham at the time of her death.

5. Karl Mannheim to Oldham, two-page "Moot" mimeograph, circulated to "Moot" members prior to their April 1941 meeting in Cold Ash, England, AA.

6. "Sacrifice quotidien" is Lukács' characterization of his conversion to Bolshevism. See Kettler 1971:76.

7. Mannheim's papers at the University of Keele (KMP) contain many pages of notes towards a major work on intellectuals. The "gentleman" figures prominently. The essay on the topic published posthumously was assembled by Mannheim's editors, drawing primarily on work he had already completed before he arrived in England (Mannheim 1956).

8. Mannheim used his influence in educational circles to resist postwar democratization of the school system, being especially solicitous of the public schools.

9. After Mannheim's death in January 1947, Julia Mannheim thanked the members of the Moot for their letter of condolences: "Your letter...shows me that you have known what your circle meant to Karl. It was the spot for him to be as he was without the slightest reservations because he knew that you all wanted and do not mind if he gives himself as he is. Only in his first youth has he had something similar to this—silicet parva componere magnus. That was the circle around George de Lukács (*sic*) in Hungary before he had to leave the country because of his political belief and convictions some 27 years ago. Until the formation of the Moot he was longing for that safe and free place for the mind, soul and spirit and your circle has given that to him and I should like to bless every one of you for having taken him in so completely. You all shared his ultimate aims and endevours of what is important" (MP/15:3).

10. "The Place of the Study of Modern Society in a Militant Democracy: Some Practical Suggestions," ten-page undated manuscript, probably written in May 1940, LP. Mannheim's letter transmitting the document to Lindsay, evidently some years later, reads: "This is another short paper written at the suggestion of Sir Walter Moberly. It also refers to the Rockefeller scheme but this time I have been asked to link up my suggestions with existing institutions, possibly in London. Today, I still think that some things ought to be done for the education of new leadership in a militant Democracy, but I would perhaps alter some of my concrete suggestions." The note complicates the dating, but the best surmise is that Mannheim's "this time" is intended to express the contrast with the other enclosure, which must have been the "Rockefeller scheme" of 1934. Otherwise the "today" in the next sentence makes no sense. Problems remain because the idea of linking up with English institutions is bruited in the Rockefeller Foundation confidential correspondence on Mannheim's application, especially Kittredge's letter to Malinowski in 1935, but there is every reason to think that Mannheim's first contact with Moberly was in the Moot. Nothing came of the proposal, although Mannheim's 1945 appointment to a professorship in the Institute of Education was a surprise.

11. In notes for the "Preface" to *Ideology and Utopia*, Louis Wirth—or perhaps Shils—writes: "Mannheim's solution (*Hochschule für Politik*). The hope of a 'synthesis.' Who will do the synthesizing? The intellectuals have a moral obligation to

do it" (LWP/65:4). Established after World War I as an adult education center, the Hochschule für Poltik gained substanial Rockefeller Foundation support in 1932, when Foundation officials were persuaded by the President. Ernst Jäckh, that research and teaching were scientific, as well as uniquely valuable because of the multipartisan character of the establishment, from National Socialist to Communist (RF:1.1/717/19/77). Arnold Wolfers, an intimate of the Paul Tillich circle, was director. The faculty included Albert Salomon, Mannheim's colleague at Frankfurt, and Franz L. Neumann (RF:1.1/717/19/177). Jäckh submitted several confidential memoranda on the German political situation to Rockefeller Foundation officials in 1932 and 1933, consistently underestimating Hitler's prospects and conjuring up an image of conflict between the "socialist" and "nationalist" sides of the movement, and encouraging belief that the Röhm purge marked the wholesome elimination of the former. The Social Science office of the Foundation recommended travel funds for researchers from the *Hochschule* as late as January 3, 1938, after the research division had been long put under a Nazi director (RF:1.1/717/9/178). During 1931 and 1932, the *Hochschule* published a periodical covering the major part of the newspapers, exposing bias and promoting synthesis.

12. Michael Polanyi remained a participant in the meetings organized by Oldham as "in part a successor to the Moot" at Christmas 1947, Easter and Christmas, 1948. The topics were increasingly religious. At the last meeting in this series, Polanyi offered a paper on atheism. Oldham wrotes him beforehand, agreeing with one of the other speakers "who is keen, as I have always been and as our experience of 'the Moot' confirms, that we should, if possible, have one or two non-Christians in the group, provided we can find the right people" (Oldham to Polanyi, May 13, 1948, MP/15:4). Occupying this tolerated outsider role during his time, Mannheim could not have achieved the "communion" he vainly sought.

13. "Militant democracy" epitomizes Mannheim's abandonment of the philosophical scruples that inform his Weimar efforts to overcome relativism without sacrificing the critical insights that inform his Weimar efforts to overcome relativism without sacrificing the critical insights that destroyed earlier trust in the "basic value" he here postulates as generally shared. Not coincidentally, Mannheim's term was adopted in the German Federal Republic (*"streitbare Demokratie"*) to characterize a controversial security regime—including a prohibition of public employment for certain categories of individuals—justified as serving to exclude anti-democratic organizations from the political process, thus averting the fate of Weimar (Jaschke 1991).

14. The neo-Freudian theorists Mannheim follows are the principal targets of Herbert Marcuse's attack, a generation later, on the "totalitarianism" of "repressive tolerance." Mannheim is himself, as noted, a *bête noire* of Marcuse and his colleagues in the Institute of Social Research.

15. A sidelight on the ambitious ethos in the Social Sciences Division of the Foundation is provided by O'Brien's extension of those remarks: "It is also very striking to me to see the exceptionally high regard with which the Foundation is universally regarded. As a corollary to this, I am also deeply impressed with the significant role the Foundation can play at the present time as a group which may not only lend moral support, which I think has a real and critical value at present in connection with our future activities, but which also, if it corrals its forces and unifies them, may do much in the way of initiating and carrying through experiments of study of the future social order. A great deal for the future peace of

Europe and of the world may be done" (DPO'B to SMG. RF:RG6.1/281.1/40/ 471).

16. In his memoirs, Huxley contends that the Rockefeller Foundation initiated the invitation to the United States after hearing of his group's work on war aims. "Though the USA was not yet in the war, and though there was a large volume of American public opinion in favor of non-intervention," he writes, "shrewder men like the Rockefeller trustees realized that the country would eventually be drawn into the conflict. They couldn't avow it publicly, but got me, a citizen of a nation already at war, and a person who knew the USA well, to talk on post-war planning" (Huxley 1970: 1/257).

17. In addition to O'Brien, Kittredge in Paris and Willits in New York interested themselves in the plans for coordinating new social science research in Britain, although New York attention concentrated on renewed funding for established programs at Oxford, Chatham House, and the London School of Economics. See the correspondence in RF:RG6.1/281.1/40/491, with some items in folder 421.

18. The question of Mannheim's departure from the LSE drops out of Carr-Saunders' correspondence with the Rockefeller Foundation at the end of 1939, when severe budget cuts were partly restored after negotiations with Sir Walter Moberly. Mannheim retained his salary, although he did little teaching. His access to research assistance was determined periodically by the University Research Committee. Cleeve to Lindsay, March 6, 1942, (LP).

19. The phrases quoted by Harris are credited to a memorandum in the Conservative Party Archives, CRD 058, Margaret Godley to R.A. Butler, May 29, 1940: "Points arising from an interview," May 28, 1940 (Harris 1986: 258).

20. The editors of *New Society* unjustly use the catchphrase, "Mannheim was ultimately a utopian of the right" to summarize a complex characterization of Mannheim's thought by Jean Floud (1966). Floud's actual critique of Mannheim's "legislative" excesses—as distinct from his diagnostic ingenuity—is epitomized by the more interesting contention that he "never realized the difference between democratic planning and planning for democracy" (Floud 1966: 98). A liberal economist writing in 1943 associates Mannheim with Keynes in maintaining that the concept of laissez faire both writers attack in the name of planning is fundamentally misconceived, and that, properly understood, Adam Smith's reformist position does not preclude argument on the merits of their substantive proposals for changes in the framework conditioning the market (Schwartz 1943). After quoting Mannheim on the distinction between "deliberately refraining from interference" and "the purposeless non-interference of the laissez-faire society," Schwartz gibes: "When Adam Smith advocated the abolition of the exclusive privileges of corporations, the repeal of the statute of apprenticeship and of the law of settlements that was purposeless interference of the laissez faire type. Today it would be deliberate planning for freedom." In mock self-reproach for failing to relabel his own policy proposals he concludes, "I could get a popular hearing...and recognition as an advanced progressive if I changed my name, grew a beard and called myself a purposeful planner for freedom" (Schwartz 1943:216n).

21. The negotiations on the project are tedious and often disappointing to Mannheim. But he was not an easy partner. He resisted deadlines and space limitations, and he appeared to be playing Chatham House off against LSE, to enhance his uncertain standing with the Research Committee. The story can be traced in Lindsay's Papers (LP). The posthumous *Freedom, Power and Democratic Planning* is a

reworking of the draft Mannheim left at his death. Julia Mannheim contended that Shils had denied the editors a portion of the manuscript.

22. Interview with Jean Floud on March 2, 1976 (AA). Mrs. Floud has written extremely well on Mannheim and has been the only commentator to notice the importance of Jászi to Mannheim. As Jean McDonald, she worked with him on the revision of *Ideology and Utopia* and joined him for a summer of work in Budapest in the late 1930s, where he and his wife used to spend many holidays. See for example Floud 1959.

23. Eliot asked Herbert Read's opinion about the draft of a review of Mannheim's *Diagnosis of Our Time* he had prepared for *Theology*. He thanked Read for his reassurance because he wanted to make it "as 'velvet' as possible." He remains unhappy, he said. "On the one hand it seems a duty for a detached critic to warn people against swallowing their Mannheim whole; and on the other I feel a peculiar unwillingness to wound Mannheim. He is a sensitive person, he has suffered rebuffs, he is unhappily uprooted, and he is terribly concerned about the dangers he apprehends. And one feels, not only admiration, but a warmth of affection for him which is not explained either by the length of the acquaintance or any particular intimacy of an explicit kind" (April 3, 1943, Eliot to Read, AA)

Conclusion
Sociology as a Vocation

Coming to maturity in a uniquely brilliant site of the European-wide dispute between rational social reform and radical cultural renewal, Mannheim learned not only the substantive issues of the controversy but also the literary and philosophical experimentation that charted its course. The most prized of Georg Lukács' younger companions, he could also believably assure Oscar Jászi twenty years later that he was his "old follower." After the first of the brutal discontinuities shocking his project, Mannheim left Budapest for Heidelberg and the legacy of Max Weber. He became a sociologist. But sociology was contested ground, and Mannheim needed his essayistic gifts for irony in his campaign for a sociology to address the striving for civil polity. "There are situations ripe for compromise," was his slogan, and he found a fascinated but critical hearing among younger intellectuals for the theorizing behind that unexciting proposition. As teacher, he bred students rare in the old German universities—devoted but contentious. Ousted by Hitler, Mannheim brought his project to England, stripped of many assets that made him an outstanding public intellectual for enlightenment: faith in the Kantian idea of a universal history with cosmopolitan intent, command of subtle language and the essay, a public. Mannheim's English career is his least attractive phase, and the most important to understand. What distorts his thinking afflicts ours, although we may scorn his clumsy language of elites, masses, and social techniques. Among his English associates and students, those who learned from Mannheim did so by bargaining. And that is the ultimate survival skill for enlightenment.

Our study is a public biography with theoretical intent. Because transactions with publics are constitutive of Mannheim's thinking, his project is analyzed by tracking his negotiations with various audiences. The book covers Mannheim's dealings with Lukács and Jászi in Budapest; with Alfred Weber, Leopold von Wiese, Franz Neumann, Paul Tillich,

Adolf Löwe, and his students in Weimar Germany; with Louis Wirth, Edward Shils, and professional American sociology; and with sociologists and Christian social thinkers in England. The analysis is informed by dilemmas of history and theory, science and rhetoric, freedom and technical control—the themes of liberalism since John Stuart Mill, who haunts this book. The objective is to learn how to get light from Mannheim's mind. The end is an opening.

Learning from Mannheim

Mannheim attracts studiers who do not think that agonic exchanges and provisional accommodations are inconsistent with inquiry, thinkers who do not draw a categorical line between bargaining and argument, between strategic and discursive communications.[1] Productive encounters with Mannheim take on the character of negotiations. This applies no less to those who meet him only through his writings, if they are sufficiently intrigued to think they may find something of value there. Mannheim's expressly "experimentalist" and "essayistic" forms frustrate fundamentalist literal readings. It may be impossible to be a "Mannheimian." But there is little to be gained by inventing one's own Mannheim from dead words on the page. His is hardly a name with which to conjure in the anterooms of professional influence. It does not pay to pass as a Mannheimian. To learn from Mannheim means to retrieve his design and acknowledge a measure of dependence on it, then engage his thinking not in purified discursive dialogue but in the exploration of possibilities on common ground.

To view contacts between instructors and learners as implicitly bilateral discussions aiming at settlement is to recognize the reciprocal play of power and resistance present in communications and the element of decision in learning. But this does not presuppose a uniform calculus of interests, an equivalence of power, or a binding contractual exchange. The processes, the forms and the terms of settlement will vary. Despite Adam Smith's early intuition that "the principle in the human mind on which the disposition of trucking is founded...is clearly the natural inclination everyone has to persuade" (Smith [1762–63] 1978: 352), legal analogies are more pertinent than economic ones. And the relevant legal models are more likely to be found in the diversity of personal, reciprocal, partial, and conditional relations in Gierke's law of associations than in the standard forms of rationalized private law. The settlements in question respect substantive standards of status, as well as substantive constraints on procedures. The parties cannot compromise their standing as actors worthy of intellectual recognition, and rational objections, when invoked, can never be denied their authority. Since traditional measures of these elements are in doubt, the bargain to bargain will always imply some working arrangement about these contested but irreplaceable substantive norms (Fisher, Ury, and Patton 1991: 91). Studying a thinker like Mannheim entails coming to an understanding with him. Intellectual historians speak of "influences"; but this concept is imprecise and unrevealing. Our aim is to acknowledge the power relations between texts and interpreters, while emphasizing elements of structured reciprocity in the transactions.

Mannheim's last doctoral student, Viola Klein, shows the possibilities of learning from Mannheim. As a postgraduate student aiming at a career as a professional sociologist, she differs from Mannheim's women students in Frankfurt (Kettler and Meja 1993). Herself a refugee from Czechoslovakia, with a literature degree and journalistic experience, she had little in common with the English-educated students who found Mannheim stimulating but dauntingly alien. Jean Floud, for example, has been forthright about her mixed feelings about Mannheim as professor in England. No student could have known him better. She helped Mannheim revise Edward Shils' draft translation of *Ideology and Utopia* (Mannheim 1936a: xi [acknowledgments to Floud under her unmarried name, Jean McDonald]) and of *Man and Society in an Age of Reconstruction* (Mannheim 1940: xxii), and, although her own supervisor was Morris Ginsberg, she took several courses with Mannheim (Floud 1959: esp. 53–54. See also Floud 1963). In a letter, she recalls pangs of discomfort with his manner and concludes, "One could put much down I suppose to the fact that his dealings with us were so un-English" (AA). This aroused a certain "resistance" among English students, "whilst being attracted to him for the kind of question he asked and the issues he raised." "Interestingly," Floud adds, "I think Mannheim must have been aware of the resistance he aroused. During the war I ran into him in Oxford where I was working and he had come for a conference. We had a brief conversation in the street and he said, 'We must meet again. I want to discuss teacher-student relations with you.'" This ingenuousness clashed with his simultaneous insistence on "his status as Herr Professor" and heightened the puzzlement. Klein may have shared Floud's need to create some distance between herself and Mannheim, as Floud speculates, and both women contributed to British sociology, but Klein's background was different and the attempt to clarify her relationship to Mannheim entered directly into her sociological work.

Klein (1908–1973) was born in Vienna but moved to Bohemia as a child. She was educated at the universities of Vienna, the Sorbonne and Prague, where she obtained a DPhil. with a thesis on Céline, and at the University of London, where she received a PhD in 1944 for the work that became *The Feminine Character: History of an Ideology* (1946). After a variety of miscellaneous and underpaid positions, she held research appointments at the London School of Economics and at the University of Manchester before gaining an appointment as lecturer in sociology at the University of Reading in 1964. She was reader there when she retired a few months before her death. The title of a well-known collaboration with Alva Myrdal—*Women's Two Roles: Home and Work* (Myrdal and Klein 1956)—epitomizes her principal professional preoccupations (cp. Bok 1991: 225–30; see Klein 1958; Klein 1961; Klein 1965a; Klein 1965b), an emphasis underlined in an obituary in *The Times*: "She was director or the inspiration of many surveys and studies of women at work" (October 18, 1973: 20). By sociologists, she is credited more broadly with many significant contributions to the sociology of women before the outburst of new interest in this subject in the 1970s (Crouch 1984; Spender 1982: 502-6). And it is her dissertation that has been repeatedly published in England and the United States—with an American edition three years after the original (1949), a second English and American edition in the last years of her life (1971 and 1972), and a third edition in 1989—and translated as well. The encounter with Mannheim documented in Klein's dissertation helps account for the narrowing of her focus in later years, underlining the need to attend carefully to the conditions under which earlier generations of women scholars sought their own voice.

Klein came upon Mannheim in the late 1930s at the London School of Economics, when his Frankfurt conception of the sociologist's "mission" had undergone substantial change. The principal objective is no longer to counter heteronomous factors obscuring self-recognition and autonomy. Sociology must aim to overcome crises of social integration, to foster "mobilization," and to deliver the principal resources for planning. Although Klein agrees that "ideas of 'Reconstruction' and 'Planning' have given a new purpose to our contemporaries," she insists with special urgency, following Margaret Mead, that "it is at this phase that the reminder of the dangers of uniformity and the warning to plan for diversity are timely" (Klein 1946: 207 and 136). Her emphasis on diversities distinguishes her recommendation from Mannheim's spatial image of providing for pockets of free activities in his proposed "planning for freedom" (Mannheim 1940). Questions about the "own peculiar ways" of diverse social actors retain a vitality for Klein that they have largely lost for Mannheim.

Mannheim's new distrust of the very striving for success and the rise of groups through organization that had been central motifs in his earlier conception of a "mission" to enhance group self-consciousness among women and others stems from his diagnosis of the German disaster. In his lecture to the 1935 Annual Conference of the Institute of Sociology on "The Place of Sociology," Mannheim revealingly revises his 1930 "ambition" thesis (Mannheim [1930] 1952). Having stressed the limits on the amount of organization a social structure can tolerate, he links upward striving to competition and concludes that an excess of such striving by individuals and groups may produce crisis and collapse: "It is possible that the arrest of individualization in Germany today...can be explained as a reaction against too great an increase of the former vital activity of the people, which has become disproportionate to the absorbing power of the existing social order" (Mannheim 1936b: 187). These fears explain his new emphasis on integrative citizen-education, at the risk of self-defined diversities. In the same year, Mannheim offered a five-lecture course entitled "Woman and Her Place in Society" at the London School of Economics, in which he echoes but reinterprets the materials of his Frankfurt historical sociology lectures, notably using women's family roles as reference points for examining other types and aspects of women's lives. He now opens with the "puzzle" that while the history of women can be defined as a history of domination, the widespread acceptance of subordinate positions by women epitomized in the enthusiasm for Nazi family values makes it unclear whether the concept of domination properly applies.[2] Mannheim leaves his question unexpectedly open.

Mannheim's changed emphasis also emerges in a 1941 essay on "The Problem of Youth in Modern Society." In his Amsterdam and Frankfurt lectures, youth rank with women and intellectuals as a group that sociology aims to render self-aware. Now he sums up his "general analysis": "Youth is an important part of those latent reserves which are present in every society. It depends on the social structure whether these reserves, and which of them, if any, are mobilized and integrated into a function" (Mannheim 1943: 36). As in his Frankfurt lectures, Mannheim draws on his sympathetic awareness of the women's movement to develop an "example" for his argument:

> All of us know that the greatest oppression in history is not that of the slaves, serfs or wage-earning laborers, but that of women in patriarchal societies. And yet the sufferings and the resentment of these women remained meaningless throughout the many thousand years as long as they were sufferings of the millions of individual women in isolation. But their resentment at once became creative and socially relevant when in the movement of the suffragettes these sufferings and sentiments were integrated, thus contributing to the recasting of our views concerning the place and function of women in modern society. In the same way…it was only when [the dissatisfactions of other oppressed classes] were integrated into a movement which not only tried to express bitterness but attempted to formulate a basis of constructive criticism that the random feelings and actions were transformed into social functions. (Mannheim 1943:34)

The passive voice prepares us for Mannheim's conclusion that the example illustrates only how "latent reserves can be mobilized and creatively integrated into society," and not how groups can act against oppression. The essay ends with a plea for retaining the British Public Schools, while cautiously democratizing their bases of recruitment, and not with a promise, as in 1932, of validating youth's experience in the youth movement (*Jugendbewegung*). In his sociology of education lectures in later years, accordingly, Mannheim welcomed what he called the closer coordination between school and home: "In girls' schools we now have a comprehensive course in domestic studies and even in grammar schools where there has been a tendency to prepare the intellectually abler girls in academic studies only, teachers now recognize much more than they used to that they have a responsibility to the future girl undergraduate as a wife and mother as well" (Mannheim and Stewart 1962: 131). Mannheim, lecturing to his Frankfurt undergraduates in 1932, had not spared "unworldly preachers and teachers" who promulgate the ideology of domesticity, especially in a vocabulary of "responsibility" (KMP).

Klein (1946:18) is firm in her call for "a new feminine type, distinct from the prevailing Victorian ideal of the submissive and 'respectable' wife,'" and she pointedly asserts that "the 'emancipation of women' would have to be followed by the 'emancipation of men' from their notion of a dependent, domesticated and receptive wife" (Klein 1946: 158). Ruminating on Virginia Woolf's question about "the relative paucity of feminine achievements in the arts and sciences," she opines that active discouragement is not the only "impediment to female creativeness" and points to "domestic affairs, not on account of the time and energy they demand, but for the state of mind they produce" (Klein 1946:181), their education for "diffusion" rather than concentration of thought. Despite such sharp questioning of conventional opinions that Mannheim is now more willing to incorporate for the sake of the larger mobilization he hopes to inspire, Klein finds much in Mannheim to her purpose.

Klein is intrigued by Mannheim's analytical figures of the cognitively privileged perspective of the outsider and the discrepancy between ideology and experience. She departs from Mannheim's English adjustments by returning the analytical themes to the theoretical context of the sociology of knowledge, with its reflexive concerns about the epistemological status of social scientific doctrine. Klein was not caught up in the Weimar situation that shaped the contrast between the politicized "Mannheimer from Heidelberg" males, intrigued but ultimately unpersuaded by an approach that jeopardized the rationales of their strategic perspectives, and the women in Frankfurt, satisfied to appropriate the self-knowledge opened to them by the method of sociology as a "science for living," before moving on. Despite her ultimate commitment to social science as a profession, she writes for long stretches in the essayistic mode that sustained Mannheim's more ingenious early intellectual experiments. She takes more from Mannheim, perhaps, because she has more confidence in her ability to use it in her own way.

The complexity of Klein's design bears the marks of Mannheim's "dialectical" strategizing in the essays comprising *Ideology and Utopia*. At first glance, she is simply investigating the ideological character of thought about "feminine character," including scientific thought. But she complicates matters by the social-psychological claim that women, as an "outgroup," are especially vulnerable to conditioning by the social expectations strengthened by such ideological "science," so inquiry into ideology may paradoxically enhance knowledge about women. Sociology of knowledge, she suggest, can revise ideological doctrines to make them contribute to "relationist" objectivity about the matters they discuss. This feature of the work often perplexes sociologically trained commentators.[3] When Klein writes that "only after all these [ideological] influences have been revealed and a comparison between the many ways of approach to the problem of femininity has been made, will a really sound and well-founded judgment on the elusive 'feminine character' be possible" (Klein 1946:4), she echoes claims that Mannheim increasingly abandoned in his English discussions of the sociology of knowledge. In a striking footnote to a 1929 discussion of political education, Mannheim nudges the reader to recognize that he has derived the "correct" answer about the "best" solution from his sociology-of-knowledge inquiry into ideologies about theory and practice. If he could only explicate the logic underlying this surprising result, he maintains, he would achieve the objective he is seeking: "A real situational analysis of a style of thought should be able to assess its validity" (Mannheim [1929] 1952: 159n.). But Mannheim (1936a) deleted this passage from the English translation of *Ideology and Utopia,* while Klein implicitly retains its aspirations.

At times, Mannheim and Klein mean nothing more by such assertions than that cultural narrow-mindedness or emotional bias distort scientific work and that their effects must be purged before scientific claims can be usefully assessed, but such method presupposes a theory of objective scientific method and presumably cannot be carried into effect without the application of suitable scientific tests to the reformulated propositions. Elsewhere, they mean that the sociology of knowledge makes ideological doctrines yield hidden insights into the historical circumstances of their promulgation. But clearly, to the consternation of many critics, they often also mean something more, as when Mannheim terms the sociology of knowledge the "organon of politics as a science."

Klein is not a philosophical writer. Her original formulations of the relation between her sociology-of-knowledge inquiry and her efforts to say something about "the innate characteristics and potentialities of women" (Klein 1946:2) scarcely captures the verve or the contents of the commentaries on Ellis, Weininger, Freud, Mead, and others that comprise the principal chapters of her work. She concludes the series of methodological comments: "The coordination and sociological examination of different formulations of the same problem as attempted in this study, is one of the various methods which can be adopted [for inquiring into femininity]. Its chief aim is to outline the scope of the problem and, by indicating its different aspects, to make possible a closer understanding and higher degree of objectivity" (Klein 1946:171).

In the "Preface to the Second Edition" of *The Feminine Character*, she sounds perplexed:

> It seems...that the reading public, by and large, was not prepared to take [the author's] word for it that the book was concerned with an analysis of existing theories about feminine psychology rather than being itself a psychological study of women. The misunderstanding of the author's intentions went so far that some critics—Rose Macaulay among them—accused her of using "secondary sources" instead of doing "original research," when in fact the investigation of those sources was the very object of the exercise. I hoped, nevertheless, to be able to learn something new, and to be able to make a constructive contribution to the solution of the "enigma" femininity by comparing and coordinating what other authorities who studied the matter had to say. (Klein 1972: xv)

In fact, Klein is stronger when writing essayistic commentary than when reflecting on method.[4] This applies to Mannheim's sociological writings as well. But the relationship between the essay and substantial intellectual work is ambiguous for Mannheim's models in sociology. While Max and Marianne Weber both express their admiration for Lukács' *Soul and Forms* ([1911] 1971), Max Weber repeatedly cautions Lukács that he has no chance of securing a habilitation at Heidelberg unless he outgrows the "essayistic disposition" displayed most defiantly in the introduction to that work, "On the Essence and Form of the Essay" (Lukács 1986: 204-5, 263-65). Mannheim bowed to such strictures in most of his academic work, at least in his programmatic statements.

The principal justification for emphasizing methodological issues is that Mannheim reacted oddly to Klein's manifest invocation of the looser but more ambitious sense of his sociology of knowledge. Klein prefaces her book by gratefully acknowledging that "The original idea and plan of this book arose out of the lectures and seminars of Dr. Karl Mannheim, and were developed in frequent discussions with him." And Mannheim not only published the book in his International Library of Sociology and Social Reconstruction, but also contributed an eight-page foreword. Yet in that introduction Mannheim virtually ignores Klein's deployment of the sociology of knowledge, limiting himself to the somewhat patronizing observation that "this aspect of the present study will, I suppose, be obvious and interesting to everyone, as hardly anything is more stimulating than the realization that our social life is full of phantasies." "From the point of view of the sociologist," he asserts, now using the term in the sense of his new "mission," the book merits attention mostly because "it is an experiment in working out a new pattern of research which I first tried to develop with research students in 1930 at Frankfurt University and have since continued, and which I should call Integrating Research. Its task is to combine different aspects of the same problem which previously have been dealt with only in water-tight compartments" (Mannheim in Klein 1946:vii)." The next six pages are devoted to a regrettably pompous summary of Mannheim's more recent hopes in this respect, altogether without reference to the book. Only in the last paragraph does Klein reappear, and only to receive faint praise for this "entirely tentative and exploratory" study, which is not to be judged as if "one were to expect from a single person at the beginning of a venture the exactness and final answers which would be feasible only if a great team of explorers were to study the various fields. As a matter of fact, in an exploratory study it is an advantage to leave loose ends. This creates scope for scientific imagination to throw new light upon known facts and to explore so far unobserved interrelations among them" (Mannheim in Klein 1946:xiv).

Not surprisingly, when Viola Klein wrote the preface to the second edition, she suddenly remembered that her "interest in the ideological element of knowledge had been aroused...by C.H. Waddington's book *The Scientific Attitude*, widely discussed at the time." Then she insists that "It was, I think, mainly because of this aspect of my study that the late Karl Mannheim took a genuine interest in it from the beginning, offered critical and constructive comment, chapter by chapter, as it advanced, and eventually published it" (Klein 1972: xv). Dryly, and in the context of her evident irritation with reviewers who took Mannheim's foreword as their guide to her enterprise, she adds: "The tentative experiment in the 'integrative method,' whose merits Karl Mannheim set forth in his Foreword to the first edition of this book, was incidental to the above prime purpose" (Klein 1972: xvi). What is documented in this tug-of-war between Karl Mannheim and Viola Klein is above all the widening split between Mannheim's public persona as would-be reformer of English sociology and counsellor to the British elite—where the sociology of knowledge is incidental—and his continuing private activities as continental intellectual and inspiration to students, notably to women like Klein. This pattern left many misunderstandings behind, but few works as rewarding as Klein's.

The sociology of knowledge serves Klein primarily as a strategy for detotalizing the claims of systematic, scientifically legitimated thinkers. She argues that science is indeed to be understood as part of the wider historically diversified cultures in which it is variously practiced, but she does not have a reductionist holistic theory about the constitution or development of such cultures. There is no base or superstructure, except in the loose sense that theories that display the "air of impartiality and systematic method which we usually associate with the scientific attitude" (Klein 1946:6) are not exempted from being understood as part of the mental activity of emotional, interested, culturally adaptive, partisan human actors. To speak of sociology of knowledge operations on scientific thought, as we have earlier done, is an unwarranted formalization of Klein's diversified moves against absolutes. The activity of moving discussions towards "relationist" objectivity turns out to be mostly a matter of converting sweeping, methodologically grounded validity claims into a mixture of fallible, contestable arguments and mere localized opinions. The "ideological" dimension of theories is uncovered to permit untrammeled encounter with the ideas the theories may also contain.

This does not mean that Klein fails to recognize scientific structures. In fact, her book is divided according to scientific disciplines: Havelock Ellis and biology; Otto Weininger and philosophy; Sigmund Freud and psychoanalysis; Helen Thompson, L.M. Terman, and C.C. Miles and experimental, psychometric psychology; Mathias and Mathilde Vaerting and a Marxism-derived historical approach; Margaret Mead and anthropology; and W.I. Thomas and sociology. It should be noted, however, that the first edition also includes an appreciative essay on a naturalistic novel about three generations of women. It is not anachronistic to say that Klein treats the disciplines as discourses, about which it is equally permissible to ask why just this way of organizing information about women comes into prominence when it does and whether its organizational and critical framework has some intrinsic merits that give its conclusions special weight.

Klein traces the ideological dimensions in the theories she treats variously to the actual condition of women at a time, to the ideology about women pervasive in a historical site, and to the idiosyncratic psychological makeup of the theorists in question. In talking about Ellis, for example, she remarks his appreciation for changes underway and marvels at his courage in legitimating sexuality as scientific subject, notwithstanding his temperamentally cool personal relationship to this force in human evolution. She situates his ideas in the early twentieth-century ideological dispute between proponents of equality and equal value, but she does not think that this discredits his attempts to identify structural differences based in differential contributions to the sexual dimension of evolution. There is nothing shocking about the fact that people are led to think systematically by problems that arise in their experiences; the need is merely to locate their thoughts within their proper context and accordingly to reinterpret their claims. In criticizing Weininger and Freud, on the other hand, Klein discredits most of their theories by uncovering how greatly they are moved by their social identities and evident psychological peculiarities, in her view, to absolutize a patriarchal regime under threat; yet she simultaneously credits them with special insights into women subjected to that regime. The psychometricians are cartographers of a given pattern and guides to accommodation, which has its justifications. Marxist historians contribute by bringing out the domination in relations that Klein believes to be more multidimensional, but they are led to exaggeration by their dedication to drastic reversals in social order. Finally, she thinks, the agenda in her time is set by a world of organization and planning, and Thompson and Mead must be understood in the context of keeping the new developments from simply reinforcing an unchanging man's world by new social technologies.

Women become a subject for separate study by both men and women because of developments in all three dimensions, including importantly the rise of women and the emergence of women's ideologies. They are studied by the methods of sciences because those sciences are instruments for the rationalization of bourgeois society, but also arenas for conflicts about its form. Studies of women show this dual character of scientific inquiry especially well because the status of women touches deep emotional issues for both men and women. These converge on the question whether women are fundamentally different from men, the question of "feminine character."

Klein aligns herself with a woman's stake in this question and a woman's perspective on it. Like other comparatively disadvantaged "outgroups," she maintains, women are especially vulnerable to damage from the stereotyping that insiders use to stigmatize and perpetuate such a status. "To be judged, not as an individual, but as a member of a stereotyped group," she asserts, "implies an incalculable amount of restrictions, discouragement, ill-feeling, and frustration" (Klein 1946: 175). Their sight may also be sharpened by their situation, and their commitments broadened. She writes:

All these groups have a vital interest in the promotion of a humanitarian, universalist outlook, in the abolition of discrimination against people on account of their race, creed, sex or nationality, and in a legal order that puts right before might. If it be assumed that the general trend of social development goes in the direction of humanism, democracy and internationalism, it may therefore be said that these groups represent a progressive element.

But she quickly adds, parenthetically: "The issue is somewhat obscured in the case of women, by the fact that in the course of centuries women have developed many substitute gratifications which they consider privileges and to which they cling emotionally more than to equal rights" (Klein 1946:174). "Such self-defeating satisfaction is not the only distortion in perspective to which socially stigmatized groups are liable. Klein argues against Otto Weininger (1903), for example, that exclusivist identification with their groups is not unique to Jews and women, but a reaction to marginality or "out-group" status and a reflection of the stereotyping indulged in by the dominant in-group. In this connection, she cites Jewish self-hatred, black color-consciousness, and cultivated women's detestation of women's groups as part of the ambivalence of marginality, an adopting of majority standards. Jewish overeagerness to be considered as having arrived and the pattern that Alfred Adler identifies as the "masculinity complex" among women show that compensatory ambition may arise, to the hurt of the victimized (Klein 1946: 174). Klein summarizes without critical objections a series of rather nasty characterizations of women—not all of them referring to the past only—in the writings of W.I. Thomas, whom she treats as the representative of her own "sociological" approach. "Under a system of male control, where self-realization is secured either through the manipulation of the man or not at all," she reports, "her intelligence expressed itself in the form of cunning, a typical characteristic of disqualified persons" (Klein 1946: 155). Approvingly, she quotes Thomas: "The remedy for the irregularity, pettiness, ill-health and unserviceableness of modern woman seems to lie on educational lines. Not in a general and cultural education alone, but in a special and occupational interest and practice for women, married and unmarried. This should be preferably gainful, though not onerous nor incessant" (cited in Klein 1946: 158). While outsider status fosters critical thinking, in sum, Klein believes it also urgently stands in need of it.

Viola Klein: Work, Eros, Sociology

Three themes in Klein's inquiry into the search for a feminine character are noteworthy, both because of their intrinsic interest and because of the light they shed on Mannheim's projects. We shall consider, first, Klein's rejection of the strand in feminism that wholly depreciates women's links to home and family, especially because this theme becomes the center of her work for the rest of her career as sociologist. In the extended contemporary sense, Klein is certainly a feminist. When she uses the term, however, she almost always has in mind the Individualist phase of the women's movement. "Before the development of Individualism," she writes, "the problem of women's emancipation...could not arise; after its decline and the move towards a society which thinks primarily in terms of social welfare, it could, in its original form, not survive" (Klein 1946:102–3); it "was incidental to the struggle of the rising bourgeoisie for political power and social ascendancy" (Klein 1946: 23). Second, we shall look more closely at Klein's careful treatment of women's emotional needs, her attention to themes of erotic attachments, and, in this connection, her striking continued openness to the possibility of a distinctive feminine makeup, despite her conclusion that almost everything said about it refers in fact to qualities either functionally dependent on socially defined roles or ideologically imposed by men. And, finally, we shall return to our point of departure, the question of parallels between women and intellectuals and their respective openness to sociology. Klein, we shall see, was Mannheim's last student but also the most important for our study, precisely because she negotiated her own terms, as a woman, in her relationship with his work and influence.

Mannheim in his Frankfurt lectures had traced women's ideological crisis to the discrepancy between a persistent ideology of housewifely virtue and the actual functioning of modern households as undemanding consumption centers, especially among the middle class, Klein instead juxtaposes that "sentimental cult of domestic virtues" to a reality where ever more women are either employed or unmistakably confronted by the fact that they are kept "on a level of unpaid drudgery" (Myrdal and Klein 1956: 137). While "the place in which the Feminist Movement was born was not the factory nor the mine, but the Victorian middle-class drawing room" (Klein 1949: 262), the "lady" does not figure in her analysis as either problem or promise. Klein implies that a feminist ideology of emancipation through access to the labor market cannot by itself meet the psychological needs of women. Organized feminism is distorted by its formative focus on the "struggle for the right to work." The initiatives originally taken by unmarried middle-class women took an "anti-masculine turn" out of political necessity, but married women felt left "out of account." "This was, naturally, a miscalculation," Klein concludes, "and it confronted thousands of girls with the alternative either of sacrificing their ideals of justice, equality, and women's rights, or of resigning their claim to love" (Klein 1946: 197–98). From the beginning, moreover, "while middle-class women were fighting for equality, working-class women demanded differential treatment" (Klein 1946: 15). Feminists attracted comparatively few—and never the young—and their employment aims were attained "simply by force of practical necessity, and because their claims were in accordance with the general trend of social development" (Klein 1946: 25). Many working class women had no choice about subjecting themselves to the labor market, and middle class women found growing opportunities, first because of wartime labor shortages in 1914–18 and after 1940, and second because of the rise of new jobs. Social service work originally performed by volunteers became professionalized as it was recognized as a social necessity, especially under conditions of wartime and postwar social disorganization: "It is obvious that a society which depends more and more on activities of an administrative character can very well make use of human qualities which were not considered essentially masculine prerogatives" (Klein 1946: 27). This link between the changing status of women and the emergence of the welfare state is central to Klein's analysis, and it is one of the areas where she anticipates recent feminist research.

Women at work are commonly engaged in "women's work," but remain in "a ready-made culture which by its origins and peculiar character is masculine" (Klein 1946: 35; see Myrdal and Klein 1956: 75). They suffer special frustration in the workplace as well as at home. Women are trapped not only by the preponderance of poorly paid jobs and the obstacles to advancement, partly owing to women's divided commitments between home and work, but also by the requirement that they justify their positions by masculine standards: "Being just as good as someone else is not a source of self-confidence: At the first crisis, whether individual or national, such persons will feel superfluous and will be prepared to relinquish their work" (Klein 1946: 35). The problems are compounded for the marriageable by cross-pressures between vocational expectations and the qualities sought by marriage partners. "If this happens she is likely to feel frustrated," Klein writes, "and often she will curse 'emancipation' which has deprived her of the simple happiness of husband, child and home" (Klein 1946: 34). Klein's attitude towards such a response is complex. She protests against the media and the scientific ideologists that inculcate a romantic distortion of woman as validated by attracting males and decries circumstances bringing it about that "it is still an easier and more profitable career for most women to marry than to work" (Klein 1946:29), but she also respects the deep roots of the feminine pattern.

She is troubled by the success in Germany of the motto: "Women, back to the Homes" (1946: 34, 204). Klein evidently shares Mannheim's belief that key Nazi slogans are indicators of serious defects not only in classical liberal ideology or institutions, but also in progressive designs. In Mannheim's case, the most important such slogan is "a valid will is sufficient for valid knowledge," which he views as a caricature of the insight upon which sociology of knowledge rests, but also as a warning against its radical relativizing potential. While Klein sees through the fact that women oppose the feminist call for equality and full emancipation from the bonds of home in important measure because "it attacked, in women, those symbols which they had developed as substitute gratification for their lack of real power, and which were no less close to their hearts than the feeling of superiority was to man's" (Klein 1946:23), she is not satisfied that the ties of home are nothing but a trap for women. Klein's inquiry into the "feminine character" strives to go beyond the exposé of male ideology precisely because the question about women's distinctiveness puzzles her. To overcome the discrepancy between the ideology of home and the reality of work requires more than an adaptive new ideology. Work and home must both better suit women's needs.

Her choice of scientific ideologists to interrogate, as well as her introductory comments, indicate that she thinks some important truth may be hidden in ideological commonplaces about woman's emotional priorities. Speaking in her own voice, she remarks about the origins of the women's movement: "Love and marriage being the main concern of women, it was only natural that their revolt should not have sprung from thirst for knowledge or a desire for freedom or adventure, but that, first of all, it should have been expressed as a protest against the humiliation of having to barter their love for support" (Klein 1946:20). Klein is confident that the emotional configurations that have been treated as natural attributes of the feminine character are historically constituted and subject to change. In planning changes, however, she urges considerate attention to the valuable capacities and satisfactions which accompanied the historical formation of living women.

Klein is least guarded about her thoughts on this analytically most complex issue, and perhaps about her own youthful experiences, in the appendix on *The Rebel Generation*, a prewar novel by Jo v. Amers-Küller. Her first degree was in literature, after all. She justifies her report on the story of three generations of Dutch women as "an illustration to the main theme: how the idea of femininity has been transformed" (Klein 1946:183); but her commentary is more than descriptive. She distinguishes the three phases covered in the book: the time around 1840, the Biedermeier period she calls the age of the "subjected" woman; 1872 marks the activity of the "emancipating"; and 1923, the time of writing, is the time of the "emancipated" woman. Klein follows her author in emphasizing the drudgery of the productive household, the patriarchal absolutism that prevailed, and the illusions about romantic love. Emancipation was above all "an unbolting of the gates of the family prison" (Klein 1946:193). The acceptance of the cultural norm of success, as well as the conscious strategy of putting the interests of spinsters first, meant that the securing of work outside the home was overvalued as a goal. The rebel generation became individualized and shared the exhilaration of accomplishment, but their successors felt cheated.

Without objection, Klein summarizes her author's narrative, "This generation is rationalist, practical, realistic, and fed to capacity...with scientific theories—but they are emotionally starving and devoid of any ideals" (Klein 1946:201). The young people envy the old spinsters. Disappointment extends through all three domains observed in the novel. Patriarchal authority is broken, but it is replaced by nothing more than an attitude of mutual noninterference and disinterested observation between parents and children "which could in a sense be called 'scientific,' because it involves an objective, personally disinterested attitude of experimental observation, diminishes the causes of friction within the family and avoids painful conflicts—but it occasions the emotional dissatisfaction which is the main trouble of the elder as well as of the younger generation" (Klein 1946:202). The attitude to work becomes negative and disillusioned due in part to letdown after exaggerated hopes and in part from lack of adequate opportunities. Finally, according to Amers-Küller: "Underneath a surface of conscious modernism, expressing itself either in the form of skepticism, frivolity, or cynicism, smolders unconsciously the longing for an unaltered romantic ideal of love which these women certainly would be ashamed to admit even to themselves" (Klein 1946:204). At this point only, Klein openly demurs. She challenges the author's assumption "that the romantic pattern of love is the true expression of an unchangeable instinct" and offers for consideration the view that the conflict is a mark of transition "in which new ideas, though rationally accepted, have not yet been completely assimilated and still meet with emotional resistance on the part of the unconscious self" (Klein 1946:205).

She maintains that her generation has passed into a new phase and is gaining "new purpose" from ideals of "Reconstruction" and "Planning" (Klein 1946: 207). The defining problem of this phase, she maintains, is not in the sphere of intimate relations between the sexes. In a dismissive comment on Otto Weininger's misogynist mystifications, she confidently remarks "The idea of sexual union as the misuse of a woman 'as a means instead of as an end in herself' is certainly no less revolting today than it was forty years ago. But what Weininger was unable to envisage, imbued as he was with Victorian morality, has since become the more or less generally accepted ideal: the union in common partnership, of two free individuals, equal in their rights" (Klein 1946:70). Having chosen not to marry, she leaves no doubt that the talk about forlorn young women and "spinsters" is obsolete. The threat is not women's frustrated longing for romantic love, but the possible destruction of the individual—"the Individual whom it took centuries to form and who has been the distinctive characteristic of modern Western Civilization" (Klein 1946:207). In the tradition of Harriet Taylor Mill, Klein distinguishes classical liberal "individualism" that annihilates variety for the sake of equality, from protection of "individuality" (Mill and Mill 1970; Mill [1859] 1977). The latter implies special precautions to safeguard the "qualities traditionally regarded as feminine" because "the gradual admission of women into a man-made society involves the risk of the universal adoption of one, the masculine, pattern" (Klein 1946:136).

Klein's conception of the planned society is sometimes hard to distinguish from that of Mannheim. Investigating the utilitarian rationale behind Helen B. Thompson's pioneering empirical investigation of "mental sex differences" between male and female college students, she observes:

> The question was no longer one of capability but became one of social expediency.... The problem as it presents itself to us today is...what are the limits to which society can go in granting women equality without endangering its continued existence and the happiness of individuals.... The problem of women presents only one particular instance exemplifying the transition from the individualism of the liberal society to the organization of the planned society. (Klein 1946:102)

But Klein's standard of the "happiness of individuals" signals an additional emphasis that is significantly different from Mannheim, whose conception of "planning" is propounded as a response to a looming social catastrophe, and whose conviction that society is faced by a crisis of integration does not lessen after the defeat of fascism. In consequence, her study of women's "two roles" addresses not only social priorities but also women's desires:

> On the one hand, they want, like everybody else, to develop their personalities to the full and to take an active part in adult social and economic life within the limits of their individual interests and abilities. On the other hand, most women want a home and a family of their own.... The technical and social developments of the last few decades have given women the opportunity to combine and to integrate their two interests in Home and Work.... No longer need women forego the pleasures of one sphere in order to enjoy the satisfactions of the other. (Myrdal and Klein 1956: xii–xiii)

Klein's emphases on welfare, happiness, women's wants and pleasures as goals of planning resemble her discursive treatment of sociology of knowledge: in both cases Klein detotalizes and relativizes Mannheim's universalistic, ontologically grounded sociological designs. As Jean Floud writes about Julia Mannheim-Láng, Karl Mannheim's wife, Klein too was simply "more insightful and delicate in human relations than Karl."

Perhaps paradoxically, the effect was to make her a sociologist in a more conventional, professional sense, as witness her subsequent career as policy-oriented empirical social scientist. Klein is the only one of Mannheim's students who expressly takes up his parallel between women and intellectuals (Kettler and Meja 1993), and in attacking the stereo-typing that reflects and consolidates the "outsider" status of women, she also calls into question the unique "mission" of intellectuals. The latter may indeed have a distinctive ability "to become articulate about pro-cesses which in their contemporaries have not yet reached to the level of consciousness" (Klein 1946: 67), as was strikingly the case with the Jewish intellectuals of Vienna, in the decades that produced Weininger and Freud, but also Arthur Schnitzler and Karl Kraus. But that capacity does not protect them from accepting many features of the dominant culture, especially when they are not subjected to an oppression "so aggressive as to alienate or frustrate them" (Klein 1946: 66). That such brilliant intellectuals as Weininger and Freud can promulgate a dualism between men and women that gives metaphysical status—idealist or materialist—to artifacts of a history of oppression manifestly drawing to a close, according to Klein, clearly shows that outsider status cannot possibly provide a warrant for cognitive validity. Knowledge is grounded in dispassionate inquiry according to appropriate method. That leaves sociology free to be one of several activities that figures in the constitu-tion of a human life rather than presuming to be its consciousness.

The relationship between sociology and the essayistic discourse of social theory exemplified by Mannheim's own promulgation of sociology's "mission," as well as by Klein's first book, is not a relation-ship of mutually exclusive opposition. Nor are they the contradictories in a dryadic dialectic, waiting to be transcended. They are distinct struc-tures that can be bound together only discursively in a rich variety of constitutions. Constitution is ultimately the paradigm that most adequately comprehends the key relationships examined in this study: intellectuals and politics, Mannheim and his students, work and home, men and women. The potential is present in Mannheim's thought; it is brought out in Klein's responses.

Klein's acute and detailed critique of Freud, as well as her sharp en-counter with Weininger, linger over their insights into bisexuality. She writes, approvingly:

> Weininger's conception of intermediate sexual forms ("sexuelle Zwischenstufen") is both in its origin and in its intention individualistic.... It creates scope for an infinite range of individual possibilities.... At the same time it conforms to the scientific aim of reducing qualitative differences to quantitative ones. It opposes those superficial generalizations which label a person characterologically "Man" or "Woman" according to his, or her primary sex characteristics and without con-sideration of characterological dispositions. (Klein 1946: 58)

Similarly, in addressing Freud's theory she begins by ironically accosting his conception of bisexuality, satirizing his "gallant gesture towards women which is quite an amusing example of chivalry entering a scientific argument" (Klein 1946: 80). Freud had casually mentioned his theory of infantile bisexuality while defending himself against charges of masculine bias, allowing that a woman who challenges him may indeed be more "masculine" than "feminine" and thus exempt from his strictures about feminine passivity. Klein regards this version of bisexuality as a blatant example of the "attitude of masculine superiority," underlined by his gesture. But she nevertheless notes that the bisexuality in question is "the corner-stone in Freud's libido-theory" and expands on its significance:

> The bisexuality of all living organisms is one of the more recent discoveries of biological science.... It means, in short, that every individual has, at least potentially if not actually, the characteristics of both sexes, but normally develops the one set to a greater extent than the other. There is no clear-cut line between absolute masculinity and absolute femininity, but reality presents us with a mixture of both in different proportions. (Klein 1946:80–81)

What vitiates the insights into bisexuality in both Weininger and Freud, according to Klein, is, first, that the concept is overshadowed by the dualistic rhetoric of polarization that carries the work (Weininger) or applied primarily to a transitory developmental stage (Freud) and, second, that the male and female components are stereotyped generalizations of existing unequal development and social roles. The longest quotation in the book, offered in both English and German, is Simmel's analysis of the power factors that shape the illusion that historically male qualities represent the universal, objective, and human, while the female is simply "the other" (Simmel 1984).

Klein criticizes Karen Horney for doing nothing more than reversing the valences, regarding the woman superior and generative because of her child-bearing role. She rejects "class struggle" in theoretical or social life (Klein 1946:143); and seeks to foster the greatest possible range of complex accommodations between differentiated factors. In an acknowledged departure from the "framework" of her study, which generally denies itself the right "to enter into discussion" with the speakers analyzed "or to supply examples in support of their cause," she invokes Virginia Woolf to support Margaret Mead's plea to "recognize the whole gamut of human values" in recreating "rich and contrasting values" without "artificial distinctions, the most striking of which is sex." Woolf, according to Klein, "was said to have written the finest English prose of her time and…was tormented by the conflict of being a woman." She then quotes Woolf, in her own cause as well as Mead's: "It is fatal to be a man or woman pure and simple; one must be woman manly or man womanly. It is fatal for a woman to lay the least stress on any grievance; to plead even with justice any cause; in any way to speak consciously as a woman" (Klein 1946: 137). Woman's "own peculiar way," it seems, is to break with the pattern that Simmel described as taking "the male sex as the universal human norm," to free herself from the condition that compels her, as Simmel says, almost always to be aware of herself as a woman, while a man rarely thinks of himself as other than simply human. That response to Mannheim's undertaking to bring women to consciousness is a marvelous surprise.

In Klein's subsequent work, that effort became stereotyped by the demands of service professionalism—women's work. But her thought denies us the luxury of passing over the imperatives of human circumstances. Klein is linked to Mannheim by bonds that are close but limited in their scope and without decisive effect on independent assertion and development. She brings a bargaining mode right into her scholarship, in her encounters with writers on "the feminine character" and ultimately in her uses of Mannheim's sociology of knowledge. If there is an asymmetry arising from the tutelary relationships between Mannheim and his students, the asymmetry is localized in time and object-domain. There is no submission to domination. Power and resistance are paired. Mannheim made strides in moving from a substantialist approach to women, however historized, to an approach that understands conflict and bargaining in the diverse institutions mediating relations between men and women. But the middle-class family and the presumed problems of the wife remained paradigmatic for him. His women students went beyond him, although further in analyses and practice than in theoretical reflection. All of them illustrate the fact that making a genuine partnership out of a relationship often merely tutelary requires an accommodation full of reservations and quirky assertiveness. They could use Mannheim's work because they had work of their own.

Biography and Theory

Mannheim implicitly challenges the method of the present book in the "Introduction" to *Man and Society*. Arguing the need for problem-oriented integration among the social sciences, he distinguishes between the habits of mind of "irresponsible laymen" and those appropriate to the new breed of sociologists he hopes to engender:

> We must try to create a period of theoretical integration, an integration that must be carried out with the same sense of responsibility which the specialists always feel in approaching their particular problems.... [In the absence of scientific integration], the solution of [the most] vital questions fell into the hands of political dogmatists and literary essayists, who...rarely have had the benefit of the tradition and training that is needed for the responsible elaboration of scientific facts.... The literary essayist tries to achieve a kind of private synthesis, the key to which lies in the chance biographies of individual writers, rather than in the evidence of scientifically studied material. (Mannheim 1940:31)

Doing justice to Mannheim, we think, requires a less polemical and less dichotomized understanding of the relationship between scientific and literary dimensions of intellectual production than he himself proposes, an interweaving of biographical information with theoretical analysis and due attention to Mannheim's own dependence on the methods of the literary essayist. Self-clarification and diagnostic clarification of the environing "times" are consistent principles of Mannheim's actual approach, as distinct from the programmatic statements on methods of theoretical integration in *Man and Society*. His works retain the marks of their philosophical and literary provenance. The notion of the sociology of knowledge as an "organon for politics as a science," for example, depends on an adventurous conception of theoretical grounding and historical development. Yet the result is a fascinating projection of the ideological process and of its possible transformation. Mannheim's ingenious essayistic response to a constellation in the political situation yields insights and is a stimulus to systematic investigation. The overly dramatized topos of "crisis" in the later work in England, in contrast, inclines him towards such forced simplifications as between "mass" and "elite," even while it gives vigor to his diagnostic writings.

His conjunction of "responsibility" with the work of "specialists" in the paragraph quoted above recalls his preoccupation with Max Weber's distinction between the vocations of politics and science, and his attachment of Weber's political ethical predicate to the vocation of science calls for a synthesis of both. Political scientists who are also scientific politicians must display responsibility towards the facts of their situations, self-understanding as well as external circumstances. This requires them to adopt a mode of rationality that aims beyond Weber's strictures on scientific objectives, a mode that is sensitive to problems of rhetorical consequences beyond the problems of communication alone. In the language of Mannheim's early theory of cultural sociology (Mannheim [1922–24] 1982), political knowledge is a mode of the "conjunctive" knowledge that constitutes meanings relevant to action.

For Mannheim, science contributes to the choice of action not only by guiding the selection of means adequate to the ends actors prefer but also by helping actors identify their places in meaningful situations. Practical knowledge competent to guide choice must consequently have the force to make those it addresses expose the myths of their own identities and identify the discrepancies between their beliefs and their experiences. As Mannheim indicates in the "Preliminary Approach" to *Ideology and Utopia*, his conception reformulates the ancient Socratic injunction to self-examination, and it implies, as Plato saw, a complex therapeutic encounter between the teacher and the taught. Sociologists and those they seek to enlighten must risk themselves in the character formed by the "chance biography" of each, but they must so structure their encounter as to lead to a common knowledge, made possible by the new situation they have jointly created, as prefigured in the Platonic dialogues. Mannheim's sociological accomplishments must be understood in the context of his work on both problems. His own attention to his situation, the conditions determining his communication with a relevant public as well as the larger historical setting, was integral to his theoretical strategy.

It is a tragic feature of Mannheim's story that these considerations drew him ever more towards formulations which rendered his own project obscure, as witness the distinction between "laymen" and "specialists" in the passage above. and the very notion of "thought at the level of planning" to which it refers. His most original contribution is the suggestion that "ideologies" approximate to the structures of practical social knowledge by virtue of the features that make them radically inadequate as scientific theories and that make them comprehensible only in the context of their social functions. Mannheim's later retreat from that suggestion follows from the intrinsic difficulties arising from his proposal and from the demands made on him by his late liberal political project and by the changed circumstances of his life.

Relating Mannheim to the situations and audiences he addresses, accordingly, is not meant to reduce his work to an artifact of his biography or to class Mannheim with those he calls "laymen." His was a life in and for sociology in a deeply instructive sense. He was a creative sociologist, and, as Jean Floud has observed (AA), he was one of the last of the "major figures" in the discipline, recognized as an inescapable presence by professional social science as well its wider public. Commenting on her own affinities to Mannheim, Claudia Honegger mourns Mannheim as the last representative of "a German tradition in sociology that sought to combine theoretical questions with empirical analyses, sociological knowledge with social experience. Its program envisioned a dialectics between experience and knowledge, commitment and distance, interpretation and structural analysis."[5] Mannheim's best essays interrogate the discipline as much as they utilize the discipline to interrogate the social world. His great and constitutive question was whether sociology can provide the integral and comprehensive practical knowledge required by liberalism to survive the disruptive irrationalities first anticipated by its critics and then brutally realized in the events of the twentieth century. Mannheim's tragedy as a thinker was that in his mature years he was forced to pursue his inquiry under conditions that often made his past accomplishments appear irrelevant and useless, even to himself. Like many victims of National Socialism, he assumed a share of the blame, disavowing Weimar culture (Gunnell 1993).

Throughout his work, Mannheim maintained that there was a spirit of the age to be uncovered, that he could bring that spirit to the consciousness of the public most immediately affected by it, and that communion with that spirit would provide valid and efficacious knowledge. Like the young John Stuart Mill, who was also inspired by the notion of a spirit of the age, Mannheim searched for consensus among the best minds of the age, and for ways of expanding the influence of those who had been brought to agreement. The practical side of this resembles the attitude and design of the politician, but Mannheim's premises embody a conception of nonconflictual politics in which there is in fact no room for politicians. Ciceronian statesmanship is required; but such statesmanship paradoxically presupposes the recognition for which it is supposed to lay the foundation (Cumming 1969: I.203).

Mannheim's search for the spirit, the synthesis, the consensus he saw incipiently emerging, produced a handsome, nonsectarian openness towards ideas from many sources. But it also led to insistence that there is "something more" to each of the ideas tapped, so that conflicting demands for acceptance from the intellectual sources used did not have to be seriously entertained. The appearance of an emerging consensus is created by a "slippery" relationship to other minds: curious, engaged, responsive, but never taking them on their terms. More arbitrator than negotiator by temperament, finally, he would put the thoughts of others in a schematized development, or he would subject key concepts to a "change of function." It was unnecessary to criticize others; it was enough to correct and balance what they said by drawing on something said by someone else. All participants were seen as sharing the same condition or expressing the same spirit.

In Central Europe, the spirit was heir to the *logos* of German Humanism, vaguely apprehended by the diverse idealist philosophies but in need of being made social flesh. In England, it was the underlying ethos of the gentleman that could revive democracy, leadership, and responsible control, restoring health after the smoldering crisis. The gentlemanly ethos would have to be sublimated, so as to be less bound by time and place, but it already combined practical responsibility and mental cultivation, Mannheim thought, and this combination was the key to substantive rationality. Much of Mannheim's reasoning about gentlemen rested on illusion. Mannheim's dependence on those who shared these illusions weakened his critical insight and, especially in the English setting, diminished his capacity for self-reflection.

In Germany, Mannheim spoke a language with resonant cultural appeal: his audiences filled in meanings, and ambiguities stimulated them to think about their own uncertainties. The essay form Mannheim used encouraged appreciation of diverse approaches and fostered reflection on that diversity. At times, as in *Conservatism*, Mannheim experimented with such designs as Müller's bipolar dialectic, mediating between opposites without claiming to have reintegrated them in a transcendent synthesis. At other times, he considered pluralistic philosophical alternatives. But throughout he treated the human world of thinking and acting as superior to his own intellectual constructs. He sought knowledge to inform creative action, not to take its place. Using the idiom of sociology, he achieved results like those of the literary essayists of his time. If he had not been expelled from Germany, he might have turned to good use the substantial responses and criticisms he was getting from people of his own generation like Hannah Arendt, Norbert Elias, Max Horkheimer, Herbert Marcuse, Hans Speier, and Paul Tillich (Meja and Stehr 1982, 1990). His work might have become more rigorous, as philosophy or history or sociology, or it might have attained greater power and forthrightness while remaining within the genres of critical essay and commentary. But the English adjustment exacted great costs. He was bound to be misunderstood, and to feel himself misunderstood.

Mannheim's persistence was marvelous, his determination was to be heard and to be accepted as a guide. In the "Preliminary Approach" to *Ideology and Utopia*, he offers the parallel with Socrates; then there is the "mission of the refugee," the Sociologist in the Summa of the Moot, the summoner to international reconstruction. Yet in addition to the influential writings and the influenced people, there are also appalling misunderstandings. Mannheim's achievements would do honor to any thinker about society. The vagaries of his thinking matter only because his sociological accomplishments are so important. The flaws appear great and had bad effects on the direction of the work itself because of Mannheim's aspirations and his conception of what he was about. Mannheim presents a dilemma to the sociological profession, unfinished business, as Hegel, Marx and Weber were unfinished business for Mannheim. Yet in the present unsettled state of sociology, where divisions into static "camps" appear ever more outdated, there may be a new capacity for recognizing in Mannheim not only a key innovator in sociological inquiry but also a representative figure whose difficulties cannot be smoothed out by interpretation. They can only be addressed by taking up the work of critical self-reflection where he was deflected from it.

Notes

1. Cp. Habermas [1981] 1984, 84-100. The question under which conditions "rhetorical" discourse is compatible with cognitive designs pervades the history of Western philosophy since Plato's dialogues. Readings of those dialogues that are sensitive to Socrates' irony question the confidence with which academic philosophy supposes the rhetoricians to have been confounded. Such awareness need not imply a relativistic inversion of the manifest argument; it may instead lead to a search for the qualitative distinctions between modes of rhetorical exchanges, as well as recognition of dependencies among participants and the constitutional politics—bargaining about bargaining—embodied in the recorded exchanges.
2. The 1935 calendar of the LSE lists the books recommended for Mannheim's class. Authors include: Westermarck, Goodsell, O.T.Mason, Malinowski, Mead, Donaldson, Buecher, Bradley, Putnam (*The Lady*), Goncourt, Pinchbeck, Halle, Lion, Hellersberg, Calverton and Schmalhausen, and Marianne Weber (KMP).

3. Characteristically, the introduction to the 1972 American edition summarizes "New Research on Women," rather than new research on the sociology of knowledge. Dale Spender (1982: 502–6), on the other hand, condemns the failure of male-dominated scholarship to allow Klein's original exposé of ideology to be recognized . Leaving aside the benighted *Punch* reviewer who found in 1946 that the book "seems unnecessarily bereft of feminine subtlety and charm" (H.K.1946: 426), early reviewers were respectful but uncertain. Reviewing the 1949 American edition, M.J.V. (1949: 401), asserts that "the main portion of Dr. Klein's stimulating book is devoted to the objective of discovering whether 'there are traits which can be called typically feminine, what these traits are, and whether they have always tended to be regarded as characteristic of women.'" Judy C. Tully's review of the 1972 edition opens by saying that the "stress on the sociology of knowledge is a major strength of the book" but asserts that most will be interested in "Klein's other aim": "She specifically sets out to clarify the idea of femininity, to describe what is thought to be the feminine character" (Tully 1974: 203–4). Florence Rockwood Kluckhohn (1950) comes closest when she praises the thoughtfulness and moderation of the work and says that while Klein does not offer a new theory of femininity, "she does us the service of holding up to reflective thought—both hers and our own—the varying and conflicting theories of a number of well-known and frequently quoted writers." Janet Sayers' (1989) introduction to the third edition of Klein's book is regrettably unhistorical in several judgments, an ironical failing because she singles out Klein's historical sensitivity. She remarks, for example, that Klein failed to gain an appointment like Mannheim's notwithstanding her two doctorates, presumably because she was not male. But Mannheim was a world-renowned scholar, and his appointment nevertheless smelled of charity, denying him professorial privileges. Her dismissive comments on Céline's "nihilism" and later anti-Semitism neglect the potentially rewarding question about Klein's earlier interest in his work.

4. Klein's strongest essays are the chapters on Ellis, Weininger, Freud, and Mead, as well as the surprisingly fresh historical survey. The following paragraph from the last of these illustrates the clever blending of informed commonplaces and insights: "There is a peculiar affinity between the fate of women and the origin of social science, and it is no mere coincidence that the emancipation of women should have started at the same time as the birth of sociology. Both are the result of a break in the established social order and of radical changes in the structure of society; and, in fact, the general interest in social problems to which these changes gave rise did much to assist the cause of women. Both, too, were made possible by the relaxation of the hold which the Christian Churches had for centuries exercised over people's minds. But the relation of woman's emancipation to social science does not only spring from a common origin; it is more direct: the humanitarian interests which formed the starting-point of social research, and practical social work itself, actually provided the back-door through which women slipped into public life" (Klein 1946: 17).

5. Honegger's apt characterization was offered in an interview (AA). Her more immediate interlocutor is Michel Foucault (Honegger 1991).

Bibliography

Abel, Theodore. [1929] 1965. *Systematic Sociology in Germany: A Critical Analysis of Some Attempts to Establish Sociology as an Independent Science.* New York: Octagon Books.

Abel, Theodor. 1933. "[Review of] Leopold von Wiese, *System der allgemeinen Soziologie.*" *The Annals of the American Academy of Political and Social Science* 169:212.

Abrams, Philip. 1968. *The Origins of British Sociology*, 1834-1914. Chicago and London: The University of Chicago Press.

Adler, Max. [1922] 1982. "Wissenschaft und soziale Struktur." In Volker Meja and Nico Stehr, eds., *Der Streit um die Wissenssoziologie*, Erster Band, pp.128-57. Frankfurt: Suhrkamp.

Adorno, Theodor W. [1951] 1969. *Minima Moralia* Frankfurt: Suhrkamp,

Adorno, Theodor W. 1986. "Neue wertfreie Soziologie." *Gesammelte Schriften*, 20:1. *Gemischte Schriften 1.* Frankfurt: Suhrkamp.

Antrick, Otto. 1966. *Die Akademie der Arbeit in der Universität Frankfurt/ Main.* Darmstadt: Eduard Roether Verlag.

Bacharach, Samuel B. and and Edward J. Lawler. 1981. *Bargaining: Power, Tactics, and Outcomes.* San Francisco: Jossey-Bass.

Bannister, Robert C. 1987. *Sociology and Scientism: The American Quest for Objectivity, 1880-1940.* Chapel Hill and London: The University of North Carolina Press.

Becker, Howard. 1932. *Systematic Sociology: On the Basis of the Beziehungslehre and Gebildelehre of Leopold von Wiese.* Adapted and amplified by Howard Becker. New York: John Wiley & Sons.

Becker, Howard. 1938. "Mannheim's *Ideology and Utopia*," *American Sociological Review* 32:260-62.

Becker, Howard and Harry Elmer Barnes. 1938. *Social Thought from Lore to Science.* New York: D.C. Heath.

Beloff, Max. 1985. "Intellectuals." In Adam Kuper and Jessica Kuper, eds., *The Social Science Encyclopedia,* pp.401-2. London, Boston and Henley: Routledge & Kegan Paul.

Benseler, Frank. 1965. "Ein Lokalpatriot der Kultur." In F. Benseler, ed., *Festschrift zum achzigsten Geburtstag von Georg Lukács*, pp.13-26. Berlin and Neuwied.

Beveridge, Lord. 1960. *The London School of Economics and Its Problems*. London: George Allen and Unwin.

Bok, Sissela. 1991. *Alva Myrdal: A Daughter's Memoir*. Reading MA: Addison-Wesley.

Borinski, Fritz. 1984. "Hermann Heller: Lehrer der Jugend und Vorkämpfer der freien Erwachsenenbildung." In Christoph Müller and Ilse Staff, eds., *Der Soziale Rechtsstaat*, pp.89-110 Baden-Baden: Nomos Verlagsgesellschaft.

Bracher, Karl Dietrich. 1960. *Die Auflösung der Weimarer Republik*. 3rd ed. Villingen: Ring Verlag.

Branford, Sybella Gurney. 1927. Review essay, "Victor Branford, *Science and Sanctity*," in *Sociological Review* 19:4(October): 335ff.

Brym, Robert. 1980. *Intellectuals and-Politics*. London: George Allen & Unwin.

Bulmer, Martin and Joan Bulmer 1981. "Philanthropy and Social Science in the 1920s: Beardsley Ruml and the Laura Spelman Rockefeller Memorial, 1922-29," *Minerva* XIX, 3 (Autumn): 347-407.

Burke, Kenneth. 1937. "[Review of] *Ideology and Utopia*." *The Nation* 143:131 (October 1, 1937).

Burke, Kenneth. 1945. *A Grammar of Motives*. New York:Prentice Hall.

Cattell, R.B., J.I. Cohen, and R.M.W. Travers, eds. 1937. *Human Affairs*. London: Macmillan.

Clark, G. N. 1942. "Principles of Research Organization," *Agenda. A Quarterly Journal of Reconstruction* I, 1 (January 1942): 91-95.

Clarke, Fred. 1940. *Education and Social Change*. London: The Sheldon Press.

Collini, Stefan. 1979. *Liberalism & Sociology: L.T. Hobhouse and Political Argument in England 1880-1914*. Cambridge: Cambridge University Press.

Congdon, Lee. 1983. *The Young Lukács*. Chapel Hill and London: The University of North Carolina Press.

Congdon, Lee. 1991. *Exile and Social Thought: Hungarian Intellectuals in Germany and Austria, 1919-1933*. Princeton: Princeton University Press.

Craver, Earlene.1986. "Patronage and the Directions of Research in Economics: The Rockefeller Foundation in Europe, 1924-1938," *Minerva*, XXIV, 2-3 (Summer-Autumn): 145-333.

Crouch, C. 1984. "Klein, Viola." In Wilhelm Bernsdorf and Horst Knopse, eds., *Internationales Soziologenlexikon*, vol. 2, p.425 Stuttgart: Enke.

Cumming, Robert Denoon. 1969. *Human Nature and History* Chicago and London: University of Chicago Press.

Cumming, Robert D. 1973. "Is Man Still Man?" *Social Research* 40,3:481-510.

Curtius, Ernst Robert. [1929] 1990. "Sociology—and its Limits." In Volker Meja and Nico Stehr, eds., *Knowledge and Politics*, pp.113-20. London and New York: Rouutledge.

Damico, Alfonso J. 1978. *Individuality and Community. The Social Thought of John Dewey.* Gainesville: University Presses of Florida.

Davie, George. 1991. *The Scottish Enlightenment and Other Essays.* Edinburgh: Polygon.

Deutsche Staatsrechtslehrer. 1927. "Die Gleichheit vor dem Gesetz im Sinne des Art. 109 der Reichsverfassung. In *Veröffentlichungen der vereinigung der deutschen staatsrechtslehrer.* Heft 3, pp.2-62. Berlin and Leipzig: De Gruyter, 1927.

Dewey, John. [1930] 1962. *Individualism Old and New.* New York: G.P. Putnam's Sons.

Dewey, John. [1935] 1960. *Liberalism and Social Action.* New York: G.P. Putnam's Sons.

Du Toit, Pierre and Willie Esterhuyse. 1990. *The Myth Makers: The Elusive Bargain for South Africa's Future.* Halfay House: Southern Book Publishers.

Duprat, G.L. 1934. "Comptes Rendu," *Revue Internationale de Sociologie,* 42. Année, I–II (Jan-Feb): 1; III (Juin 1934):143.

Duprat, G.L. 1935. "Analyse de la 2e Sèrie des Communications (reçue avant le 1er Julliet 1935," *Revue Internationale de Sociologie,* 43. Année: 449-466.

Dymes, Dorothy M.E., ed. 1944. *Sociology and Education.* Malvern: LePLay House Press.

Elias, Norbert. [1933] 1983. *The Court Society.* Oxford: Basil Blackwell.

Elias, Norbert. [1939] 1978-82. *The Civilizing Process: The History of Manners* 2 vols. New York: Urizen.

Elias, Norbert. 1990. *Norbert Elias über sich selbst.* Frankfurt: Suhrkamp.

Eliot, T.S. 1947. "Professor Karl Mannheim." *The Times,* 25 January 1947.

Erd, Rainer, ed. 1985. *Reform und Resignation, Gespräche über Franz L. Neumann.* Frankfurt: Suhrkamp.

Faris, Robert E.L. 1967. *Chicago Sociology 1920–1932.* San Francisco: Chandler Publishing Company.

Fisher, Roger, William Ury, and Bruce Patton. 1991. *Getting to Yes: Negotiating Agreement Without Giving In.* New York: Penguin Books.

Floud, Jean. 1959. "Karl Mannheim." In A.V. Judges, ed., *The Function of Teaching. Seven Approaches to Purpose, Tradition and Environment,* pp.40-66. London: Faber and Faber.

Floud, Jean. 1963. "Karl Mannheim and the Sociology of Education." *Sociologische Gids. Tdschrift voor Sociologie en Sociale Onderzoek.* 10,3: 123-31.

Floud, Jean. 1966 "Karl Mannheim," *New Society,* 29 December: 96-98.

Foitzik, Jan. 1985. "Zwei Dokumente aus dem Untergrund." *Internationale Wissenschaftliche Korrespondenz zur Geschichte der deutschen Arbeiterbewegung,* 21,2: 142-82.

Fraenkel, Ernst. 1929. "Kollektive Demokratie," *Die Gesellschaft* 6, 8 (August): 103–18.

Fraenkel, Ernst. 1968. "Vorwort zum Neudruck." In *Zur Soziologie der Klassenjustiz.* Darmstadt: Wissenschaftliche Buchgesellschaft.

Frankel, Jonathan. 1981. *Prophecy and Politics. Socialism, Nationalism, and the Russian Jews, 1862–1917.* Cambridge: Cambridge University Press.

Freudenthal, Margarete. [1934] 1986. *Gestaltwandel der städtischen, bürgerlichen und proletarischen Hauswirtschaft.* Frankfurt: Ullstein, 1986.

Freund, Gisèle. 1936. *La Photographie en France au 19e siècle.* Paris: Maison des Amis des Livres.

Frisby, David. 1976. "Introduction to the English Translation." In Theodor W. Adorno et al., *The Positivist Dispute in German Sociology*, pp.ix–xliv. London: Heineman

Gábor, Éva. 1983. "Mannheim in Hungary and in Weimar Germany." *Newsletter of the International Society for the Sociology of Knowledge* 9,1/2 (August): 7–14.

Gerth, Hans. [1935] 1976. *Bürgerliche Intelligenz um 1800. Zur Soziologie des deutschen Frühliberalismus.* Göttingen: Vandenhoeck & Ruprecht.

Gerth, Hans. [1937] 1985. "Speier's Critique of Karl Mannheim." *State Culture and Society*, 1,3: 198–208.

Gerth, Hans and C. Wright Mills, eds. 1958: *From Max Weber.* New York: Oxford.

Ginsberg, Morris. [1932] 1948. "Recent Tendencies in Sociology," reprinted as chapter five of *Reason and Unreason in Society.* Cambridge, Mass.: Harvard University Press.

Ginsberg, Morris. 1936. "The Place of Sociology." In *The Social Sciences: Their Relation to Theory and in Teaching*, pp.190–207. London: LePlay House.

Ginsberg, Morris. 1937. "Psychology and Sociology." In J.E. Dugdale, ed., *Further Papers on the Social Sciences: Their Relations in Theory and in Teaching*, pp.105–25. London: LePlay House Press.

Gluck, Mary. 1985. *Georg Lukács and His Generation, 1900-1918.* Cambridge, Mass. and London: Harvard University Press.

Greenberg, Karen 1985. "The Search for the Silver Lining: The American Academic Establishment and the 'Aryanization' of German Scholarship." In *Simon Wiesenthal Center Annual*. Volume 2, pp.115–37. White Plains, N.Y.: Kraus International Publications.

Greffrath, Mathias. 1979. *Die Zerstörung einer Zukunft.* Reinbek: Rowohlt.

Greven-Aschoff, B. 1981. *Die bürgerliche Frauenbewegung in Deutschland. 1894–1933.* Göttingen: Vandenhoeck & Ruprecht.

Gunnell, John. 1993. *The Descent of Political Theory.* Chicago: University of Chicago Press.

H.K. 1946. "The Feminine Character." *Punch* (May 15): 426

Habermas, Jürgen. [1981] 1984. *The Theory of Communicative Action*, volume 1: *Reason and the Rationalization of Society*. Boston: Beacon Press.

Habermas, Jürgen. 1992. "Soziologie in der Weimarer Republik." In Helmut Coing et al., *Wissenschaftsgeschichte seit 1900*, pp.29-53. Frankfurt: Suhrkamp.

Halperin, Natalie. 1935. *Die deutschen Schriftstellerinnen in der zweiten Hälfte des 18. Jahrhunderts*. Quakenbrück: Handelsdruckerei C. Trute.

Harris, Jose. 1986. "Political ideas and the debate on State welfare, 1940-45. In Harold L. Smith, ed., War and Social Change, pp.233-63. Manchester: Manchester University Press.

Haselbach, Dieter. 1990. "Franz Oppenheimer." In Heinz Steinert, ed., *Die (mindestens) zwei Sozialwissenschaften in Frankfurt und ihre Geschichte. Ein Symposion des Fachbereichs Gesellschaftswissenschaften aus Anlaß des 75-Jahre-Jubiläums der J.W. Goethe-Universität Frankfurt. 11./12. Dezember 1989*, pp.55-71. Frankfurt: Studientexte zur Sozialwissenschaft 3, Johann-Wolfgang-Goethe Universität.

Haussig, Frieda Elisabeth. 1934. *W. H. Riehl. Ursprünge der mittelständischen Soziologie in Deutschland*. Koblenz: Görres Druckerei.

Hayek, Friedrich. [1941] 1952. *The Counter-Revolution of Science*. Glencoe: The Free Press.

Honegger, Claudia. 1990. "Die ersten Soziologinnen in Frankfurt." In Heinz Steiner, ed., *Die (mindestens) zwei Sozialwissenschaften in Frankfurt und ihre Geschichte. Ein Symposion des Fachbereichs Gesellschaftswissenschaften aus Anlaß des 75-Jahre-Jubiläums der J.W. Goethe-Universität Frankfurt. 11./12. Dezember 1989*, pp. 88-89. Frankfurt: Studientexte zur Sozialwissenschaft 3, Johann-Wolfgang-Goethe Universität.

Honegger, Claudia. 1991. *Die Ordnung der Geschlechter. Die Wissenschaften vom Menschen und das Weib*. Frankfurt and New York: Campus.

Honegger, Claudia. 1993. "Jüdinnen in der frühen deutschsprachigen Soziologie." In Mechtild M. Jansen and Ingeborg Nordmann, eds., *Lektüren und Brüche. Jüdische Frauen in Kultur, Politik und Wissenschaft*, pp.178-95. Wiesbaden: Hessische Landeszentrale für politische Bildung.

Honegger, Claudia. 1994. "Die bittersüße Freiheit der Halbdistanz. Die ersten Soziologinnen im deutschen Sprachraum." In Theresa Wobbe and Gesa Lindemann, eds. *Denkachsen. Zur theoretischen und institutionellen rede vom geschlecht*, pp.69-85. Frankfurt: Suhrkamp.

Horkheimer, Max. [1931] 1990. "A new concept of ideology?" In Meja and Stehr, *Knowledge and Politics*, pp. 140-57. London and New York: Routledge.

Horowitz, Irving Louis. 1988. "Zwischen der Charybdis des Kapitalismus und der Szylla des Kommunismus: Die Emigration deutscher Sozialwissenschaftler." In Ilja Srubar, ed., *Exil, Wissenschaft, Identität: Die Emigration deutscher Sozialwissenschaftler, 1933–1945*, pp. 37–63. Frankfurt a.M.: Suhrkamp

Horváth, Zoltán. 1966. *Die Jahrhundertwende in Ungarn*. Budapest: Corvina.

House, Floyd N. 1933. Review of Becker/von Wiese and Eubank, *The American Journal of Sociology* 38 (July-May): 128–30.

Iremonger, F.A. 1948. *William Temple, Archbishop of Canterbury*. London: Oxford University Press.

Jaschke, Hans-Gerd. 1991. *Streitbare demokratie und innere sicherheit*. Opladen: Westdeutscher Verlag.

Jászi, Ocar. 1908. *Art and Morals*, 2nd ed. Budapest.

Jászi, Oscar. 1923. *Magyarians Schuld, Ungarns Sühne. Revolution und Gegenrevolution in Ungarn*. Munich: Verlag für Kulturpolitik.

Jay, Martin. 1973. *The Dialectical Imagination: A History of the Frankfurt School and the Institute of Social Research, 1923–1950*. Boston: Little Brown.

Kadarkay, Arpad. 1991. *Georg Lukács: Life, Thought, and Politics*. Cambridge, Mass. and Oxford: Basil Blackwell.

Kahn-Freund, Otto. 1981. *Labour Law and Politics in the Weimar Republic*. Oxford: Basil Blackwell.

Káradi, Eva, and Erzsébet Vezér, eds. 1985. *Georg Lukács, Karl Mannheim und der Sonntagskreis*. Frankfurt: Sendler.

Käsler, Dirk. 1981. "Der Streit um die Bestimmung der Soziologie auf den Deutschen Soziologentagen 1910–1930." In Rainer M. Lepsius, Hrsg., *Soziologie in Deutschland und Österreich 1918–1945*, pp.199–244. Opladen: Westdeutscher Verlag.

Käsler, Dirk. 1984. *Die frühe deutsche Soziologie 1909 bis 1934 und ihre Entstehungs-Milieus*. Opladen: Westdeutscher Verlag.

Käsler, Dirk. 1991. *Sociological Adventures: Earle Edward Eubank's Visits with European Sociologists*. New Brunswick and London: Transaction Publishers.

Kettler, David. 1967. "Sociology of Knowledge and Moral Philosophy: The Place of Traditional Problems in the Formation of Mannheim's Thought," *Political Science Quarterly* 82, 3(1967).

Kettler, David. 1971. "Culture and Revolution: Lukács in the Hungarian Revolutions of 1918/1919," *Telos* 10:35-92.

Kettler, David. 1984. "Works Community and Workers' Organization: A Central Problem in Weimar Labour Law." *Economy and Society* 13, 3: 278ff.

Kettler, David and Volker Meja. 1993. "Their 'Own Peculiar Way': Karl Mannheim and the Rise of Women." *International Sociology*, 8, 1 (March):5-55.

Kettler, David, Volker Meja, and Nico Stehr. 1982. "Introduction: Karl Mannheim's early writings on cultural sociology." In Karl Mannheim, *Structures of Thinking*, pp.11–29. London: Routledge and Kegan Paul.

Kettler, David, Volker Meja, and Nico Stehr. 1986. "The Design of *Conservatism*." In Karl Mannheim, *Conservatism*, David Kettler, Volker Meja, and Nico Stehr, eds., pp.1–26. London and New York: Routledge & Kegan Paul.

Klein, Viola. 1946. *The Feminine Character: History of an Ideology*. London: Routledge and Kegan Paul.

Klein, Viola. [1946] 1989. *The Feminine Character: History of an Ideology*. 3rd ed. with an introduction by Janet Sayers. London and New York: Routledge.

Klein, Viola. 1949. "The Emancipation of Women: Its Motives and Achievements." In BBC Third Programme Lectures, *Ideas and Beliefs of the Victorians*, pp.261–67. London: Sylvan Press.

Klein, Viola. 1958. *Working Wives; a survey of facts and opinions concerning the gainful employment of married women in Britain, carried in co-operation with Mass Observation Ltd.*. London: Institute of Personnel Management, Occasional Papers, No. 15.

Klein, Viola. 1961. *Employing Married Women*. London: Institute of Personnel Management, Occasional Papers, No. 17.

Klein, Viola. 1965a. *Women Workers: Working Hours and Services: A Survey in 21 Countries*. Paris: Organisation for Economic Cooperation and Development (Employment of Special Groups, 1).

Klein, Viola. 1965b. *Britain's Married Women Workers*. London: Routledge & Kegan Paul.

Klein, Viola. 1972. "Preface to the Second Edition." In *The Feminine Character: History of an Ideology*. 2nd ed. Urbana, Chicago and London: University of Illinois Press.

Klingemann, Carsten. 1986. "Soziologen vor dem Nationalsozialismus. Szenen aus der Selbstgleichschaltung der Deutschen Gesellschaft für Soziologie." In Josef Hülsdünker und Rolf Schellhase, Hrsg., *Sozialgeschichte. Identität und Krisen einer 'engagierten' Disziplin*, pp.59–84. Berlin: Duncker & Humblot.

Klingemann, Carsten. 1992. "Social-Scientific Experts—No Ideologues. Sociology and Social Research in the Third Reich." In Stephen P. Turner and Dirk Käsler, eds., *Sociology Responds to Fascism*, pp.127–54. London and New York: Routledge.

Kluckhohn, Florence Rockwood. 1950. Review of Viola Klein, *The Feminine Character*. *The American Journal of Sociology* 56: 88–89.

Kojecky, Roger. 1972. *T.S. Eliot's Social Criticism*. New York: Farrar, Straus and Giroux.

König, René. 1984. "Über das vermeintliche Ende der deutschen Soziologie vor der Machtergreifung des Nationalsozialismus." *Kölner Zeitschrift für Soziologie und Sozialpsychologie* 36,1:42.

König, René. 1987. *Soziologie in Deutschland*. Munich: Carl Hanser.

Kraft, Julius. 1929. "Soziologie oder Soziologismus?" *Zeitschrift für Völker psychologie und Soziologie* 5: 406–17.

Krohn, Claus-Dieter. 1987. *Wissenschaft im Exil: Deutsche Sozial-und Wirtschaftswissenschaftler in den USA und die New School for Social Research*. Frankfurt and New York: Campus.

Kuckhoff, Greta. 1972. *Vom Rosenkranz zur Roten Kapelle*. Berlin: Verlag Neues Leben.

Laski, Harold. 1936. "Political Theory and the Social Sciences." In *The Social Sciences: Their Relation to Theory and in Teaching*, pp.115–128. London: LePlay House.

Lepsius, M. Rainer. 1979. "Die Entwicklung der Soziologie nach dem Zweiten Weltkrieg 1945 bis 1967." In Günther Lüschen, ed., *Deutsche Soziologie seit 1945*, pp.25–70. Opladen: Westdeutscher Verlag.

Lepsius, M. Rainer. 1981. "Die Soziologie der Zwischenkriegszeit: Entwicklungstendenzen und Beurteilungskriterien." Pp. 7–23 in Lepsius, *Soziologie in Deutschland und Österreich 1918–1945*. Opladen: Westdeutscher Verlag.

Lindsay, A.D. 1943. *The Modern Democratic State*. London: Royal Institute of International Affairs.

Lindsay of Birker (A.D. Lindsay). 1952. Review of *Freedom, Power and Democratic Planning*. In *British Journal of Sociology*, 3:85-6.

Loader, Colin. 1985. *The Intellectual Development of Karl Mannheim: Culture, Politics, and Planning*. Cambridge: Cambridge University Press.

Löwe, Adolf. 1935. *Economics and Sociology*. London: George Allen and Unwin.

Lowe, Adolph 1937. *The Price of Liberty: A German on Contemporary Britain*. London: The Hogarth Press.

Lowenthal, Leo. 1987. *An Unmastered Past*. Berkeley: University of California Press.

Löwy, Michael. 1979. *Georg Lukács - From Romanticism to Bolshevism*. London: New Left Books.

Lukács, Georg. [1911] 1971. *Soul and Form*., Anna Bostock, trans. Cambridge, Mass.: The MIT Press.

Lukács, Georg. [1923] 1968. *History and Class Consciousness*. Cambridge, Mass.: The MIT Press.

Lukács, Georg. [1924] 1971. *Lenin: A Study on the Unity of His Thought*. Cambridge, Mass.: The MIT Press.

Lukács, Georg. [1933] 1982. *Wie ist die faschistische Philosophie in Deutschland entstanden?* Budapest: Akadémia Kiadó.

Lukács, Georg. 1986. *Selected Correspondence. 1902–1929.* Judith Marcus and Zoltan Tar, eds. New York: Columbia University Press.

Lukacs, John. 1988. *Budapest 1900.* New York: Grove Weidenfeld, 1988.

Luthardt, Wolfgang. 1984. "Politiktheoretische Aspekte im Werk von Hans Kelsen." In Richard Saage, ed., *Politische Konzeptionen der Sozialdemokratie zwischen den Weltkriegen.* Frankfurt: Suhrkamp.

Luthardt, Wolfgang. 1986. *Sozialdemokratische Verfassungstheorie in der Weimarer Republik.* Opladen: Westdeutscher Verlag.

Macgregor, D. H. 1942. "Actual War Influences on Reconstruction," *Agenda. A Quarterly Journal of Reconstruction,* I, 1 (January 1942): 3–12.

M.J.V. 1949. Review of Viola Klein, *The Feminine Character. Sociology and Social Research* 33: 401–2.

MacIver, Robert M. 1938. "*Ideology and Utopia* by Karl Mannheim," *The American Historical Review,* 43: 814–17.

Mannheim, Karl. 1917. Review of Ernst Cassirer, *Freiheit und Form: Studien zur deutschen Geistesgeschichte. Athenaeum* (Budapest), 3:409–13.

Mannheim, Károlyi, 1918. *Lélek és kultura.* Programelöadás a II. szemeszter megnyitása alkalmából a Szellemi Tudományok Szabad Iskoláján. Bp. Benkö Gyula Könyvkereskedése.

Mannheim, Karl. [1918] 1964. "Seele und Kultur." In *Wissenssoziologie,* ed. Kurt H. Wolff, pp. 66–84. Neuwied: Luchterhand.

Mannheim, Károlyi. [1918] 1985. "Georg Simmel als Philosoph." In Karádi and Vezér, eds. *Georg Lukács, Karl Mannheim und der Sonntagskreis,* pp.150–53. Frankfurt: Sendler.

Mannheim, Karl. [1919a] 1985. "Die Grundprobleme der Kulturphilosophie." In Karádi and Vezér, eds., *Georg Lukács, Karl Mannheim und der Sonntagskreis,* pp.206–31. Frankfurt: Sendler.

Mannheim, Károlyi. [1919b] 1985. "Ernst Bloch, Geist der Utopie." In Karádi and Vezér, eds., *Georg Lukács, Karl Mannheim und der Sonntagskreis,* pp.254–59. Frankfurt: Sendler.

Mannheim, Karl. [1920] 1993. "A Review of Georg Lukács' *Theory of the Novel.*" In Kurt H. Wolff, ed., *From Karl Mannheim,* pp.131–35. New Brunswick and London: Transaction Publishers.

Mannheim, Karl. 1921–1922. "Heidelbergi levelek i & ii," *Tüz* (Vienna), 1, 1921: 46-50; 1922:91–95. German translation, "Heidelberger Briefe." In Karádi and Vezér, eds., *Georg Lukács, Karl Mannheim und der Sonntagskreis,* pp. 73–91.

Mannheim, Karl. [1921] 1964. "Beiträge zur Theorie der Weltanschauungs-Interpretation." In *Wissensoziologie,* pp.91–154. Berlin und Neuwied: Luchterhand.

Mannheim, Karl. [1921] 1993. "On the Interpretation of Weltanschauung." In Kurt H. Wolff, ed. *From Karl Mannheim*, 136-87. New Brunswick and London: Transaction Publishers

Mannheim, Karl. [1922] 1953. "Structural Analysis of Epistemology." In *Essays on Sociology and Social Psychology*, ed. Paul Kecskemeti, pp. 15-73. London: Routledge and Kegan Paul.

Mannheim, Karl. [1922a] 1964. "Zur Strukturanalyse der Erkenntnistheorie." In *Wissenssoziologie*, pp.166-245. Berlin und Neuwied: Luchterhand.

Mannheim, Karl. [1922b] 1964. "Zum Problem einer Klassifikation der Wissenschaften." In Kurt H. Wolff, ed., *Wissenssoziologie*, pp. 155-65. Berlin und Neuwied: Luchterhand.

Mannheim, Karl. [1922-24] 1982. *Structures of Thinking*. David Kettler, Volker Meja, and Nico Stehr, eds., Jeremy J. Shapiro and Shierry Weber Nicholson, trans., London: Routledge & Kegan Paul.

M[annheim] K[arolyi]. 1924. "Levelek az imigràciòbol," *Diogenes* 1(1924): 13-25; 2(1924):20-23.

Mannheim, Karl. [1924] 1964. "Historismus." In *Wissenssoziologie*, pp.246-307. Berlin and Neuwied: Luchterhand.

Mannheim, Karl. [1924] 1952. "Historicism." In *Essays in the Sociology of Knowledge*. London: Routledge & Kegan Paul Ltd.

Mannheim, Karl. [1925] 1952. "The Problem of a Sociology of Knowledge." In Mannheim, *Essays on the Sociology of Knowledge*, pp. 134-90. London: Routledge & Kegan Paul.

Mannheim, Karl. [1925] 1986. *Conservatism: A Contribution to the Sociology of Knowledge*, David Kettler, Volker Meja, and Nico Stehr, eds., David Kettler and Volker Meja, trans. London and New York: Routledge & Kegan Paul.

Mannheim, Karl. 1927. "Das konservative Denken." *Archiv für Sozialwissenschaft und Sozialpolitik* 57, 1: 68-142, 2: 470-95.

Mannheim, Karl. 1928. "Der sechste deutsche Soziologentag in Zürich." *Frankfurter Zeitung* (October 5): 1-2.

Mannheim, Karl. 1929. *Ideologie und Utopie*. Bonn: Cohen.

Mannheim Karl. [1929] 1952. *Ideologie und Utopie*, 3rd ed. Frankfurt am Main: Schulte-Bulmke.

Mannheim, Karl. 1929a. "Die Bedeutung der Konkurrenz im Gebiete des Geistigen." In *Verhandlungen des sechsten deutschen Soziologentages vom 17. bis 19. September 1928 in Zürich*, pp. 35-83. Tübingen:J.C.B. Mohr.

Mannheim, Karl. [1929] 1993. "Competition as a Cultural Phenomenon." In Kurt H. Wolff, ed., *From Karl Mannheim*, pp. 399-437. New Brunswick and London: Transaction Publishers.

Mannheim, Karl. [1929a] 1993. "Problems of Sociology in Germany." In Kurt H. Wolff, ed., *From Karl Mannheim*, 438-46. New Brunswick and London: Transaction Publishers.

Mannheim, Karl. [1930] 1952. "On the Nature of Economic Ambition and Its Significance for the Social Education of Man" (1930). In Karl Mannheim, *Essays on the Sociology of Knowledge*, pp. 230-75. London: Routledge & Kegan Paul.

Mannheim, Karl. [1931] 1952. "Wissensoziologie," *Ideologie und Utopie*, 3rd ed. Frankfurt am Main: Schulte-Bulmke.

Mannheim, Karl. [1931] 1953. "American Sociology." In *Essays on Sociology and Social Psychology*, pp. 185-94. London: Routledge & Kegan Paul.

Mannheim, Karl. 1932a. *Die Gegenwartsaufgaben der Soziologie* Tübingen: J.C.B. Mohr (Paul Siebeck).

Mannheim, Karl. 1932b. "Die geistige Krise im Lichte der Soziologie," *Stuttgarter Neues Tageblatt* (December 31).

Mannheim, Karl. [1932]. 1993. "The Sociology of Intellectuals," in *Theory, Culture & Society* 10,3 (August): 69-80 .

Mannheim, Karl. 1934a. "Persverslag van den Universitairen leergang gehouden van 12-27 September 1933," *Algemeen Nederlandsch Tijdschrift voor Wijsbegeerte en Psychologie* 27 (January): 32-39.

Mannheim, Karl. 1934b. "The Crisis of Culture in the Age of Mass-Democracies and Autarchies," *Sociological Review* 26,2 (April): 105-29.

Mannheim, Karl. 1934c. *Rational and Irrational Elements in Contemporary Society*. Hobhouse Memorial Lecture. London: Oxford University Press.

Mannheim, Karl. [1934] 1953. "German Sociology (1918-1933)." In *Essays on Sociology and Social Psychology*, pp. 209-28. London: Routledge & Kegan Paul.

Mannheim, Karl. 1935a. *Mensch und Gesellschaft im Zeitalter des Umbaus*. Leiden: Sijthoff.

Mannheim, Karl. 1935b. "Friedrich Tönnies." *Encyclopedia of the Social Sciences* 15: 106-7.

Mannheim, Karl. 1936a. *Ideology and Utopia*. London: Routledge & Kegan Paul.

Mannheim, Karl. 1936b. "The Place of Sociology." In *The Social Sciences: Their Relation to Theory and in Teaching*, pp, 164-89. London: LePlay House.

Mannheim, Karl. 1937. "The Sociology of Human Valuation: The Psychological and Sociological Approach." In J.E. Dugdale, ed., *Further Papers on the Social Sciences: Their Relations in Theory and Practice*, pp. 171-91. London: LePlay Press.

Mannheim, Karl. 1940. *Man and Society in an Age of Reconstruction.* London: Routledge & Kegan Paul .

Mannheim, Karl. 1943. *Diagnosis of Our Time: Wartime Essays of a Sociologist.* London: Kegan Paul, Trench, Truebner & Co.

Mannheim, Karl. 1945. "The Function of the Refugee," *The New English Weekly*, 27, 1 (April 19):5-6.

Mannheim, Karl. 1950. *Freedom, Power and Democratic Planning*. New York: Oxford University Press.

Mannheim, Karl. 1952. *Essays in the Sociology of Knowledge*, ed. Paul Kecskemeti. London: Routledge & Kegan Paul Ltd.

Mannheim, Karl. 1953. *Essays on Sociology and Social Psychology*. Paul Kecskemeti, ed. and trans. London: Routledge & Kegan Paul.

Mannheim, Karl. 1956. "Towards the Sociology of the Mind: An Introduction." In *Essays on the Sociology of Culture*, Ernst Mannheim, ed., in cooperation with Paul Kecskemeti, pp. 15-89. London: Routledge & Kegan Paul.

Mannheim, Karl. 1964. *Wissenssoziologie: Auswahl aus dem Werk*, ed. and intro. by Karl H. Wolff. Berlin and Neuwied: Luchterhand.

Mannheim, Karl. 1971. "Karl Mannheim's Letters to Lukács, 1910-1916," *The New Hungarian Quarterly*, XVI, 57 (Spring): 93-105.

Mannheim, Karl and W.A.C. Stewart. 1962. *An Introduction to the Sociology of Education*. London: Routledge & Kegan Paul.

Marcus-Tár, Judith. 1982. *Thomas Mann and Georg Lukács*. Budapest: Corvina.

Marcus, Judith, and Zoltán Tar, eds. 1986. *Georg Lukács: Selected Correspondence, 1902-1920*. New York: Columbia University Press.

Marshall, T.H. 1936. "Report on the Teaching of the Social Sciences." In *The Social Sciences: Their Relation to Theory and in Teaching*, pp. 29-54. London: LePlay House.

Marx, Karl and Friedrich Engels. 1956. *The Holy Family or Critique of Critical Critique*. Moscow: Foreign Languages Publishing House.

Mathiesen, Ulf. 1990. "Kontrastierung/Kooperationen: Karl Mannheim in Frankfurt (1930-1933)." In Heinz Steinert, ed., *Die (mindestens) zwei Sozialwissenschaften in Frankfurt und ihre Geschichte*, pp. 72-87. Frankfurt: Studientexte zur Sozialwissenschaft 3, Johann-Wolfgang-Goethe Universität.

Meja, Volker. 1975. "The Sociology of Knowledge and the Critique of Ideology," *Cultural Hermeneutics* 3:57-68.

Meja, Volker and Nico Stehr. 1982, eds. *Der Streit um die Wissenssoziologie*, 2 volumes. Frankfurt: Suhrkamp

Meja, Volker and Nico Stehr. 1990, eds. *Knowledge and Politics: The Sociology of Knowledge Dispute*. London: Routledge

Merton, Robert K. [1941] 1968. "Karl Mannheim and the Sociology of Knowledge." In *Social Theory and Social Structure*, pp. 543-62. Glencoe: The Free Press.

Merton, Robert K. [1949] 1968. *Social Theory and Social Structure*, enlarged ed. Glencoe: The Free Press.

Meusel, Alfred. [1928] 1982. "Die Konkurrenz in soziologischer Betrachtung. Gedanken zum 6. Deutschen Soziologentag." In Volker Meja, and Nico Stehr, eds., *Der Streit um die Wissenssoziologie*, pp. 402-13. Frankfurt: Suhrkamp.

Mill, John Stuart. [1844] 1965. *Principles of Political Economy: With Some of Their Applications to Social Philosophy.* Toronto: University of Toronto Press.

Mill, John Stuart. [1859] 1977. "On Liberty." In *Essays on Politics and Society.* Toronto: University of Toronto Press.

Mill, J.S. 1924. *Autobiography.* New York: Columbia University Press.

Mill, John Stuart. 1881. *A System of Logic*, 8th ed. Philadelphia: Harper and Brothers.

Mill, John Stuart and Harriet T. Mill. 1970. *Essays on Sex Equality*, ed. by Alice Rossi. Chicago: University of Chicago Press.

Miller, Susanne. 1978. *Die Bürde der Macht.* Düsseldorf: Droste.

Mountford, Sir James. 1972. *Keele: An Historical Critique.* London: Routledge & Kegan Paul.

Myrdal, Alva & Viola Klein. 1956. *Women's Two Roles. Home and Work.* London: Routledge & Kegan Paul.

Nelson, Rodney D. 1990. *The Reception and Development of the Sociology of Knowledge in American Sociology, 1936-1960.* Ph.D. Dissertation, University of Toronto.

Nettl, J.P. 1969. "Ideas, Intellectuals, and Structures of Dissent." In Philip Rieff, ed., *On Intellectuals*, pp. 57-134. New York: Doubleday.

Neumann. Franz. 1923. *Rechtsphilosophische Einleitung zu einer Abhandlung über das Verhältnis von Staat und Strafe.* Unpublished Disseration. Faculty of Law. Frankfurt/Main.

Neumann, Franz. 1929. "Gegen ein Gesetz zur Nachprüfung der Gesetzmäßigkeit von Reichsgesetzen," *Die Gesellschaft. Internationale Revue für Sozialismus und Politik*, 6,6 (June): 517-36.

Neumann, Franz L. 1936. *The Governance of the Rule of Law.* Dissertation, London School of Economics.

Neumann, Franz. 1986. *The Rule of Law: Political Theory and the Legal System in Modern Society.* Leamington Spa, Heidelberg, and Dover: Berg.

Newman, Michael. 1993. *Harold Laski: A Political Biography.* Basingstoke: Macmillan.

Odum, Howard W. 1951. *American Sociology: The Story of Sociology in the United States through 1950.* New York: David McKay.

Oppenheimer, Franz. [1928] 1932. "Tendencies in Recent German Sociology," *The Sociological Review* 24, 1-3: 1-13, 125-37, 249-60.

Parsons, Talcott et al. 1961. *Theories of Society: Foundations of Modern Sociological Theory.* II. Glencoe: The Free Press.

Pels, Dick. 1993. "Missionary Sociology between Left and Right: A Critical Introduction to Mannheim's Theory," *Theory, Culture & Society* 10,3 (August 1993): 45–68.

Pois, Robert A. 1976. *The Bourgeois Democrats of Weimar Germany.* Transactions of the American Philosophical Society, New Series 66:4. Philadelphia: The American Philosophical Society.

Polanyi, Michael. [1939] 1945. *Rights and Duties of Science.* Occasional Pamphlet No. 2 of the Society for Freedom in Science [Oxford].

Popper, Karl. [1944] 1951. *The Poverty of Historicism.* London: Routledge & Kegan Paul.

Radbruch, Gustav. 1914. *Grundzüge der Rechtsphilosophie.* Leipzig: Quelle & Meyer.

Radbruch, Gustav. 1922. *Kulturlehre des Sozialismus.* Berlin.

Revue Internationale de Sociologie. 1932. 40. Année, Nos. I–II (Jan.-Feb.): 1–7.

Rohner, Ludwig. 1966. *Der deutsche Essay.* Neuwied: Luchterhand.

Roth, Guenther. 1988. "Marianne Weber and Her Circle. Introduction to the Transaction Edition." In Marianne Weber, *Max Weber. A Biography*, pp. xv–lix. New Brunswick: Transaction Books.

Rubinstein, Nina. [1933] 1989. *"Die Französische Emigration nach 1789. Ein Beitrag zur Soziologie der politischen Emigration".* Frankfurt: Unpublished Doctoral Dissertation.

Rüschemeyer, Dietrich. 1981. "Die Nichtrezeption von Karl Mannheims Wissensoziologie in der amerikanischen Soziologie." In M. Rainer Lepsius, ed., *Soziologie in Deutschland und Österreich 1918–1945*, pp. 414–26. Opladen: Westdeutscher Verlag.

Rutkoff, Peter M. and William B. Scott. 1986. *New School: A History of the New School for Social Research.* New York: The Free Press.

Sárközi, Mátyás. 1986. "The Influence of Georg Lukács on the Young Karl Mannheim in the Light of a Newly Discovered Diary." *Slavic and Eastern European Review* 64(3): 436-37.

Savigny, Friedrich C. 1892. *Vom Beruf unserer Zeit für Gesetzgebung und Rechtswissenschaft.* Freiburg: J.C.B. Mohr.

Sayers, Janet. 1989. "Introduction." In Viola Klein, *The Feminine Character*, 3rd edition, pp. ix–xxxiv. London: Routledge.

Scheler, Max, ed. 1924. *Versuche zu einer Soziologie des Wissens.* Munich: Duncker & Humblot.

Schelting, Alexander von. 1936. Review of *Ideologie und Utopie, American Sociological Review* I, 4 (August): 664-74.

Schivelbusch, Wolfgang. 1982. *Intellektuellendämmerung: Zur Lage der Frankfurter Intelligenz in den zwanziger Jahren.* Frankfurt: Insel.

Schwartz, G. L. 1943. "Laissez-Faire," *Nineteenth Century and After,* 134 (November): 209-220.

Scott, Drusilla. 1971. *A.D. Lindsay, A Biography.* Oxford: Basil Blackwell.

Shils, Edward A. 1941. "Irrationality and Planning: A note on Mannheim's *Man and Society in an Age of Transformation.*" *The Journal of Liberal Religion* II:148-53.

Shils, Edward A. 1947. "In Memoriam: Karl Mannheim 1893-1947." *Erasmus* 1,4 (February 15): 195-96.

Shils, Edward. 1948. *The Present State of American Sociology.* Glencoe: The Free Press.

Shils, Edward A. 1968. "Karl Mannheim." In *International Encyclopedia of the Social Sciences,* vol. IX, pp. 557-62. New York: The Free Press.

Shils, Edward A. 1970. "Tradition, Ecology, and Institution in the History of Sociology," *Daedalus* 99, 4 (Fall): 760-825.

Shils, Edward. 1973. "*Ideology and Utopia* by Karl Mannheim," *Twentieth-Century Classics Revisited. Dœdalus,* 103, 1 (Winter): 83-89.

Shils, Edward. 1980. *The Calling of Sociology.* Chicago and London: The University of Chicago Press.

Shils, Edward. 1981. "Some Academics, Mainly in Chicago," *The American Scholar* (Spring): 179, 196.

Simonds, A.P. 1978. *Karl Mannheim's Sociology of Knowledge.* Oxford: Clarendon Press.

Simmel. Georg. [1908] 1968. *Soziologie: Untersuchungen über die Formen der Vergesellschaftung,* 5th edition. Berlin: Duncker & Humblot.

Simmel, Georg. 1984. *On Women, Sexuality and Love,* ed. by Guy Oakes. New Haven and London: Yale University Press.

Sinzheimer, Hugo. 1976. *Arbeitsrecht und Rechtssoziologie.* Frankfurt and Cologne: Europäische Verlagsanstalt.

Sklar, Martin J. 1988. *The Corporate Reconstruction of American Capitalism, 1890-1916.* Cambridge and New York: Cambridge University Press.

Smend, Rudolf. 1928. *Verfassung und Verfassungsrecht.* Munich and Leipzig: Duncker & Humblot.

Smith, Adam. [1762-3] 1978. *Lectures on Jurisprudence.* Oxford: Oxford University Press.

Söllner, Alfons. 1984. "Leftist Students of the Conservative Revolution: Neumann, Kirchheimer, and Marcuse," *Telos* 61 (Fall): 55-70.

Sombart, Nicolaus. 1955. "Henri de Saint-Simon und Auguste Comte." In Afred Weber, ed., *Einführung in die Soziologie.* Munich: Pieper.

Soziologisches Kollektiv [1930] 1986. "'Die Wolke' oder 'Politik als Wissenschaft.'" In H.E.S. Woldring, *Karl Mannheim,* pp. 391-403. New York: St. Martin's Press.

Speier, Hans. [1930] 1990. "Sociology or Ideology?" In Volker Meja and Nico Stehr, eds., *Knowledge and Politics*, pp. 209-22. London: Routledge.

Speier, Hans. 1937. "The Social Conditions of the Intellectual Exile." *Social Research* 4, 2 (May): 316-28.

Speier, Hans. [1937] 1985. "Karl Mannheim's *Ideology and Utopia*," *State, Culture and Society* I, 3 (Spring): 183-97.

Speier, Hans. 1938. "The Social Determination of Ideas," *Social Research* V (July): 182-205.

Speier, Hans. 1952. *Social Order and the Risks of War*. New York: G. W. Stewart.

Speier, Hans. 1989. "Karl Mannheim as Sociologist of Knowledge." In *The Truth in Hell and Other Essays on Politics and Culture, 1935-1987*, pp. 35-49. Oxford: Oxford University Press.

Spender, Dale. 1982. *Women of Ideas and What Men Have Done to Them*. London: Routledge & Kegan Paul.

Tillich, Hannah. 1973. *From Time to Time*. New York: Stein & Day

Tillich, Paul. 1983. "Das Frankfurter Gespräch." In Paul Tillich *Briefwechsel und Streitschriften*, pp. 314-69. Frankfurt: Evangelisches Verlagswerk.

Troeltsch, Ernst. [1921] 1925. "Die Revolution in der Wissenschaft." In *Aufsätze zur Geistesgeschichte und Religionssoziologie*. Tübingen: J.C.B. Mohr (Paul Siebeck).

Troeltsch, Ernst. 1922. "Der Historismus und seine Probleme." In *Gesammelte Werke*, vol. 3. Tübingen: J.C.B. Mohr.

Truhel, Käthe. 1934. *Sozialbeamte. Ein Beitrag zur Sozioanalyse der Bürokratie*. Sagan: Herzögliche Hofbuchdruckerei Benjamin Krause.

Tully, Judy C. 1974. "Sex Roles: A View from the Past," *Contemporary Psychology* 19: 203-4.

Vierkandt, Alfred. 1931. "Was die Wissenssoziologie uns lehrt." *Pädagogische Warte*, Heft 9.

Vierkandt, Alfred. 1932. *Handwörterbuch der Soziologie*. Stuttgart: F. Enke, 1931.

Wagner, Gerhard and Heinz Zipprian, eds. 1994. *Max Webers Wissenschaftslehre*. Frankfurt: Suhrkamp.

Weber, Marianne. 1907. *Ehefrau und Mutter in der Rechtsentwicklung*. Tübingen: J.C.B. Mohr.

Weber, Marianne. 1919. *Frauenfragen und Frauengedanken*. Tübingen: J.C.B. Mohr.

Weber, Max [1906] 1989. "Zur Lage der bürgerlichen Demokratie in Rußland." In *Zur Russischen Revolution von 1905. Max Weber Gesamtausgabe* I/10, ed. Wolfgang J. Mommsen with Dittmar Dahlmann, pp. 86-279. Tübingen: J.C.B. Mohr (Paul Siebeck).

Weber, Max. 1922. "Wissenschaft als Beruf." In *Wissenschaftslehre*. Tübingen: J.C.B. Mohr (Paul Siebeck).

Weininger, Otto. 1903. *Geschlecht und Charakter*. Vienna: Wilhelm Braumüller.

Wiese, Leopold von. 1928. "Einsamkeit und Geselligkeit als Bedingungen der Mehrung des Wissens." In Max Scheler, *Versuche zu einer Soziologie des Wissens*, pp. 218-29. München und Leipzig: Duncker & Humblot.

Wiese, Leopold von. 1929a. "Vorbemerkungen." In *Verhandlungen des Sechsten deutschen Soziologentages*, pp. vii-ix. Tübingen: J.C.B. Mohr (Paul Siebeck).

Wiese, Leopold von. 1929b. "Die Konkurrenz, vorwiegend in soziologisch-systematischer Betrachtung." In *Verhandlungen des Sechsten deutschen Soziologentages*, pp. 15-35. Tübingen: J.C.B. Mohr (Paul Siebeck).

Wiese, Leopold von. 1931. *Soziologie. Geschichte und Hauptprobleme*. Berlin: G.J. Göschen'sche Verlagshandlung.

Wiese, Leopold von. 1935. "Social Theory and Social Practice," *Human Problems of Social Planning*, Publications of the American Sociological Society, XXIX, 3 (August). Chicago.

Wiese, Leopold von. 1935a. [Review of] Karl Mannheim, *Mensch und Gesellschaft im Zeitalter des Umbaus. Zeitschrift für Nationalökonomie* VI, 4: 565-71.

Wiese, Leopold von. 1936. "Der gegenwärtige Entwicklungsstand der allgemeinen Soziologie," *Reine und Angewandte Soziologie. Eine Festgabe für Ferdinand Tönnies zu seinem achzigsten Geburtstage am 26. Juli 1935*. Leipzig: Hans Buske Verlag.

Wiese, Leopold von. 1936a. *Sozial, geistig und kulturell. Eine grundsätzliche Betrachtung über die Elemente des zwischenmenchlichen Lebens*. Leipzig: Hans Buske Verlag

Wiese, Leopold von. 1948. "Karl Mannheim(1893-1947)," *Kölner Zeitschrift für Soziologie und Sozialpsychologie* 1:98-100.

Wiese, Leopold von. 1957. *Erinnerungen*. Köln und Opladen: Westdeutscher Verlag.

Wiggershaus, Rolf. 1986. *Die Frankfurter Schule*. Munich: Hanser.

Wilbrandt, Robert. [1928] 1990. "Discussion of Karl Mannheim's 'Competition' paper at the Sixth Congress of German Sociologists (Zurich, 1928)." In Volker Meja and Nico Stehr, eds., *Knowledge and Politics*, pp. 86-106. London and New York: Routledge.

Williams, Raymond. 1976. "Intellectual." In *Keywords*, pp. 140-42. London: Fontana/Croom Helm.

Wilson, Charles H. 1937. Review of *Ideology and Utopia* by Karl Mannheim. *Sociological Review* 29,4 (October): 414-19.

Wirth, Louis. 1935. "The Future of Regional Planning," *Human Problems of Social Planning*, Publications of the American Sociological Society, XXIX, 3, (August). Chicago.

Woldring, Henk. 1986. *Karl Mannheim: The Development of His Thought*. New York, St. Martin's Press.

Wolff, Kurt H. [1971] 1993. "Introduction: A Reading of Karl Mannheim." In *From Karl Mannheim*, 2nd expanded ed., pp. 1–123 New Brunswick and London: Transaction Publishers.

Wolff, Kurt H. 1974. *Trying Sociology*. New York: Wiley.

Wolff, Kurt H. 1978. "Karl Mannheim." In Dirk Käsler, ed., *Klassiker des soziologischen Denkens. Zweiter Band: Von Weber Bis Mannheim*, pp. 286–387. Munich: Verlag C.H. Beck.

Wolff, Kurt H. 1989. *O Loma! Constituting a Self (1977–1984)*. Northampton, Mass.: Hermes House Press.

Wolff, Kurt H. 1991. *Survival and Sociology*. New Brunswick and London: Transaction Publishers.

Wolin, Sheldon. 1960. *Politics and Vision*. Boston: Little, Brown & Co.

Zaret, David. 1994. "Max Weber und die Entwicklung der theoretischen Soziologie in den USA." In Gerhard Wagner and Heinz Zipprian, *Max Webers Wissenschaftslehre*, pp. 352–66. Frankfurt: Suhrkamp.

Ziffus, Sigrid. 1988. "Karl Mannheim und der Moot-Kreis." In Ilja Srubar, ed., *Exil, Wissenschaft, Identität: Die Emigration deutscher Sozialwissenschaftler 1933–1945*. Frankfurt: Suhrkamp.

Zinn, Alexander. 1992. "Gehaßt oder Instrumentalisiert? Soziologie im Dritten Reich aus der Perspektive des Reichsministeriums für Wissenschaft," *Zeitschrift für Soziologie* 21,5 (Oktober): 347–65.

Index

Abel, Theodore, 203
Academic disciplines (esp. sociology), 1, 27, 31, 41, 49, 51, 56, 67, 73, 89, 92, 110, 113, 120, 132, 159, 171, 182-85, 190, 199, 201, 203, 206-9, 211, 216, 227-8, 230, 235-6, 240, 247, 250, 285, 317, 319. *See also* American sociology, British sociology, German sociology
Adler, Alfred, 305
Adler, Max, 92-93
Administration and management, 103, 137, 139, 150, 170, 190, 243, 244
Adorno, Theodor W., 109, 113, 140-43, 145, 285-86
Ady, Endre, 34
Aesthetics, 11, 14, 19, 34-38, 40, 50, 54, 63-64, 71, 73, 82, 103, 108, 178, 213
Agenda, 274, 304
Alienation and homelessness, 14, 36, 40, 44, 79, 85, 204, 223, 255
American Journal of Sociology, 197, 200, 202, 210, 219, 226, 243
American Sociological Review, 8, 208-10, 227, 228
American Sociological Society, 203, 209-11, 220, 227, 228, 243
American sociology, 183, 193, 197, 198, 200-2, 208, 214, 220, 226-7, 236, 240, 244, 250, 294. *See also* Academic disciplines
Amers-Küller, Jo van, 309-10
Anti-positivism, 14, 40-41
Anti-semitism, 33, 168, 243, 320
Arendt, Hannah, 3, 27, 95, 318
Aristophanes, 122
Art (fine arts), 34-35, 45, 48, 66, 107-8, 119, 130, 139-40, 157-58, 176, 286-87

Art (knowledge-based practice; not science), 156-58, 171
Ascoli, Max, 226
Authoritarianism, 6, 27, 164, 180, 248-49
Autobiography, 173, 189

Bacon, Francis, 116, 153
Bain, Read, 225, 226, 228-31, 235, 242
Balázs, Béla, 87
Becker, Carl Heinrich, 144
Becker, Howard, 202, 208-11, 213, 219, 240
Benda, Julien, 82
Bentham, Jeremy, 256
Bergsträsser, Arnold, 178
Beveridge, William Henry, 188, 195, 240
Bildung (cultivation), 21, 26, 48, 107-8, 126, 127, 130, 135, 161, 175, 189, 318
Bildungskultur, (culture of the cultivated) 48-49
Biography, 1, 210, 287, 293, 314-16
Blumer, Herbert, 198-99
Bourgeoisie, 24-25, 39, 46-47, 69, 72-78, 79, 92, 95, 97, 99, 129, 132, 267, 304, 306
Bramstedt, Ernest K., 181
Branford, Victor, 183-84
Branford, Sybella Gurney, 183-84.
Brinkmann, Carl, 50, 144
British Sociological Society, 183
British sociology, 182, 183, 296. *See also* Academic disciplines
Buber, Martin, 104, 287
Budapest, 2, 11, 17-18, 27, 30, 39, 41, 88-91, 103, 107, 112, 139, 249-50, 256, 260, 273, 287, 290, 293